EX LEBRES

THE FREE PRESS

New York   London   Toronto   Sydney   Singapore

"We Wrecked the Place"

CONTEMPLATING AN END TO THE
NORTHERN IRISH TROUBLES

JONATHAN STEVENSON

THE FREE PRESS
A Division of Simon & Schuster Inc.
1230 Avenue of the Americas
New York, NY 10020

Designed by Carla Bolte

Manufactured in the United States of America

10 9 8 7 6 5 4 3 2 1

Library of Congress Cataloging-in-Publication Data

Stevenson, Jonathan, 1956–
    "We wrecked the place": contemplating an end to the Northern Irish troubles /
Jonathan Stevenson.
        p.   cm.
    Includes bibliographical references and index.
    ISBN 0–684–82745–X
    1. Northern Ireland—Politics and government.   2. Northern Ireland—
Social conditions.   3. Peace movements—Northern Ireland.   4. Violence—
Northern Ireland.   5. Irish question.   I. Title.
DA990.U46S774 1996
320.9416—dc20
                                                      96-18302
                                                        CIP

FOR LIONEL

Where would the Irish be without someone to be Irish at?

—Elizabeth Bowen, *The House in Paris*, 1935

CONTENTS

AUTHOR'S NOTE

Though an American, I have lived in Belfast since September 18, 1993—a little more than a month before the Provisional Irish Republican Army's Shankill bombing, which killed nine Protestant civilians. With this book, I provide a history and analysis of the "troubles" in Northern Ireland—that is, the low-intensity guerrilla conflict that occurred more or less continuously between the Catholic civil protests in 1968 and the declaration of the loyalist ceasefire on October 13, 1994. I also try to determine how the damaged peace process will shake out, and how the Northern Irish people might keep themselves from slipping back into the idiom of ritual political murder.

The conflict was triangular. It operated between the republican paramilitaries and the British security forces (army and police), between republican and loyalist paramilitaries, and, to a lesser extent, between loyalist paramilitaries and security forces. My principal sources are the men and women who did most of the killing: former paramilitaries from both the republican and the loyalist sides. Although the IRA ended its seventeen-month ceasefire by bombing London's Canary Wharf on February 9, 1996, before that date virtually all of the paramilitaries and peripheral parties I interviewed believed that relative peace would endure pending a political settlement. For the first time, then, the players were able to speak about the troubles retrospectively. This circumstance, I think, produced an unprecedented expansiveness and forthrightness in their remarks. Notwithstanding Canary Wharf, most of my subjects still have hope that the gains of seventeen months of peace will be salvaged and built upon.

In a divided society, when an outsider like me encounters enthusiastic candor in both camps, it tends to mean that each is angling for partisan approval. To a degree, that is true in Northern Ireland. But the Northern Irish—Catholic or Protestant, nationalist or unionist, republican or loyalist—also possess a native gregariousness and a transcendent fascination with their own little war. They are not inclined to play down either a grievance or a triumph. These qualities have made my task both easier and more enjoyable than it might have been elsewhere. I am grateful to the people I interviewed for their openness.

Jonathan Stevenson
Belfast, June 1996

DRAMATIS PERSONAE

REPUBLICANS

JOSEPH CLARKE. Grew up in middle Falls, republican west Belfast. Joined Provisional Irish Republican Army (IRA), 1970. Interned, Long Kesh, August 1971 to July 1974; suffered severe physical and psychological abuse by British army; sued in Belfast High Court, got £12,500 settlement. Re-interned, Long Kesh, December 1974 to November 1975. Active member, IRA, through 1990. Now runs a garage in west Belfast. Member of Sinn Fein.

CAROL CULLEN. Grew up in north Belfast, a broadly mixed area where one-fifth of troubles killing took place. Joined youth wing of Provisional IRA (known as Fianna Eireann), 1979. Joined Provisional IRA, 1981. Caught and arrested attempting to blow up a police station, January 1989. Convicted of possession of explosives, sentenced to nine years in Her Majesty's Prison Maghaberry. Served four and a half years. Released September 1993. Married while in prison to Anthony McIntyre. Now lives in west Belfast with him and her two children. Runs counseling center for republican ex-prisoners. Member of Sinn Fein.

TOMMY GORMAN. Grew up in middle Falls, republican west Belfast. Joined Provisional IRA, 1970. Interned, December 1971. Escaped from the prison ship "Maidstone," 1972. Re-interned, Long Kesh, 1973 through 1975. Became field operations officer, 1st Battalion (Andersonstown), Belfast Brigade, Provisional IRA. Arrested 1978 for possession of

---

Note to readers: This "cast" includes only the people who are most prominently featured in the book. For a more comprehensive list of sources, with briefer biographical sketches, see the backmatter Interviewees section.

heavy-caliber ammunition, convicted, sentenced to three years in H.M.P. Maze. Served three years. On the H-block blanket protest, 1978 to 1981. Released 1981. Arrested 1981 for possession of a large bomb, convicted, sentenced to nine years in the Maze. Served five years. Released 1986. Graduated from Queen's University of Belfast. Now a community worker in west Belfast, runs a cross-community project with ex-loyalist paramilitary Billy Hutchinson. Member, Sinn Fein.

LEO GREEN. Grew up in Lurgan, County Armagh. Brother John executed by loyalist group run by renegade British intelligence officer, 1975. Arrested for murder of policeman, 1977, convicted, sentenced to life imprisonment in H.M.P. Maze. Served seventeen and a half years. On H-Block blanket protest, 1977 to 1981. One of seven prisoners to go on fifty-three-day hunger strike, October to December 1980. Officer commanding, Provisional IRA prisoners, 1986 to 1987. Released 1994. Now works in Prisoner-of-War Department, Sinn Fein.

BRENDAN "THE DARK" HUGHES. Grew up in mixed Grosvenor area of west Belfast. Nicknamed "The Dark" by British army on account of swarthy appearance. Joined Provisional IRA, 1970. Interned, Long Kesh, June 1973, with Gerry Adams. Escaped in a garbage truck to Irish Republic. Returned December 1973 to Belfast under an assumed identity, as a toy salesman, to become officer commanding, Belfast Brigade, Provisional IRA. Arrested May 1974 for possession of ammunition, explosives, and documents likely to be used by terrorists; convicted; and sentenced to fifteen years in the Long Kesh compounds. Served twelve years. Officer commanding, Provisional IRA prisoners. Charged with rioting, convicted, and transferred to H-blocks in 1978. On H-block blanket protest, 1978 to 1980. One of seven prisoners to go on fifty-three-day hunger strike, October to December 1980. Released 1986. Now lives in west Belfast. Member, Sinn Fein.

SEAN LYNCH. Grew up in rural County Fermanagh, in mixed area near the border with the Republic of Ireland. Joined Provisional IRA, 1973. Arrested 1986 by British army, after taking five bullets in a gunfight with an elite Special Air Services unit. Blinded in one eye. Charged with possession of explosives and possession of firearm with intent, convicted, and sentenced to twenty-five years in H.M.P. Maze. Officer commanding, Provisional IRA prisoners, H.M.P. Maze. Scheduled for release in early 1999.

ANTHONY MCINTYRE. Joined youth wing of Provisional IRA, 1973. Joined Provisional IRA, 1974. Arrested for IRA membership, 1974; escaped. Caught, convicted of attempting to escape, and sentenced to two years in Long Kesh. Released November 1975. Became officer commanding, Provisional IRA, for lower Ormeau Road area of central Belfast. Arrested February 1976 for the murder of a loyalist paramilitary; convicted; sentenced to life imprisonment in Long Kesh compounds. Moved to H-blocks for trying to escape. On H-block blanket protest, 1978 to 1981. Earned B.A. in politics in prison. Released 1992. Now pursuing Ph.D. in politics, Queen's University of Belfast. Married to Carol Cullen. Member, Sinn Fein.

JACKIE MCMULLAN. Grew up in heavily republican Andersonstown estate, west Belfast. Joined youth wing of Provisional IRA, early seventies, later Provisional IRA itself. Arrested May 1976 for the attempted murder of a policeman, convicted, and sentenced to life imprisonment in H.M.P. Maze. On H-block blanket protest, 1976 to 1981. One of the last six participants in the 1981 hunger strike; without food for forty-seven days when strike was called off. Released 1992. Now works in Prisoner-of-War Department, Sinn Fein.

KEVIN "BAP" MCQUILLAN. Grew up on lower Falls, later Ballymurphy. Joined Irish Republican Socialist Party, political wing of the hard-line Irish National Liberation Army, becoming IRSP Belfast chairman. Arrested and detained over fifty times under the Prevention of Terrorism Act and held for eighteen months on remand (i.e., pending trial) in Portlaoise prison in the Irish Republic for INLA membership and a suspected bombing in Dublin. Lives on the "peace line." Attacked once in internal feud (McQuillan himself shot in the head and back, recovered; brother shot in the head, paralyzed), and twice by Ulster Freedom Fighters (McQuillan hurt, brother lost two fingers). Now a community activist, nurse, and, as IRSP leader, one of several prominent hard-line republicans skeptical of IRA ceasefire. Favorite line: "A revolutionary is a dead man on leave."

ELLA O'DWYER. Grew up in rural County Tipperary, Republic of Ireland. Joined Provisional IRA as a college student in Dublin, in the wake of the 1981 hunger strike. Arrested as a suspected member of the IRA active service unit that tried to kill Margaret Thatcher in Brighton, taking out five of Thatcher's colleagues instead. Tried on explosives charges, convicted, and sentenced to life imprisonment. Earned bachelor's and master's degrees in literature at University College, Dublin. Now pursuing doctorate in literature through University of Ulster at Coleraine, while serving sentence in H.M.P. Maghaberry, Northern Ireland.

DONNCHA O'HARA. Grew up in Ardoyne, north Belfast. Joined the Provisional IRA in early seventies. An "own-goal": Premature bomb explosion blew off his right arm, blinded him in right eye, paralyzed right side. Arrested in 1974 for the bombing of a store in central Belfast, in which a woman was killed. Convicted of murder and sentenced to life imprisonment. Served seventeen years. On H-block blanket protest. Released 1991. Now a Sinn Fein press officer.

JOHN PICKERING. Grew up in heavily republican Andersonstown estate, west Belfast. Joined youth wing of Provisional IRA in early 1970s, later Provisional IRA itself. Interned, 1972 to 1975. Arrested August 1976 after shoot-out with policemen following attempt to blow up police station in Belfast. Charged with corresponding terrorist offenses and with earlier murder of seventy-seven-year-old Protestant man, convicted of murder, and sentenced to life imprisonment in H.M.P. Maze. Served eighteen years. On H-block blanket protest, 1976 to 1981. One of the last six participants in the 1981 hunger strike; without food for twenty-six days when strike was called off. Released 1994. Now works in Prisoner-of-War Department, Sinn Fein.

GARY ROBERTS. Grew up in the Short Strand, a Catholic enclave of largely Protestant east Belfast, and later Andersonstown. Cousin and fourteen others died in Ulster Volunteer Force's 1971 bombing of McGurk's Bar in north Belfast. Joined youth wing of Provisional IRA, early seventies, later Provisional IRA itself. Arrested 1976 for his part in the barroom execution of a sixty-four-year-old Protestant man. Convicted of murder, sentenced to imprisonment "at the Secretary of State's pleasure" (life imprisonment for a minor). Served fourteen years. On H-block blanket protest, 1976 to 1981. Released 1990. Became fluent in Irish in prison, graduated from Queen's University of Belfast after release. Now teaches Irish at Falls Road Irish-language primary school.

UMBERTO SCAPPATICCI. Grew up in Newry, County Down. Joined Provisional IRA, mid-seventies. Arrested 1975 for the murder of a soldier, convicted, and sentenced to life imprisonment. Served fourteen years in the Long Kesh compounds. Released 1988. Now runs a community youth project in heavily republican Twinbrook, south of Belfast.

LOYALISTS

GLEN BARR. Grew up on the "Waterside," the Protestant part of Derry. Co-founder of Ulster Defense Association in Derry. Political advisor to

Ulster Defense Association, 1971 to 1979. Ran the 1974 Ulster Workers' Council strike that brought down the short-lived power-sharing government and forced Westminster to resume direct rule. Now a businessman and community activist in Derry.

ALEX CALDERWOOD. Grew up in heavily loyalist Shankill Road area. Joined youth wing of the Ulster Defense Association, 1979. Arrested several times. Confessed 1981 to sectarian murder of a Catholic man, whom he beat to death with a cinder block. Convicted of murder, sentenced to imprisonment "at the Secretary of State's pleasure" (life imprisonment for a minor) in H.M.P. Maze. Served eleven years. Became born-again Christian in prison. Severed paramilitary ties in prison, transferred voluntarily to nonparamilitary wing at H.M.P. Maghaberry. Released 1992. Now a community worker on the Shankill Road.

JIMMY CREIGHTON. Grew up in north Belfast. Member, Ulster Defense Association, 1971 to 1983. Andy Tyrie's bodyguard. Now a community worker in Glencairn, Belfast.

DAVID ERVINE. Grew up in heavily Protestant east Belfast. Joined Ulster Volunteer Force, 1972. Arrested 1974 for possession of explosives, convicted, sentenced to eleven years in Long Kesh compounds. Served five and a half years. Released 1980. Now political spokesman for the Progressive Unionist Party.

WILLIAM GILES. Grew up in heavily Protestant east Belfast. Joined Ulster Volunteer Force, 1976. Arrested 1982 for shooting murder of Catholic man, convicted, sentenced to life imprisonment in H.M.P. Maze. Earned B.A. in psychology in prison. Now serving out his sentence.

BILLY HUTCHINSON. Grew up in heavily loyalist Shankill Road area. Joined youth wing of Ulster Volunteer Force (known as Young Citizen Volunteers), 1972. Worked at Mackie's (site of President Clinton's first scheduled stop in Belfast). Arrested 1974 for double murder of two Catholic half-brothers, convicted, sentenced to life imprisonment in Long Kesh compounds. Served sixteen years. Officer commanding, UVF prisoners, 1977 to 1990. Earned B.A. in social science in prison. Released 1990. Now a west Belfast community worker, runs inter-community project with ex-Provisional IRA man Tommy Gorman. Leading member, Progressive Unionist Party.

EDDIE KINNER. Grew up in heavily loyalist Shankill Road area. Joined youth wing of Ulster Volunteer Force (known as Young Citizen Volunteers), 1973. With Martin Snoddon, arrested 1975 (age seventeen) for murdering a Catholic woman in a gun and bomb attack on a republican bar in north Belfast. A third UVF man, George Brown, was killed. Kinner was badly injured in the attack. Convicted of murder, sentenced to imprisonment "at the Secretary of State's pleasure" (life imprisonment for a minor). Served thirteen years in the Long Kesh compounds. Earned B.A. in computer science in prison. Released 1988. Now runs the computer training program for the Northern Ireland Association for the Care and Resettlement of Offenders (NIACRO); prominent member of the Progressive Unionist Party.

Tommy Kirkham. Grew up in Protestant "Docklands" area of Belfast, later north Belfast. Joined Ulster Defense Association, 1972. Arrested 1973 and convicted of possession of ammunition, served two and a half years in the Long Kesh compounds. Released 1976. Community activist. Member, Newtownabbey District Council, 1989 to 1993. Now a prominent member of the Ulster Democratic Party.

Gary McMichael. Grew up in predominantly Protestant Lisburn, County Antrim. Son of John McMichael, co-chairman of the Ulster Defense Association, who was assassinated by the IRA in December 1987. Now leader of the Ulster Democratic Party.

Ronald McMurray. Grew up in central Belfast (Donegall Pass). Joined Ulster Volunteer Force, 1974. Confessed in 1977 to the 1974 bombing of the Rose and Crown bar, in which six Catholics were killed and twenty-six patrons were injured. Convicted of murder, sentenced to imprisonment "at the Secretary of State's pleasure" (life imprisonment for a minor). Served thirteen years in the Long Kesh compounds. Earned B.A. in psychology in prison. Released 1990. Now counsels young offenders for NIACRO.

Billy Mitchell. Grew up in Ballyduff, County Antrim, north of Belfast. Founding member of "revived" Ulster Volunteer Force; subsequently on brigade staff. Arrested 1976 for murder of two Ulster Defense Association men during loyalist feud. Convicted of murder, sentenced to life imprisonment, served fourteen years—first six in Long Kesh compounds, then renounced paramilitary membership and finished sentence in nonpolitical wings in the H-blocks and H.M.P. Maghaberry. Now a community worker in north Belfast and a leading member of the Progressive Unionist Party.

William "Plum" Smith. Grew up in the militantly loyalist Shankill Road area. Held rank in Red Hand Commando, a small paramilitary group with links to the Ulster Volunteer Force. Arrested 1972 for the attempted murder of a Catholic man, whom Smith and an accomplice shot fourteen times. Convicted, sentenced to ten years, served five years in the Long Kesh compounds. Released 1977. After release a labor activist at Harland and Wolff shipyard, now a community worker and prominent member of the Progressive Unionist Party.

MARTIN SNODDON. Grew up in Protestant estate of Suffolk, southwest Belfast. Joined Ulster Defense Association, later Ulster Volunteer Force. With Eddie Kinner, arrested 1975 for murdering a Catholic woman in a gun and bomb attack on a republican bar in north Belfast. A third UVF man, George Brown, was killed. Snoddon was burned and deafened in one ear. Convicted of murder, sentenced to life imprisonment. Served fifteen years in the Long Kesh compounds. Earned B.A. in computer science in prison. Released 1990. Now in charge of providing free computer training and services for a Belfast charity. Also involved in setting up advice center for loyalist ex-prisoners.

GUSTY SPENCE. Grew up in heavily loyalist Shankill Road area. Served in British army, saw combat in Cyprus. Discharged 1961. Founding member of "revived" Ulster Volunteer Force, 1965. Officer commanding, UVF, Shankill Road. Arrested 1966 for murder of Catholic barman Peter Ward, who is often called the first victim of the troubles. Convicted of murder, sentenced to life imprisonment in Crumlin Road Prison, Belfast. Served nineteen years. Moved to Long Kesh, 1971. Officer commanding, UVF prisoners, 1971 to 1977. Renounced violence in prison. Released 1985. Without question the greatest loyalist folk hero and most influential loyalist ex-prisoner. Now a leading member of the Progressive Unionist Party.

MICHAEL STONE. Grew up in Protestant east Belfast. Known as "Rambo." Ulster Defense Association freelance operator, 1970s and 1980s. In March 1988, armed with an assault rifle and grenades, staged one-man kamikaze attack at Milltown Cemetery in west Belfast on mourners of three IRA members killed by SAS in Gibraltar. Killed three people. Arrested on the spot after being beaten by mob, convicted of murder, sentenced to life imprisonment in H.M.P. Maze. Officer commanding, UDA prisoners from east Belfast; UDA prison spokesman. Now serving out his sentence.

ANDY TYRIE. Grew up on the Shankill Road, later Ballymurphy. Forced to move to Glencairn after 1969 disturbances. Chairman, Ulster Defense

Association, 1973 to 1988, during which period several attempts were made on his life by both republicans and loyalists. Arrested and held on remand numerous times in Crumlin Road Prison, Belfast, on terrorist charges. Now owns and runs several stores in east Belfast.

JOHN WHITE. Grew up in mixed west Belfast area of New Barnesley; forced to move to Shankill Road when Catholics petrol-bombed house. Joined Ulster Defense Association, 1971. Arrested 1972 in Britain on weapons charges; held on remand in Brixton prison for one year; charges dropped. Interned 1973 to 1975, Long Kesh. Arrested 1975 in stolen car, convicted, sentenced to three years in Long Kesh; served eighteen months. Held high rank in "Ulster Freedom Fighters," the illegal paramilitary wing of the UDA. In 1977, during police interrogation confessed to brutal 1973 stabbing murders of Catholic Belfast city councilman Paddy Wilson and his Protestant woman friend Irene Andrews. Convicted of murder, sentenced to life imprisonment in Long Kesh. Served sixteen years. Officer commanding, UDA prisoners. Earned B.A. in social sciences and postgraduate degree in criminology in prison. Released 1993. Leading member, Ulster Democratic Party.

PROLOGUE:

SEVENTEEN MONTHS

Over twenty-five years have passed since the Provisional Irish Republican Army—known provincially as the Provos—began its terrorist campaign against British rule in Northern Ireland. On August 31, 1994, the IRA declared a unilateral ceasefire. In response, on October 13, 1994, the loyalist paramilitaries, whose counterterrorist operations supported British rule, announced a ceasefire of their own. Both ceasefires were open-ended. The quarter-century of guerrilla conflict quaintly known as the troubles was ostensibly over.

"We went to jail, our people hunger striked, we suffered in protest, we died, and we killed an awful, awful lot of people in the process—we killed British soldiers, we killed an awful lot of RUC [Royal Ulster Constabulary], we lost an awful lot of our own lives, and we blew up London, we blew up Belfast, we wrecked the place. Now we're back to where we started." So says Anthony McIntyre. He is now a doctoral candidate at Queen's University of Belfast, but in 1976 he was convicted of murdering a loyalist paramilitary and he spent the next seventeen years in prison for the greater glory of the Provisional IRA. McIntyre pleaded not guilty. He is not jailhouse cute about his innocence. "For legal reasons, I just don't admit guilt. If you said I was guilty in your book, I wouldn't sue for libel." McIntyre was guilty. He is not ashamed of it.

McIntyre still does not want to be a British subject. He never learned *God Save the Queen* in school. When, as a nine-year-old, he was braced by a gang of adolescent Protestant boys in the Sandy Row section of Belfast, and asked to sing the British national anthem on demand, he came up mute. "I got a powerful beating," he remembers. His pal, David Young, was four years older and a Brit. Young crooned, and walked away unscathed. Their friendship atrophied.

The working-class Protestants of Sandy Row were not merely unionists, but loyalists: they were willing to fight and die to keep Northern Ireland

1

British. McIntyre lived on the lower Ormeau Road—not as militantly union-ist as nearby Sandy Row, but then still largely Protestant. "There was a sectar-ian undertone from the very start," he asserts resentfully. "Loyalists drew an 'X' on our door because we were the only Catholics on that street at the time." Angry Catholic youth responded with the Provisional IRA in 1970.

In 1971, at age fourteen, McIntyre joined Fianna Eireann (pro-nounced "feenah-err-*on*"), the youth wing of the IRA. Although he ex-celled in school and actually qualified for the college preparatory curricu-lum—highly selective in Northern Ireland—he had lost all interest in academic pursuits in favor of military ones. Working as an apprentice ter-razzo layer, McIntyre's avocational activity consisted mainly of rioting, throwing rocks and the occasional petrol bomb at police and soldiers, and providing logistical support for the IRA proper by carrying messages or weapons. In 1973, aged sixteen, McIntyre lied about his age—the IRA minimum for active service was seventeen—and joined the A-team. Within months, he was arrested on a charge of IRA membership and taken to a home for young offenders. He escaped in thirty minutes.

The IRA sent McIntyre down to Dundalk, a town just over the border in the Republic of Ireland. He was too itchy to stay holed up and returned to Belfast a day later. The police caught him, and he was sentenced to two years in prison. He did eighteen months, and upon his release in November 1975 im-mediately resumed active service, as "officer commanding" (OC) of the Provi-sional IRA in the lower Ormeau area. Three months later he was charged with the murder of a forty-five-year-old Protestant man named Kenneth Lenaghan.

"You can find his death indexed in this latest book out.[1] It was the 27th of February, 1976. That'll be there," he says. From a big, lumpy man with an outsized head, thick glasses, and a scruffy beard, the confirmation of an execution seems like a joke. In 1995, McIntyre looked more like a school-teacher than a lethal guerrilla. On his wrist, a professional tattoo of a beautiful bird covers a jailhouse etching of "Mackers" (his nickname), as if to suggest he has decided on a higher calling. He himself seemed to view the killing of Kenneth Lenaghan as an episode in another world, involv-ing another Anthony McIntyre, of which he needed a reminder provided by the book. "In the index it says he was killed by the IRA, and he was a member of the UVF [Ulster Volunteer Force]," he droned, distantly. The syllables "I-R-A" came out as "E-raangh," in a nasal riff even more forbid-ding and extreme than the standard Belfast accent.*

---

*In west Belfast slang, the IRA has evolved into, simply, "the 'Ra."

Lenaghan was a bouncer at the Victor Bar, a Protestant hangout in McIntyre's neighborhood, and was shot from a car while standing in front of the place. He held rank in the local branch of the Ulster Volunteer Force, the more secret and exotic of the two principal loyalist paramilitary organizations. Among the other neighborhood Protestants also in the UVF was Ron McMurray, an exact contemporary of Anthony McIntyre. Like McIntyre, Ron was something of a freak, finishing secondary school with seven "O-level" qualifications* while most working-class teenagers got none. What moved him conclusively to violence was a Provisional IRA atrocity.

A friend of Ron's and another fellow named Robert Collins got drunk and drifted into a Catholic part of north Belfast—easy to do, as that quadrant is a segregated sectarian patchwork. Mistaking Collins for a British soldier, the Provos tortured him, cut off his tattoos, and sadistically sent the inked patches of skin to his family. Then they killed him. McMurray's friend was shot in the head and remains brain-damaged. Incensed, McMurray joined the UVF in 1974. He was arrested only once— for accidentally shooting a friend with a nine-millimeter pistol—before committing what he calls "the main act": blowing up the Rose and Crown Bar on the Ormeau Road with two accomplices on May 2, 1974. The explosion killed six Catholics and injured another twenty-six people.

The police rousted McMurray over the next three years, but didn't have enough evidence to hold him. Though he is tall and muscular, his pale gray eyes, skin to match, and protruding ears betray both his intelligence and his vulnerability. In 1977, McMurray confessed. Because he was only sixteen when he did the bombing, he could not legally be sentenced to life imprisonment and instead served his time "at the secretary of state's pleasure"—or SOSP. McMurray spent thirteen years inside. "I reckon I was very lucky," he comments. "I wanted to believe that my actions would stop republican violence, but obviously they didn't. The UVF had attempted to go political, and had obviously failed. That depressed me. But what had occurred to me by the time I confessed was, when you kill someone you kill them for the rest [of] their life. There's no going back on that." McMurray's soft voice trails into inaudibleness.

---

*U.K. schools offer teenagers qualifications at two academic levels. At age sixteen, a student may take tests in several basic subjects that were formerly called "O-levels" but are now grouped under the heading "General Certificate of Secondary Education," or GCSE. Two years later, the student can take "A-levels," which are more difficult tests primarily for college admission.

In early 1995, as McIntyre voiced his stinging frustration and McMurray issued his profound remorse over the futility of the troubles, the British army withdrew daytime foot patrols from west Belfast. Officers of the Royal Ulster Constabulary (the official police force of Northern Ireland, generally known as "the RUC") took off their flak jackets and laid down their assault rifles. Security guards stopped searching purses and shopping bags in department stores. A sleek new Catholic church opened on the posh Malone Road, right next door to the fortified barracks of the all-Protestant Royal Irish Regiment, who left the gates open during the Christmas season without fear of IRA bombings or strafings. Representatives of Sinn Fein* and the loyalist paramilitaries began talking to British government officials about how to get to the negotiating table.

The "marching season" began on Easter Sunday. The Falls Road parade commemorating the Easter Rising was perfunctory and dispirited—a good sign. On the following day, the Apprentice Boys of Derry, a unionist group, showed little resistance when the RUC diverted their parade from a nationalist area of Belfast's lower Ormeau Road, where loyalist paramilitaries had gunned down five innocent Catholics in 1992. So far so good. In June, the Belfast City Council elected a Catholic nationalist deputy lord mayor for the first time in Northern Ireland's seventy-five-year history. Better yet.

The first post-ceasefire sectarian backsliding occurred in July. Private Lee Clegg, a member of the British army's elite Parachute Regiment, was released from prison after serving only four years of a life sentence for murdering a teenage Catholic car thief, Karen Reilly. Terrorists convicted of murder serve at least fourteen years. Catholic west Belfast erupted in anger. IRA men, normally brutal enforcers of public order, turned a blind eye. Over two hundred cars were hijacked, many of them torched. A week later, the RUC and seven thousand Protestants clashed in Drumcree, twenty-five miles west of Belfast, over the rerouting of a Protestant march through a Catholic area; the police got rough and fired a few plastic bullets. Later that month, RUC men donned riot gear to repel an unruly nationalist mob protesting a Protestant march on the lower Ormeau Road; thirty-one people were injured. This was real proto-troubles stuff, reminiscent of the 1969 summer riots that inaugurated twenty-five years of violence.

By October 1995, however, the province's big story was whether Presi-

---

*The Provisional IRA's political wing. Pronounced "shin-*fane*." "Sinn Fein" means "ourselves alone" in Irish.

dent Clinton or the Power Rangers, a group of costumed, acrobatic children's entertainers, would turn on the Christmas lights at Belfast City Hall. The nationalist minority, generally Catholic, viewed Clinton as an equalizer and credited him with facilitating peace. They wanted him to throw the switch. Unionists, largely Protestant, resented American meddling and backed the Power Rangers. After a comical debate in the city council, nationalists prevailed. True to form, Washington had a bigger-and-better evergreen sent over from Nashville.

On November 30, Clinton finally arrived for the first visit ever of a sitting U.S. president to Northern Ireland. After an impromptu stroll down the Shankill Road, Clinton entered Mackie's engineering plant, which sits near the thirty-foot-high corrugated iron "peace line" that separates Catholic and Protestant west Belfast, to give his keynote speech. Adorable Catherine Hamill, a nine-year-old Catholic girl in blonde curls and pinafore, told President Clinton how her "first Daddy" was killed in the troubles and how her "Christmas wish is that peace and love will last in Ireland forever." Bill himself wiped a tear from his cheek and hugged Catherine as she sat down next to him on the podium. After Mackie's, the president enjoyed a quick schmooze with Sinn Fein president Gerry Adams on the Falls Road. Hours later, the nationalist crowd in Derry* frenetically waved plastic American flags. Belfast street vendors sold blow-up baseball bats decorated with stars and stripes.

The Clinton visit became the closest thing to a group encounter the Northern Irish had ever had. Northern Ireland, now happy, was front-page news again. The people basked in their fame, now for peace rather than violence. At Belfast City Hall, the majestic Victorian hub downtown, eighty thousand spectators—one-twentieth of the province—came

---

*Derry is Northern Ireland's second city, located in County Londonderry and 70 percent Catholic. Although both city and county are still officially called "Londonderry" by unionists and the British government, both places are now known as "Derry" to most of their inhabitants, Protestant as well as Catholic, and in common parlance throughout the province. The political sensitivity of the city's nomenclature has caused some consternation to outsiders. Lord Mayor John Kerr, a nationalist, suggested to President Clinton's advance team for his 1995 visit that he refer to it as "this city of Derry, which some people call Londonderry." But city councillor Gregory Campbell, a strong unionist, advised Clinton to use "the proper and legitimate term of Londonderry" if "he want[ed] not to cause offense." Other possibilities included "the Maiden City" and "the city on the banks of the Foyle." See "Name Game Is a Verbal Minefield," *Irish News* (Belfast), October 27, 1995, p. 1. In the event, the president settled on calling the city "Derry," but the county "Londonderry." Throughout this book, with reckless abandon, the city is called Derry.

out to hear Belfast-born Van Morrison sing Celtic soul and watch the president illuminate the pine tree from Tennessee.

On February 9, 1996, a few IRA members who had grown impatient with peacetime politics announced the end of the IRA ceasefire. Ninety minutes later, they set off a large bomb at east London's Canary Wharf, killing two civilian shopkeepers and injuring over one hundred people. Although the bombing appeared an act of near political suicide, it could not erase seventeen months of peace. During that period, ex-terrorists took the opportunity to consider the past twenty-five years with greater detachment and honesty than ever before. Many conceded the fruitlessness of the troubles, and resolved not to repeat it. This book records and interprets their reflections, in the hope of making the lessons they have learned more difficult to discard.

CHAPTER 1

SINS OF THE FATHERS

Officially, the troubles began in 1969. Yet as with everything Irish, centuries of history animate the present and recent past. The island's heritage is speckled with violent events, which serve as justifications for more violence. Depending on the context, republicans and loyalists will assert that relevant history starts at the Norman conquest (1171), the Irish rebellion in Ulster against Protestants (1641), Oliver Cromwell's evangelistic terror against Catholics (1649), King William's victory at the Battle of the Boyne (1690), Wolf Tone's United Irishmen rebellion (1798), the Easter Rising (1916), partition (1921), the founding of the new UVF (1966), the Catholic civil rights movement (1968), the August riots in Belfast (1969), or the IRA split (1970).

At street level, one of the provocations of the troubles occurred each 12th of July, when unionists have long flown British flags from their homes. Provincial law was complicitous. The Flags and Emblems (Display) Act (Northern Ireland) of 1954 gave private property owners an absolute legal right to display a Union Jack, but empowered policemen to order any other flag or emblem removed to prevent a breach of peace. In practice, the flag or emblem which the police would take down was invariably an Irish tricolor. The act was not formally repealed until 1987, but long before that the IRA took matters into its own hands. The recollection fills Anthony McIntyre's chest: "Even in early 1971 I remember, at around internment* time, there were still people in the [Ormeau Road] area that

---

*In response to growing terrorist activity, Westminster authorized internment without trial in 1971. On August 9 of that year, the British army rounded up 342 republican suspects, and imprisoned them in the Long Kesh military camp, south of Belfast, and on the prison ship Maidstone in Belfast harbor. Many of the initial internees were old IRA men (including Gerry Adams's father) who may have been active in the forties and fifties but were not involved with the new Provisional IRA; 104 were released within two days; only

hung out their Union Jacks on the 12th of July. And some done it in a very defiant manner and kept them out. A duo of houses in particular kept it up for the whole of the summer—until the IRA shot up the houses."

The 12th of July is the height of Ulster's six-month "marching season," during which loyalist groups stage over 2,500 parades. The holiday marks the date when, in 1690, the forces of King William of Orange, a Dutch Protestant who married into the British royal family, vanquished the army of the actual heir, King James II, a Catholic. After driving him from the British mainland, King William established Anglo-Protestant domination in Ireland. Protestants like to point out that King Billy had the support of a papacy that didn't want to get involved in island politics. Catholics shoot back that Oliver Cromwell's genocide forty years earlier trumps any weakness of will on the part of the Pontiff in the game of political equity. Besides, most republicans are lapsed Catholics, anyway, so who cares what the Church did?

The year 1690 remains the watershed of British rule in Ireland. Subsequently, the so-called Protestant Ascendancy ruled Ireland for three hundred years. They derived largely from "New English" folk who settled in Ireland during the early seventeenth century via colonial expropriation, or "plantation." The distinctly Protestant plantation of this period was consciously designed to root British rule in Ireland. Pre-Reformation "Old English" settlers, though also imperious, were Catholic and thus had assimilated too comfortably to guarantee the British territorial security. With their Church of Ireland established as part of the Anglican Church, "New English" Protestants promised hegemony through religious antagonism.

Though a one-sixth minority, the Ascendancy owned most of Ireland. From 1689, the Ascendancy controlled the Irish parliament, which between 1695 and 1727 enacted the Penal Laws roundly oppressive of Catholics. In particular, Catholics were not allowed to vote until 1793. After the Act of Union in 1801, Ascendancy Protestants dominated Britain's Irish administration at Dublin Castle until the end of the nineteenth century. In the Ascendancy mind, Ireland was nothing less than a Protestant nation.

Presbyterians were the other main Protestant group to settle in Ireland.

---

two were Protestant. But internment continued, and British intelligence improved; well over a thousand more, including some loyalists, were arrested and detained between August 1971 and December 1975, when internment ended. The policy proved an unmitigated law-enforcement and public-relations disaster by alienating the nationalist community and galvanizing violently inclined young men. Troubles violence peaked in 1972, the second year of internment.

Although some Presbyterians too were plantation settlers, before and after the Ulster plantation of the early seventeenth century many emigrated (primarily from Scotland to Ulster*) on their own, often to escape religious prejudice. Indeed, heavy Scottish Calvinist immigration to Ulster during the latter part of the seventeenth century is the factor primarily responsible for the greater Protestant numbers in Northern Ireland now. The Presbyterian Church of Ireland constitutes the single largest Protestant denomination in Northern Ireland. Yet Presbyterians were in no way part of the Ascendancy. They were less educated and less wealthy than the Ascendancy, who resented their religious iconoclasm and felt threatened by their industriousness, denying them the right to hold political office from 1704 until 1780 and continuing a degree of landlord-tenant exploitation thereafter. The division between Ascendancy Protestants and Presbyterian "Dissenters" then is roughly paralleled by the schism between "fur-coat brigade" unionists and working-class loyalists today—at least in the iconography of many loyalists.

Presbyterians, though not actively persecuted, were denied some of the same privileges denied Catholics. In 1798, Presbyterians and Catholics became tenuously allied as nationalists in Wolf Tone's United Irishmen. But Presbyterian nationalists never fully trusted Catholics and saw salient differences in the Catholics' agenda, such as their inclination to cozy up directly to the English in order to marginalize the Protestant Ascendancy. Doctrinally, Presbyterians were more vehemently anti-Catholic than Ascendancy Protestants. And Presbyterian nationalism was hardly uniform. In locales where Catholics outnumbered Protestants, or where heavy action had occurred during the 1641 Catholic rebellion, Presbyterians eschewed the United Irishmen and in fact leaned towards virulently anti-Catholic organizations.[1]

Most notably, in 1795 the Peep o' Day Boys, a group of Protestant vigilantes, routed the Catholic Defenders in an agrarian skirmish known

---

*Ulster is one of the four provinces of Ireland recognized since the Norman conquest in the twelfth century, the other three being Connaught, Leinster, and Munster. Over the course of the English plantations, Ireland was further divided into its present thirty-two counties; the province of Ulster comprised nine counties. At partition, in order not to dilute their majority, Protestant politicians declined three of Ulster's nine counties. They are Cavan, Donegal, and Monaghan. The six counties of Northern Ireland are Fermanagh, Armagh, Tyrone, Londonderry, Antrim, and Down. Schoolchildren learn the names through a mnemonic acronym: FAT LAD. Nevertheless, northern Protestants often call Northern Ireland "Ulster." Catholic nationalists resent this use of the name "Ulster" and even the designation "Northern Ireland," often referring to the area as "the north of Ireland" or, more defiantly, "the six counties."

(grandiosely) as "the Battle of the Diamond." The victory led to the founding of the Orange Order. The original purpose of that organization was to galvanize Protestant farmers against Catholics competing for land, but over time the Orange Order bred in urban as well as rural Protestants a broadly exclusionary attitude towards Catholics that infiltrated politics. Seven Orangemen elected to Westminster during the 1886 home rule crisis effectively started the Ulster Unionist Party (UUP), still Northern Ireland's largest, and the Orange Order has dominated unionist politics ever since. At present, the Orange Order has about 100,000 members.[2]

In the near-century between the Wolf Tone rebellion and the inception of the home-rule movement, Presbyterians, who were mainly farmers and laborers, decisively came to see the economically competing Catholic minority as a threat. This pressure compounded the Puritanical suspicion they had always harbored towards Catholics and nudged Presbyterians closer to the Protestant Ascendancy. Presbyterians always placed the highest value on their independence, and still do; transient phases of nationalism have been essentially prudential and self-preservative. After 1798, Westminster and its Ascendancy partners saw Catholics—accurately—as the critical disruptive force in Ireland. Presbyterians were worried about their civil rights and employment. But having settled in Ireland recently compared to Catholics, they did not have such strong inclinations toward nationalism. Accordingly, the British helped neutralize their fears about political freedom by granting them the right to stand for political office in 1780—forty-nine years before Catholics. Unlike Catholics, Presbyterians always had the right to vote. Ascendancy Protestants, who owned most of Ulster's businesses, hired Protestants preferentially.

Ulster took on a different character from the rest of Ireland. During the eighteenth century, the "black north" industrialized and the agrarian south did not; this had not a little to do with the enterprising nature of Protestants raised on Adam Smith. Ulster benefited from linen exports to England, while the Irish wool industry collapsed. The tenant rights movement at the very root of Irish nationalism got a head start in Ulster, which, as of 1850, was the only place in Ireland where the coveted "three F's"—fair rent, fixity of tenure, and free sale of leasehold—were already widely practiced.[3] By then, Ulstermen were both more prosperous and more liberated than Catholics elsewhere in Ireland. Ulster, on balance, did not need Irish nationalism. British nationalism served the province better.

Catholic triumphalism in the 1850s emanating from Daniel O'Connell's emancipation reforms (including the right to sit in Parliament, granted in 1829) dovetailed with the disestablishment of the Church of Ireland in 1869 to further bevel the edge between Presbyterians and Ascendancy Protestants. By 1886, the famine and other factors had rendered Irish nationalism, in the form of the first home-rule bill, a decisively Catholic phenomenon. Ulster Protestants were marginalized, and Presbyterians closed ranks with the ruling-class Anglican Protestants against nationalism. Blue-collar Prods were prepared to accept the political leadership of their Protestant employers in exchange for jobs. Those employers, in turn, had a vested interest in the union.

The rest of Ireland, being generally poor, provided no appreciable market for Ulster's manufactured goods. Instead, they found their way, duty-free, for both direct consumption and re-export, principally to mainland Britain. From industrialization forward, Ulster identified prosperity with the union. Conversely, Ulster was by turns economically, politically, and militarily important to Great Britain. By 1849, the linen industry imported 250,000 tons of British coal annually. By the 1880s, the Conservative government at Westminster needed unionists to safeguard its power and ever since they have periodically "played the Orange card" by reassuring Ulster unionists that the North would remain British. In World War I, Ulstermen died in droves at the Somme. During World War II, Northern Ireland produced 140 warships, 10 percent of the United Kingdom's merchant fleet, 1,500 heavy bombers, and an abundance of other ordnance.[4] There was, therefore, a quid pro quo. Effecting and maintaining partition guaranteed Britain the fruits of Ulster, and vice versa.

One hundred and fifty years after the Battle of the Boyne, another historically divisive event bisected the nineteenth century. In autumn of 1845, the fungus *Phytophthora infestans* attacked the Irish potato and touched off the Great Famine. Over the next seven years, Ireland's population dropped by over two million—one-quarter of the island's population—through disease, starvation, and emigration. Irish orthodoxy has it that the British government cared so little about the largely Catholic peasantry that it willfully neglected them to death. As such, the famine has served Irish nationalism by sustaining Catholic distrust of the British. But Roy Foster, the leading revisionist historian, argues that British public works and price-control policies, though obviously inadequate, merely tracked effective measures taken by the government to fight previous famines of smaller scale. Foster also notes that Irish farmers' inability to diversify and expand before the potato blight amplified its effects. Although direct relief eventually did materialize in 1847, Foster admits that the payments were too little too late, and had been inhibited by the notion entertained by some in London that Irish shiftlessness made so severe a laissez-faire corrective economically necessary.[5]

The famine entrenched Anglophobia in Ireland, and even the revisionist interpretation does not completely exonerate the British. In her recent book, *This Great Calamity,* post-revisionist historian Christine Kinealy resurrects British disregard as the prime cause of what nationalists often call "the Irish holocaust."[6] Others have followed her lead. A group called Dublin Against Royal Tour (DART), for example, protested Prince Charles's first visit to the Republic of Ireland in June 1995—in part because of Britain's stewardship of Ireland during the famine. The famine was one of several themes of the West Belfast Community Festival, which began on August 6 of that year and ran for two weeks. Community workers saw the festival, then in its eighth year, as a vehicle for affirming Catholic west Belfast's Irish culture. But in the matter of the famine, culture drifts into politics: the famine indisputably has shaped Ireland right up to the present moment, yet to the nationalist community it was not a natural disaster at all but a grand case of callousness by the British government. A new mural next to An Culturlann, the Irish language and culture center on the Falls Road, declares: "There was no famine."

Tommy Gorman, an ex-IRA bomber twice interned and twice convicted, and ex-UVF life-sentence prisoner Billy Hutchinson work together on the Springfield Intercommunity Development Project. The project's aim is to foster the exchange of information and ideas between the Protestant community on the Shankill Road and the Catholic community on the Falls Road, with an eye toward better mutual understanding. For the festival, Gorman says, "we were trying to get some link-up with the Shankill for them to do murals depicting the famine and how it affected people. I mentioned it to Billy and he said, we know nothing about it, it wasn't taught in our schools." The famine hit Ulster first and killed thousands of Protestants, but affected heavily industrialized Ulster least. Thus, the event also helps explain why so many Catholics flocked to an area predominantly inhabited by Protestants.[7] These are precisely the kinds of facts Gorman's and Hutchinson's project is designed to disseminate, but most Protestant community leaders opted out of the festival.

The IRA and Sinn Fein can credibly trace their roots to the Irish Republican Brotherhood, founded right after the famine in 1858. Thus, when the troubles began in 1969 republicans had a long and rich, though not untainted, history. The party originally known as "Sinn Fein" was founded in 1905 by a group of nationalists dissatisfied with the pace of agitation for home rule set by the Irish Parliamentary Party, the constitutional nationalists who had been angling for Irish self-determination since the famine. In the ideological spirit of the early decades of this century, when many now infamous "isms" were boiling, Sinn Fein became increasingly revolutionary. The party shared members with the covert Irish Republican Brotherhood (IRB), a cadre of which staged the Easter Rising of 1916. This was the defining moment of modern republican resistance to British rule, in which republicans led by Patrick Pearse took over downtown Dublin for five days. The Rising in turn allowed Sinn Fein, led by Michael Collins while Eamonn de Valera was in prison for his part in the Rising, to supplant the Irish Parliamentary Party as the strongest in Ireland in 1917.

De Valera, once free and installed as president of Sinn Fein, reinforced Sinn Fein's commitment to democracy for public consumption, while Collins secretly re-formed the IRB and other clandestine rebel societies into the IRA. The IRA fought the Anglo-Irish war to an ambiguous conclusion with the Anglo-Irish Treaty of 1921—after 1690, the most important year in Northern Irish history. The treaty certified the partition of Ireland's thirty-two counties into the largely Catholic twenty-six-county Irish Free State (eventually the Republic of Ireland) and six-county Northern Ireland, which harbored the bulk of the island's Protestant population and remained part of the United Kingdom.

Sinn Fein barely squawked about partition until after the treaty was signed—in the 1918 Irish parliamentary elections, Sinn Fein largely ignored the fears of both Catholics and Protestants in Ulster[8]—yet the prospect of partition was flagrantly manifest from the moment the first home-rule bill was presented to Parliament in 1886. After the general election of December 1909, Irish nationalists, with eighty-four MPs, held the balance of power over the Liberal government. So co-opted, the government ambivalently supported home rule and introduced a home-rule bill in 1912. Legislation in 1911 had contracted the House of Lords' power from veto (which had saved the unionists in the past) to mere amendment and delay. But the opposition Conservative Party believed passionately that the imposition of home rule on Ulster was an abuse of a parliamentary majority. When unionists threatened massive armed rebellion, they enjoyed the unexceptionable support of the Conservatives, who were gaining dangerously on the Liberals in popularity. Thus, through political leverage, unionists were able to secure Westminster's support for partition as compromise.

In principle, partition was approved by both houses of Parliament in May 1914. The debate was over form: the Commons' bill favored temporary exclusion by county option, the Lords' amendment permanent exclusion of all nine Ulster counties. Herbert Asquith, the prime minister, was inclined to split the difference, with the solution of permanent exclusion of the four counties with Protestant majorities, but debate on the Ulster question was suspended by agreement when World War I broke out in August. In September the home-rule bill was enacted as the Government of Ireland Act of 1914, with the proviso that it would not come into operation until the war had ended and special legislation had been passed for Ulster. The Government of Ireland Act of 1920, which finally effected partition, arose on the strength of the 1914 Act.

With World War I over, the Conservative Party, as the senior member of the ruling coalition, actually needed unionists less than it had before. But in the climate of open Anglo-Irish warfare, the once dominant Irish Parliamentary Party—constitutional nationalists opposed to partition— had lost all but six of its eighty-four prewar seats in parliament in the 1918 elections. By the same token, a permanent political solution had become more urgent. Unionists had taken twenty-six seats, including twenty-two of Ulster's total of thirty-seven. Sinn Fein won only three seats in the six counties that would become Northern Ireland, but with the remaining seventy-three seats out of Ireland's 105 aggregate, had replaced the Irish Parliamentary Party as nominally the strongest Irish party.

In 1919, Sinn Fein thus established the Dail Eireann* (consisting of all Irish MPs except those representing Dublin University) as the independent government of Ireland. Sinn Fein regarded partition under the 1920 Act as an unsatisfactory monarchist answer to the national question. The party deemed the Dail the only proper solution and accordingly followed a policy of abstention from Westminster. This left the unionists as the loudest Irish voice by far in parliament. Sinn Fein, then, can be seen as a central culprit in the passage of the 1920 Act. Thanks in part to Sinn Fein's institutional silence, unionists were able to strengthen their majority position in the putative state. The 1920 Act provided for a six-county devolved government—which republicans call "gerrymandered"—and

---

*Pronounced "doll err-*on*" and meaning "parliament of Ireland."

barred reunification absent the popular consent of the six counties—which republicans call the "unionist veto."[9]

During the run-up to the treaty, David Lloyd George, the British prime minister, gave unionists private assurances that the six counties would remain under unionist control. Eamonn de Valera, then president of Sinn Fein and of the first Dail, effectively conceded partition as a temporary salve that a "Boundary Commission" authorized by the treaty would dissolve piece by piece. A three-man Boundary Commission, appointed in 1924, concluded that the Treaty contemplated only minor changes to the border. An embarrassed Dublin government acquiesced to the dissolution of the Commission in December 1925. But the foundations for permanent partition had already been laid when the treaty was signed by Michael Collins and de Valera's five other delegates under Lloyd George's threat of a resumption of war.

Lloyd George's ultimatum may have been a brutish power play, but that's beside the point: partition was a *fait accompli* long before.[10] Legal and administrative partition was firmly in place before the treaty was signed in December of 1921.[11] A separate Northern Ireland administration had been set up in 1920 by authority of the outgoing Anglo-Irish government at Dublin Castle. Inaugural parliamentary elections for Northern Ireland in May 1921 had yielded forty unionist seats against twelve nationalist ones, creating an essentially one-party state, and the new Northern Ireland parliament was opened in Belfast on June 22, 1921. The second Dail—composed of Sinn Feiners—narrowly *approved* the treaty. In the Irish election that followed, the pro-treaty side won a decisive victory.

Sinn Fein and the IRA then each split into respective pro- and anti-treaty factions which then squared off. The anti-treaty IRA resorted to civil war to stop the new government from taking office, and denounced all successive Dails as illegitimate. The war, however, was fought not because the treaty copper-fastened partition, but because, thanks to the requirement of fidelity to the Crown, it failed to deliver a true "republic." Self-evidently, it was the anti-treaty Sinn Fein/IRA, not the unionists, who behaved without regard to democracy. The anti-partition faction of the IRA lost the civil war, and became completely marginalized. In 1923, pro-partition Sinn Feiners formed Cumann na nGaedheal, which is now Fine Gael (pronounced "finneh-*gale*"). In 1926, de Valera left the remaining anti-partition Sinn Fein and founded Fianna Fail (pronounced "feenah-*fall*"), to which more pragmatic IRA and Sinn Fein members defected. Fianna Fail and Fine Gael would become the Republic of Ireland's two major parties. The virulent anti-partitionists had been pushed aside for the time being.

Partition also marginalized militant unionism in Ulster. No vote on partition had been taken within the six counties, but on September 28, 1912, 471, 413 unionists from the nine counties of Ulster signed "Ulster's Solemn League and Covenant," pledging their refusal to recognize home rule. Unionists soon engineered the mass armament of the original UVF (in 1914, 100,000 strong, with 24,000 rifles and three million rounds of ammunition). The UVF threatened insurrection to thwart Irish home rule and preserve the union of Ulster and Britain. In March 1914 came the so-called Curragh mutiny. Some fifty-nine officers in the British regional army command for Ulster informed their commander-in-chief that they would not enforce home rule against Ulster, and London felt compelled to assure them that they would not be asked to do so. Already Downing Street had come under too much pressure from the unionists to accord home rule to all thirty-two counties as a unit.[12] The First World War put home rule on hold, and the UVF was rolled into the British army as the 36th (Ulster) Division. At the Battle of the Somme, the 36th took inordinately high casualties. But contrary to republican lore, Ulster's sacrifice at the Somme in July 1916 had nothing essential to do with establishing partition, which in essence occurred beforehand.

After the civil war, the old IRA split over partition. One wing accepted a six-county Protestant stronghold as the unavoidable cost of a twenty-six-county Irish Free State, while the other stubbornly insisted on a thirty-two-county unitary socialist state and characterized anything short of that as merely "provisional." Compromisers who won the civil war carried their realpolitik through to 1949, when a new coalition government declared the twenty-six-county Irish Free State a full-fledged sovereign republic—in part, with a view to coaxing the IRA away from violence. But from 1956 through 1962, the IRA tried to resuscitate Irish reunification with a border bombing campaign, though an indifferent Catholic population made indigenous recruitment anemic. The IRA gave up and hawked a nonviolent political strategy.

When mass arson and rioting emerged in August 1969, mummified local IRA cadres comprised only about sixty men, most of them old and halfhearted, too weak to protect Catholics in Belfast and Derry. The defining slogan on walls of the Falls Road was "I.R.A. = I Ran Away." In December 1969, after London had sent in British troops (but before loyalists had started their campaign of killing Catholic civilians), young republicans got a testosterone boost. They split from the extant IRA, and formed the Provisional IRA, its military strength centered heavily in

Belfast, to mount more effective armed resistance. Those who declined to join the new group were dubbed the Official IRA.*

By the time the troubles broke out, members of the original Ulster Volunteer Force of 1912, many of whom fought in the First World War, were either dead or decrepit. Their sons were young and healthy. One such son, Gusty Spence, had himself enlisted in the British army, and was discharged a corporal in 1961 after seeing combat in Cyprus. Spence returned home to the Shankill Road—an area adjacent to the Falls Road, exclusively Protestant and unexceptionably loyalist—and an inherited job as a stager at the Harland and Wolff shipyard. There was agitation for Catholic civil rights afoot. Spence believed his community was threatened, and in 1965 he and a few other working-class veterans started a secret vigilante group. For prestige, they cadged the name "Ulster Volunteer Force." Military backgrounds were just enough to make the name stick with a patriotic and suggestible Shankill Road crowd.

According to McIntyre, "the UVF under Gusty Spence was four or five drunks on the Shankill." Spence issues no direct denial. But he says: "There were vigilantes on both sides. The Provisional IRA came out of the Central Citizens' Defense Committee"—a Falls Road community action coalition that began in 1969. In other words, the troubles begat their own terrorist groups, whatever anyone says about history.

Nobody disputes the origins of the Ulster Defense Association, the largest of the paramilitary organizations in Northern Ireland: it was born in 1970 as the coalescence of local vigilante groups. Some UDA men

---

*After a brief feud with the Provisional IRA, the Official IRA declared a permanent ceasefire in 1972. The Provisional IRA became the largest and most effective of the paramilitary organizations—loyalist or republican—that operated during the troubles. Between 1969 and its ceasefire on August 31, 1994, the Provisional IRA was responsible for 1,778 deaths—well over half the total. Among republican groups, the Irish National Liberation Army (INLA) ranked a distant second, claiming 122 lives during the same period. For comparison, the loyalist paramilitaries killed a total of 946 people through their ceasefire on October 13, 1994, while the security forces killed 357 people. The political counterpart of the Provisional IRA is properly called Provisional Sinn Fein, of which Gerry Adams is president. Official Sinn Fein (the official IRA's political wing) was strongly socialist and opposed to physical force, and has branched into the Workers Party and the Democratic Left. These parties and Provisional Sinn Fein have negligible political support in the south, but Provisional Sinn Fein has commanded 10 percent of the vote in Northern Ireland since the 1981 hunger strike. In this book, "IRA" refers to the Provisional IRA and "Sinn Fein" means Provisional Sinn Fein, unless a clear indication to the contrary is given. The terms "Provo" and "Shinner," also used in this book, are the common colloquialisms, respectively, for a member of the Provisional IRA and a member of Provisional Sinn Fein.

sneer at the UVF's cheap claim on Ulster's posterity. "The UVF carried that tag of 'UVF' from 1912. We thought that was disloyal," explains Jimmy Creighton, a former member of the UDA. "The original UVF, you know, 750 of them went from the Shankill area, and seventy-five came back. Gave their lives for this country and for England, and were glorified. With all the books that's writ about them and the medals and so on—to use that name I thought was not the proper thing to do."

Republicans and loyalists alike forge the ore of history into sledgehammers with which to bludgeon each other. That passes for politics in Northern Ireland. Gusty Spence's pet line: "Compare the lies and you can approximate the truth in Northern Ireland." You can also opt out of this coy Irish game and take a stab at stating some facts. Fact: the troubles started locally, with Catholic civil rights protests. Fact: the troubles happened because an abused Catholic community lashed back and a competing (though less abused) Protestant underclass reacted in kind. Fact: the IRA revived the objective of a united Ireland to give the Catholic civil insurgency added momentum. Fact: the loyalist paramilitaries exaggerated the threats to Protestants from Dublin to give their own movement greater urgency. Fact: paramilitary deeds ennobled these causes and created Doppelgänger loops of illogic—people died over militant republicanism and loyalism, therefore these stances must be valid.

The paramilitaries' antics evolved like a spectator sport. Without expressly approving murder, nationalists rooted for the IRA as they would the Glasgow Celtics. Likewise, unionists boosted the UVF and the UDA as they might the Glasgow Rangers. Jimmy Creighton, then a UDA man and now a community worker, remembers the banality of the conflict. He lived in north Belfast. "You know, there can never be an acceptable level of violence, but we had become accustomed to it. The TV was on, and we're sitting here talking, they say the man has been shot in Ardoyne—must be a Catholic. If it came out that it was a Catholic—desperate, but so what? But if it came out it was a Protestant—fucking rotten bastards, he was only in there trying to help them. We justified the violence. Every person on God's earth. Not just paramilitaries, everybody. I was sitting talking to a woman one night and there was a young Catholic fellow shot in Ardoyne, and she made a comment to me—she said, did you see the fucking shop they had? And I says, what's that got to do with him being dead? She says, nothing, but did you see the shops they had, we haven't got shops like that. That's how immune people became to violence."

John Lyttle, the son of recently deceased Shankill Road UDA brigadier

Tommy "Tucker" Lyttle and now a journalist with London's *Independent,* eloquently recalls the cheap romanticism the troubles released and then fed off. "Suddenly, we were living inside the reports we saw on the television news, which had the odd, almost Brechtian effect of distancing you from things you might have actually participated in: a riot, for example. The result was a kind of documentary unreality. That, and a sort of vicious glamour which would increasingly loosen moral constraints and permit previously unimaginable behavior. Men who traditionally read only thrillers, spy novels, war books, and James Bond—like my father— and whose cinematic tastes ran to gangster flicks and the rough justice of the Western, now had the chance to star in their own home-grown, patriotic versions of heroic fantasies. They took their chance."[13]

The troubles-gawkers included not just the working classes in the thick of the conflict, but also the middle class that escaped the troubles virtually unscathed and international onlookers as well. Catholic Irish-Americans, especially at the grass-roots level, have long been entranced by the IRA because it makes being Irish seem romantic, dangerous, and sexy. For more than a hundred years, Irish nationalist movements, including the Provisional IRA, have drawn huge proportions of their finances from Catholic Irish-Americans, who also supported Irish neutrality in both world wars.

There are at least 38 million Americans, 15 percent of the population, that claim Irish descent. About half of them originated in Ulster, and most of that group are Protestant. Their ancestors came over primarily in the eighteenth century, when Presbyterians in Ireland were disenfranchised as Catholics were. These immigrants were mainly anti-British, and participated widely in the Revolutionary War. Though in the fullness of time the descendants they left behind were better treated by the Crown and came to value the union, the Ulster Protestant diaspora are too far removed, too assimilated, or too ambivalent to care about Ulster's union with the United Kingdom now. Catholic Irish-Americans date back mainly to the famine of the 1840s; the perceived wounds at London's hands are fresher.

Over the past twenty-five years, the troubles have been an overblown conflict, but not a trivial one. Native comparisons to Beirut or Bosnia may be melodramatic, yet they are not utterly silly with respect to the first seven years. In the period from 1969 to 1976, Belfast and Derry sometimes verged on civil war, at least on a guerrilla level. During those eight years, about 1,800 people were killed—well over half of the total number. But after 1976, political violence dropped precipitously, and averaged only eighty-six deaths annually through October 13, 1994, the date of the loyalist ceasefire.

That translates to a murder rate of about 60 per 1,000,000 people, which most American metropolitan police chiefs would welcome. Belfast has always been far safer than New York. In terms of pure carnage, the troubles came to little more than a protracted gang war. Even counting paramilitaries, the criminal element in Northern Ireland is minuscule compared to that of the United States, one in 800 versus one in 250 being incarcerated. Indeed, the generation of children that bore witness to the troubles have not turned into the "monsters" that some American sociologists predicted they would become.[14]

In addition to national roots, there are two reasons Americans have sustained an unusual interest in the troubles. First, white folks harbor an inward-looking fascination about other white folks fighting still other white folks—it's not supposed to happen much anymore. Second, nationalist immigrants and their descendants in the United States make out the lot of Catholics in Northern Ireland to be worse than it really is.

In February 1996, for example, San Francisco mayor Willie Brown organized a boycott of Bushmills Irish whiskey. Prompted by the John Maher Irish-American Democratic Club, Brown launched the protest by pouring a bottle of Bushmills down the sewer to impel the distillery to fix its "shameful record" of "anti-Catholic" employment habits. Bushmills is in north County Antrim, a densely Protestant area of Northern Ireland. The plant employs about one hundred people. Fewer than ten are Catholic, but most of the work force has been employed there for years, and business is mildly contracting. Bushmills is in full compliance with the Fair Employment Commission, which has received no complaints. In areas like 70 percent Catholic Derry, there are businesses with work forces at least as skewed in the other direction. The U.S. firm United Technologies, for example, in its Northern Ireland automotive parts plant employs over 95 percent Catholics—at last count, 1,070 Catholics versus eleven Protestants.[15] Californians are unlikely to forgo driving until the imbalance is remedied. John Hume, Northern Ireland's most revered Catholic politician, is from Derry. He wrote Mayor Brown explaining that the Protestant share of Bushmills employees was demographically "natural" and asking him to call off the boycott.[16]

On the western side of the Atlantic, the central misconception is that if the IRA has continued its campaign for twenty-five years, circumstances in Northern Ireland must merit the carnage. The Falls Road, Americans imagine, is all bomb craters and bullet holes, when in reality most of the leveling that has occurred in recent years is from vigorous urban renewal—substantially in Catholic areas. U.S. congressmen and state legislators insist on affirmative action for Catholics, when Hume proclaims the policy not only unnecessary but divisive and uneconomic. It is not uncommon to hear uninformed Americans exclaim that the British should leave Northern Ireland and let those poor Catholics have their freedom, even though roughly one million people—60 to 65 percent of the province's population—are Protestant, consider themselves British, and want to stay that way. Many Americans seem to think these "unionists" want a united Ireland, when in fact the "union" they desire is the existing one with the United Kingdom. Others cherish the conceit that Northern Irish politics are impossibly complicated, and the cliché that enmity between Catholics and Protestants is intractably deep-rooted. Neither is true. That the troubles never reached high-intensity warfare suggests as much. Seventeen months of peace seemed to prove the case.

Nonpolitical murder was negligible in Northern Ireland before and during the troubles. In the decade prior to the troubles, murders in the province *totaled* thirty-seven.[17] So 1969 and its aftermath were terrible shocks to the existing order. Certainly nobody expected the guerrilla conflict to continue for twenty-five years. When construction began in the early seventies, Her Majesty's Prison the Maze, the high-security penitentiary for paramilitary prisoners, had an expected life-span of ten years. Thus, the architects didn't think to design the blocks with slanted roofs, so they are constantly water-damaged and under repair.

Yet post-ceasefire Northern Ireland differs from the recent pre-ceasefire version more in spirit than in substance. From 1976, the troubles were a tinker-toy war, notable more for the hit-and-run cowardice of the participants than for sheer bloodshed. Northern Ireland, in P. J. O'Rourke's droll phrase, was "heck's half-acre."[18] In 1994, the final year of the troubles, there were eighty-two murders. In the year following the loyalist ceasefire, there were twenty-four.[19] The drop is statistically significant, but did not drastically affect the quality of life. How the troubles ended is scarcely a puzzler, for there wasn't much real fighting to halt. The harder question is why the troubles—that is, the steady drip of indigenous terrorism over the constitutional status of Northern Ireland—lasted for so long.

A key reason was republican tradition. All it needed was the spur of the August 1969 riots to reacquire critical momentum. "I had a strong sense of being a victim," says McIntyre. "We always felt that Protestants could come into our areas but we couldn't go into theirs, we were always getting beat up. I didn't know what a unionist was, but I knew that they were people who give us trouble. That, mixed in with the romantic side of it, the exciting side of it, informed a certain intellectual nerve that was in me." The old IRA fought the Anglo-Irish war and the Irish civil war between 1919 and 1923 and staged periodic guerrilla operations between 1924 and 1969. McIntyre's generation of republicans had a warm trail of extralegal agitation to follow.

The loyalists' trail was colder. In 1969, loyalists had only a tentative history of extralegal paramilitarism. They did, however, have a strong sense of entitlement to Ulster born of heavy sacrifices for Britain during two world wars. Ron McMurray recalls the feeling. During the two-week-long general strike of 1974, engineered by the loyalist paramilitaries with the cooperation of loyalist-dominated trade unions, he says, "my area was totally and absolutely sealed off. The best I can describe it is wartime—a wartime spirit, everybody sticking together. It was a reenactment of the Second World War again. So it was good, it was good times. I don't mean to sound facetious about it. As a teenager, you know, I felt supreme power. I felt good that I was doing something which I thought was positive, something which was dangerous, exciting, romantic. I was carrying a gun. There's something else about being able to carry a gun, and also the fear of being shot dead. There was an adrenaline buzz to it."

Add to that a collective sense of noble purpose: "It actually was a consensus thing too—you felt you were part of a larger community," says McMurray. "One of the main motives for a lot of people was that you were doing something for your community in that we perceived an attack on our community or our identity. So therefore, being young, rough, and tough, we could defend all of the people—our parents, our friends—by actually going out and engaging in this violent behavior."

McIntyre and McMurray both testify that their motives were more hormonal than political, and their concerns more communitarian than constitutional. As a practical matter, they were concerned mainly about territory. Next came romance and historical tradition. Politics—that is, whether Northern Ireland stayed British or became Irish—was farther down on each man's list. And religion itself came in dead last. Territory ranked first because republican and loyalist paramilitaries were almost exclusively working-class. Whereas middle-class people always had the option of England or Ireland, blue-collar folks never had the vocational expectations that would allow them to leave Northern Ireland easily. In a place the size of Connecticut, this lack of cross-border mobility mattered. Many believed the only alternative was to stand and fight.

So who was responsible for the troubles?

Even during the height of the bloodletting, active paramilitaries never numbered more than a thousand on each side at any one time. Neither side had a substantial electoral constituency, but each had what might be called a "passive constituency" that was very broad—that is, communities that would not affirmatively or openly support paramilitary violence but would accept whatever advantages terrorist attacks offered to their larger political objective. At ground level, these groups therefore were inclined to acquiesce rather than oppose. Tolerance at the community level was essential to allow the conflict to continue in Belfast and Derry, where terrorism was heaviest. These cities are segregated on an atomized level—neighborhood by neighborhood—which necessitated conflict in very close quarters.* Without at least some local support, the paramilitaries could not have staged attacks with the frequency that they did, and they could not have evaded the security forces as successfully. For example, although paramilitaries sometimes had to commandeer "safe houses," sympathizers often provided them voluntarily.

As for the apparent substance of the conflict, strictly religious lines are blurred in Northern Ireland. IRA men are not particularly devout ("I don't want the Catholic Church telling me I can't get a divorce," ex-Provo lifer Donncha O'Hara admits), and neither are most Protestant paramilitaries. On the other hand, Ulster Protestants generally are the most church-going in the world, and find divorce and abortion almost as distasteful as Catholics do. Many loyalists were in fact sympathetic with the 1981 Catholic hunger strikers led by Bobby Sands, and said so at the time. Some loyalists now admit that they should have joined the strikers insofar as loyalists wanted precisely what the republicans were agitating for against the state—namely, prisoner-of-war status. It's probably true that Protestants culturally are less inclined than Catholics toward self-sacrifice, and less prone to nuanced legal interpretation, but the conflict in Northern Ireland is hardly about the moral right to starve to death or the niceties of language. It is about tribal power.

---

*The rest of Northern Ireland is geographically segregated on a much broader scale. Catholics compose the majority of the population west of the River Bann, which bisects the province, while Protestants hold an even larger majority east of it.

"It's not a religious conflict—no one's getting shot over transubstantiation or Mary worship," says Billy Mitchell, ex-UVF life-sentence prisoner and now a studious Christian. "If you take Catholicism and Protestantism as spiritual entities, you should expect that Catholics would be more amenable to being subjected. I mean it's a totalitarian church where certainly all the lines of communication come down through the Pope—you should have a subjected people, who are used to being subjected. Protestants should be more radical, more innovative, more risk-taking, and more devil-may-care. But it doesn't work out like that." In Ulster, in fact, quite the opposite.

The operative division is between British and Irish. Ever since 1690, history has transformed the Irish problem into a nagging colonial conflict between the occupiers and the occupied. Religion is not writ large in Ulster now, the way it was three hundred years ago. Instead, its influence is micro-behavioral—like, as Mitchell puts it, "something working away at the back of the mind that molds the whole person."

The British presence, both direct and through unionist institutions, was and still is paramount. The "B-Specials," an all-Protestant police auxiliary force, abetted Protestant mobs during the August 1969 riots. Thereafter the Brits' military and legal excesses were many. Beginning in 1969, as many as 21,000 British troops at a time were deployed in Northern Ireland. Soldiers on foot patrol strong-armed innocent Catholics, and sometimes took salacious pleasure in frisking teenaged girls. Elite paratroopers shot dead fourteen unarmed Catholic civil rights protesters in Derry on "Bloody Sunday" in 1972—Northern Ireland's Kent State. Twenty years later, Private Lee Clegg was released after serving only four years of a life sentence for the murder of a Catholic teenager—in stark contrast to the Birmingham Six and the Guildford Four, who were wrongly convicted of IRA bombings and served prison terms exceeding fifteen years.

These transgressions both riled up the IRA and gave it credibility with the larger Catholic population. Joe Clarke, who held rank in the Belfast Brigade of the IRA for two decades, was interned along with 341 other suspected republicans in the massive British army swoop in August 1971.[20] Clarke tuned and raced rally cars before joining the IRA. He is built like a cube, and his broad face wears the imperturbable look of the cheerful Mick who'd keep smiling as he took a crowbar to his tormentor. This manly countenance would not have sat well with British troops entrusted with the emasculation of the incipient republican movement. After forty-eight hours of the third degree— "slapping you about a bit and asking you the same old questions over and over again"—he and four others were handcuffed together with hoods placed over their heads.

As Clarke tells the story: "We were then put into helicopters, and they seemed to go for an hour, ninety minutes. Then one of the soldiers said, 'Have you seen what the Americans do to the Vietnamese, throwing these guys out of helicopters? Well, that's what's going to happen to you.' And the next thing, I was thrown out of the helicopter while it was still hovering. It was only hovering about six feet in the air, but we didn't know that because we had hoods on our heads." Clarke was then questioned further, forced to stand spread-eagled against a wall for three days straight, a single bright light shining in his eyes as "white noise" hissed. When he stonewalled his interrogators, they kicked his back and the inside of his legs. Now hallucinating, Clarke attacked them, and they cuffed his wrists and ankles so tightly they bled. Then the soldiers bound his feet to his buttocks and dropped him on a concrete floor from about four feet directly on his knees. Internally, they swelled with fluid and bled. During a week of this brand of interrogation, Clarke was given bread and water twice. He lost sixteen pounds. He never broke. He still limps.

As one of "Twelve Hooded Men," Clarke filed a claim with the Belfast High Court, which in two cases found the security forces guilty of degrading treatment and awarded damages in 1974. Clarke himself settled for £12,500, then about $25,000. Four years later, the European Court of Human Rights pronounced the security forces' "five techniques" used for "interrogation in-depth" inhuman and degrading treatment. These techniques included prolonged hooding, extended physical discomfort, "white noise," sleep deprivation, and denial of food and water. It would have been difficult for a dirty-tricks operative to script better propaganda for the Provisional IRA. The republicans turned the British penchant for hardball to even greater advantage during the 1981 hunger strikes. The election to Parliament of Bobby Sands, who soon after became the first hunger striker to die, established the IRA's foothold, through Sinn Fein, in Northern Irish politics.

In turn, the IRA was the lifeblood of loyalist paramilitaries and unionist politicians. Throughout much of the troubles, London did not seem to entertain any real prospect of a political solution but sought only to preserve a certain military peremptoriness over a misbehaving colony. In December 1971, as the troubles reached their peak, British home secretary Reginald Maudling had fatuously and cynically set as the goal of Britain's Northern Ireland policy merely "an acceptable level of violence"[21]—which history eventually revealed as eighty-six dead per year.

Later on, the administration of the state during Britain's direct rule of Northern Ireland became far more equitable than it was during the fifty-year tenure of Northern Ireland's devolved assembly. Installed at partition and known simply as "Stormont," the assembly was christened "a Protestant parliament for a Protestant people" by Sir James Craig, the first prime minister of Northern Ireland. Due to the rising violence, Westminster suspended Stormont in March 1972 and began to govern Northern Ireland through a Northern Ireland secretary of state and his ministers. They spend, on average, roughly one-fifth of their time in Northern Ireland. The administrative machinery of Northern Ireland's government was constituted in a Northern Ireland Office (NIO) and several executive departments. The NIO is responsible for matters particular to Northern Ireland and reserved by statute—notably, security and political affairs. The executive departments are collectively much larger, as they embrace the civil service, through which economic and financial matters and human services are conducted.

Both the NIO and the departments are based, as the old government was, at Stormont Castle in east Belfast. This building is a grandiose neo-Gothic extravagance opened in 1932. It looks as though it was designed by Albert Speer. From the iron gates at the roadside a wide, tree-lined driveway dips slightly and then ascends dramatically about five hundred yards up a hill to a six-pillar facade fronting a massive five-story white granite rectangle flying the Union Jack.

Under Stormont, the province enjoyed near-dominion status. In the direct-rule arrangement, the NIO and the Northern Ireland departments essentially became proxies. They have no legislative power, no power to modify or delay House of Commons legislation, no taxing power, and only limited executive discretion. They are accountable to Westminster and Whitehall through the Northern Ireland secretary of state, a member of Parliament of ministerial rank, and his ministers.

Direct rule was interrupted for five months in 1974, when Brian Faulkner, the last Stormont prime minister, established a power-sharing executive to complement a new seventy-eight-member Stormont assembly elected in 1973 on Westminster's initiative. The loyalist strike in May 1974 ousted the experimental administration, and direct rule resumed. In 1982, Westminster instituted another salaried, elected Northern Ireland assembly with an eye toward developing "rolling devolution"—that is, a gradual, ad hoc resumption of self-government by the assembly on the basis of 70 percent super-majorities. Although the NIO participated through committees, the assembly was hobbled by nationalist abstention-ism and unionist boycotts. After the Anglo-Irish Agreement was signed in November 1985, the Assembly simply became a platform for dissent. The NIO withdrew its committee staff, and Westminster dissolved the Assem-bly in June 1986, just before fresh elections were to take place. Northern Ireland has been represented in the House of Commons since the incep-tion of the state. At present, for Northern Ireland there are seventeen MPs—thirteen unionists and four nationalists. For the next parliamen-tary elections, the province's allotment of seats in the House of Commons will increase to eighteen.

The Anglo-Irish Agreement established Ulster's majority as the opera-tive determinant of Northern Ireland's constitutional status, but also cre-ated an "Intergovernmental Conference" through which Dublin has a con-sultative role in Northern Irish affairs. Constitutional nationalists saw the arrangement as a happy compromise; unionists considered it the first step to a united Ireland. They regarded as empty the Republic's acknowledg-ment of the six-county consent, because of articles 2 and 3 of the Irish Re-public's constitution, which claim all thirty-two counties as national terri-tory and oblige the Irish government to effect reunification. The unionists overreacted.* Based permanently in Maryfield near Stormont Castle, the Intergovernmental Conference came to nothing more than a few south-erners, under heavy guard, issuing the odd atrocity denouncement and playing a lot of cards. Republicans more accurately saw the Anglo-Irish Agreement as a fair attempt by Margaret Thatcher, in the wake of the hunger strikes and the IRA's assassination attempt in Brighton, to render the republican movement impotent and short-circuit reunification by force. Hence, Sinn Fein and the IRA were determinedly undeterred from

---

*Given southern apathy about reunification and the concession of six-county consent, ar-ticles 2 and 3 are merely aspirational. Nevertheless, in November 1985, 100,000 people gathered at Belfast City Hall in protest. The buzzphrase of unionism became "Ulster Says No!" During July 12th celebrations in 1986, Sandy Row residents were burning Margaret Thatcher in effigy, and protesting loyalist mobs clashed with police. Two and a half years later, with Ulster Unionist Party funding, Chris McGimpsey and his brother Michael brought a lawsuit before the Dublin High Court challenging the validity of the agreement on the basis of the inconsistency between Dublin's recognition of unionist consent as a re-quirement of reunification and the Irish Constitution's territorial claim to all thirty-two counties of the island. They lost despite a convincing argument, and have cleverly used the judicial defeat to strengthen the unionist contention in Westminster that Dublin cannot be trusted. What the unionist community remembers is the vehemence of the complaints, not their substance.

waging their armed campaign. Since it was signed in 1985, the agreement has proven practically ineffectual, and emotionally inflammatory. In short, it has caused far more trouble than it has alleviated.

During direct rule, Westminster has enacted tough antidiscrimination laws that have made a substantial, if not wholly curative, impact on nepotistic and Protestant-biased hiring practices. This was always one of Northern Ireland's most egregious problems. Working-class Protestants claim that housing improvements have unfairly favored Catholics. Jimmy Creighton runs a community project in Glencairn—a grim pebble-dash housing estate known as Belfast's South Bronx. "We have people living in maisonettes up there with no heat, and they spend the whole winter living in one room with an electric fire," he says. "Now, the housing conditions on the Catholic side have been addressed. There's been reverse discrimination here. Don't punish us for something somebody else did. We've been blamed for the sins of what's happened for the past seventy fucking odd years."

The Brits' bottom line was to behave honorably on their own terms. That meant two things. First, they righteously defended their Protestant wards with military aggressiveness and political rigidity, when flexibility might have spelled an end to armed conflict sooner. Second, though, they heeded the legitimate complaints of Catholics whom Britain's Protestant clients had marginalized for fifty years. Throughout the troubles, London tried to draw republicans into politics and away from violence. Through the ill-fated 1974 power-sharing executive, the British government sought to make the nonviolent constitutional nationalists of the Social Democratic and Labour Party (SDLP) full partners with unionists in government. In the same year, the Brits made Sinn Fein a legal political party in the hope that the party would contest 1975 elections for a constitutional convention. Sinn Fein declined, and, beneath the pall cast by the 1974 loyalist strike, the convention was a resounding flop.

Like many neocolonial powers, the Brits were well-intentioned and sophisticated in their approach to Northern Ireland. And like many such powers, by parsing the equities they ended up achieving little in the way of permanent resolution. With the Downing Street declaration of December 1993, Britain relaxed its claim on the sovereignty of Northern Ireland and left it essentially to the people of the province. This concession, finally, was enough to get Sinn Fein and the IRA to suspend the republican armed campaign.

Neither republican nor loyalist terrorism has worked in Northern Ireland. Although Britain might not have been as aggressive about redressing Catholics' civil rights had the IRA not bombed the mainland and targeted British political leaders, neither might the Brits have been so intent on disempowering the Provos and everybody they claimed to speak for. Rather than advance either cause, terrorism made Northern Ireland unappealing to both sovereign powers regardless of which side perpetrated it.

Consequently, the paramilitaries decided they'd best declare for peace lest events and attitudes render them politically obsolete. Gerry Adams must have concluded—correctly—that the unionists rather than the Brits drive constitutional politics in Northern Ireland. Stepping up the IRA's military campaign would only produce greater political intransigence in the unionists and stiffer martial resolve in the Brits. (After the IRA's Shankill bombing in October 1993, in which nine Protestant civilians were killed, several savvy commentators were pushing for selective internment.) The IRA could not hope to come out on top in a military escalation. On the other hand, Sinn Fein had developed electoral support of about 10 percent in the twelve years since the hunger strikes. Combine it with the 25 percent mandate of the SDLP, and nationalists could confront unionists with greater internal strength than ever before. Moreover, in Adams's apparent calculation, a renunciation of violence by the IRA would enlist Washington's power (through the Irish nationalist "mafia" there) to soften the Brits and thereby involve Dublin in a nascent peace process.

The IRA cessation boxed in the loyalists: they had always claimed that their terrorist campaign was strictly reactive, so credibility demanded that they stop when the Provos did. At the same time, the ex-paramilitaries that led the fringe loyalist parties saw a positive opportunity to divorce themselves from staid unionism by matching Sinn Fein's high visibility and trumpeting the neglected concerns of the Protestant working class. In early 1995, there were more Shinners and loyalist ex-prisoners flying across the Atlantic than there were Brits and unionists. Belfast newspapers extolled former IRA chief of staff Martin McGuinness's dress sense and ridiculed the loud sweaters worn by UVF-man-turned-politician David Ervine. These were exciting and unprecedented developments, and kept the most dynamic element of Northern Ireland in the headlines without the earlier cost. Republicans and loyalists, of course, still seek opposite constitutional ends for Ulster. But violence had produced tedium and yielded to the inspirational novelty of a fragile peace.

The ex-paramilitaries' rough pedigrees mean that their Camelot as peacemakers will be a brief one. The former "men of violence" will keep their historic resonance, but their direct control over politics will fade once Ulster's voters decide on a permanent settlement. This reality may help explain the otherwise bewildering Canary Wharf bomb. As long as the threat of terrorism remains acute, its political stewards enjoy the formidable power either to comfort the population or to intimidate it—just as they did during the troubles.

CHAPTER 2

REPUBLICAN PROVOCATIONS

Most republicans were hardened in their youth by some act of callow bigotry. To hear some of them tell it, they never met with anything but juvenile venom from Protestant kids. Anthony McIntyre gets thumped because he can't sing Britain's favorite tune. He learns about the IRA from his father and a Jimmy Cagney movie called *Shake Hands with the Devil,* and figures out what's behind the 12th of July nastiness in the neighborhood. Then come the all-Protestant B-Specials and the British army to clinch his hatred. McIntyre is an IRA volunteer. For many young Catholics sectarianism was far more cruel. Carol Cullen, who is married to McIntyre and did five years for an attempted RUC station bombing, lost her infant brother Gerard when he suffocated from tear gas the British army pitched into her family's house during the internment sweep in August 1971. Eighteen months later, her father was shot in the legs by loyalists. His father had been murdered by loyalists along with seven other men while working on the ship *Argentina* at Harland and Wolff in the late 1940s. Leo Green's brother John, also an IRA man, was executed in 1975 by loyalists led by a renegade British intelligence officer. The Ulster Freedom Fighters murdered Joe Clarke's brother Padraic in 1992.

Still others found themselves under a cloud of violence, though not directly touched by it. Gary Roberts, who served fourteen years for his part in the murder of a sixty-four-year-old Protestant and for trying to escape, got the same treatment as McIntyre in the east Belfast neighborhood of Tiger Bay when he let slip a Catholic "haitch" instead of a Protestant "aitch" reciting the alphabet on demand en route to his home in the Short Strand. By itself, the occasional beating was not enough to drive Roberts to the guerrilla life. His great-grandfather, though a Catholic, was killed at the Battle of the Somme. The man his great-grandmother then married, Henry Cromie, was decorated in the First World War. At partition, as Roberts tells it, "his elder brother, who was also a decorated war hero, was

31

shot dead by loyalists in a totally wanton sectarian attack coming back from work in the shipyards, because they didn't want Catholics working in the shipyards." In 1971, Henry Cromie's eldest grandson and Robert's uncle, James Cromie, was about to turn fourteen. On December 4, he was blown up along with fourteen other Catholics at McGurk's Bar in the New Lodge section of north Belfast. The "Empire Loyalists," later revealed to be a UVF *nom de guerre,* claimed responsibility.

Recalls Roberts: "Mrs. McGurk was killed, her fourteen-year-old daughter was killed, her brother was killed, most of the people who died were elderly or married couples. That's the sort of bar it was. If you were sitting at the bar and you swore or cursed you were thrown out—that's the sort of person Mr. McGurk was. And my great-grandfather, one day he brought me into the parlor—politics were never spoken about, and this was the first I knew about his war history—brought me into the parlor and showed me his war medals. And he says, 'I fought for their Empire, and this is the thanks I get,' pointing to a picture of his grandson who had been murdered."

Set this against the backdrop of a weird kind of calculated distance at which Protestant children put their Catholic contemporaries. Where Roberts grew up in east Belfast, "all my friends would have been Protestants—all of the wee lads my age would have been Protestants. I would have played cricket with them and football with them, and then when I went to school I would have played Gaelic [football] and hurley. Okay, it was no problem. But come every 12th of July, for about two weeks before and two weeks after, I did not have a friend on the street. Come the 12th, they would just hit me with some sort of mad fever. There was hardly a day that went past when I wouldn't get hit or abused in some way. And after the 12th it was all grand again, we all got on great again."

Brendan Hughes, born in 1948, was involved in paramilitary activity from almost the beginning of the troubles, joining the Provisional IRA right after the split. Interned with Gerry Adams, Hughes escaped from Long Kesh in a garbage truck, got across the border, changed his appearance, and fashioned a new identity. "It was taken from *The Day of the Jackal,*" he says. Hughes returned to Belfast as one Arthur McAllister, bought a house on the exclusive and then largely Protestant Malone Road, masqueraded as a toy salesman—and resumed his position as commander of the Belfast Brigade of the Provisional IRA. In May 1974, after five months undercover, he was arrested in possession of plans for civil war— what the British called a "doomsday plan." "I actually thought they were going to execute me for treason, because they talked about it, and one of the solicitors said they possibly might." Instead, he was sentenced to fifteen years in prison, where he became an officer commanding (OC) and led the first of the republicans' two hunger strikes.

Hughes is one of a handful of genuine IRA folk heroes, but he neither looks the part nor flaunts his status. IRA alumni call him "the Dark" on account of his swarthy appearance. (Before he joined the republican movement, as a merchant seaman on a bender in England, Hughes was almost shot dead by drunken British soldiers who suspected him of being an Arab terrorist.) At forty-seven, he's mustachioed and turning gray, he's gaunt and chain-smokes. He lives off the dole and occasional manual labor, and organizes the Irish music program for the West Belfast Community Festival. Hughes is soft-spoken, no hatred burns in his voice. He once was a warrior, but not because he loathed Protestants.

Hughes grew up in the Grosvenor Road area, a sectarian no-man's-land bounded by Belfast city center, Protestant Donegall Road and Sandy Row, and the Catholic lower Falls, and now bisected by a six-lane motorway. His early memories are fond, bordering on sentimental. "My school friends obviously were Catholic, but I run around with Alex Higgins, the snooker player [World Snooker Champion, 1972 and 1982; known as "the Hurricane," the John McEnroe of snooker]. He's a Protestant, but we used to run around together when we were teenagers. We'd get a couple of bob [small change] together by going around to refuse bins and collecting scrap metal and going to the shipyard and selling it, or collecting buckets of skins [potato peelings to be used as fodder] for the pigs. And then we went over to the Jam Pot snooker hall and Higgins would have conned someone for a couple of bob, and then we went to the bookie's to try and win some more money that way. We had that relationship, but then when it came to July, the marching period, we sort of drifted. But then again, on the 11th night, we all used to have a bonfire at the bottom of Blackwater Street."

For Brendan Hughes and those of his vintage, pre-troubles Belfast was more like Tom Sawyer's Hannibal, Missouri, than Ice Cube's south central Los Angeles. Tommy Gorman lived in the middle Falls on Iveagh Street, about six blocks south of Hughes. Gorman's father was a professional soccer player and something of a local celebrity. Most Catholics then would have favored Gaelic football over soccer, which is the big British sport, so Mr. Gorman's team (called "Belfast Celtic") was mainly Protestant. For that reason, he was treated like an honorable Prod, to use the diminutive but not necessarily derogatory term for a Protestant. Mr. Gorman drank with Protestants. Although in 1961 more than half the houses in Northern Ireland had no fixed baths, hot-water taps, or indoor toilets,[1] Mr.

Gorman got a house with all these amenities. And in the off season, he worked undisturbed at Harland and Wolff—the shipyard that built the *Titanic* and until the sixties Northern Ireland's largest private employer.

The Gorman family felt comfortable enough with the unionist establishment that Tommy's older brother Jack joined the RUC. Remembers Tommy: "To me it was a bit of a shattering because there were none of us as much of a prankster as what he was, especially with the RUC. I remember him riding into the house with his shoes off after being chased by the cops. At that time the shoes were these loafers, you know, loose shoes, so to run fast you had to remove your shoes. Many's the day he arrived in the house breathless, with his shoes in his hand after being chased by the cops. He was a bit of a prankster. He used to stand on the corner and shout at the cops, and the cops would chase him. It was a bit of a game, you know. I was surprised when he joined the cops, but it didn't bother me that much because at the time there was no troubles as such." In the early seventies, Gorman also had a brother in the British army and another who tried to enlist in the royal navy. Gorman was in the IRA. "All four branches of the service were represented," he quips.

Hughes and Gorman didn't know each other, but after they finished secondary school, both joined the merchant navy—a popular option among working-class Belfast men. When Hughes returned to Northern Ireland in 1969, Protestants were already fleeing the Grosvenor Road area. One of his boyhood Protestant friends, Dennis Meek, was still there. "Me and him fought," Hughes recalls wistfully. "I remember coming back to the house after fighting at the bottom of the street and Denny Meek getting sent back by his mother to fight me again, and he came back. Three times we fought on the same day, and we remained friends up until 1969, when the conflict started. I remember being in real conflict with meself then. I remember crowds coming over, Catholic families being burned out all over the place. I was on the other side of the Grosvenor Road. A crowd of Catholics came over to burn Malt Street down—it was the street that Denny Meek lived in. I remember stopping at the Grosvenor Road and finding myself in real conflict because I was in the middle of a Catholic mob going to burn down Protestant houses, houses of people who were friends of mine."

Gorman too came back to Belfast in 1969, married, and moved to the same area where McIntyre and McMurray lived, then largely Protestant. For Gorman, the bubble burst during the notorious August riots when he witnessed the RUC leading loyalist mobs onto Divis Street in the lower Falls to burn houses down. "There's one thing that I remember, this is what sticks in my head," he says. "At one point, there was a charge and countercharge on Divis Street that night, and I got caught behind enemy lines and hid in the doorway of a shop. A line of cops run past me with their Sten guns pointing into the ground, slapping into the ground, and just firing into the ground. Five or six of them, with the mobs behind them. I said to myself, what are they firing into the ground for? It was only with experience that I realized they were firing into the ground so that the ricocheting bullets couldn't be traced to any particular weapon. So anybody shot was getting hit with bits of bullet and it could never be traced to the particular weapon. You know, I thought to meself, Jesus Christ, they're trying to murder the people, but they were trying to keep themselves clean at the same time." During the mid-August disturbances, the RUC in fact killed four Catholic civilians.

Such episodes, in sufficient number, turn a low-intensity conflict into a long-term nightmare.

With his sloping mustache, long hair, and denim car-coat, Tommy Gorman looks younger than his fifty-odd years. He is impishly warm in manner and appearance, and carries his small frame with the confidence of a large man who thinks in black-and-white, can't imagine defeat, and loves his mother. When the RUC visited a school in the middle Falls to preach restraint, he recalls, "I said to my mother, well, I'm going 'round to put these bastards out. She says, your brother's a cop. I says, aye, and if he's fucking down there I'll chase him, too. She says to me, son, you'll get six months, because at the time six months was the ordinary sentence for rioting. I says, Ma, before this is finished everybody'll get their six months. So she kept reminding me there before she died, like, son, you done your six months before the whole street." Jack Gorman quietly resigned from the RUC in early 1972. At about the same time, Tommy and six others escaped from the prison ship *Maidstone* in Belfast Harbor three weeks after being interned, fleeing to Dublin and appearing at a republican rally. He carries a photograph of himself and three co-escapees. All three were killed in the troubles.

Hughes's principal memory of 1969 was the way republican vigilantes stopped a Catholic mob from retaliating against marauding Prods. At the same time, he felt both literally and metaphorically abandoned by Protestants who'd once been neighbors. "By July 1970 the majority of Protestants had moved from this area into Sandy Row or other largely Protestant areas. This became almost a ghost town, with empty houses, burnt-out houses. A lot of these Protestants when they left burnt the houses themselves, so's Catholics couldn't move into them. We're talking about maybe thirty, forty streets. They were all just desolated." His girlfriend, a Protestant, moved away. And in his recollection, it was the British occupation that conclusively forced Catholics and Protestants to take sides. "Here you had British troops coming in to keep Protestants and Catholics apart, and they were stationed at the top of the street. I'm standing in the street with the soldiers and Protestant friends, and we were not in total conflict in 1969. It's a hard thing to understand now, but that's the way it was happening. But by 1970 that would all change."

The arrival en masse of the British army served to confirm the underdog position of the Catholics, and acted as justification for full-blown revolt. Says Hughes: "The Provisionals were seen as Catholic, nationalist, reactionary—and to a large extent they were. I certainly reacted to the situation, I was a Catholic, and I seen the Catholic community under attack. My whole reason for joining the Provisionals at that time was not to bring about a thirty-two-county democratic socialist republic, and I had no ideology at that time. We were a reactionary force." That's an admirable admission. Republicans generally brand loyalists the reactionaries, casting themselves as lofty idealists who embraced the affirmative goal of a united Ireland from the start.

The truth is, untangling the cause of the onset of the troubles in 1969 is extremely difficult. Mutual hatred had been in place since partition, but occasional sectarian violence did not add up to anything more than Arab terrorism in the West—until Crown forces stepped toward martial law and gratuitous beatings became the stuff of weekly legend. On the other hand, it was only a handful of Provisionals—and not the nationalist population at large—that decided a military campaign was necessary to vindicate Catholic civil rights. Further leveling the republican myth of immaculate populist conception, Hughes points out that what cast him irreversibly into a revolutionary was not loyalist or British brutality, but an Official IRA assassination—of his cousin and mentor, Charlie Hughes, officer commanding of the Provisional IRA, Belfast Brigade, Second Batallion (Lower Falls).*

---

*In the early to mid-1970s, the Belfast Brigade of the Provisional IRA was divided into three active battalions. The First Battalion covered the upper Falls, Andersonstown, and Ballymurphy; the Second caught the middle and lower Falls; and the Third embraced north Belfast and the Short Strand. (The so-called "Fourth Battalion" was composed simply of IRA prisoners.) In 1976, a system of operationally independent cells adopted for security reasons theoretically superseded the hierarchical military structure, though in practice it did not work particularly well. Eventually, the IRA became organized into small "active service units" within larger "companies." In these particulars, the loyalist paramilitaries basically emulated the IRA.

He was the first casualty in the feud between the Provisionals and the Officials. "I remember at Charlie's funeral, being angry that the leaders of the movement were not going out and taking stronger action against the Officials." Brendan replaced Charlie as OC in early 1971. The Provisionals did take reprisals against the Officials, and 1971 was the first year of heavy British army casualties—to wit, forty-eight. Many of the killings occurred on the lower Falls. "The lower Falls rapidly became one of the best areas for guerrilla war because it was all warren-holes and back yards," Hughes reminisces. "At one point it was a free area that the British army did not come in, unless they come in in real heavy force. You got a warning almost right away where they were, through word of mouth. Many's a time when I'd walk down the street and an old woman would have come out and thrown holy water around you, blessed you. There was a perception that you were going to jail, or you were going to be killed, and you sort of accepted that."

Had the neighborhood fun and games stayed confined to Provos, soldiers, and cops, the troubles might never have reached critical mass. But in summer 1971, the Brits made their seminal gaffe: internment without trial. "It patently was a mistake. That's a matter of history now," says one prison official. The measure hit not only at the Provos, but also at their families and their neighbors. Because army intelligence was so poor, most of the 342 suspects rounded up in the first swoop weren't even active Provisionals, but merely middle-aged ex-Officials who themselves had been interned during earlier, tamer incarnations of the conflict. "When internment came, they arrested my father, who had a record from the forties," remembers Hughes bitterly. "They hit Number Three Blackwater Street and arrested him, and they took him out in his bare feet. They took him to Girdwood Barracks and they held him for I think it was two days."

After Hughes had spent almost two years on the run, the Brits finally caught up with him on the Falls Road and arrested him along with Tom Cahill and Gerry Adams. Hughes didn't quite get the Joe Clarke treatment, but the abuse he experienced was enough to entrench his hatred of the British more deeply. During seven hours of questioning, Hughes was beaten and then tied to a chair while two intelligence officers rapped his fingers with an upholstery hammer until they swelled to the size of kielbasas. Then a very tall, distinguished looking man in a suit came into the interrogation room, smiled at Hughes, pulled a .45 automatic from his belt, put it to Hughes's head, and pulled the trigger—on an empty chamber. Adams received similar treatment. Finally they were flown to Long

Kesh* by helicopter. "It was home," recalls Hughes. "Long Kesh wasn't a dreaded place for me. It was just coming out of interrogation, right, and you get into Long Kesh and you hear the boys shouting, you hear the friendly voices. It was a great relief to be there."

In one stroke, the British army created a pantheon of martyrs for the next generation of young Catholics to worship. Monsignor Denis Faul, the Dungannon priest who catalogued British abuses of republicans and first brought them to the world's attention, insists: "The last twenty-five years was not about the border, I repeat, not about the border. Forty thousand Catholics in Belfast were driven out of their homes all along the shores of Lough Neagh and portions of west Belfast. The youngsters don't forget that. And then the British Army were brought in and the Provos started against the British Army and to recruit the young Catholics in the streets. All of them were arrested or interned, and you had Bloody Sunday.† The use of torture from '71 to '79 was quite extensive. Amnesty International had to come over twice; we had to go to the European Commission on Human Rights to give a report on human rights. We have records of at least two thousand torture cases, and there were 150 innocent people killed in the past twenty-five years. In other words, the Catholics joined because they were ill-treated, unjustly ill-treated. They shouldn't have joined, it was a trap, they walked into the trap. I know one young fellow who was sent to jail on very serious charges, and somebody

---

*Long Kesh was the name of the internment camp and military-style compound prison outside of Belfast, replaced by a conventional cellular facility, the Maze, when Britain withdrew the paramilitaries' political status in 1976. All republicans call the Maze "Long Kesh" or "the Kesh" in defiance of the Brits' denial of status. Loyalists generally do not, although they do refer to the old facility (still extant but unused) as Long Kesh.

†January 30, 1972; Bloody Sunday is the British misdeed that fixed Northern Ireland firmly in world headlines, and convinced Catholics generally that they would be fairly treated only in a united Ireland. The event remains the singularly abiding nationalist obsession. To quell an illegal and unruly anti-internment march staged by the Derry Civil Rights Association through the Catholic part of the city known as the "Bogside," soldiers from the First Battalion of the Parachute Regiment fired into the crowd and killed thirteen unarmed Catholic civilians and one seventeen-year-old IRA volunteer. Demonstrators later burned down the British embassy in Dublin, and nationalist MP Bernadette Devlin slugged British Home Secretary Reginald Maudling in Parliament. An official British investigation produced what nationalists still regard as a whitewash. Lord Widgery concluded that nobody would have been hurt had the illegal demonstration not occurred, and that the soldiers had been fired on first—though none of the victims was found to have been handling weapons. No soldier was ever held to account for his actions.

asked him why did he get involved. He says, you've never seen the British army in the streets of Balwatertown. If you live in this guy's village, and the British army ill-treats your father—you know, put him up, make him stand with his hands out, and then beat him all over and bring their hands up between his legs and bash him on the privates—you'll want to be a Provo and join the IRA to get back at them."

When security forces are unconstrained by civil rights worries, their members become miniature tyrants. The British have generally respected such rights. But there was a genuine civil emergency in Northern Ireland during the early seventies. The government descended from the Magna Carta, John Locke, and John Stuart Mill was inclined to look the other way when jailhouse tormentors supplanted mild-mannered bobbies. Umberto Scappaticci, for example, lived in heavily Catholic Newry. His parents were middle-class shop-owners, his father a second-generation Italian immigrant. On account of his first cousin Freddie's known IRA involvement, in the early seventies the army hassled his father, "lifted" Umberto several times, and gave him the third degree. Although he was not in fact involved then, the rough interrogations gave him motivation. By early 1976, he had joined the Provos, become officer commanding of an active service unit, been arrested for murdering a soldier, and been sentenced to life imprisonment.

Although Britain's troop deployments in 1969 were designed to control disturbances for which Protestants were as immediately responsible as Catholics, the army bolstered Protestant sectarianism. Donncha O'Hara's father worked for a Protestant butcher in north Belfast. In 1971, just before internment, when he showed up for work he was turned away by a sign on the wall spurning Catholics. Though hardly the stuff of full-blown political revelation, this personal experience—combined with everyday street abuses by the security forces and peer pressure to do something about it—turned Donncha into a Provo. Within months, he was skipping school so he could throw rocks at the British army and set cars on fire. Within three years, he was serving a life sentence for murder.

There is an alternative explanation for the troubles marketed in the United States by Gerry Adams. According to him, the Provisionals' armed confrontation with the British was a natural progression from the "one man, one vote" protests launched in 1968. All adult citizens of Northern Ireland were entitled to vote in national elections. In local elections, however, the vote was limited to property-tax payers and their wives, which meant owners of property or "householders." Businesses also got up to six votes, depending on the value of their property.[2] This was not discrimination against Catholics per se. There was a Protestant working class also disenfranchised by the householder vote. But the voting laws did have a larger discriminatory impact on the Catholic population as a whole because there were far more Protestant than Catholic property owners and businessmen, and these laws facilitated gerrymandering—most egregiously in Derry, where, despite a two-to-one ratio of Catholics to Protestants in the electorate, unionists had controlled city government since partition.[3]

These problems were significantly ameliorated in February 1969, when Captain Terence O'Neill's liberal unionist government, fulfilling a campaign promise, instituted a "one man, one vote" policy for local as well as general elections. Many of the Provos' main players, like Hughes and Tommy Gorman, did not even participate in the original 1968 demonstrations—they were too busy venting wanderlust in the merchant navy like nice, normal boys. Although it is true that Catholics continued their civil rights marches, emboldened by the "one man, one vote" victory and inspired by the American black movement, civil rights had nothing inherent to do with armed republicanism. To Adams, however, explaining republicanism in terms of civil rights is politically useful, chiefly because what happened a month before O'Neill instituted universal suffrage circumstantially linked civil rights to violence, and violence to the constitutional question.

In January 1969, the People's Democracy, a radical civil rights group started by students at Queen's University of Belfast in late 1968, brought Catholics together for a four-day, Selma-style march from Belfast to Derry. Two hundred loyalists (half of them off-duty members of the B-Specials, the RUC auxiliary force) attacked the marchers at Burntollet Bridge in County Derry, sending thirteen of them to the hospital. The People's Democracy's co-founder and leading light was Bernadette Devlin (later McAliskey). In 1969 she became the youngest female MP in British history. Dubbed a "mini-skirted Castro" by unionists and an "Irish Joan of Arc" by republicans, Devlin was later shot and badly wounded by loyalists. The involvement of the B-Specials and the failure of the RUC regulars to protect the demonstrators at Burntollet Bridge convinced Devlin and other radicals that civil rights for Catholics could not be upheld in a partitioned Ireland, and she said so publicly and defiantly. Thus, violent Protestant resistance encountered by Catholics in their civil rights march appears to justify armed republicanism, even though their principal demand—one man, one vote—was attained a month later. It was the threat to the border posed by Catholic radicals, not the recognition of Catholic civil rights per se, that panicked the Protestant community into sectarian agitation.

In any event, the violence had begun. The next step was the institutionalization of violence. During the sectarian riots in Derry and Belfast eight months later,* the few men that had guns, left over from the border campaign of the fifties and sixties, called themselves the IRA. Republicanism was then merely a latent rebel tradition that could be called upon to rally Catholics—as it was by Devlin and others.

The 1916 Easter Rising had established a unitary socialist state as the Irish nationalist desideratum. The fusing of socialism and nationalism was the brainchild of James Connolly, the military commander of republican forces in Dublin during the rising who was executed a month later. The combination was unusual for the times, when leftist revolutions were largely anti-state and exalted the global proletariat over borders. Nationalism and socialism iconoclastically converged in Ireland because Britain historically had deprived the island of her nationhood by depriving her natives of their land. Since the early plantations, Protestants from the mainland, bound to the Crown by legislative favoritism and religious affiliation, constituted a one-sixth minority but owned five-sixths of Ireland. Thus, on April 8, 1916, Connolly wrote in *The Workers' Republic:* "The cause of labour is the cause of Ireland; the cause of Ireland is the cause of labour. They cannot be disseevered. Ireland seeks freedom. Labour seeks that an Ireland free should be the sole mistress of her own destiny, supreme owner of all material things within and upon her soil."[4] Then, as now, republican socialism was strictly subservient to Irish nationalism.

Loath to risk popular criticism for timidity that the IRA had drawn after August 1969 but before the split, the Provisional IRA seized on the

---

*Catholic civil rights protests in Derry gave way to outright agitation by the time the Apprentice Boys marched on August 12th to celebrate the slamming of the city gates on the Catholic forces of King James 280 years earlier. Two days of riots in Derry primed Belfast for the same. Catholics feared a Protestant purge; Protestants feared a Catholic insurrection. Protestant hysteria and Catholic resistance in west Belfast reached critical mass on August 15. On the lower Falls Road, the Catholic ghetto, angry young men flung petrol bombs at each other, and Protestant mobs crashed Catholic barricades. By the 16th, the Royal Ulster Constabulary had shot dead four Catholic civilians in Belfast, and British troops had been rapidly deployed to Derry and Belfast. At least seventy-two Catholics and sixty-one Protestants suffered gunshot wounds. Some 1,505 Catholic families were forced out of their homes, versus only 315 Protestant families.

proud tradition of 1916. In its inaugural public statement in January 1970, the Provisional IRA dedicated itself to the "provisional" thirty-two-county socialist republic "proclaimed at Easter 1916, established by the First Dail Eireann in 1919, overthrown by force of arms in 1922 and suppressed to this day by the British-imposed six-county and twenty-six-county partition states."[5] By 1972, the Provos had demonstrated their toughness and resolve. The People's Democracy produced a detailed policy statement proposing a secular all-Ireland republic and the dissolution of the two states that existed by virtue of the Government of Ireland Act of 1920, which effected partition. Although actual electoral support for the Provisional IRA did not materialize until the 1981 hunger strikes, the organization had in fact garnered significant interstitial popular support during the preceding decade.

The birth of modern Irish republicanism should be recorded as the accidental and unhappy confluence of valid civil rights protest and convenient myth. The move both serviced Irish history and gave terrorism an idealistic face. But by restrictively defining the recognition of Catholic civil rights in terms of the border, the development also sidelined that original goal in favor of the far less realistic aim of erasing the border. Republicans effectively abandoned the modest strand of reform that began with "one man, one vote." In 1973, for example, voting in Northern Ireland was made still more equitable to nationalists when a proportional representation system was adopted for nonparliamentary elections. Although proportional representation ensured a nationalist share in elected bodies, republicans considered such advances substantively "petty." In their view, they couldn't afford to think otherwise. Sinn Fein leaders suspected that they could not compete electorally with the nonviolent nationalists of the SDLP, whose political mandate was enhanced by proportional representation. To republicans, the only valid majority would have been 51 percent or more of the entire thirty-two-county Ireland. Consequently, in the seventies republicans opted out of six-county politics.

Throughout the next twenty years, the republican movement invested much of its political energy in opposing what it called "partitionist nationalism"—that is, any supposed political solution, like the 1974 power-sharing executive known as "Sunningdale" after the town where the arrangements were worked out, or the 1985 Anglo-Irish Agreement, both supported by the SDLP, which conditioned a united Ireland on the approval of a six-county majority while establishing a consultative role for the Irish government in Northern Irish affairs. Though initially hostile, unionists came to accept proportional representation and, to some degree, power-sharing on the executive level. During the troubles, therefore, the empowerment of northern nationalists was not the crux of the conflict. The real problem was republican absolutism. It had sharpened unionist fears of any Irish dimension, and concentrated histrionic unionist defiance on Dublin. Thus, unionists as well as republicans opposed Sunningdale and the Anglo-Irish Agreement because these arrangements humored the Republic—even though, on balance, they also favored the preservation of the union. Republicans had now artificially raised the stakes of the Catholic civil rights movement from local conditions to national sovereignty.

For years, of course, the unionist establishment continued to provoke locally. Discrimination in employment—public and private, through nepotism as well as outright bigotry—was pervasive until the eighties. Tommy Gorman's father admonished him that if he didn't tell employers he lived on the Falls Road, he'd have good chance of getting a job because his surname didn't sound especially Catholic. Then, finally, direct-rule reforms gave the Fair Employment Commission (FEC) for Northern Ireland—the administrative agency that enforces antidiscrimination laws—some teeth. There is still an imbalance—Catholics remain twice as likely as Protestants to be unemployed. But the discrepancy is substantially structural: the province's industry is concentrated in Protestant areas, where many Catholics are still afraid to venture, and the economy is contracting, making job creation a struggle. Within these limits, the FEC is slowly ameliorating the employment discrimination problem. Nevertheless, job bias was one fundamental cause of the troubles that persisted throughout their duration.

BORN AND BRED: THE CHILDREN OF THE TROUBLES

By the late sixties housing discrimination was insignificant, and practiced as much by Catholics on Protestants as vice versa. Thereafter, both the IRA and the loyalist paramilitaries took to "allocating" houses in their respective areas of control—often to heavyweights in their own organizations. The Andersonstown estate, a sprawling square-mile expanse of two-storey brick cottages built to house working-class Catholics at the top of the Falls Road in the fifties, never welcomed blue-collar Protestants. Unlike Hughes's neighborhood on the Grosvenor Road, Andersonstown just a mile and a half away was both insular and exclusionary, and had little use for the RUC, which was almost completely Protestant. The layout of the estate collapses inwardly in a dense array of self-contained enclaves bounded by dead-end streets and roiled by diversionary crescents, which makes it ideally suited to ambushes and traps. The RUC's most heavily fortified station sits at the northern tip of the estate, and even after the IRA ceasefire RUC patrols have not generally ventured into Andytown on foot. As the Provisional IRA soared into folklore, Andytown became its natural breeding ground. Gerry Adams now calls it home. Two of its products are Jackie McMullan and John Pickering. Both served life sentences in the Maze.

"This would have been a new estate in the fifties and sixties," says Pickering. "Now, you have the older areas as you move in towards the center of the town—the likes of the Falls, the lower Falls, the New Lodge Road, Ardoyne—they would have different experiences. Andersonstown in them days was a big brand-new estate for newly married couples or young families, you know. Because there wasn't a high level of criminal activity in these areas, the RUC never really had the men in. They never enjoyed any hospitality or anything in these areas. We never really seen the RUC in these areas until the late seventies." Whereas Tommy Gorman's brother Jack could join the RUC without incurring the hostility of his community, an Andytown man couldn't get away with it. McMullan can recall only one fellow from the area, James Heaney, who actually became a policeman. He was slain by the IRA in 1976 outside his mother's home, just a few doors down from the McMullans'. "I don't want to be talking insultingly of the dead," McMullan declares, "but even as a kid he would have been an outsider, an oddball. He wasn't one of the boys then." Any Andytown native who joined the RUC was branded a "Castle Catholic"—that is, a quisling in the service of the British.

Pickering and McMullan got their limited experience with Protestants through pilfering apples from orchards on the Malone Road and in attenuated encounters at the movies. At age fourteen, McMullan remembers, he had to dash from the theater early because management routinely played *God Save the Queen*—that song again—at the end of the film. He and any other self-respecting Catholic would have refused to stand to show allegiance, and then would have been beaten up outside the theater. At about that time, McMullan and a friend were arrested and "slapped about" for sticking out their tongues at a policeman, but he says the experience left no particular mark. "At that stage, I think the lines had already been clearly drawn," he remarks.

Fundamentally, IRA men were community-minded segregationists. Paramilitarism to them was an extreme form of social work. Rather than escaping Protestant triumphalism to England itself or the Republic of Ireland, they sought to better their native home. The strongest and deepest influence the republicans had in this direction was the sense of destiny and exclusivity that nationalist history gave them: the dedicated few could win back their turf from the British through blood sacrifice. The sanguine words of Patrick Pearse, who led the 1916 Easter Rising and was the first of sixteen Irish republicans to be executed by the British after the rebellion was suppressed, still decorate building facades on the Falls Road: "Life springs from death, and from the graves of patriot men and women spring living nations. The defenders of this Realm have worked well in secret and in the open. They think that they have pacified Ireland. They think they have purchased half of us and intimidated the other half. They think they have foreseen everything, think they have provided against everything; but the fools, the fools, the fools!—they have left us our Fenian dead, and while Ireland holds these graves, Ireland unfree shall never be at peace."*[6]

Contemporary republicans seize on Pearse's words as a prophecy of the troubles, a prescient warning that partition would never douse the wrath of true Irish patriots. Is this true? Is the peace process of the nineties the inevitable conclusion of a fight that began in 1916? If so, why did the troubles wait until 1968 to begin? The line soldiers of the IRA, as Hughes suggests, were not always nationalist ideologues. Visions of a united Ireland, at least in 1968–76, were often little more than a justification for reactive populist violence that then gave it an irrepressible lift. "I don't remember ever being taught republicanism or anything. I remember shouting at the cops when I was about eight or nine, 'Up the rebels!'" recalls Jackie McMullan. "The national question was a progression from defending the area. In 1969, right, you're eleven and twelve, thirteen, you see it on the television—civil rights marchers being batoned by B-Specials, et cetera, et cetera. Marches, special demonstrations being banned. You're sitting watching that, your parents are in the house, they're watching it, too. They're up to a million,† you're up to a million. There's people getting burnt out of—Catholics getting burnt out of areas in the east and north of the city and flooding into Andersonstown. There were refugees, like, thousands moved up into some trees at schools, different schools. There was barricades put up by the local men, my father included, [who]

---

*The Fenians were nineteenth-century Catholic rebels.

†Argot meaning highly agitated.

formed vigilante committees manning the barricades. So you're eleven, twelve, thirteen. You're part of all that. There was excitement to it as well. And all my friends, like, you would have been involved in it, and the men would have been chasing you away from the barricades, but you wanted to become part of it. It developed from that, I think. Then the national question did explode onto the agenda then, 1970, 1971, and you became involved in that, as did all your friends."

To be sure, the "lift" of nationalism should not be underestimated. Though garden-variety nationalists never openly condoned violence, they loved the romance of rebellion. Armed republicanism may have had marginally more popular support than constitutional nationalism throughout the early and mid-seventies,* but it then lost steam due to the attrition of a Catholic population to whom violence may have sounded good but, up close and over time, became distasteful. It was a nonviolent republican protest—the 1981 hunger strike—that revitalized nationalism and injected it into Northern Irish politics proper. Amid the fervor of violence and the radical nationalism of Sinn Fein, the eyes of republicans became the only eyes that still viewed the United Kingdom as a world power, defeatable only by virtual supermen. Notes one keen observer: "[P]roclamations about British might crushing helpless Catholic waifs [reflect], perversely, a belief in Britain, loyalty to the Crown. In actual fact, Westminster is a tawdry, has-been capital once victorious over the Spanish Armada, now reduced to claiming the midget Falkland Islands as a serious military coup. Why, west Belfast is the last place on earth where the British Empire still exists."[7]

On the other side, the one shibboleth that may well be true is that the Provisional IRA is the most effective terrorist organization in observed history. "The Provos were undoubtedly the professionals in the whole game," concedes Glen Barr, co-founder of the Ulster Defense Association (UDA) in Derry. "They're the most professional paramilitary organization the world has ever seen, without a shadow of a doubt. And for all sorts of reasons—the romanticism, the propaganda, unbelievable." The IRA has

---

*It is impossible to say for sure, since Sinn Fein—the political party representing armed republicanism—did not contest elections in Northern Ireland until the 1981 hunger strike. The theory behind this nonparticipation was that the "provisional" pre-partition government proclaimed during the Easter Rising and established in 1919 by a newly empowered Sinn Fein remained the only valid authority in Ireland. Running for office in any other government—especially a British one—was thought to undermine that contention.

moved a great power to assume direct control of a leftover colony that is admittedly of no economic or strategic value to that power. But by the same token, the IRA has perversely achieved too much by embarrassing Britain into an intransigence which at times has matched the unionists'.

From a British standpoint, the Provos' depredations demand stubborn honor rather than the benign acquiescence that constitutional nationalists might have hoped for. While the Brits surely want the mainland safe, there is no proof—wish it though the IRA might—that the republican campaign really precipitated the civil reforms of direct rule, or that the incrementalism of the SDLP wouldn't have produced them on its own. At the end of the day, sadly, the only salient conclusion to be drawn about the effect of IRA terrorism is that Northern Ireland is no closer to uniting with the Irish Republic than it was in 1974, when nationalists *and unionists* established a power-sharing government in which the south had a nominal voice, only to have it collapse after five months under the pressure of the loyalist strike.

A BETTER CLASS OF TERRORIST?

Granting the IRA's impact, there has nevertheless been a litany of messy operations, as with any Beirut-style conflict. Donncha O'Hara, now a Sinn Fein press officer, was convicted of a murder resulting from a bombing near Belfast City Center. Pickering, with four others, was caught red-handed trying to blow up an RUC station in south Belfast, and arrested after a shoot-out and siege that lasted several hours; he was later charged with murdering the seventy-seven-year-old owner of a garage, William Creighton. Jackie McMullan tried to snipe an RUC reserve officer in a south Belfast park, missed, and was apprehended minutes later as his accomplices sped off in a car. Gary Roberts, having ceased active service in the IRA, supplied the gun used in the execution-style murder of sixty-four-year-old Henry Scott in a pub in Dunmurry, a Belfast suburb. The IRA men had forced the man's grandson at gunpoint to lead them to Farmer's Inn, where they shot him in the head as he sipped a drink. Tommy Gorman was imprisoned four separate times, the last for possession of a large bomb, and admits to participating in operations which may have killed people.

Most Provos shed no tears over their victims. O'Hara doesn't even remember the name of the person he was convicted of killing, recalling only that it was "some woman." Pickering says he was framed for the murder he was charged with, but covers all bases with the indignant comment that the septuagenarian *some* Provo shot in the groin "interfered with the IRA volunteers." Says Roberts now of his victim: "He had a history of loyalist involvement," which supposedly consisted of providing the UVF with intelligence about Catholics traveling through Protestant areas. To the offense of bomb possession, quips Tommy Gorman, "I pleaded guilty—unashamedly guilty, just as Wolf Tone pleaded 'unashamedly guilty' for his republicanism in 1798."

Gorman's wisecrack is revealing. IRA men do their best to spin history toward their plight as prisoners rather than their acts as guerrillas. The British unwittingly cater to this dodge by mistreating them. Take Roberts. As far as he's concerned, his arrest in 1977 was a showcase for his family values and martyrdom. "My family home was raided, and I had a gun and ammunition upstairs. I took responsibility for it because my mother was also arrested, so I immediately took responsibility for the possession of that weapon. I was brought then to the Springfield Road police station and I was badly beaten there. I didn't know that they had released my mother, and all's I could think of was that my mother was being charged and kept in the middle of this, and that meant five younger brothers and sisters aged from thirteen to seven were left with no parents. My father was dead. They released her that night from Springfield Road, but they didn't tell me this, and then they moved me from there to Lisburn police station, where the brutality continued. I signed a statement for the police which they had written. I didn't know what was in it until I saw it a year later."

Unlike Joe Clarke, Roberts does not look tough. He is blond and doughy, and though he acts haughty in that magisterial republican way, his resistance appears brittle. He must have looked a feast to cops and soldiers hardened by seven years of IRA targeting. In the statement, Roberts admitted that he was in possession of the weapon for a period of three weeks, that the gun went out to active service units on several occasions, and that it was used to shoot certain people. After twenty-four hours of interrogation, he actually confessed to a lot more. According to Roberts, the police slapped him, spat on him, cursed at him, dragged him by the hair. They would send in a doctor who would declare Roberts fit, then came back and beat him some more. They stuck a gun in his mouth and up to his head. "At one stage I went through an actual story of how I got hired to do these murders. That's how bad of a state they had me in—that I admitted them, I told them, but I didn't even know where they happened. They had me in such a bad state that if they'd have said to me, we know you shot President Kennedy, I'd have said, Oswald's innocent, I did it."

A republican volunteer is also likely to point out that whereas loyalists have predominantly targeted Catholic civilians indiscriminately, republicans customarily hit only "legitimate" military targets like soldiers, policemen, and loyalist paramilitaries. Thanks to Sinn Fein propaganda, most of the world subscribes to this pristine generality. The facts are more complicated. The only targets loyalists *have* are civilians; there is nobody in Northern Ireland directly opposed to the union who wears a uniform. This feature is part of the nature of pro-state terrorism. Republicans, by contrast, oppose the state and have had correspondingly easy pickings. The loyalist presumption—admittedly, simplistic and brutal—has been that every Catholic civilian supports republican terrorism, and is therefore a logical, if not a legitimate, target. While loyalists would have preferred killing republican paramilitaries, they were hard to identify, so ordinary Catholics had to suffice. In fact, republican paramilitaries found it almost as difficult to nail down active loyalist paramilitaries as vice versa, the score being a close twenty-eight to twenty-seven in favor of the loyalists.

The principle on which Sinn Fein rhetoric assumes the moral high ground is that Protestant civilians who don't serve the British cause are not proper targets. Of the 1,755 total victims attributed to the Provisional IRA through 1993, only 1,006 were British soldiers, policemen, or prison officers, leaving 749 who by the IRA's putative criterion must have been accidents. The Protestant casualty list includes common folk whose only anti-republican act (outside of possibly voting unionist) was working for a living: the IRA has killed thirty-three civilians simply because they entered into contracts with the government to build facilities for the security forces, or labored on construction projects under such contracts. As the troubles went on, the Provos modified their standard, but never missed a beat of sanctimoniousness.

On January 17, 1992, a unit of the IRA's County Tyrone brigade blew up eight Protestant workmen at Teebane Crossroads with a 1,500-pound bomb as they returned home by bus for the weekend after working on a bomb-damaged RUC station. It was the worst Provo atrocity since the Remembrance Day bomb in Enniskillen, over five years earlier. A day later, the IRA issued a statement characterizing the dead men as "Crown force collaborators" and reiterated its seven-year policy of using "military action" to discourage Britain's "cynical use" of civilians for work in its security installations. "That Britain has continued in spite of previous operations to exploit nonmilitary personnel in this fashion," the statement went on, "is a measure of its total disregard for the safety of those it deems expendable."[8] Although the Provos themselves admitted their targets were "nonmilitary," Gerry Adams chimed in that the massacre was "a horrific reminder of the failure of British policy in Ireland."[9]

Steve Bruce, an unusually perceptive student of the troubles, has no time for this kind of calculated hubris.

> [T]he republican definition of a legitimate target expands to include not just serving members of the police and army but also retired members of the police and army, members of the families of policemen and soldiers, civilians who work for the security forces, publicans and shopkeepers who supply policemen and soldiers, and any civilian who happens to frequent any establishment with a service clientele (the girls who danced with off-duty soldiers at the Droppin' Well pub in Ballykelly,* for example). And with the Enniskillen bombing† we have the addition of anyone who attends a memorial service to soldiers who died in wars quite unconnected with Northern Ireland.[10]

Bruce's point is also quantifiable. There have been many baldly sectarian republican killings scarcely different from the sectarian assassinations loyalists have engaged in. The most horrifying of these was the Kingsmills massacre in January 1976, when the IRA set up a bogus checkpoint, stopped a van carrying thirteen workmen, took the two Catholics aside for mercy, and machine-gunned the remaining eleven Protestants; only one survived.

On this score, the authoritative source on troubles deaths, journalist Malcolm Sutton, has himself been taken in by Sinn Fein's sanitization of the IRA's *modus operandi*. In his *Index of Deaths* for the troubles, he counts only 133 IRA killings as "sectarian," which he defines as "deliberate killing of Protestant civilians." Not included in that number are 142 civilians killed during attacks on British forces or who were mistaken for British forces, 118 civilians killed on commercial property due to premature bomb explosions or inadequate warnings, 48 civilians murdered on the British mainland, 15 innocent bystanders killed, another 12 civilians killed for no ascertainable reason, 8 legal officials, 7 Protestant civilians killed in street disturbances, 3 businessmen, 3 civilians shot at IRA road-

---

*December 1982, Irish National Liberation Army. Five of the girls were killed, along with eleven soldiers and a teenage boy.

†November 1987, IRA. Eleven Protestants dead.

blocks, one witness to a Provo operation, one RUC *applicant,* one man mistaken for a civilian contractor, and one civilian instructor employed by the Prison Service. Add to these the 33 civilian contractors, and the "non-sectarian" civilians taken by the IRA come to 393. With the 133 "sectarian" murders, that makes 526 civilians killed by the IRA because of some connection, intentional or circumstantial, with the unionist or British establishment. When the tally of the Irish National Liberation Army (INLA) is added,* it brings the republicans' outright "sectarian" total to 151, their total in Sutton's other subcategories to 417, and the grand total of civilian dead to 568. This is merely sectarianism by proxy, no matter how it's packaged.

Consider the 1979 "execution" of Lord Mountbatten, along with his wife and two grandchildren. The IRA rigged a remote-controlled bomb to his yacht off County Sligo, turning it into matchsticks. On the same day, the Provos tallied the highest military score in the history of the troubles—eighteen British soldiers, by two bombs, at Warrenpoint. Why bother with a seventy-nine-year-old life peer who never had anything to do with partition or the governance of Northern Ireland? Bobby Sands offered the feeble answer that Mountbatten saw what was happening in Northern Ireland but never did anything about it.[11] The same goes for Mother Teresa. The real reason is that the sheer random senselessness of the killing would make Westminster sit up and take notice. That is terrorism *par excellence.* And what made Mountbatten an especially suitable target was that he was a British *Protestant* whose continued association with Ireland recalled pre-partition Anglo-Irish dominion. Again, sectarianism by any other name is sectarianism. The fact that it has some strained political peg only makes it smell a little better.

The republicans' civilian body-count of 568 is more than half the number of bona fide military targets they have liquidated, and only 145 short of the loyalist paramilitaries' total of 713 sectarian killings. This record hardly reflects the disciplined operation of a precision guerrilla machine. The republicans' conceit is that they have a moral edge on loyalists

---

*For some unexplained reason, Sutton lumps the loyalists' murders together but separates the IRA's and the INLA's. Like the UVF and the UDA, the republican groups have essentially the same objectives and have used roughly the same methods. Feuds between each of these sets of paramilitaries have been centered on primacy within the movement rather than a dispute over military tactics. The Official IRA declared a ceasefire in 1972, but still accounted for twenty-three civilian deaths; these are not included in the total of 568 given above.

because their emotions are "positive" and loyalists' "negative"—because republicans have the affirmative goal of a united Ireland, while loyalists have only the passive objective of maintaining the status quo. "There's a basic difference between the two types of conflicts, you know," waxes Jackie McMullan. "Republicans were fighting for something, whereas [loyalists] were fighting to resist something, which doesn't require any sort of inventiveness, imagination, creativity." Republicans might well have been more diabolical. In October 1990, for example, they forced a civilian army employee to drive his van into a vehicle checkpoint, killing five soldiers along with the driver. But such "proxy bombs" were not palpably more inventive, imaginative, or creative than loyalist methods.

Neither were the Provos more selective than the loyalist paramilitaries. Compare terrorist operations in which three or more civilians were killed. During the years of the heaviest killing (1971–79), loyalists murdered twenty-six in Dublin (three simultaneous car bombs), fifteen in McGurk's Bar (bomb), seven in Monaghan (car bomb), six in the Rose and Crown (bomb), six in the Strand Bar (bomb and shooting), six at the Ramble Inn (shooting), five in the Chlorane Bar (shooting), five in the Top of the Hill Bar (shooting), four at Casey's Bottling Plant (shooting), four at the Hillcrest Bar (car bomb), three at the Imperial Hotel (car bomb), three members of the Miami Showband (shooting), three on Cliftonville Road (bomb), three in Killyliss (booby trap bomb), three in a social club in Bleary (shooting), three in McGleenan's Bar (bomb and shooting), three in Greyhillan (shooting), three in Ballydougan (shooting), three in Ligoniel (shooting), three in Clancey's Bar (bomb), three at the Whitefort Inn (bomb), three on Hillman Street (petrol bomb), three at the Silverbridge Inn (bomb and shooting).

In the same time frame, republicans killed twenty-one in Birmingham, England pubs (bombs), twelve in the La Mon House Restaurant (incendiary bomb), ten at Kingsmills (shooting), nine in Claudy (car bombs), seven at the army base in Aldershot, England (Official IRA bomb), six in the Newry Customs Office (bomb), six on Railway Street in Coleraine (car bomb), five on Brougher Mountain (land mine), five in the Tullyvallen Orange Hall (shooting), four on Anderson Street (bomb), four in the Bayardo Bar (bomb and shooting), four on Donegall Street (car bomb), four at the Mountainview Tavern (bomb), four at the Oxford Street bus station (car bomb), four at the Balmoral Publishing Company (bomb), four at the Stag Inn (shooting), four (including Lord Mountbatten) in County Sligo (bomb), three on the Ormeau Road (bombs), three on Cavehill Road (car bomb), three in Herron's drapery shop, three in The Store Bar (shooting), three on the M-62 motorway in Yorkshire, England (bomb), and three at the Central Bar (shooting).

This comparison yields a raw score of 131 to 123 "in favor of" republicans. The republicans were no more discriminating, killing 11 Catholics in those attacks while the loyalists also killed 11 Protestants. Republicans make a great deal of the fact that some of their biggest kills were unintentional, having resulted from late warnings or premature explosions (the La Mon and Claudy, for example), or from attacks aimed at military personnel (Brougher Mountain, Yorkshire)—as if these excuses exonerate them from having intentionally put people in harm's way in the first place. Northern Irish courts, like American courts, call that murder, too.

"Quite often the outcome of a republican operation is as bad as if not worse than a loyalist one," admits McIntyre. "For the victims of the Shankill bomb,* it doesn't matter that the people who killed them came in without the intention of doing so. As far as they're concerned, they're in the same boat as the people at Greysteel." He also concedes that in 1975 the IRA was overtly sectarian. "In my eyes," Tommy Gorman agrees, "we had a very dodgy leadership at that time. We were being dragged into a sort of sectarian scenario which a lot of us fought against—that this is not right, we don't go out to fucking stiff Prods, we're not out to shoot up bars, we're supposed to be in a revolution, a struggle for national independence." In 1976, Gorman was asked if he would consider becoming OC

---

*For the Shankill bomb, the IRA tendered the excuse that it went off prematurely and was intended to hit a meeting being held at UDA/UFF headquarters upstairs. The IRA press statement added: "We regret all innocent deaths and we understand the grief felt by the loved ones of all those who died today. We reiterate our policy of not allowing ourselves to be dragged down the cul-de-sac of sectarian warfare." The IRA then allowed as how "today's operation . . . went tragically wrong." Quoted in "IRA Claims Target Was UFF Meeting," *Irish Times* (Dublin), October 25 and 26, 1993, p. 6. The IRA's claim simply doesn't add up logically: although the bomb did detonate earlier than intended, any effective warning would have allowed UFF men to evacuate with everyone else and thwarted the IRA's stated military goal. Moreover, the design of the device permitted a maximum of only 11 seconds between priming and explosion. (See Eamonn Mallie and David McKittrick, *The Fight for Peace: The Secret Story Behind the Irish Peace Process* [London: Heinemann, 1996], p. 197.) This short fuse and the extent of the damage—in addition to the nine Protestants killed, fifty-eight were injured—indicate that casualties would have been inevitable even with a warning. At best, therefore, the Provos intended to take out the UFF group and any other Protestants who happened to be nearby; at worst, they wanted to kill as many innocent Protestant civilians as possible. Their unctuous apology and nonsectarian disclaimer are entitled to no weight or credence whatsoever.

of the Belfast Brigade of the Provisional IRA. He said he'd take the post only if sectarian operations were phased out. Brigade staff never followed up the offer. At the time, the Belfast OC was Billy McKee, whom Gorman calls "an arch-Catholic bigot." According to McIntyre, "there is still a sectarian element within the republican movement, unpalatable as it may seem." In fact, there has been from the Provisional IRA's inception. In the best book yet written on the IRA, Bishop and Mallie report that many of McKee's proto-Provos painted the IRA's southern leaders as "sinister" and "atheistic," objected to their dropping the rosary from IRA commemorations, and shared with the Provisionals' first chief of staff, Sean Mac Stiofain, an "incoherent, God-fearing brand of socialism."[12] Sean O'Callaghan, an ex-IRA man from the Irish Republic now serving a life sentence for murder, testifies that the "awful sectarianism" of Northern Irish Provos drove him to resign from the organization. "After about eighteen months in Northern Ireland," he says, "I realized that I was taking part in a sectarian war directed primarily against the Protestant, unionist people."[13]

In the matter of sectarianism, Gorman and McIntyre are unusually candid. Most republicans try to wash their hands of outright sectarian hits, like the Bayardo Bar and the Mountainview Tavern, blaming them on aberrational elements. Even confessional ex-Provisionals like Gorman tend to explain away sectarian operations as missteps teased out by the loyalists or the Brits. One of the men sentenced to life for the Bayardo Bar hit is Brendan "Bik" McFarlane—now, with over twenty years inside, the longest-serving prisoner in the Maze. McFarlane and his accomplices strafed the Shankill Road pub with machine-gun fire, tossed a bomb into the place, and shot patrons as they fled the ensuing fire. The building almost completely collapsed. As the perpetrators made their getaway, they fired on women and children waiting at a taxi stand. All told, five people died and forty-four were injured.[14]

McFarlane became one of the IRA's stalwart prison leaders. Gary Roberts defends him to this day. "Och, come on ahead," he sneers. "Lenny Murphy* told us in prison in 1976 that he'd just been at the Bayardo Bar ten minutes previously, that the UVF staff, Belfast, had just finished a meeting at the Bayardo Bar. The bar was being used as headquar-

---

*Leader of the Shankill Butchers, a gang of brutal sectarian serial killers who operated under the banner of the UVF. Murphy was shot dead by the IRA in 1982, almost undoubtedly with loyalist complicity.

ters by the UVF. The IRA went out to hit that, they were ten minutes late. That's not sectarian." Although the Bayardo was in fact a known UVF haunt, the IRA nailed only one UVF man and four innocent Protestants.

And despite Gorman's sentiments, McFarlane has hardly been marginalized. He was OC of the IRA prisoners during the hunger strike, and micro-managed the staggered sequencing of the prisoners' fasts for maximum effect. Result: ten men dead and a propaganda coup for the Provos. Monsignor Denis Faul, who broke the hunger strike, remembers him as "a good leader, in total control. He was a nice fellow, too; he had a nice manner with him. A friendly, kindly sort of fellow. I wish the Pope would pick the bishops as well." (McFarlane had in fact been to seminary in the Republic before joining the Provisionals.) Brendan Hughes defends his friend with fractious reasoning: "He has suffered for many, many years, and still does, because it was a sectarian conflict we allowed ourselves to get trailed into by British Intelligence to show the whole world, especially America, that here you had two tribes blowing the hell out of each other, and here's us trying to to stop them."

Even when vintage republicans like Gorman, Hughes, and McIntyre admit that the Provos went through that sectarian epoch in the mid- to late 1970s, they add that since then IRA operations have been aimed almost exclusively at getting the British out of Northern Ireland. While the Provos have been more selective, they've still killed plenty of innocents. The Enniskillen bomb (1987), the land mine at Teebane Crossroads (1992), and the Shankill bomb (1993) respectively claimed ten, eight, and nine Protestant civilians.

The truth is that both groups are tribal. That is, each sees the other side as inherently inimical to itself and therefore untrustworthy as an equal partner in governing Northern Ireland. This attitude secretes venom, and the republican strain is at least as potent as the loyalist one. UVF and UDA men hate Catholics because they are the other side. IRA men hate Brits and unionists for the same reason. Republicans have the rhetorical luxury of saying that Brits and unionists do not include all Protestants— that republicans themselves aren't sectarian—only because London and the unionist majority hold formal governmental power over them and therefore are obvious pulse-points for a Protestant constituency.

Had Britain declined direct rule in 1972 and instead cut Northern Ireland loose, there is little doubt that in the relative anarchy that would have ensued, the Provisionals would have been randomly whacking Protestants just as the loyalist paramilitaries were arbitrarily killing Catholics. The Provisionals' so-called ceasefire in 1975, when the security forces partially stood down, proves as much: over a period of just under fourteen months dissident Provos broke ranks and indulged in rampant tit-for-tat sectarian murder, killing 72 Protestant civilians as the loyalists killed 109 Catholics. As much as Gorman and Hughes would like to blame the carnage on a few misguided chiefs, a fair number of rank-and-file volunteers were also involved, including Anthony McIntyre. "The killing of innocent civilians does not appeal to me now," he reflects, "but I'm not saying that at one time it didn't appeal to me. It did appeal to me at one time."

The anarchy would not, of course, have lasted interminably. Here, again, the British military was a provocateur. Had the unionists been left without British military support, the troubles probably would not have gone on for twenty-five years. Anti-Protestant sentiment among Catholics, having fermented for perhaps three hundred and fifty years, is still less durable than contempt for the British, which began over eight hundred years ago. Motley influences have produced in the Provos an attitude that is at bottom sectarian, but turbocharged by their hatred for the British. That hatred, in turn, has a basis both in republican heritage and in the actual British military presence since 1969.

Beyond reinforcing sectarianism, demonizing the Brits has done strange things to republicans' capacity for rational thought. Sean Lynch is present OC of IRA prisoners in the Maze. On April 26, 1986, he and Seamus McElwaine were caught by an elite Special Air Service unit of the British army as they were trekking across wet farmland in Roslea, County Fermanagh, about to detonate an IRA land mine under a passing army patrol. Led by McElwaine, a Maze escapee, their active service unit had waged a guerrilla campaign against the army of sniping and mining along the border, living in barns and outhouses and acquiring the status of legend and the wrath of the Brits in the process. McElwaine was shot dead, and Lynch was hit five times, mainly in the abdomen. He was also blinded in the right eye, and he has several scars on his face. A big, raw-boned man of evident physical power, Lynch evaded capture for a few hours. He says, with impenetrable indignation, that the SAS would have executed him as they did McElwaine because the shoot-to-kill policy was in effect. A British army back-up team picked up Lynch, and he spent four months in the hospital, then four months on remand. He admitted participating in the gunfight, and was convicted of possession of explosives and possession of a firearm with intent, and sentenced to twenty-five years in the Maze.

Like most IRA men, Lynch believes that republicans are entitled to special treatment. By his reasoning, the world should tolerate the IRA's carrying out a shoot-to-kill policy but condemn the security forces for doing the same. Unlike many IRA men, Sean Lynch has the profile and track record of an authentic soldier: when he was arrested, he was living off the land and "on the hoof" guerrilla-style, targeting the British army. (He still sports a red ready-for-action crewcut.) The rules of engaging the security forces established by the IRA dictated shoot to kill—that is, if a volunteer encountered a British soldier or a policeman and could fire on him with a reasonable chance of escape, he should end the uniformed man's life with a bullet. Period. This applied to any military personnel in any posture—armed or unarmed, on duty or off duty, combat-ready or standing down. Most Provo hits on soldiers and cops during the troubles were not made in pitched battles at all, but through hit-and-run snipings or bomb attacks. Many of these, in turn, involved off-duty men walking along the street, driving in civilian cars, or fraternizing in public establishments. In total, between 1969 and 1994 republicans outkilled the security forces 1,064 to 141—a ratio of better than seven to one.

The IRA's border campaign against RUC and British army personnel in 1985 and 1986, in which Lynch was a main participant at the time of his arrest, resulted in the deaths of forty-eight soldiers and policemen. Of these, fifteen were off-duty and eleven were shot or blown up in barracks; only twenty-two were on active patrol. Nevertheless, Lynch expresses outrage at the very idea that the British army or the RUC might have applied the same rules of engagement to unarmed or disarmed IRA volunteers. He seems to think that the Brits and the police should not be allowed to be as ruthless as the IRA. The general argument against a shoot-to-kill policy for the security forces, of course, is that the state organs of law enforcement must operate on a higher ethical plane than terrorists. But it was the IRA that established the nebulous terms of battle during the troubles. For the terrorists themselves to castigate the other side for adopting those terms recalls the casuistry of the man who murders his parents and then pleads for judicial clemency on the ground that he's an orphan.

In the end, to an outside observer, what matters is that it is historically arguable that the Brits or the Prods were the original instigators, and virtually all republicans are fully convinced of their cause. For them, the recursive algebra of history, not any single act, justified the armed struggle. As far as republicans are concerned, with each epoch the merits of Irish history have leaned more and more decisively against Protestants and their claim to Ulster. Thus, republicans consider their conduct predestined. They are quick to say that their responses to violent stimuli were Pavlovian—in the same situation today, they'd do the same thing.

Yet republicans would not want to be anyone else. They revel in martyrdom. They get to be Irish at the whole world. Carol Cullen is typical. "There's no apologizing for being a republican," she says. "I just don't feel that I'm any different from anyone else. I just feel that my life has been shaped by different factors and that I've been put on a different course. I have no regrets." Past age fifty, Tommy Gorman insists, "if the same situation was maintained, and there was no fundamental change, and the Brits remained with the same dogmatic attitude and the unionists remained with the same intransigent position of refusing to recognize our elected representatives and to afford us parity of esteem, I would have no hesitation in taking up arms again, because I have no wish to let my sons and my grandchildren grow up in this society."

CHAPTER 3

LOYALIST REACTIONS

THEORY AND PRACTICE

On June 21, 1973, republicans murdered a dull-witted sixteen-year-old Protestant boy named David Walker. Two members of the Ulster Freedom Fighters (UFF), the illegal paramilitary wing of the then-legal Ulster Defense Association (UDA), reacted. They had been shadowing a Catholic Belfast city councillor named Paddy Wilson for several weeks. Though married with children, Wilson appeared to be "keeping company" with a Protestant woman, Irene Andrews, a civil servant and one of Northern Ireland's leading ballroom dancers. In the thickly sectarian atmosphere of 1973 Belfast, when Protestants regarded the IRA's new campaign as nothing less than a Catholic declaration of war, the mixed, extramarital relationship alone made Wilson and his mistress prime targets. He was also a founding member of the fledgling SDLP, a rising nationalist voice, and election agent for Gerry Fitt, the party's leading light. Wilson had publicly proclaimed his abhorrence of firearms, and made known his refusal to carry one at a time when many Ulster politicians packed guns. To the loyalist paramilitaries, Wilson was the perfect target. Numbed and fortified with drink, on June 26 the two UFF men abducted Wilson and Andrews outside a downtown Belfast bar, forced them to drive to a remote quarry north of the city on Upper Hightown Road, and killed them.

Later that night, the *News Letter,* one of Belfast's three dailies, received the following telephone message: "This is Captain Black of the UFF. Last night, we assassinated Joseph Cunningham because he was passing information to the IRA. Tonight, we got Senator Paddy Wilson and a lady friend. The bodies are lying on the Hightown Road. After the IRA have murdered a retarded boy, we are not going to stand any longer for what those animals have done to us in the past four years. There will be more deaths in reprisal."[1] According to the police, the caller was "on the edge of hysteria."[2] The next day Paddy Wilson was found stabbed thirty times, his throat cut, his head nearly severed. Miss Andrews was stabbed twenty times. Forensic evidence suggested that the nonlethal lacerations were inflicted before each victim died.

According to "Captain Black," the Wilson-Andrews murders were reactions to the execution of David Walker. But because the slayings were almost ceremonially violent, they were also terrorist acts. As such, the Wilson-Andrews murders represent both the theory and practice of loyalist violence.

Loyalist violence is only partly reactive. Loyalists, as much as republicans, appreciate the stark efficiency of the terrorist act as an instrument of preemptive deterrence.

"Captain Black" was a play on the name of John White, who in the seventies was one of the highest ranking members of the UFF—a quietly ruthless leader whom loyalist prisoners told McIntyre they would "follow to hell and back." He had been arrested on the mainland for trying to purchase almost a million dollars' worth of illegal arms, and served a year on remand in Brixton Prison before he beat the charges. In June 1973, the UFF had just surfaced and had claimed a number of murders. Already a known UDA man and under heavy suspicion, White was then being snatched at least once a week and questioned about his paramilitary activities. For this reason, he couldn't carry a gun. "My philosophy then was, if you're going to kill someone, it doesn't matter what method you use. With the ferocity of [the murders] we also wanted to instill in Roman Catholics that we mean business. It was a message to the Roman Catholic community that if youse continue to slaughter our people, this is what's going to happen to youse, so youse put pressure on your people to stop, and we'll stop."

In 1976, racked with guilt, John White confessed to the murders. He served over sixteen years of a life sentence, and was released in 1993. He is now a leading member of the Ulster Democratic Party, which aims to build a constituency of working-class loyalists. White is bald and bespectacled, and appears Poindexter-ish. Though of medium height and solidly built, he is not physically prepossessing. He speaks quietly and thoughtfully about the murders, and his account is free of the "controlled rage" he admits he felt then. "I suppose now Paddy Wilson would be called a member of the pan-nationalist front. My analysis then was that he supported the concept of a united Ireland; the IRA were trying to pursue a united Ireland; therefore, by his rhetoric, he was supporting the IRA. It may have been warped at that time, but that was the way I viewed it when I was twenty-two years of age."

Loyalists had not yet coined the term "pan-nationalist front" in the early seventies, but they did view the entire nationalist community—that is, those advocating a united Ireland by peaceful means as well as armed republicans—as a well-oiled machine primed to destroy Ulster's union with Britain. They traced this pervasive strength to Catholicism, and tended to believe that their own Protestant state could not marshal the power to match it. "Catholics have this history of the armed struggle, they have this homogeneous society, whereas Protestantism is very frag-mented," says Billy Mitchell, a Royal Air Force veteran and an original member of the revived UVF sentenced to life for the murder of two loyal-ists from the rival UDA during a feud. "In the nationalist community you have this solidarity, and that's why it was easy for us to talk about a pan-nationalist front. When you looked at the nationalist community, you seen the church was there to give spiritual guidance—a solid church, not a split, fragmented church, but a unified one; the SDLP, the so-called constitutional nationalists, were there to give the respectability and the brains; and then you had the republicans to produce the muscle. Even though they disagreed—they ripped the back out of each other—when an issue come up, they all come together. In Protestantism, that doesn't happen."*

White, Mitchell, and their comrades believed that the security forces were not up to the task of containing the IRA, and therefore that they, as loyalist paramilitaries, had to step in. American right-wing vigilantes

---

*Note the definitions Mitchell uses. In Northern Ireland, "republicans" have traditionally been those, like the IRA, who advocate a united Ireland through armed force. Their prin-cipal political party is Sinn Fein. "Nationalists" or "the nationalist community" include not only republicans but also constitutional nationalists, who have always wanted Ireland united by peaceful political means. Their main party is the Social Democratic and Labour Party (SDLP). Symmetrically, "loyalists" have customarily believed in extralegal armed re-sistance to the republican campaign. During most of the troubles, loyalists as such had no political parties. Recently, however, the so-called fringe loyalist parties materialized. These are the Progressive Unionist Party (PUP), led by former UVF men; and the Ulster Demo-cratic Party (UDP), led by former UDA men. "Unionists" or "the unionist community" embrace not just loyalists but also mainstream unionists, who oppose loyalist paramili-tarism as well as republicanism and prefer to leave the republican problem to the security forces. Their political organizations are the Ulster Unionist Party (the province's largest) and Ian Paisley's Democratic Unionist Party. After the ceasefires, the distinction between republicans and nationalists, and that between loyalists and unionists, obviously became blurred. Since Canary Wharf, these distinctions are turning stark again.

often take action over some essentially personal loss—the killing of their local beat cop, the slaying of a neighborhood grocer in a robbery—that convinces them of the inadequacy of U.S. law enforcement. The same goes for loyalist paramilitaries. "The violence emanating from the loyalist paramilitary organizations was a defensive tactic," White explains. "It was to try and instill in the Roman Catholic community in general that the IRA were responsible for the death and destruction, so the Catholics in those communities would put pressure on the IRA to desist from what they were doing, and the loyalists would stop immediately." While loyalist violence was "reactive" insofar as it was prompted by IRA violence, it was also strategic insofar as it was intended to reward the IRA for restraint. Says White now: "The case has been proven; that's what did happen—when the IRA called the ceasefire, the loyalists responded shortly after that with their own."

John White also says that "there was a methodology behind the violence that I perpetrated, because I wasn't a violent person." He maintains that the "ferocity" of the Wilson-Andrews murders was intended to shock and frighten the Catholic community. Yet beneath White's twin towers of defensive reaction and military calculation was a foundation of deep-seated sectarian animosity. He was raised in the tradition of the [Anglican] Church of Ireland; his mother was Ulster working-class stock, his father a pensioned British soldier who was disabled for most of John's youth and died when John was nineteen. "I remember my mother, an uneducated working-class woman, saying to me, Son, we don't go into a united Ireland, and me saying, why not, Mammy, and I remember her saying, because you'll not get a job, and you'll probably not get a house, and they'll murder us, you know. And my Da, he just had a confirmed hatred for Roman Catholicism. I remember one time my brother brought a Roman Catholic to the house, a girlfriend, and my Da told her to get out of the house and not come back again. So, you know, I thought there must be some genuine fears there, when even my Da was saying, no bringing Taigs* home to this house." To his recollection, at the start of the troubles mixed couples were pressured to leave the Shankill.

The sectarianism White's parents taught him was reinforced when Catholics drove his family out of New Barnesley in far west Belfast, then

---

*Among working-class Protestants in Northern Ireland, "Taig" is the most popular derogatory term for Catholics, from an English rendering of the Gaelic Christian name "Tadhg."

petrol bombed their new house on what became the peace line. Others came by their bigotry even more dramatically than White. Alex Calderwood lived on Brown Square in the lower Shankill. In 1971, as the troubles got under way, a British army barracks was established there. Calderwood, then nine and a gregarious child, hung around the barracks and ran errands for the soldiers. He became such a fixture that they gave him a little uniform and a wooden rifle. Effectively, Calderwood was the mascot of the Brown Square barracks. On March 10, 1971, three off-duty Scottish soldiers were enticed into a car by Catholic lads promising girls and a good time. When the enticers stopped the car and the group got out to urinate, they shot the soldiers once each in the back of the head and dumped them in north Belfast. At army expense, Calderwood flew with the bugler from Brown Square barracks to Scotland for the funeral. "I had to ask questions and one of them was, who killed the three Scottish soldiers?" recalls Calderwood. "I was told that it was the IRA. So I once again asked another question: who's the IRA? And I was told, it's the Fenians,* or the Taigs, or the Roman Catholics. So basically, from a very early age, I grew up hating Roman Catholics."

Calderwood's teenage years were marked with spontaneous brutality against Catholics. When he was fourteen, on a cross-community trip to the Netherlands, he beat up so many Catholic boys that the chaperones had to park him in a Dutch mental hospital for two weeks, until the holiday was over. Along with his sectarianism, his learning disorders, his taste for alcohol, his 225-pound bulk, and his utter fearlessness (which he now calls "stupidity") made him a natural for the local branch of the UDA— again, then an ostensibly legal organization with an illegal paramilitary wing (the UFF) that dominated its activities. "From fourteen through sixteen years of age, my life was one of growing up through violence—people were being murdered, the police was being murdered, the army was

---

*Another epithet for Catholics, stemming from the Fenian Brotherhood, groups of Irish immigrants in the United States and Britain who, prompted by the famine, organized against British rule in Ireland in the mid-nineteenth century. Members of the indigenous Irish Republican Brotherhood, forerunner of the IRA, also became known as Fenians. The gentler, but still pejorative, middle-class term is "R.C."—for "Roman Catholic." For their part, Catholics refer negatively to Protestants as "black bastards." This term alludes to the "Black-and-Tans," vindictive auxiliary police recruits sent in by the British during the Anglo-Irish war in the twenties to reinforce the dwindling Royal Irish Constabulary. They earned their nickname from their makeshift uniforms—half army khaki, half RIC green-black—and their reputation through rampaging sprees of brutality against Irish civilians.

being murdered, people in my community was being murdered. I lived right on the so-called peace line between the Shankill Estate and Unity Flats,* and fourteen to sixteen we just got constant rioting all the time. They would have broke our windows, and we'd have broke theirs, and more people would have got involved into a whole big riot, stuff like that. Sixteen years of age, I looked around me, I seen that a lot of my friends were joining the junior paramilitaries. At that particular time we used to get these blue jackets with a wee fur collar on them, so I says I'll have one of them. At least I felt I could belong to something then. So I joined the UDA at sixteen." Calderwood's family had also been involved. His uncle, William "Buckie" McCullough, UDA brigadier on the Shankill, was shot dead by the INLA in October 1981.

At seventeen, Calderwood was walking along the Shankill Road after an evening at his drinking club. Several of his UDA buddies had a couple of Catholic lads pinned up against a wall. One ran off, and they left Calderwood there to take care of the remaining captive. He took the lad to a derelict garage and beat him to death with a cinder block. It was the first loyalist killing of 1980. The Catholic fellow, twenty-year-old Alexander Reid, had no connection with the IRA. He had gotten drunk and mistakenly clambered into the wrong taxi.

Then, through a series of epiphanies, Calderwood disavowed his sectarianism. Only five days after the Reid murder, Calderwood was arrested for a burglary and sentenced to a year in the Hydebank Young Offenders Center in Belfast. On his first day there, he refused to make his bed and belted the guard who tried to make him do it. He was placed in solitary confinement for the next five months. After that, he found himself sharing a cell with a Catholic lad from Unity Flats, who had been convicted of robbing a bank. The Catholic was enterprising, and soon convinced Calderwood to set aside his prejudice by offering to make Calderwood's bed if he would provide muscle for a jailhouse protection racket. For the next seven months, Calderwood and his Catholic friend extorted cigarettes and food out of other prisoners too scared of Calderwood to refuse their demands.

Shortly after the two were released, the Catholic boy came to visit Calderwood on the Shankill Road, where they smoked a couple of joints and had a few drinks. Calderwood's uncle heard that he had a Catholic visi-

---

*A Catholic estate between the Shankill and Falls Roads, razed in the early nineties. An "estate" is a public housing area.

tor and sent two UDA men in balaclavas* to execute the Catholic boy. Although Calderwood himself had rejoined the UDA, he stood up for his friend, who was grudgingly allowed to leave the Shankill unharmed. In pleading the Catholic boy's case, Calderwood argued to his uncle that his chum was "just an ordinary Taig" with no IRA connections. Calderwood soon realized that the boy he had beaten to death just a year earlier fit the same description. Remorse set in. Three months later, Calderwood turned himself in to the RUC and confessed to the Reid murder. He resigned from the UDA in prison, swore off drink and drugs, and experienced Christian rebirth. He now runs a community youth activity center on the Shankill Road, and has established his bona fides sufficiently to win public funding.

As an apparent Neanderthal-turned-evangelical, Calderwood is almost a caricature of the loyalist gunman. The common understanding among Protestants as well as Catholics is that loyalist killers typically have no political philosophy beyond an uninformed phobia of Catholics and a united Ireland. They often do their deeds while intoxicated, and frequently see the religious light in prison. This portrait contrasts with that of the IRA gunman, who is seen as a savage, but nonetheless militarily disciplined, true believer who kills cops and soldiers primarily, and hits Protestants only if they impede the path to a united Ireland. This standard distinction has some small basis in fact, but in general it is unfair to loyalists and too charitable to republicans.

"I admit that I was a sectarian bigot," says Calderwood. "It was my background and the society that programmed me in a sense, but I was responsible for what I done. I was a bigot and I hated Catholics. But the IRA will never admit that they hated Protestants. But they do. The Bayardo Bar on the Shankill was blew up, and there was men and women shot in the street, and that was done in the name of republicanism. I would say that the top republican who done that—Bik McFarlane—became a republican when he went to prison, because he educated himself to be a republican. But he was just a Catholic bigot when he done that bombing." Calderwood's point is not that he was as good as McFarlane, but that McFarlane was as bad as Calderwood. His own sectarian violence ultimately derived from the IRA's killing of the three Scottish soldiers in 1971. McFarlane hit the Bayardo Bar in retaliation for the UVF's murder

---

*Knitted woolen hoods that cover the head, neck, and part of the shoulders, exposing only the eyes. Named for an 1854 battle in the Crimean War, a balaclava can serve the same purpose as a ski mask.

of three members of the Miami Showband two weeks earlier. Both men were conditioned to violence by customary tribal insularity and suspicion, but driven to violent deeds by other specific acts of violence perpetrated by their putative enemies. In prison, Calderwood got religion while Mc-Farlane got republicanism.

PROTESTANT SECTARIANISM

Virtually all northern Catholics and a surprising number of middle-class Protestants see loyalists as less intellectual and political and more brutal and venal than republicans. Their view is that loyalists are really criminals and republicans revolutionaries, and it's an impression the rest of the world largely shares. But neutral parties argue that the truth is far murkier. "I don't think you can generalize in that way, I really don't," says Marty Rafferty, a Quaker social worker who counsels both loyalist and republican prisoners on adjusting to incarceration and release. "I think on both sides you have people who were committed out of a sense of principle, you know. Certainly in the seventies, I don't think either republicans or loyalists were very political then. They were reacting only to what happened in their communities. The Catholic might be reacting to the army activity, or the harassment, or the perceived injustices in their local community, and the loyalists would be reacting to a bomb that went off and it appeared nobody was doing anything. And I think both of them were really motivated by family or community things, and it was only later in prison that they put political reasons to all of that and became politicized."

Many loyalists were forced from their homes by Catholic agitation, as White was in New Barnesley. Tommy Kirkham, who joined the UDA at seventeen and promptly served two and a half years in Long Kesh on a weapons charge, had to move after an IRA bomb wrecked his house. Some loyalists may have been beaten up by Catholics as children, but most, like Kirkham, didn't even meet their first Catholic until they started working in their mid-teens. Most loyalist animosity toward Catholics probably has a firmer basis in community indoctrination than in maltreatment by Catholics or an aggressively sectarian upbringing.

Ex-UVF man Billy Hutchinson was convicted of shooting two Catholic half-brothers dead on the Falls Road in 1974. He maintains they were active IRA men, though that's never been publicly proven. Hutchinson paints a relatively wholesome picture of his conditioning. "Growing up on the Shankill, you learnt your politics on the streets then, sure you didn't learn them in the house. There would have been a few households, but there would have been very few households which would have, you know, preached in terms of unionism. It's different from republican areas, where you'd have had strong republican families." Hutchinson's father, who made his living as a bookie, was a socialist and voted for whatever pro-labor party stood *against* mainstream unionists. His mother cleaned houses and "voted unionist because her father and mother did it."

Hutchinson's loyalism developed not in the home, but in debates at Mackie's, an engineering firm which sits on the peace line and has generally employed more Catholics than the average Belfast concern. "Whenever I started working in Mackie's, it was really the first time I came into contact with Catholics my own age, and it was the first time I was in, I suppose, a structured environment where there were Catholics. Whenever I was younger, my father would have took me to the Falls Road to look at pictures or to go to a park or to visit Catholic houses, but, I mean, I wouldn't really have had much talking to people. I was quite shy." That's not difficult to imagine. Hutchinson is handsome, with high cheekbones and an aquiline nose that seems to go on forever. He is lithe and soft-spoken. He might appear almost feminine, until his flinty self-confidence and imperturbable intellect register. Then he comes off like an Eagle Scout or a war hero. It is difficult to imagine that this teetotaling marathon runner ever saw himself as a sectarian killer. What fueled loyalists like Hutchinson was the notion that the Catholic bigotry against Protestants in the south was at least as bad as the Protestant bigotry against Catholics in the north.

William "Plum" Smith, who served time with Hutchinson for attempted murder, remembers the early days of the troubles as something like the dawning of a prophesied apocalypse. "In the seventies these communities were close-knit communities," he says gruffly. "You still had the extended family situation, and word-of-mouth and rumor was far more valid than printed matter or television. But there's no one thing, it was the whole situation at that time. You had segregated schools, you had segregated areas, you had a whole history dealt down to you by word-of-mouth about troubles, the IRA, and all that—that was all part of your dogma the whole way through your life. So whenever the bogeyman appeared in 1970, this was the bogeyman we were told about. The bogeyman appeared and the rest became part of life—there was thousands and thousands, I mean, the vast majority of people were involved in it. So when your community felt threatened, you felt threatened."

David Ervine's experience drives home the point. He grew up in east Belfast—almost exclusively Protestant and the heart of working-class loyalism. He was never beaten up or displaced by Catholics. By his own account, he was as disposed to philosophical thought then as he is now—which is to say, considerably. But he couldn't stand idly by as the two communities slugged it out. "I think my fundamental memories of that time are of agonizing about what I was going to do, and I think that my movement towards the loyalist paramilitaries coincided with the birth of my son and the death of my father. There was intercommunal violence, numbers of people being found dead were tortured and all manner of things, on both sides. And I think there was a feeling within me that I had to take sides." After steering clear of the paramilitaries for four years, Ervine joined the UVF in 1972. In November 1974, he found himself tied with a long rope to the ankle of an RUC bomb disposal officer who was holding Ervine at gunpoint while he gingerly removed from the trunk of David's car a detonator, a fuse, and five and a half pounds of commercial gelignite. Ervine served over five years in Long Kesh for possession of explosives.

Sectarianism, where it existed in the home, was more often subtle than in-your-face. Eddie Kinner, another ex-UVF prisoner, recalls that before the troubles his parents never promoted anti-Catholicism and socialized regularly with a mixed couple, but privately expressed a distrust of the woman, who was Catholic. "My mother at that stage would say, she's all right, but I wouldn't turn my back on her." Certainly there were tribal pressures. Although the woman's testimony helped the elder Kinner beat a rioting charge, he refused to push her case in a loyalist bar after the bartender refused to serve her a drink. Kinner's father was a member of the Orange Order. "That's a sectarian organization," he admits, "and therefore you'd have to conclude that he was sectarian."

Many working-class Protestants were members of the Orange Order, the Royal Black Preceptory, or the Apprentice Boys of Derry, although these organizations are predominantly middle-class. All three groups are exclusively Protestant. Their ostensible purpose is to celebrate Ulster Protestant culture affirmatively and to strengthen community cohesion and voluntarism—much like the Masons, the Shriners, the Elks, or the Kiwanis Club. But the three groups were founded in the spirit of Protestant territorial triumphalism. The original "apprentice boys" numbered thirteen Presbyterian lads who slammed the gates of Derry on the besieging forces of King James II in 1689, crying "No surrender!" The Orange Order was formed in 1795 in County Armagh to consolidate rural Protestant landowners against Catholic rivals after Protestant vigilantes defeated their Catholic counterparts in "the battle of the Diamond." The Royal Black Preceptory is basically the senior level of the Orange Order, to which Orangemen are promoted once they have completed established institutional rituals. In such a contentiously divided society, these institutions perforce took on a sectarian character.* Their annual series of marches inevitably proved offensive to the nationalist community. Although not violently inclined during the troubles, these fraternities are without question doctrinally anti-Catholic.

Veterans, fathers and grandfathers, often planted a military seed in their sons. Ex-UVF lifer Martin Snoddon's father was a member of the Ulster Defense Regiment and, in his regular job as a municipal bus driver on the Falls Road, carried a pistol in his hip pocket. Again, this kind of example was not sectarian in itself, but the IRA campaign sometimes transmogrified it into militant anti-Catholicism. "Most of my background came from my grandfather," says Tommy Kirkham with pride. "I spent an awful lot of time with my grandfather. He was a fervent member of the 5th Royal Irish Fusiliers. During the First World War they went through Gallipoli, and he was wounded there and sent back home. They then reformed and were sent out to France. He fought at the Somme before being sent to Belgium, and he was wounded a second time at the Second Battle of Ypres."

Most Irish Catholics adopted a position of neutrality during the First World War and did not enlist in the British army. Then the Irish Republican Brotherhood attempted to land twenty thousand rifles from Germany to arm the Easter Rising in 1916. Finally, the Irish Free State was officially neutral during the Second World War. These three factors all tend to make an Ulster veteran's Protestantism distinctly anti-Catholic. Of his grandfather, Kirkham remembers: "He was a staunch Protestant. When coming back from the war, he was a member of the A-Specials and then subsequently the B-Specials.† He was a member of the Apprentice Boys, the Or-

---

*Their opposite Catholic number is the Ancient Order of Hibernians, which traces its roots to the 1641 Catholic rebellion in Ulster. The AOH, however, is less integral to northern Catholicism than the Orange Order is to Ulster Protestantism.

†After partition, the old UVF was mustered into the three police reserve units, exclusively Protestant, of the Ulster Special Constabulary. The A-Specials were attached full-time to the RUC for six-month periods; the B-Specials were part-time (and the most numerous); and the C-Specials were for emergencies. In the 1930s, the A- and C-Specials were disbanded and the B-Specials became permanent RUC auxiliaries. Following their excesses on the lower Falls in 1969, the nine-thousand-strong B-Specials were disbanded, reformed into the Ulster Defense Regiment, and placed under military control. Catholics still considered the UDR sectarian, and republicans killed 230 members and ex-members between 1970 and 1992. In 1992 the UDR and the Royal Irish Rangers were combined to form the Royal Irish Regiment.

ange and the Black institutions." A richer Protestant pedigree couldn't have been manufactured. When Tommy Kirkham says, "I've always been in my heart a soldier," he can't help but mean a *Protestant* soldier.*

ULSTER PROTESTANTS: A MINORITY AT HEART

Myriad cultural forces reinforced Protestant sectarianism. That foundation of bigotry, in turn, enabled loyalists to muster the ruthlessness required to carry out an especially cynical and brutal counterterrorist campaign. But it was not sectarianism alone that moved loyalists to hit Catholic civilians at random. The loyalist paramilitaries were motivated to a significant extent by the urgency of physically defending and avenging a community victimized by republican aggression. After 1969, republicans attacked that community continually. The Shankill area and east Belfast were fairly difficult for the IRA to penetrate, but other Protestant areas were surrounded by Catholic neighborhoods, and thereby isolated. The Suffolk Estate in southwest Belfast, for example, is flanked by three of the strongest republican areas—Andersonstown, Lenadoon, and Twinbrook. Martin Snoddon lived in Suffolk during the seventies.

"Suffolk was unique," recalls Snoddon, a bluff, strapping redhead. "It was completely cut off from any other Protestant area, it didn't back onto any other Protestant area. It was actually very, very isolated up where it is, surrounded on three sides by the nationalist republican community. Two very good friends of mine, classmates, lived at the top of Lenadoon, and they were coming into school and telling us about being intimidated and not being able to go out at night because there was this Catholic gang coming down from the other end of Lenadoon who were giving them hammerings and things. So a few of us decided, right, we're going to go up some night—we'll have a bit of a barney, you know, we'll have a bit of a dig. Which we did, you know, we went up and there was a lot of punches thrown and whatnot. That was my first sort of personal involvement with fighting the enemy."

---

*Around November 11, Remembrance Day (Veterans' Day in the United States), most adults in the United Kingdom honor fallen veterans of the two world wars by wearing red paper poppies in their lapels. The most unanimous among observers of this tradition are Ulster Protestants. Correspondingly, almost all northern Catholics leave their lapels unadorned. The IRA's Remembrance Day bombing in Enniskillen in 1987 amplified the division.

Snoddon's paramilitary activity began to take shape when he joined a local vigilante group, which became part of the UDA. But to Snoddon's way of thinking, the UDA was not militant enough. "I was transporting guns, making pipe bombs, this type of thing. They might have had a few guns, but the guns were rarely if ever fired in anger or in defense. The security forces appeared on the scene maybe half an hour or an hour after an incident. So I wanted to do more." He and a group of friends went three miles north to the Shankill and joined the Young Citizens' Volunteers—the youth wing of the UVF. Unlike the UDA, the UVF seemed to have a distinguished history. Its predecessor in name had helped stave off Irish rule in Ulster by threatening armed resistance in 1912, and fought valiantly for Britain in World War I. More recently, Gusty Spence had revived the UVF as a secret, illegal loyalist paramilitary group to combat the Provisional IRA's renewed threat to Ulster's union with Britain. This reincarnation had acquired its honored place in 1966, five years before the UDA was even formed, when Spence went to jail for shooting Peter Ward dead. The UDA threatened to kill Snoddon for defecting, but retreated after he came back at them with UVF muscle.

On March 13, 1975, as Snoddon, George Brown, and Eddie Kinner raked a north Belfast IRA hangout called Conway's Bar with gunfire, the bomb that was to be the *coup de grace* exploded prematurely. Snoddon was blown out of the bar. The only person they killed was Marie Doyle, a thirty-eight-year-old patron and mother of IRA volunteer Mary Doyle, who was later one of the three female hunger strikers in Armagh jail who complemented the male prisoners' 1981 hunger strike. Snoddon's pants were burned off, his penis singed, his hair scorched. He was deafened permanently in one ear. And his back was on fire. A mob chased him, but he was caught by the RUC, who beat him both on the scene and at the police station. Snoddon collapsed without talking, and was taken to the hospital. Kinner and Brown were also injured, and Brown died several weeks after the attack. When Snoddon learned that an innocent civilian had been killed, he was shattered. "I felt disgusted with myself that a woman had been killed in that incident. If there had have been ten Provisional IRA men killed, I would have probably smiled and said, well, to hell with them, you know, that's where they're trying to send us. But I hadn't went out to kill any women."

Though a Protestant along with 65 percent of Ulster's population of 1.6 million, Snoddon did not feel like part of a majority. Instead he felt besieged. Even in the constitutional context, Ulster Prods are a small minority both within the United Kingdom and within the island of Ireland as a whole. They feel, collectively, as much like a minority as northern Catholics do.[3] As a consequence, they hang onto what republicans call the "unionist veto"—the right of Northern Ireland's majority, as opposed to the island's majority, to decide its constitutional fate—in a spirit of desperation rather than complacency. Republicans have always been able to draw eager and inspirational support from the United States. Meanwhile, unionists have stood alone in the face of Great Britain's growing apathy for a province whose turmoil seems terminal.

Hence, vulnerability, not mere stubbornness, accounts for what is commonly known as "unionist intransigence." If this is true, then why, many wonder, have unionist politicians taken so long to explain it? They seem to have nurtured the fantasy, stoked by Margaret Thatcher, that Northern Ireland is "as British as Finchley."* The answer lies in loyalist naiveté, and with the Reverend Ian Paisley.

In the early days of the troubles, most loyalists had not developed any political theory to back up the visceral compulsion to defend their turf. Not one of the loyalists interviewed for this book felt the need to formulate such a theory until he got to prison. Before that, the rightness of liquidating dissidents and their supporters was simply taken for granted. Loyalist paramilitaries regarded themselves as adjuncts to the security forces. The government did not unequivocally disabuse them of the notion. The UDA was not declared illegal until 1992. Despite Gusty Spence's pre-troubles murder conviction, the British government actually legalized the UVF between October 1974 and October 1975 in the hope that it would become politicized. Prison was the reality check. "I suppose that the main thing for me was that it was at that point in time that I started looking around and I seen that it was the British crown that I was being punished by," says Eddie Kinner. "For a loyalist it was a difficult thing to realize. I think for nationalists it's very easy to go in there and say, it's still the same old system that's picking on us."

When unincarcerated loyalists did use politics to justify their actions, they got it ready-made from Ian Paisley. Paisley is a Christian fundamentalist who trained rigorously for three years in the Reformed Presbyterian Church in Belfast, and was ordained there. For most of his career, however, he has styled himself a "Free Presbyterian"—of an evangelical sect

---

*Finchley is a suburb of London, England. It is Thatcher's former constituency.

which institutionally has nothing to do with the mainstream Presbyterian Church. His followers call him "Dr. Paisley"—a title that comes from a mail-order Doctor of Divinity degree from an American "degree mill," Pioneer Theological Seminary of Rockford, Illinois, and an honorary doctorate from Bob Jones University in South Carolina.[4] Paisley is basically an honest bigot, railing fire-and-brimstone against "popery" and "the whore of Rome" and fiercely resisting any attempts to involve the Catholic minority in mainstream Northern Irish politics.

Paisley built up his influence with the Protestant working class as Catholics began to wage their civil rights protests in the mid-sixties—that is, during the run-up to the troubles. While the border issue had always overshadowed class politics, Paisley did work harder than most unionist politicians to make sure the working class was taken care of. But this he did quietly. Rhetorically, he banished bread-and-butter issues to the distant periphery by casting the specter of papist Ireland up against Ulster's pewter skies. Catholics not only threaten your way of life, he thundered, they will destroy your Protestant values and your identity as Ulster Scots. His cant demonized Catholics in the insinuating, sententious way of the seductive demagogue.

In 1966, when a priest (and several Protestant clergymen) persuaded the Ballymoney town council to cancel a Free Presbyterian election meeting on the ground that the local people collectively deplored its message of intolerance toward Catholics, Paisley retorted as follows: "Priest Murphy, speak for your own bloodthirsty persecuting intolerant blaspheming political religious papacy but do not dare to pretend to be the spokesman of free Ulster men. You are not in the south of Ireland. Go back to your priestly intolerance, back to your blasphemous masses, back to your beads, holy water, holy smoke and stinks and remember we are the sons of martyrs whom your church butchered and we know your church to be the mother of harlots and the abominations of the earth."[5] In the height of the troubles, Paisley's rhetoric was nothing short of incitement. "Christ was not a man of peace," he bellowed from his pulpit. "Be violent for Christ's sake, to defend the faith which he himself defended with his fists."[6]

Hardly subtle, but to simple working folk he was a great communicator. "Paisley was a homespun man who seemed to communicate horizontally and he spoke the people's language," remembers Mitchell. "Although he probably had more content and body to what he had to say, I just identified with Paisley because of the personality. Obviously that molded a lot of my thinking then. And I think that Paisley's whole political philosophy came over in catchphrases." Steve Bruce, Paisley's most probative biographer, sardonically calls him "the prophet in the political wilderness."[7] He hypnotized a generation that had never thought for itself. "Protestants were conditioned that your clergyman done your theological thinking, your politician done your political thinking, your boss done your economic thinking, you just followed suit," says Mitchell. Was he sectarian? "Well, being honest, yes. I mean, I got my politics from Paisley." Having a rebel culture of long standing, Catholics were not saddled with the same baggage of intellectual inertia.

Paisley set the tone of troubles politics. Following his example, politicians saw actual or potential victimhood as the most exploitable characteristic in the electorate. Andy Tyrie witnessed it happening at ground level. "Why can we work together, Catholic and Protestant, live together, meet on holidays, then come back here and fight? Because people who are politicians have been left over and never change—because they felt that they had to adopt that sectarian attitude, Catholic and Protestant, for to maintain support. See, what happened was, there was the Ulster Unionist Party, then Dr. Paisley come in proclaiming hard-line attitudes to the nationalist community. He got people elected, he was taking it off unionists, so people started to think, that's how you got elected."

The larger public began to justify violence not on the basis of any political objective, like keeping the union with Britain or reuniting Ireland, but instead *because they did it to us.* "Look, you know, I'm a moderate unionist, but I've got to tell you now, my whole body's full of sectarian bones, and there's a sectarian gunman in all of us trying to get out," says a frank Chris McGimpsey, city councillor for Protestant west Belfast. "Some of us have managed to keep him in and have managed to rationalize our anger and divert it into ways which were lawful rather than unlawful, but there is no line drawn." In other words, the self-perpetuating motive of revenge gave the troubles an extrapolitical vitality.

Paisley's inordinate power in Ulster does not derive from the fact that unionists are religious zealots, though some are. Since the Irish home rule movement began over a hundred years ago, the overriding concern of Ulster Protestants has been to remain British for a cumulation of reasons that are political, cultural, and economic as well as theological. Paisley gives unionists neat, sturdy packaging in exchange for ideological license. Thus, Protestants' vehement unionism fuels Paisley's evangelical Protestantism—not, as some suppose, the other way around. Although the relationship is symbiotic, Paisley has exploited loyalist ignorance.

Ian Paisley has never had any direct involvement with the principal loyalist paramilitary groups.* He is a member of the British Parliament, a member of the European Parliament, and the founder and leader of the third-largest political party in Northern Ireland, the Democratic Unionist Party. Yet his political activism has generally been limited to bombastic sermons from the pulpit of his huge Martyrs' Memorial Church in east Belfast, and jingoistic statements to the press of the "No surrender!" variety. His street agitation has been infrequent but dramatic: in 1964, he and his supporters compelled the RUC to wrest an Irish tricolor from the window of the old Sinn Fein election office on the Falls Road; in 1969, he blocked a civil rights march in Armagh, for which he served six weeks in jail; and in 1981, on a County Antrim hillside, he organized a demonstration against Anglo-Irish cooperation in which five hundred Protestant men brandished their gun licenses. For loyalist paramilitaries, the first two acts may have been sources of pride, but the last was an embarrassment.

While he ignited the entire Protestant population by trumpeting (indeed, championing) its isolation, Paisley's palaver spoke more to the Protestant shop-owners than to the loyalist paramilitaries. There has for decades been a tremendous class distinction between loyalist talkers and loyalist terrorists—the latter worked for the former but didn't think like them. Most loyalist paramilitaries had decent blue-collar jobs. Gusty Spence was a stager at Harland and Wolff, where he erected the high scaffolding needed to build ships. John White was a carpenter. Billy Hutchinson was a lathe operator at Mackie's, the engineering firm. Marty Snoddon was a manual laborer, Eddie Kinner a plumber's apprentice. During the bulk of Stormont's tenure, Northern Ireland was economically healthy, and Protestant lads

---

*The UDA and the UVF have recruited mainly from Belfast and vicinity. They have not found favor among rural Protestants, who tend to be more evangelical than urban dwellers and thus to judge "men of violence" harshly. Reacting to the hunger strike and the IRA's murder of unionist MP Robert Bradford, in late 1981 Paisley organized a short-lived popular resistance movement styled the "Third Force" ("Turd Force," snickered one authentic paramilitary) that held a few rallies and set up the odd roadblock. In 1986, after the Anglo-Irish Agreement was signed, Paisley gave a vague, wink-and-nod public endorsement to Ulster Resistance, a nascent group of rural paramilitaries. When berets bearing the group's insignia were found in a County Armagh arms cache in 1988, Paisley disavowed any knowledge of illegal activity by the group. Five months later in Paris, three Ulster Resistance members, a South African diplomat, and a U.S. arms dealer were arrested while in possession of stolen missile parts manufactured by Short Brothers in east Belfast. Allegations arose that the group intended to trade missile technology for South African guns. Ulster Resistance has not resurfaced since.

were assured of work. Their employment became the tacit quid pro quo of their votes, which went mainly to the representatives of the unionist middle class who ran the businesses that employed the paramilitaries.

"The business people were mostly unionists, so you voted for unionists and you were maybe getting first preference for a job," explains Billy Mitchell. "What it would mean in reality was, you were a Catholic, you were being punished for your disloyalty, and we Protestants were being exploited for our loyalty. So you had big factories saying, okay, we'll give you a first-preference job here, but it's low-paid, bad working conditions. And if you complained—once you started to complain about your wages and your working conditions, you were promptly told, if you don't like it there's a hundred Catholics out in the street that will take your job tomorrow."

Although working-class Prods were more secure in their lot than their Catholic counterparts, it was a squalid lot indeed. Because of the pronounced class division and superimposed lack of upward mobility, the Protestant ethic in Northern Ireland acquired an acquiescent anti-intellectual dimension. Most Protestants did not graduate with academic qualifications, and weren't encouraged to. Eddie Kinner, though demonstrably bright, did very poorly in school and left at age fifteen. But when Ulster's economy skidded in the sixties, seventies, and eighties, unemployment around the Shankill (though not in east Belfast, the industrial center) was almost as bad for Protestants as it was on the Falls for Catholics. The loyalist community found itself lacking intellectual capital to fall back on. Loyalist prisoners saw this happening from their cells, and consequently developed a strong educational culture in the compounds.

Between 1960 and 1985, employment in manufacturing dropped 45 percent, by 82,000. Half of that decline, along with a 39 percent fall in construction employment, came in the last seven years of that period. The linen mills that had anchored Ulster's economy for two hundred years all closed by the sixties, rendered obsolete by synthetic textiles. Ultimately, the synthetic-fibers plants that replaced the linen mills struggled against foreign competition. Harland and Wolff employed 26,000 in 1945 but less than 4,000 in 1985, and stays open only with a hefty annual government subsidy.[8] Alex Calderwood counted on a blue -collar job; his father had worked the shipyard until a back injury put him permanently on the dole. Alex was functionally illiterate when he entered prison. Calderwood, like the rest of the loyalist working class, wanted to hang on to what he had. As that became increasingly little, he became increasingly desperate.

Loyalist terrorism arose not from counterrevolutionary politics so much as from fear. Billy Mitchell makes no excuses, but he is also quick to say that the ultra-nationalist line that republicans were peddling to Catholics partially validated Protestant paranoia. "I was being told that republicanism is wrong, that Catholicism was wrong, that there was a pan-nationalist conspiracy, and I didn't question it. I'm not saying that—this is where it can get a wee bit complicated—today I can still see a pan-nationalist conspiracy. But what the problem was in those days, there were certain grievances that the Catholic population had that Protestants also had, and it wasn't all the Protestants' fault that they weren't tackled by the government. If the civil rights movement hadn't sectarianized civil rights, Protestants would have got involved, too." They had shared goals and, but for parochialism and chauvinism on both sides, might have united.

Gusty Spence, like Mitchell, came to this realization only after he had spent years in prison and observed Northern Ireland from a detached vantage point. "The working class have always been on the cutting edge, you know, they've lived cheek-by-jowl, Catholic working class and Protestant working class," he says from the den of his lower Shankill house, now thickly decorated with military memorabilia and testimonials. "And invariably the interface areas which are now the peace lines became the battlegrounds. The unionists always lived in a nice, leafy suburbia, thank you very much, and if there was any threat to them, they had their police bodyguards, and so on and so forth, and all the trappings of security. So they were—like some churchmen, too—absolutely and completely out of touch with what was and is the thinking within the loyalist working class. They never really considered the working class except at election time."

Being isolated by choice, much of the middle class apprehended the troubles with detached bemusement. The few paramilitary players they deigned to socialize with were considered ugly novelties. One such player was Glen Barr. He co-founded the UDA in Derry, but always took care to stay at arm's length from the nasty end of its business. As a self-made businessman, with piercing blue eyes and a slick "black Irish" look, he was presentable. But he was never really accepted. "You know," says Barr sarcastically, "there's nothing nicer than to sit at a social gathering or dinner and pontificate—what better than to have somebody like Glennie Barr threw into the middle of it? Let's see what makes this fucker tick. Let's have a circus, let's see what makes them go."

Perversely, the insulated "chattering class" became less intolerant of the violence as time went on. "They got on with life," Barr explains. "Their kids had to get their A-levels, good grades, had to get to university. They said, don't get involved in this, don't get sidetracked. Northern Ireland will be all right." This division in the Protestant community put the Protestant working class at a disadvantage. "All of the fighting and the bombing hit the Shankill and the Falls, places like Greysteel and stuff like that," says Barr. "The middle class didn't say anything. The problem is that we've lost the talents from that community, which was making a major contribution to our political life. At the end of the day, basically you need those academic classes. But the middle class, particularly on the Protestant side, all pissed off [fled]. And ordinary working-class guys were left leaderless."

Or rather, all they had was Paisley. In recent years, he has perceptibly lost clout among the loyalist rank and file—a signal that they have started to think politically for themselves. Loyalist paramilitaries, in particular, privately resent Paisley for the two-faced manner in which he has wound them up and then condemned them. Yet in 1979, he received more votes in the election for the European Parliament than any other candidate. Stormont and then Paisley made the loyalist community reactionary through-and-through. By appearances, Billy Mitchell is the last person anyone would pick out of a lineup as a loyalist gunman. Now in his mid-fifties, he is a compact, bald man. His eyes are sunk in deep, leathery pockets, from which they radiate sadness, remorse, and wisdom salvaged from moral suffering. He admits: "A lot of people may be a wee bit dilatory at saying it, but I have no problem saying it: I do come from a reactionary past. I'm not saying that I was a born reactionary. But I believe it was the upbringing, it was this upbringing that you done what your betters told you to do, you didn't question what they done, and if they told you to fight for something, you fought for it."

Through a haze of pipe smoke, the diminutive Plum Smith—another unlikely killer, on the face of it—thus explains his activity as a paramilitary in the Red Hand Commando* in cold, clinical terms, as if in retro-

---

*A small group with close links to the UVF. In their insignia, most Protestant paramilitary groups incorporate the symbol of the "Red Right Hand of Ulster." The symbol originally signified the hand of God, but the operative legend is a corruption of that meaning. Supposedly, in pre-Elizabethan Ulster, a Gaelic chieftain from the O'Neill clan of Ulster was racing another man across a river to determine who would occupy the land on the opposite bank. When the chieftain discovered he was losing, he cut off his hand, threw the bloody thing onto the far shore, and laid claim to the land. The red hand thus signifies resolve against heavy odds, and as such embodies the "siege mentality" for which Ulster Protestants are noted. For republicans, the rough equivalent is the traditional Gaelic harp "new-strung," which was the motto of the United Irishmen—Presbyterians and Catholics led by Wolf Tone who revolted against the Protestant Ascendancy in 1798. The symbol of the hand is etched on an old ornamental harp preserved at Trinity College, Dublin. This counteradoption of two symbols common to both traditions is one of many examples of each side "hijacking" history and using it to lash the other.

spect he were watching a separate being actuated by external forces. "I got caught in the act of shooting a Catholic. It was a sectarian assassination attempt. He was shot fourteen times, and he still lived. I haven't a clue whether he's still alive. Obviously, the shooting left him paralyzed. The man wasn't targeted for any particular reason. It was sectarian—I mean, in those days, it was community against community."

The victim's name was Joseph Hall, but it barely matters to Smith. It's not that Smith is a cruel man. As most republicans consider themselves, he believes the loyalist paramilitaries to have been ordinary people in extraordinary circumstances, behaviorally conditioned by a jangled tribal society to kill the other guys, no matter who they were. "In 1969, what you had here was a complete breakdown of law and order. Although I may have committed a violent act, I wasn't a violent person as such," says Smith. "If I was born in another country which had no violence or political trouble, I would never have seen the inside of a prison. At the time, I believed I was doing right. At the time, I believed it was necessary, and I believed that I was making a sacrifice, that it was a good thing. So to say, och, I've got remorse or I feel guilty—I think that's wrong in the context of our ends." In Smith's memory, Northern Ireland in the seventies was a Skinner box for violence; bloodshed could not be helped. But his recollection is perhaps too sanguine. Early in the troubles, loyalist paramilitaries did make earnest efforts to switch from violence to politics. They were nearly successful.

GLORY DAYS

Paisley managed to rouse loyalist violence without getting his hands dirty. This does not mean, however, that the loyalist paramilitaries have always been headless, and have always been operated by remote control. Nor has their leadership always been anarchically sectarian. In prison, Spence was a strong, inspiring, and enduring officer commanding. Comparable leadership on the outside has been sporadic, but not inconsequential. Its valedictorians would be Andy Tyrie and Glen Barr, and their finest moment was the 1974 loyalist strike. The episode shows that, contrary to republican sentiment, loyalists were not always crudely reactive or inhumanly sectarian, nor reflexively anti-Catholic, nor, in Gusty Spence's phrase, "slack-jawed Neanderthals."

The strike came in response to the installation by Northern Ireland Prime Minister Brian Faulkner on January 1, 1974, with British sanction, of a power-sharing government. A year after assuming direct rule of

Northern Ireland in an effort to truncate the burgeoning troubles, Westminster had authorized a new Northern Ireland assembly. The idea was to establish a devolved government in which, unlike Stormont, power would be shared equitably between unionists and nationalists. Elections to the new assembly in June 1973 yielded a slim majority in favor of power sharing. Faulkner's government—called "Sunningdale" after the English town where British and Irish officials had met to hash out the details—would thus replace direct rule.

The theory behind Sunningdale was that Northern Ireland and the Republic of Ireland should be treated as interdependent entities. Northern Ireland was to be governed by an eleven-member "executive" composed of northern nationalists and unionists in roughly equal parts. Two tiers of officials drawn equally from Ulster and the Republic of Ireland would advise this executive and help formulate policy. Although Britain retained sovereignty over Ulster, both London and Dublin affirmed the principle that Northern Ireland's sovereign future was up to the majority of its people.

By the time Faulkner's government took power, unionists had changed their minds about power sharing. The Ulster Unionist Party's intramural council voted down the Sunningdale principles. Most importantly, in the British parliamentary elections in February 1974, an anti-power-sharing unionist coalition (known as the United Ulster Unionist Council) won more than half the total votes cast and sent eleven of a total of twelve Northern Ireland MPs to Westminster. The UDA, being against power sharing as well, had a political mandate. Tyrie was then chairman of the UDA and Barr his political adviser. They were in agreement with mainstream unionists: the Irish Republic's voice in Faulkner's power-sharing executive was a direct affront to the principle of majority rule in Northern Ireland—and, consequently, the beginning of the end.

The initial response to the executive from the loyalist community consisted of Paisley-inspired parades and riots. They only made the British indignant, and more determined to support Faulkner. Officers of the Ulster Workers Council, the province's trade union coalition, came up with the notion of a strike, but it was Tyrie and Barr who put it into action. Although the UWC nominally staged the strike, the UDA supplied both the brains and the muscle. Barr was the chairman of the strike coordinating committee, Tyrie its most influential member. Most ranking UWC men were also in the UDA, which at the time had a legal membership of perhaps forty thousand. Paisley himself, being in essence a man of words, was wary, but he had little say in the matter. Billy Kelly of the UWC simply delivered him a *fait accompli,* and Barr kept Paisley out of one morning committee meeting early in the strike because he was late. Barr and Tyrie were careful to set conditions for calling off the strike that were tailored to precisely what they saw as the power-sharing executive's principal offense—namely, the abuse of the democratic process. Specifically, they demanded new elections to the Northern Ireland assembly.

"The fact was that the democratic wish of the people was being overlooked, it wasn't being listened to," explains Glen Barr. "The overwhelming majority of the people of Northern Ireland were being pushed into a political arena that they didn't want, nor did they vote for, indeed they voted against. It was going against the democratic wishes of the people, so we decided that the only way to do something about it was to have us withdraw our support for the whole institution of the state, just to demonstrate this is what it can be like if the Protestants come together and say, no, we don't like this and we don't want it and this is what we're going to do about it. It was a public demonstration of their disapproval of what was taking place politically. That's basically what it was."

Barr and company ran the stoppage from a big house up on Horton Dean Road in east Belfast, near Stormont Castle. Without UDA squads to police the strike, everybody would have gone to work. If everyone had gone to work, the anti-executive unionists would have looked almost irreparably foolish. "The UDA created the strike," remembers Andy Tyrie fondly. "What happened was, on Wednesday morning of the strike, there was no strike. Most people were going to work, so they were. So everyone was panicking, and I says, look, we'll block the roads, take your own cameras with you, take things with you, I says, subtle intimidation. Once you're rioting, you're finished, I says, because people will use it as an excuse, saying there's the thugs, there's the hoodlums again. I said, look, in any confrontation there is with the security forces, move back. I says, move back, put a roadblock somewhere else, keep on the move, don't look for confrontation. And that's how we played it, and that's how it worked. Then the power workers got a grip of the situation, and then once we got control of the power, then we got control of the whole situation. Now the nice thing about it, in all the population, both Catholic and Protestant, there was nobody starved, everybody got everything they needed, they got their milk, they got their food, they got everything. It became almost like a festival." Intimidation for the most part was subtle. To discourage workers from crossing picket lines, UDA men took photographs of those who tested the barricades.

The UDA also showed political deftness and practical competence in running the strike. The coordinating committee made sure livestock was fed, and machinery maintained. UDA squads brought milk to children after buying it from a co-op. There were some paramilitary excesses—cars hijacked, buses burned, three Catholic pubs wrecked by drunken UDA and UVF men, and two Catholic pub owners shot dead—but for the most part the strike was staged with a fair degree of nonpartisan humanity, as Tyrie says. Nonconfrontation worked. The British army had opted out, and the RUC, being fundamentally anti-executive itself, left the UDA alone so long as the police were not directly challenged with physical force.* Within two weeks, the unionist members of the executive had resigned, and the body collapsed. Direct rule resumed.

The 1974 strike was a successful and principled rejection by working-class loyalists of nationalists, upper-class unionists, and, to an extent, even Paisley. But its resonance flagged quickly because Protestant paramilitaries were unable to sustain respectability. Having enjoyed hegemony in Northern Ireland since partition, the Protestant community, unlike its Catholic counterpart, is persistently suspicious of paramilitaries on account of its law-and-order ethic. Although Barr was elected to the reconstituted Northern Ireland assembly in 1973, he was always associated strictly with the political side of the UDA. Those with reputed paramilitary connections never fared well. Tommy Herron, vice-chairman of the UDA and one of its most powerful "hard men," was trounced in the 1973 assembly elections in east Belfast, the heart of entrenched loyalism. (Later that year he was murdered during an internal feud.)

Robert Cooper, a unionist elected to the 1973 assembly, a member of Faulkner's executive, and now chairman of the Fair Employment Commission, offers an explanation. "In the Catholic community the great heroes of the pantheon of republicanism are people who had violent careers, rebels, and therefore it is much easier for Catholics to regard people who are involved with violence as people who are worthy of support. But not in the Protestant community. And a lot of people don't vote for them.

---

*Although car bombs in Dublin and Monaghan on May 17, 1974 produced the greatest single-day carnage of the troubles—thirty-three dead—the bombings were ordered only by the UVF and had no tactical connection to the UDA's supervision of the strike. In general, the UVF's involvement in enforcing the strike was well subordinate to the UDA's, because of both the UVF's smaller size and its tentativeness about joining forces with the UDA.

There would be people who would say, well, thank God we have them, we need them, but they want to isolate them. They're like vicious dogs, Rottweilers—you are very glad to have them, but you don't want them in your house."

Ron McMurray adopts the same reasoning, but finds in the Protestant community an even more odious degree of hypocrisy. "The analogy I draw between the loyalist paramilitaries and the Protestant people is to the use of a condom," he says in complete seriousness. "It's not really talked about because it's disgusting and it's sexual and it's very private, and when it's used you just discard it. A lot of the loyalist paramilitaries, I feel, felt like that—that we could be wheeled out, that we could be used by political leadership as the big stick, but when our actions had become irrelevant or futile for the politicians, we could just be discarded. Unionist politicians actually asked for us to be hanged along with the republicans, and that produced a lot of bitterness within the ranks of the paramilitaries."

The paramilitaries did not help their own public relations cause. UVF brigade staff, for example, allowed the Shankill Butchers gang led by Lenny Murphy, a UVF man, to torture and murder up to thirty people over a five-year period in the seventies. The UDA had asked Jimmy Craig, a Shankill Road tough guy in jail for nonpolitical offenses, to take charge of the UDA group at Long Kesh early in the troubles. Once he was out, Craig maintained his links with the UDA and through its fearsome prestige became Belfast's most energetic racketeer. He also bought information from the Official IRA. Tyrie exacted no tribute from Craig, kept him off the Shankill Road, and took away his operational paramilitary authority. But he allowed Craig to run his massive extortion racket out of the Sandy Row UDA headquarters—probably to content brigadiers who were taking money from Craig and to maintain the flow of intelligence that Craig could provide. The UDA ultimately executed Craig in 1988 for his suspected complicity in the IRA's assassination of UDA vice-chairman John McMichael and several other prominent UDA men.

Both the IRA and the UVF run illegal operations—protection, robberies, kickbacks from the black-taxi services on the Falls and the Shankill. According to the RUC, the UVF and the smaller republican groups are definitely involved in some drug-dealing. The IRA appears to eschew the trade and to punish maverick entrepreneurs, and certainly does not net significant amounts from drug sales. But the RUC suspects that the Provos do take in some drug money indirectly by "licensing" a limited number of nonmember dealers and exacting tributes from them.[9] Although the RUC believes the IRA of late has brought in as much as $3 million annually from pirated videotapes, neither the UVF nor the IRA is believed ever to have netted from Northern Ireland rackets the estimated $4.5 million per year the UDA was raking in during the eighties.[10] All of this is common knowledge in Northern Ireland. But while the nationalist community excuses IRA crime as essential to its armed struggle, the unionist community tends to regard UVF and UDA crime as mere thuggery in political clothing.

After the 1974 strike, Andy Tyrie did his best to control both the activities and the image of the UDA. The fact that he remained chairman of the UDA for sixteen years without being killed (despite attempts from every quarter) or convicted of any crime (despite several arrests and detentions on remand) is one of the small miracles of the troubles. A short, roly-poly man with a thick black mustache, a fondness for aviator glasses, and a deep, kindly voice, Tyrie had a low-key, corporate style quite in contrast to the charismatic aloofness of Gerry Adams or the folksiness of Gusty Spence. "I didn't mind being chairman of the organization, but the glory and the color of it didn't really suit me," he now recollects. "So what I done is, I done my best to create people who were in the council along with me for particular jobs, which they were best suited for and liked doing. Glennie Barr looked good, he looked the part for politics. He suited that. There was other people who suited different things, and I tried to choose people for to do the jobs they enjoyed doing. So by doing that there, it kept everybody happy and it shared the responsibility." Tyrie had centralized the UDA and made it more selective. Membership fell from forty thousand in 1973 to about ten thousand in 1978.[11] But his best was not enough to keep the UDA political.

Though he recognized that its political trajectory was limited, Tyrie wanted the UDA to become as nonviolent as it could be without losing effectiveness. The 1974 strike fortified his belief that he could make headway in that direction, and in 1977, at Paisley's urging, the UDA staged another strike with the hopelessly amorphous objective of bringing about more decisive action by the security forces against the IRA. It was a fiasco. The UDA was now directly impugning the RUC. Accordingly, policemen were less tolerant and themselves confronted UDA squads directly. Within three days, most people were going to work. Power workers had voted against the strike and refused to mobilize. Ten days after it began, the strike was called off. Paisley used the UDA's intimidation as an excuse for withdrawing his support, and left Tyrie with egg on his face and the loyalist paramilitaries soberly educated about the ephemeral nature of their political clout.

Tyrie had called Glen Barr and asked him to salvage the strike. Barr refused because he thought any attempt to coerce the British government was folly. "The one thing that I'm surprised that Andy had lost and forgotten about was, we really didn't defeat the British government in '74," says Barr. "What happened was that the Faulknerite-led unionist group, they resigned because they were faced with opposition from their own people. I says to them on the phone, you don't have that cushion there this time. You're in a head-on collision with the British government. Now, what's the British government going to do? Do they acquiesce to you? And I says, I know at the end of the day your main stand is that you want greater security, I says, so they can bring twenty thousand troops in for two weeks and then take them out again, and that's your whole case. You don't have any basis for a strike—there's nothing tangible to hold onto. So there was no way they could win this thing. They just couldn't. And as I said to him, not only is it a disaster that you're going to fail, but it'll also destroy '74." So it did.

HUMBLED

The failure of 1977 destroyed a lot more as well. In 1978, Barr wrote a position paper called "Beyond the Religious Divide" which called for an independent Northern Ireland, with a written constitution, a bill of rights, and separation of powers. The UDA, by rank-and-file vote, had actually adopted independence as its official policy. The theory is that northern Catholics and Protestants are all "Ulstermen" and could function on a nonsectarian basis if unshackled from London and Dublin.

Though economically dubious, independence is an intuitively appealing notion. Barr still fervently supports the idea, and the Ulster Democratic Party—now the UDA's political front—has adopted it as its fallback position. "My statement on the whole thing is that the sovereignty of the people of Northern Ireland is an inalienable right, and that if there's constitutional status that's the subject of negotiation between two foreign governments, there's not only going to be violence but it's also a recipe for civil war," a peevish Glen Barr says now. "I maintain that we should have political diversity and constitutional unity. John Hume, with his idea of an 'agreed Ireland,' is saying political unity and constitutional diversity. I can't see the sense in that." Being a Protestant from Derry, Barr has a natural competitive feistiness toward Hume that goes deeper than ideology: Hume made Derry a Catholic town and, more than that, *his* town.

Although Barr continued to promote the idea of independence through the New Ulster Political Research Group in 1978 and 1979, after the 1977 strike the UDA lost faith in its political clout and its support for an independent Ulster remained hedged and tentative. The independence movement never acquired critical momentum.* New York civil rights lawyer Paul O'Dwyer was an Irish expatriate and staunch nationalist who had taken the hunger strikers' grievances to the European Court of Human Rights. Ironically, he had actually been retained by Barr and Tyrie to flesh out the logistics of an independent Ulster, under which the United States would serve as guarantor. O'Dwyer undertook the task largely on account of his respect for Andy Tyrie, whom O'Dwyer regards as a virtual statesman far above sectarian partisanship.

Whether that is true or not, Tyrie was limited by his environment. In his eyes, the Protestant working class had allowed its economic interests to be neglected by Stormont politicians, and then used the troubles as an opportunity to reassert their interests through paramilitary violence. But the larger Protestant community was not prepared to vote for anyone but unionist politicians untainted by violence, and therefore never allowed the paramilitary groups to gain a wide popular base. At the same time, the Protestant electorate demanded a hard line. After the Anglo-Irish Agreement was signed in 1985, the UDA published a position paper called "Common Sense," which subsumed many of Barr's ideas about constitutional democracy. The document was well received by London, Dublin, and the SDLP, but the UDA felt compelled to insist with mainstream unionists that the Anglo-Irish Agreement be suspended before political negotiations could go forward. This requirement was unrealistic, and the initiative was stillborn.

---

*The theoretical attractiveness of independence is that it yields two winners instead of the one winner and one loser that the union or reunification net. Despite the constitutional civil rights guarantees Barr envisions, however, realistically very few Catholics would support independence because they would see in it Stormont incarnate. If Catholics do become numerically strong enough to negotiate antidiscrimination guarantees that would satisfy them, they might as well push for devolved power sharing with a strong Irish dimension—or, for that matter, a united Ireland outright. Given this dynamic, independence, for all its superficial promise, appears very unlikely.

"The problem always was the unionist machinery. It was very difficult to break into," laments Tyrie. "What we done is, between me and
Glennie, we created a situation where it was possible to jump from that.
But on each occasion, when there was a riot started, the people who led
the unionists would take the opportunity to condemn you—they would
say, these are the people who are asking you to vote for them. Yet we
were also the people who were to come out and defend the status quo
what existed here." Tyrie thus saw his job as keeping a respectable—that
is, a marginally political—face on an organization which couldn't help
but stay essentially paramilitary. Unfortunately, he couldn't sustain the
effort.

Tyrie was arrested on assorted terrorist charges in 1982, held on remand for several weeks, but released at the behest of church leaders who
attested to his "moderating influence" on the loyalist paramilitaries.[12] By
then, however, the UDA had turned decisively away from politics. Although the UVF flirted occasionally with the idea of becoming a political
force, its small size, military roots, and clandestine character made this
aim even less realistic than it was for the UDA. Despite their common
cause, the two paramilitary groups did not join forces.* When they
weren't feuding, cooperation consisted merely of the local UDA command informing its UVF counterpart of planned operations, or vice
versa, for purposes of avoiding any sort of clash. Indeed, the UVF's overriding boast had always been that it was more ruthless and authentically
military than the UDA—or more precisely, the UFF, the UDA's illegal
paramilitary wing.

During its political heyday in the mid-to-late seventies, the UDA
could shrug off this gibe. Deflated by terrible electoral failures in 1981,
though, the UFF set out to prove itself the UVF's military equal. During
the last ten years of Tyrie's tenure, excluding feud killings, informant executions, and "own-goals,"† the UVF claimed forty-four killings, versus

---

*The Combined Loyalist Military Command, the body which formally declared the loyal-
ist ceasefire in October 1994, did not emerge until April 1991. The CLMC is a shadowy
umbrella organization embracing the UDA, UVF, and Red Hand Commando. It remains
unclear how much central operational authority over each group the CLMC exerts.

†Northern Ireland's snide term for people, like Shankill bomber Thomas Begley, who blow
themselves up while making, transporting, or planting bombs, adopted from the sports
expression for a soccer player who kicks the ball into his own net. During the troubles, republicans had 106 own-goals, loyalists thirty-one. Also from soccer terminology, an especially violent paramilitary is often called a "head-the-ball" or "header."

twenty-eight for the UFF. For the five years after Tyrie resigned, from 1989 through 1993, loyalist violence in general increased sharply, and the UFF was actually credited with more political murders than the UVF by a count of seventy-two to fifty-eight (though the republican body-count of 235 still was almost half again the loyalist total of 163). By the time the Combined Loyalist Military Command announced the loyalist ceasefire, the UDA was not perceptibly different from the UVF. Outlawed in 1992, the UDA had become, simply, the UFF.

In the end neither of the principal Protestant paramilitary groups was able to make the transition to politics proper, but it is also worth noting that they were sharply responsive to relaxations in IRA aggression. That is, to the extent that they were reactive, they reacted positively as well as negatively. The government introduced the policy of "Ulsterization, normalization, and criminalization" in 1976. Along with the termination of prisoner-of-war status for republican and loyalist inmates, the new policy switched primary authority over antiterrorist operations from the army to the RUC. A crackdown on paramilitaries (largely through undercover intelligence operations run by the British Special Air Service, or SAS, and the recruitment of paid informers, seven loyalist and eighteen republican, known as "supergrasses") produced more arrests and convictions, and helped reduce the number killed by republicans by more than 50 percent, from 155 in 1976 to 75 in 1977. The corresponding drop in loyalist victims was even more precipitous—from twenty-five to ten. This lends credence to the loyalist claim that they intended mainly to compensate for inadequacies in the security forces' efforts. From 1978 through 1984, republicans averaged about sixty-five killings per year, loyalists about a dozen. In 1985, loyalist murders bottomed out at four, as republican violence hit a fifteen-year low of forty-seven dead.

The rise in loyalist violence thereafter occurred principally for three reasons. First, paranoia increased due to the Anglo-Irish Agreement of 1985, which the unionist community generally perceived as an abrupt step towards a united Ireland. Although the agreement between Dublin and London sanctified majority rule in Northern Ireland on the constitutional question, it also established an advisory Intergovernmental Conference of ministers from both capitals which carried the putrid whiff of joint authority—similar to the Council of Ireland that the UDA had defeated in the 1974 strike. Loyalists thus began to feel as though not even the law supported their constitutional position, and were less inclined even to pay lip service to the law-abiding tradition of the Protestant community. Second, as explained, politics no longer interested the UDA, which accounted for the lion's share—76 percent—of the increase in loyalist hits.

Finally, the loyalist paramilitaries inferred that the IRA had shot and bombed their way to the Anglo-Irish Agreement, and decided to copy their proactive strategy to keep them from getting any farther. "If it wasn't for paramilitary groupings," concludes John White, "I think that there's a great possibility that the British government would have sold out the people of Ulster into a united Ireland." White, who as OC of UDA prisoners in the Maze was privy to strategic decisions even while in jail, says, "I still believe that violence was necessary right up until recent years, you know, but a streamlined version. I certainly condemned, without reservation, sectarian violence, absolutely. I certainly did not condemn the use of violence against the IRA, Sinn Fein, any auxiliaries, or anyone that supports the IRA. That," he adds sardonically, "is a pretty wide grouping of people to choose from."

It also sounds very much like the IRA's expansive definition of a military target. White's frank elaboration of the loyalists' military viewpoint shows starkly the conditional nature of what republicans and loyalists call nonsectarian targeting. "I have no hatred for Roman Catholics," he says. "I have a profound hatred for anyone who associates themselves with the IRA, whether they vote for Sinn Fein or whether they're auxiliaries to the IRA. I think anyone who votes for Sinn Fein is equally as guilty as the IRA people who planted that bomb on the Shankill Road. So I would have a profound hatred for quite a lot of Roman Catholics, but it's not because they're Roman Catholics." Judging by IRA deeds, a Provo would say roughly the same thing about Protestants. From 1989 through 1993, more than a quarter of those killed by loyalists were either Sinn Fein councillors or active IRA men—not exactly surgical, but far more selective than the previous twenty years' operations. The loyalist paramilitaries were learning from the IRA.*

Killings like the murders of Paddy Wilson and Irene Andrews show that loyalist paramilitary operations have been far worse than simply reactive. Political triumphs like the 1974 strike show that they also have been far better. And the late rise in loyalist violence shows, at the end of the

---

*Still, right up to the IRA ceasefire loyalists undeniably placed considerable value on sectarian mass murder designed to terrify the Catholic community. The last major atrocity was the UVF's June 1994 execution of six Catholic men as they watched the Republic of Ireland play soccer in the World Cup at a bar in Loughinisland, southeast of Belfast.

day, that at times their strategy has not been reactive at all. Arguably, the loyalists' overall strategy has been more effective than the IRA's. Leaving aside sectarian indiscipline, the loyalist practice of targeting the IRA and its supporters (broadly construed) did frighten the Catholic community and may have helped produce the IRA ceasefire. The IRA killed the security forces very efficiently but probably did less to scare the Protestant community directly. Getting the British out of Northern Ireland may prove relatively easy because of their unwillingness to take further casualties in a province in which they have declared they have no strategic or economic interest. But in its preoccupation with the Brits and its refusal to acknowledge the legitimacy of unionist consent, Sinn Fein has unrealistically dismissed the one million unionists who oppose a united Ireland.

The "new loyalists" like Ervine, Hutchinson, Kinner, and White who have emerged so conspicuously since the ceasefires say that violence should be a last resort—that political conflict can be tamed into dialogue. But if the Provos resumed a full-blooded armed campaign in Northern Ireland itself, would the loyalists "react" as they have? Hutchinson says they'd do far more. "Loyalist paramilitaries are still a force to be reckoned with. You know, if the south tried to help the IRA force a united Ireland tomorrow, Dublin would be in real trouble because they could never sustain a twenty-five-year war. They'd be lucky if they could sustain one for twenty-five months. Loyalists would do exactly the same as the IRA did and they would shift their attacks to Dublin and Dundalk, and they would go for all their financial centers. Same as the IRA did in England."

In Northern Ireland it's often said that the difference between the Provos and the loyalist paramilitaries is merely twenty-five years. That should give the IRA pause about returning to wholesale violence in the province. At the same time, the sturdiness of the loyalists' ceasefire has given credence to their claim that at bottom loyalist violence is only reactive. That may convince the IRA that continued forbearance is the best way to protect the nationalist community. The ominous question remaining is whether the Provos can be persuaded to wait for constitutional change.

CHAPTER 4

"UNDEFEATED"

LAUNDERING REPUBLICAN TERRORISM

Announcing the IRA ceasefire to a euphoric crowd in west Belfast on August 31, 1994, Gerry Adams assured them and the world that republicans were "undefeated." Two days later, in an interview with Dublin's *Irish Times,* he said that "the British government should be seeking to leave our country in a manner which leaves behind a stable and peaceful Ireland." Two days after that, at a west Belfast rally, he proclaimed that if the British would not demilitarize, "we'll do it for them."[1]

For the next seventeen months, Britain refused to clear all-party talks on a permanent political settlement without some handover of arms by the IRA. In response, Adams intimated a return to violence by the IRA should Whitehall not relent. Then came the IRA's Canary Wharf bombing. This sequence reveals the acutely tactical dimension to the IRA ceasefire: it holds Ulster hostage to the IRA's forbearance. Six days before President Clinton's celebrated visit to Northern Ireland, for example, Adams said: "What they are holding to our heads is a British gun; a return to repression; a swamping of these areas once again with British troops; and the unleashing of the loyalists."[2] This amounts to a threat. The only development likely to precipitate Adams's parade of horribles was the IRA's return to violence. British foot patrols were withdrawn from west Belfast back in March 1995. The loyalist paramilitaries stuck doggedly to their promise not to strike unless the IRA did.

Republicans are allied in their refusal to admit defeat, guilt, or remorse, at least publicly. They remain, in their magisterial self-images, freedom fighters rather than terrorists, who have worn out Britain and outmaneuvered unionists. In their heart of hearts, notwithstanding palliative rhetoric, a united Ireland remains a vested geographical right, not a democratic aspiration. Thus, republicans do not believe that the liberation of

650,000 northern Catholics through violence required even their popular approval, much less that of the unionist population.

Whether the republican movement is valid or not, its cohesiveness and resolve over twenty-five years is impressive. Their determination almost buckled in the mid-seventies, however, under the weight of two developments: the 1975 ceasefire, and criminalization.

The Provisionals announced a ceasefire in December 1974 which, after a series of extensions, putatively lasted until February 1976, when IRA hunger striker Frank Stagg died in a British jail. During that period, the government suspended internment and relaxed their enforcement measures against the IRA volunteers, refraining from harassment and arresting them only with cause. At the same time, many republicans disapproved of the ceasefire and refused to abide by it, either joining splinter groups or operating freelance. Republicans killed nineteen fewer soldiers and policemen in 1975 than in 1974, but murdered civilians at an unprecedented clip. Seventy-five civilians, mostly Protestant, were killed during the fourteen-month period, and that's leaving out informer executions and feud killings.

"About 1975 the IRA were being dragged into a whole sectarian war," concedes Tommy Gorman. "In my eyes, we had a very dodgy leadership at that time. There was some sort of semi- or quasi-ceasefire going on, or someone agreeing with the Brits. You had all these provisos—you can shoot a Brit, but you can't shoot him if he's with a cop, or you can shoot a cop if he's not with a Brit; you can't shoot them in these areas but you can shoot him on the main roads. You had all these fucking rules." Veterans of the struggle like Gorman had been somewhat deflated by the thirteen-day IRA ceasefire of June 1972, which, in spite of its brevity, created a leadership crisis punctuated by failed covert peace negotiations with Downing Street in July 1972, chief of staff Sean Mac Stiofain's shameful *faux* hunger strike (he secretly took glucose) in January 1973, the arrests of several key leaders (including Hughes), the loyalist strike, and the passage of the Prevention of Terrorism Act. Now, with a second futile ceasefire behind them, the Provos were thoroughly demoralized.

" 'Seventy-two was probably the highest level of action, and I would feel that we had them beat," laments Gorman. "At the time of the ceasefire in June/July '72, we had them on the run. The ceasefire was for giving them breathing space, like. We stopped in our tracks then. I think from this point we went downhill. I think we had them on the way down, if we had just kept on pushing. But that's it." Confirming Gorman, Hughes recounts the Provisional IRA's pre-1972 Camelot, when the British army openly acknowledged its authority in west Belfast. "I remember going into the lower Falls and ordering British troops out of the area, carrying weapons. We were all carrying weapons—the British army was carrying weapons. It was that sort of strange situation. Here you were shooting at these guys, and all of a sudden you're face to face with them telling them to get out of your area. And most of the time they did. I mean, the IRA had foot patrols out to protect the area at night."

But after the ceasefires of 1972 and 1975, the IRA was running out of steam. Between the two ceasefires, the Provos had focused their operations on obliterating the Sunningdale power-sharing executive, regarding it as an unacceptable "partition solution," but ironically the loyalist strike stole their thunder. To get the 1975 ceasefire, Westminster dangled a constitutional convention in front of the Provisionals. It was stillborn, but it bought the British time to devise a better way to fight the IRA. On March 1, 1976, criminalization began.

Paramilitaries were never pure "political prisoners" because they were in jail for violent deeds rather than just their beliefs. In fact, in 1980 Amnesty International condemned the IRA's assassinations of prison officers, declared that IRA prisoners were not "prisoners of conscience," and refused to support their dramatic attempts to secure political status. Yet from June 1972 until that March 1976, the British government itself did accord loyalist as well as republican prisoners "special category" status. Like prisoners of war, they were permitted to wear their own clothes, allowed free association, excused from prison work, and accorded more visits and parcels than "ordinary decent criminals."* The relatively unsupervised compounds for both sides had become "universities of terror," where the more knowledgable veterans taught green inmates how to make bombs, build intelligence networks, and carry out covert paramilitary operations. Considering themselves POWs in a civil war, they did not expect to be incarcerated for very long, and fixed-sentence prisoners enjoyed a standard 50 percent remission of sentence.

The termination of special-category status not only dashed the prisoners' hopes of early release, but also savaged the honor of their respective

---

*The provincial term for granny-beaters, common thieves, and the like, as distinguished from those convicted of terrorist offenses that are presumed to be politically motivated. Paramilitary prisoners, particularly republicans, generally regard ordinary decent criminals, or "ODCs," with disdain.

struggles. While politically motivated prisoners convicted of acts committed on or before March 1, 1976 stayed in the compounds or "cages" at the
old military prison camp called Long Kesh, those with post–March 1 offenses were sent to the new purpose-built cellular prison next door known
as H.M.P. Maze—or, to republicans, as the H-blocks.

Though criminalization applied to loyalists too, it had a greater practical impact on republicans. To take just one example, while special-category status was in effect, Plum Smith was sentenced to ten years for a sectarian murder attempt in which the civilian victim was maimed and
crippled; he served five years. Just after status was withdrawn, Jackie Mc-
Mullan drew a life sentence for a murder attempt on an RUC officer who
was not even hit; he served sixteen years. McMullan was the first man in
Northern Ireland to get life for merely attempting murder. In pronounc-
ing sentence, the judge said that "this was a particularly cold-blooded and
unprovoked attempted murder committed as part of a deliberate plan to
shoot policemen on duty."[3]

He was not wrong—the IRA had stepped up its campaign against the
RUC in particular precisely because of criminalization and its twin policy
of "Ulsterization," under which the RUC was given central responsibility
for antiterrorist enforcement. But that was not the IRA's only response.
Loyalists in jail tend just to "do their whack"* to get it over with, considering themselves retired from active service and ennobled as veterans.
This is in part because they cannot fight republicans from a prison wing,
and are left to oppose the very system they were trying to support on the
outside. Republicans, though, are not hamstrung in that way. Prison for
them was another battlefield. In September 1976, they organized a mass
"blanket protest" that would continue for five years. Some loyalists joined
them, but quit in July 1978 in the quite accurate belief that the protest
had become too identified with republicanism to benefit loyalists.

The Maze comprises eight H-blocks. In each H-shaped block there are
four wings, two end-to-end on each side connected by a corridor for administration and education. Each wing contains twenty-five cells that will
accommodate two prisoners each, giving each H-block a capacity of two
hundred prisoners. During the period of the blanket protest, republican
prisoners occupied five of the H-blocks. At the peak of the protest, almost
four hundred prisoners were "on the blanket"—Green, McIntyre, Mc-

---

*Northern Irish slang for "serve a prison sentence."

Mullan, O'Hara, Pickering, and Roberts included—and the number of participants never dropped below two hundred. According to Pickering and McMullan, at least 70 percent of the republican prisoners were on the blanket at any given time, and at least 90 percent participated at one point or another. During the first eighteen months of the protest, the prisoners simply refused to wear prison clothes and instead draped a standard-issue blanket over their nude bodies. As punishment for not conforming, the blanketmen were confined to their cells except for meals, bathing, and medical appointments. For the first few months of the protest, they weren't even allowed a blanket for cover during these excursions. And they were routinely beaten and cavity-searched throughout by prison guards, or "screws."

Jackie McMullan somehow wears the experience. He is tall and wiry, and keeps his brown hair in a military-style brush-cut. A dense covering of translucent freckles gives him a grainy appearance, and twenty years of smoking hand-rolled cigarettes have stained the tips of his fingers blood-red. He speaks in a solemn, even baritone. "It definitely hardened me," he remembers. "I never—honestly never—hated anybody in my life until I was sentenced and was on that protest and experienced the brutality and ill treatment. Brought up to the H-blocks, I was made to strip in front of the reception committee of about eight to ten screws, who then proceeded to surround me and slap me about the face and scream at me and hurl abuse at me. But more than anything was the total humiliation of it, because whenever you're stripped naked and standing in front of these very hostile people who are beating you and threatening to beat you to a pulp, you just feel totally and utterly vulnerable and humiliated."

If there was ever any prospect of McMullan's giving up the armed struggle, the vindictiveness of the screws during the first few months of the blanket protest extinguished it. "I was a kid, even though I was twenty, I wouldn't have been mature for me age at all. And the humiliation that was burning inside me for months, maybe years after it—and that was just the start of it, you know, you run the gauntlet, and the parade up and down the wing in front of these screws, you're naked, there's other prisoners, conforming prisoners, who are standing about. This happened every single day. They wouldn't allow us to wear any clothes outside our cell—we didn't have any clothes. So for breakfast, dinner, tea, they opened your door, you had to walk the full length of the wing down to the canteen where the other prisoners are sitting eating their grub. You were in the nude. You had to do the same whenever you were going out to get washed. Had to shave every day. I didn't shave before I went into jail, didn't need to shave, but it's a prison rule you have to shave every day. When you were going out to the doctor—they brought you out to see a doctor every week or something, and he passed you fit for punishment. Every time your cell door was opened, every time you left the cell—it might have been five, six times a day—if it was just down to do something and back up, you were naked, and there were always taunts and jibes and insults. That was my worst experience in the whole blanket. Anything that happened after that was wee buns* compared to it."

Brutality embedded the republicans' hatred of the British regime even deeper into their hearts and minds. "The British were hoping that this regime would break people. It most definitely didn't work," says McMullan. "It would have had the opposite effect. I think you can produce statistics to prove that, you know. There would have been a higher percentage return rate of ex-prisoners to the republican movement from the H-blocks than there would have been from any other period of imprisonment—the internment or anything."

The blanket protest also produced in republicans a new strain of sectarianism. It had a noble cast because it rested in part on the indisputably sadistic behavior of the screws, who were almost all Protestant. "The screws that worked with the blanketmen didn't have to work with the blanketmen," recalls John Pickering, who had been interned in the cages and witnessed a marked change in the prison guards' attitudes. "You had screws could have went and worked in a different block, but they volunteered because they were getting more money for it. Now, say you were a decent family man—no way would you work under them conditions, on that protest. During the no-wash protest we made the place absolutely stinking—we pissed out the door every day—but for an extra six quid a day they were willing to stand there. There was a lot of screws wouldn't work in it; these guys wanted it."

The explanation Pickering tenders is that the prison guards who volunteered to work in the blanketmen's wings were exacting revenge on behalf of their community. "Prior to the introduction of the criminalization policy in 'seventy-six, in the cages the prisoners had their own command structure, done all their own thing," he says. "I think a lot of them people

---

*Northern Irish slang meaning "easy" or "no sweat."

who joined the security services, most of them are loyalists anyway, and when they were running about in the cages prior to the H-blocks—it must have been bubbling in them half the time, look at these bastards locked up, and my cousin was killed by whatever, but they could do nothing about it. See, the minute they got that situation in the blocks, the screws were in control. The proof of the pudding of this here is that since the hunger strikes the whole thing in Long Kesh has absolutely changed. Brutality, hostility, everything disappeared. They were cowards." But republicans got their own revenge, too. Between the inception of criminalization and the end of the hunger strike, republicans on the outside executed eighteen prison officers, including the deputy governor of the Maze, in retaliation for ill treatment of republican inmates.

The other factor that bolstered the republicans' chauvinistic sense of superiority was the loyalist prisoners' inability to sustain a protest of their own. Says Pickering: "Lenny Murphy's crowd—UVF, et cetera—tried to go on the blanket about six different times and kept failing. Whether they like it or not, the screws probably took a bit of a reddening for that, too, because that was the Protestants the first time, in a sense, trying a protest and failing. That sort of enhanced the image of republicans on protest— their durability, their resistance. Our guys wouldn't even bend."

After eighteen months the government was unmoved. The blanketmen stepped up the pressure with the "dirty protest," smearing their own excrement on the walls, floors, and ceilings of their cells. But in over a year of literally living in their own shit, the prisoners still got no favorable response from the Brits or the Northern Ireland Office, so on October 27, 1980, seven republican prisoners led by Brendan Hughes, then the IRA's prison OC, began a hunger strike that would last fifty-three days. Hughes undertook the strike without the full support of IRA leadership outside—Gerry Adams was strongly against it—out of a desperate fear inside that the republicans' stamina for the blanket was waning. "They started the force-washing in the jail—that was early 'eighty," Hughes remembers. "I believed that we had to find a way to end this, because it was humiliating, really, really demoralizing. I then started to believe we should leave the blanket because of it. It was a frightening experience. You're sitting in your cell and you have a long beard, long hair, you're filthy, and six big men come in, trail you up the wing by the feet, throw you into a bath, scrub you, shave you. They're wearing rubber gloves and all the rest. Every hair on your body they shave off, and then they throw you back in the cell. So that's when I decided we needed a hunger strike."

The prisoners made five demands. They wanted the right to wear their own clothes, to decline prison work, to free association, to better recreational and visiting privileges, and to have remission time lost on account of the blanket protest fully restored. Leo Green, an even-tempered man who has a greyish-red mustache and a gravelly voice that rolls with casual authority, was one of the seven hunger strikers. He stresses that the strike was not a publicity stunt. "Republicans in jail weren't out for any big deal, we were out for proper, sensible conditions. With the second hunger strike, there's this view that republicans went on hunger strike for propaganda. I think the experience of the first hunger strike showed that the hunger strike was about better conditions within the jail. At the end of the day, we were prepared to sort of define the political status in terms of five demands which were clearly humanitarian demands, to show that we were recognizing that the British government could wind up putting us into a political corner. And fulfilling the five demands, you know, would have allowed them to come out of it without maybe saying that they've been given political status. So basically, what I'm trying to say is that what we were after in jail was a solution, not propaganda, and the first hunger strike come about after years of struggle on the blanket."

Green's assertion about the first hunger strike is unequivocally correct. In negotiations with Hughes, the British made vague promises of partial compliance with the five demands, hinted at in a message from Humphrey Atkins, Northern Ireland secretary of state, and embedded in a long document describing prison conditions. One hunger striker, Sean McKenna, lay comatose and dying. Hughes did not want to let him perish with a compromise on the table, and called off the strike. Hours later, Hughes was presented with a far shorter document. The document merely conceded the republicans room for negotiation; it was without the representations that had looked so much like substantive compromise. At this point, the republicans became convinced that the British would not give in, and could not be trusted. The realistic objective began to change from prisoner-of-war status to sheer glory. Bobby Sands, who had replaced Hughes as OC when Hughes stopped taking food, started to plan a tactically superior hunger strike, in which prisoners would begin their fasts in a staggered sequence, rather than all at once, so as to protract the pressure on the Brits. With prisoners beginning their fasts sequentially rather than en masse, the time during which at least one person was at risk would increase about fourfold for a given number of hunger strikers. About half of the blanketmen volunteered.

Adams and the IRA army council urged the prisoners to abandon the second hunger strike, feeling that British intransigence* would make the movement look silly, whether or not prisoners took it to the limit and died. The prisoners were adamant. Sands inaugurated the second hunger strike on March 1, 1981 and died sixty-six days later. Nine more dead republicans—six from the IRA, three from the INLA—followed over the course of three and a half months. When the strike was finally halted on October 3, the battle of wills between the IRA and Margaret Thatcher had been publicly judged a standoff. Several hunger strikers had been taken off their fasts by their families. Six active strikers were left. One was Jackie McMullan, who'd been fasting for forty-seven days, and another John Pickering, without food for just short of a month.

Seventy thousand people turned out at Milltown Cemetery for Sands's funeral, and troubles violence surged. Sands had been elected to Parliament. Kieran Doherty, the seventh man to die, won a seat in the Dail. With Protestants ridiculing Sands and his brethren as "slimmers of the year," the churches debated whether a hunger strike was suicide or an act of protest with a calculated risk of death. For McMullan, the distinction is easy. Rightly, he cites the long tradition of hunger striking in Ireland as a form of moral compulsion. The practice goes back as far as the medieval Brehons, who used it as a self-help remedy for a tort or breach of contract. To the very end, Doherty was hyped on breaking the record of Terence MacSwiney, the Lord Mayor of Cork and an old IRA man, who lasted seventy-three days without food in Brixton prison during the Anglo-Irish war in 1920; Doherty missed a tie by a few hours.[4]

To the glory of the cause McMullan adds a dose of psychological realism. "What we associate suicide with is people who deliberately set out to kill themselves because they don't want to live any more. They've made a conscious decision that they can't handle life. Now, that certainly was not the case in the blocks. You're talking about dozens of healthy young men in the prime of their youth, as they say, who were full of life and whose ac-

---

*Republicans like to think that Thatcher and the British government were singularly unyielding toward men on hunger strike dying of starvation. Not true. As taoiseach (an Irish word pronounced "tish-hook" for the Irish head of state), Eamonn de Valera himself let three old IRA hunger strikers die in the forties, refusing to grant his former comrades political status.

tual love of life would have been manifested in their getting involved in the struggle. Nobody who went on the hunger strikes wanted to die. They knew there was a certain risk involved that they would cause their death on the strength of their own political beliefs. They decided to take that risk." Irish Cardinal Tomas O Fiaich, who had considerable sympathy with the republican cause, supported this position. Pickering, for his part, explains, "I wasn't even thinking about dying, I was so motivated just to strike back at the Brits."

Pickering, McMullan, and the rest only reluctantly ended their fasts— in part due to pressure from their familes that originated from Monsignor Denis Faul, who Pickering charges "was doing the Brits' work for them." Though they now agree that the strike's political value was dwindling— Pickering admits it had "ended up, rather than a hunger strike to death, a hunger strike into a coma"—they resented the priest's betrayal of a "morally correct" enterprise which they believed all Catholics should support. During the hunger strike, Monsignor (then Father) Faul was dubbed "the Menace" by IRA prisoners. Once welcomed to prison mass as the Maze's chaplain and one of the first to expose the security forces' maltreatment of republicans, Faul is no longer allowed in the H-blocks.

Many republicans were brought up strictly Catholic. Kevin McQuillan, twice jailed on charges of INLA membership and suspected bombing, was groomed for the priesthood, and his mother was buried in a nun's habit. But a substantial proportion of republicans—perhaps most of them—are lapsed Catholics. Brendan Hughes on marriage: "If two people come together, a pedophile priest isn't going to make it any holier." Most of those who are no longer practicing would trace their loss of faith to the hunger strike. Monsignor Faul, for his part, begrudges the Provos only their methods but not their madness.

"These fellows only got into prison because they're fanatical Irish patriots. These men knew they were dying for the future of their people, the release of their people from slavery. They weren't brainwashed, but they were very uncritical in their acceptance of being manipulated. Gerry knew the person who stopped the hunger strike—his political career would be dead. Poor Mickey Devine* died 20th of August, which was the day of the by-election, and Adams couldn't stop it before the by-election.†

---

*An INLA man, and the last of the hunger-strikers to die.

†A "by-election" is a special election held between regular elections in order to fill a vacancy, as would occur, for example, when an elected representative dies.

He got his MP of west Belfast. They should have been more critical. When I tried to inject that note, they didn't like it." The Sinn Fein candidate, Owen Carron, won the by-election held to replace Sands in parliament. Faul had gotten wise to Sinn Fein's cynicism. What started as an earnest prison protest, as Leo Green portrays it, ended up a propaganda opportunity which the republican leadership had seized and ruthlessly milked dry.

Still, republicans were not merely grief-stricken but angry when their comrades died. With two men dead and two on the verge, in a famous communication to an unidentified Sinn Fein official from Bik McFarlane—written on cigarette paper, wrapped in cellophane, and smuggled to the visiting area in the prisoner's anus or foreskin and outside in a female visitor's brassiere or vagina[5]—McFarlane said he felt like taking out a British commercial jet with a surface-to-air missile. The significant feature of this "comm" is the complete refusal of McFarlane to acknowledge any degree of complicity on the part of either the hunger strikers themselves or the republican movement in their deaths. "Personally I'd whack the Concorde with a Sam-7," he wrote. "Then where would we be, sez you? Oh, I don't know. Did you ever feel totally frustrated? . . . I really feel terrible just sitting here, waiting for Ray [McCreesh] to die."[6] Likewise, in their statement at the end of the hunger strike, republican prisoners proclaimed Bobby Sands "murdered by British callousness and vindictiveness" and strikers Kieran Doherty, Kevin Lynch, and Thomas McElwee "murdered by Britain." Irish Republic political parties Fianna Fail, Fine Gael, and Labour got off as mere "accessories to murder" for "[sitting] idly by."[7]

This mindset is *de rigueur* for a Provo. "He was responsible only insofar as anybody enlisted in the struggle decides to take up arms," says McMullan. "If you're talking in terms of blame, no way would I have considered or would anybody on the blocks have considered—would it even have crossed our minds—that there was any element of blame or even foolishness because we were completely and totally behind him. We were all in the same boat." The republican rationale was circularly foolproof: the hunger strikers aren't at fault because the cause is right; the organization isn't at fault because it supports the hunger strikers. Two days later, McFarlane was coolly passing "names of volunteers who are on my short list in numerical order of preference" to replace Patsy O'Hara and Raymond McCreesh, gone but still warm.[8]

During the hunger strike, neither Thatcher nor the IRA would blink because they were too much alike. Both were stubborn, imperious, self-righteous. Republicans don't agree with this observation. The standard retort would run something like IRA lifer Ella O'Dwyer's: Thatcher came from privilege, became an MP, then progressed to prime minister. She earned her power through the convenient channels of civil government. The IRA, though, got its power through the ongoing toil and suffering of war and imprisonment. Thus, Thatcher could say no without consequences while the IRA faced the deaths of volunteers. Whereas Thatcher could accede to the Provos' demands at no cost to her government's standing, the argument proceeds, the IRA had no choice but to let its men die. In the matter of the hunger strike, destiny exculpates the IRA of all guilt. But a few leaders, like Brendan Hughes, now confess to feeling some responsibility, and muse that simply extending the civil disobedience of the blanket into a more belligerent form of mass protest might also have worked.

"To be totally honest, I think it could have been done another way," he says. "I suggested that we end it, put on the prison gear, and go out and just make the whole place unworkable. If you have five hundred men who are disciplined and you can control them, you can bring any prison to a standstill. You can get almost any demand that you want if you have the discipline and the will to bring about that objective, and republican prisoners had it. I believe we could have done it at that period, but because people's attitudes had become so hardened after being there for years— and it's quite understandable—they didn't want to put on the prison gear." Instead of resorting to an Attica-type solution, though, republicans acted on a collective need for a romantic, tragic epiphany, and it worked better than pugnacity would have.

Nominally, the Brits prevailed in the hunger strike: due to family pressures rallied by Father Faul, the remaining republicans ended their fasts before Thatcher caved to any of the five demands. But the Brits knew that while they might have won the battle, the republicans won the war by gaining sympathy locally and around the world. Ten dead prisoners cast the IRA and INLA as martyred freedom fighters rather than heartless terrorists. The Iranians named a Teheran street after Bobby Sands. American donations to The Irish Northern Aid Committee—usually known as "Noraid" and the principal expressly pro-republican U.S. fundraising group— skyrocketed. Although the money technically went to Sinn Fein, no corporate wall exists between Sinn Fein and the IRA, so the IRA's military budget was almost certainly directly increased. Having secured the cry of "Uncle" required to claim victory, the British acted swiftly to forestall further protests and concomitant propaganda gains. Three days after the strike was called off, the British government acceded to two of the republicans' demands: they were allowed to wear their own clothing, and given back sentence reductions lost on account of the blanket protest. Within three months, they could associate freely within connecting wings during mealtimes, work hours, exercise and recreation periods, and weekends.

By the end of 1981, the prison work requirement was minimal, and prisoners could refuse to work with no significant loss of privileges. But now, belatedly, they took Hughes's advice. They got dressed, went out to do prison work, and proceeded to wreck the place. "We were trying to sort of make the jail come to the realization, this is costing us more than it's worth," explains Leo Green, who was OC of IRA prisoners in 1986 and 1987. When they weren't busy sabotaging machinery, they cased the layout of the Maze.

On September 23, 1983, thirty-eight IRA prisoners staged the biggest jailbreak in Britain's long history. One guard died, and six others were shot or stabbed. Nineteen of the prisoners, including Gary Roberts, were caught immediately. The other half got away—among them Bik McFarlane, who was finally extradited back to Northern Ireland from the Netherlands in 1986. "The Great Escape" became yet another dignifying legend. Afterwards, the prison administration confined republican prisoners to the blocks and ended prison work. "Weaponry was made in the workshops and they used all of the facilities to do things that we didn't want them to do," admits Duncan McLaughlan, deputy governor of the Maze at the time of the escape. "We just stopped them working. It just was not worth it." Although the prison administration pleads practicality rather than principle as the reason for not requiring work, after the escape all five of the grievances of the first hunger strike had been redressed.

Endemic brutality from the screws also ceased. Just before the escape, the prison administration tried to integrate republicans and loyalists. Brawls and protests forced the governor to abandon the experiment, leaving as many as fifty republicans on a wing as before, but now without the vulnerability of nudity. "I knew what it was like to be dragged by ten strangers stark naked and be bent down over a mirror so that they could look right up my ass and then feel around my private parts," says Roberts. "That was humiliation that I wouldn't inflict on anybody, but we accepted screws in the wing. There was maybe three or four screws coming into our wing and there could be up to thirty, maybe more, republicans walking about that wing. We weren't going to inflict on them what they had inflicted on us, so they didn't mind working with us." Republican

prisoners had the self-control and command discipline to avoid a confla-
gration like the one at Attica in 1971. By first showing what havoc they
were capable of wreaking, then the self-restraint they could marshal, they
held the screws' fear hostage and earned their respect.

Life in the H-blocks now is much the same as it was in the cages before
special-category status was removed. The Prison Service officially claims
the reasons for the liberal post-1981 prison regime simply stem from the
security imperatives of limiting the circulation of prisoners through each
block and keeping them pacified. But republicans see full compliance
with their five original demands for what it is: a de facto concession of political status. McLaughlan admits that the current regime at the Maze
came about partly because of the H-block protests, though he also credits
Council of Europe decisions requiring better prison conditions and a
global trend towards improving them. More broadly, the former Maze
governor agrees that the Provos "work from an ideological base," and that
most would not be in jail but for the troubles—qualifications which virtually define political status. While nobody in the Prison Service would
publicly concede that the paramilitaries run the Maze, McLaughlan states
unashamedly that "you can only run a prison with the consent of the prisoners. A prison governor is not necessarily seeking their agreement, but he
is seeking their consent."

Indisputably, this shift in attitude is a direct result of the hunger
strikes. Before they occurred, the Prison Service as a matter of policy regarded paramilitaries as common criminals.

THE SPOILS OF THE BLANKET

The staying power republicans generated and showcased during the blanket protest and the hunger strike earned them an almost luxurious prison
environment, in which communality and defiance could flourish. "In
terms of jail history," says Jackie McMullan, "the blanket transformed republican imprisonment."

In the Maze, limited athletic and recreational facilities are now located
in each wing. Since late 1994, cell doors have been left open twenty-four
hours a day. Sean Lynch, the Provos's OC inside, recalls a time several
years ago when he, John Pickering, and a third prisoner were all sitting in
a cell chatting, and the governor came and told them they could not socialize three in a cell. "Now, the governor himself comes in and puts his
feet up," he brags. The republicans have established an area where only

Irish can be spoken—a "Gaeltacht"—and the prison no longer enforces the rule against Irish speaking. According to Lynch, the prisoners essentially run their own wings.

Paramilitary prisoners resist any program that smacks of rehabilitation. As a result, the Maze prison regime is nonprogressive. Even well-behaved prisoners will not accept increased freedom as a reward, since that would imply that the institution was reforming them. Apart from the "working-out scheme," under which prisoners are transferred to Maghaberry and furloughed to outside jobs during the last six months of their imprisonment, day one is like day of release—prisoners are accorded the same privileges throughout their incarceration at the Maze.

The Maze is not presently overcrowded, and everyone gets an individual cell unless he asks otherwise. Each cell is ten feet by six feet, with a mirror, cot, bookshelf, and reinforced window. Prisoners have access to prison yards (one per wing, concrete, about eighty yards by fifty yards) twelve hours a day. There is one "multi-gym" (i.e., a modular weightlifting unit with separate stations) per wing. There is one dining hall per wing, with TV and VCR. Also on each wing is "Cell 26"—a room about twice as large as a single cell which contains a TV, stereo equipment, and a library of up to three hundred books. Each wing has a microwave oven, a refrigerator, a washer, and a drier as well. The Maze contains two soccer fields and one full-size gymnasium, and they are better facilities than most secondary schools have. Each prisoner is allowed three sessions per week at these communal athletic facilities.*

All Maze paramilitary groups are run like armies, and all have formal command structures. These are not officially recognized by the Prison Service, but are recognized in fact. Owing to these structures, the prisoners are substantially self-regulating. Attempts at strict disciplinary enforcement are seen as a challenge, and are not considered by the Prison Service to be worth the aggravation unless security would otherwise be impaired. There is a pay telephone on each wing, and prisoners can use it whenever

---

*Prison officers serve as soccer referees. Gaelic football is not played because prison officers don't know the rules. Founded in 1884, the Dublin-funded Gaelic Athletic Association remains fiercely nationalistic and is the official sanctioning body for Gaelic football. One prison official reported that the GAA does not permit RUC or British army personnel to attend its matches in uniform, or to play in them. It is also against GAA rules for the organization to instruct members of the security forces on the rules of Gaelic football. The Prison Service asked the GAA to relax this restriction so that republican prisoners could play Gaelic, but the GAA refused. Hence, no Gaelic football at the Maze.

they want, twenty-four hours a day. They can buy £2 phone cards, up to ten per week, though this privilege is not closely monitored. Technically, each prisoner is allowed £15 per week spending money, but this also is not rigidly enforced. Ten percent of correspondence is "censored" (i.e., read), but the other 90 percent stamped as officially received and left unread. The authorities do not enforce any sort of moral code beyond what is required by law. While it does not furnish pornographic movies, legal soft-core pornography is permitted. Whereas prisoners on the blanket were limited to the Bible, religious magazines, and later pulp westerns, there is no longer any censorship of literature except for obvious security reasons (e.g., gun magazines). Some classes are prohibited for the same reason (e.g., chemistry). Speaking Irish is "no longer an issue"—Irish classes, in fact, are now offered.

H-block prison officers are in the wings only twice a day—for mandatory head-counts at noon and at 8:00 P.M. Otherwise, they stay in the administrative area of each block, which is incongruously known as "the circle" (from Victorian prison layouts) but in fact occupies the central bar of the "H." They carry neither guns nor truncheons, and are under standing orders not to challenge any armed prisoner. Most prison officers carry personal protection weapons outside the jail, but firearms are absolutely prohibited inside. Although a military guard force of Royal Irish Regiment soldiers provides heavy armed security for the perimeter of the prison and from guard towers, soldiers are not allowed into the prison unless invited by the governor, and no soldier is ever allowed personal contact with prisoners. Prisoners themselves associate freely within a wing and in the adjacent wing at all times, may sometimes go to other wings in the same block, but are not allowed ever to visit other blocks. For 90 percent of their needs, they need go no farther than the circle.

Back in their cells with time on their hands after the 1983 escape, republican prisoners campaigned hard for formal education privileges. Most republicans had minimal schooling. "When I went to secondary school, there was always rioting in New Lodge, Ardoyne, Cliftonville Road, so I never did a test in my life," recalls Donncha O'Hara. "I was hardly at school and had no interest in it. I'd much rather burn a bus, or throw stones at the British army, that's the type of things you got involved in when you were that age." They learned their politics on the blanket. They were not allowed books or paper, pens or pencils, so they improvised. "We used to get religious medals from the priests, and we would scrape them on the wall," Gary Roberts remembers. "Or maybe we would smuggle pens and pencils in, and we'd write on toilet roll, and keep it that way. But formal education was a privilege, and we had lost all privileges."

The privilege was finally restored in 1985. The Prison Service offered secondary school equivalency in both standard British classifications (O-levels and A-levels). It also sponsored college courses through the Open University.* Among republicans, the most popular Open University offering was the social sciences foundation course. It was seen as a tool for reinforcing political beliefs already planted during the blanket.

"Nobody I know went into the Open University just to get a degree," says Jackie McMullan, somewhat haughtily. "We did it because it was complementary to our own political education process. You'll find that 99 percent of the republican prisoners who studied at the Open University all selected courses which deal with politics, history, philosophy, as opposed to any career-orientated courses—you know, computers or whatever else they had on offer." People at the Open University recognized as much. "The Provisionals were having considerable success in their educational groups. I was always astonished at what they were doing amongst themselves, and the breadth of what they were doing," says Diana Purcell, senior counselor at the Open University. "At a certain point, they decided they needed a third party as a gauge."

At the same time, Joy Clarke, chief education and training officer for the Northern Ireland Prison Service, says that "the accreditation issue is very important to them, and they all value the certificate that they can have if they manage to get the qualification." More than 50 percent of republican prisoners take part in some formal course of study, and more than 80 percent of those wind up with degrees. Anthony McIntyre earned a B.A. in politics with first-class honors,† and is now a Ph.D. candidate in politics at Queen's University of Belfast, Northern Ireland's top school. Gary Roberts started undergraduate studies with the Open University's social sciences foundation course, and finished with a B.A. in Celtic languages and modern history from Queen's after his release. Carol Cullen completed two years of the Open University in jail, and has resumed her studies outside. The same goes for McMullan. Ella O'Dwyer—sentenced

---

*In operation for over twenty-five years in the U.K. Under the Open University system, students progress independently through course packets, supplemented by tutorials (on average, one per month) given by teachers. A bachelor of arts degree requires six credits, and usually takes prisoners six years to complete.

†Equivalent to *summa cum laude.*

to life for conspiracy to cause explosions as a member of the same active service unit responsible for the Brighton bombing that targeted Margaret Thatcher in 1984—is now pursuing a doctorate in Irish literature at H.M.P. Maghaberry.

Before the hunger strikes, many republicans regarded prison-sponsored education as an insidious attempt to brand them "criminals" by conning them into accepting rehabilitation. But by the mid-eighties, most came around to the view that availing themselves of educational opportunities amounted instead to self-transformation at the system's expense. An enlightened prison administration did nothing to disabuse them of the notion. Citing Robert Martinson's classic study of the futility of rehabilitation programs in U.S. prisons, Duncan McLaughlan, one of Northern Ireland's more liberal prison officials, refuses to claim any credit for the prison system in rehabilitating inmates.

"There isn't a pill or something that we can [administer]," he says. "My version of it is, everything works—at certain times, in certain circumstances, in certain places, with certain individuals. What we don't have is the ability to match you, as a prisoner, to the time, the place, the circumstance, the scheme, or whatever. The flip way of talking about it is, if you make a plum duff [a kind of pudding], you make the basic pastry and the dough and you put it in that corner of the room, and you stand in the other corner of the room and you have a handful of currants or whatever and you throw them, some stick and some don't, and you have no control over the ones that do. So I just totally do not accept that prisons in any way at all rehabilitate as a result of a considered approach by us. No way. The role of a prison is containment and passive, and the principal task of somebody like me is to present opportunity." Since the 1983 escape, the Prison Service has done just that.

Over twenty-five years of agitation, republican prisoners have earned the Prison Service's grudging esteem. The prison administration openly considers paramilitary prisoners political players. The peace process was heavily influenced by prisoners, who constitute a "massive power base" for the paramilitary groups, says the unnamed prison officer quoted before. This is a factor which the Prison Service bears firmly in mind in dealing with prisoners—it does not want to be responsible for "turning the war back on." Even the prison official anticipates an early release for Maze inmates.

In the meantime, IRA volunteers imprisoned in mainland Britain press to be moved to Northern Ireland. Their motivation is in part political, but they also protest that conditions in the Maze are far better than they

BEFORE THE 1994 IRA CEASEFIRE

Left: Members of the British army's Parachute Regiment, feared and loathed by nationalists, in front of a huge republican mural, lower Falls. *Hugh Russell, Irish News*

Right: A little girl greeting a British soldier during a bomb scare on the lower Falls, 1994; the obscene gesture is presumed unintentional. *Ann McManus, Irish News*

Undertaker digging the graves for the six victims of the UVF's gun attack on a Loughinisland bar, June 1994—the last mass atrocity before the loyalist ceasefire. *Brendan Murphy, Irish News*

Top: Mourners at the funeral of John O'Hanlon, a Catholic carpenter and the loyalist paramilitaries' last victim before their 1994 ceasefire. *Brendan Murphy, Irish News*
Middle: Orangemen marching past Ormeau Road bookies' shop where the UFF killed five Catholics in 1992. *Hugh Russell, Irish News*
Bottom: Mourners at the funeral of three Pentecostalist worshippers murdered in 1983 by the INLA in Darkley, County Armagh. *Brendan Murphy, Irish News*

Shankill bomber Thomas Begley, the troubles' most notorious "own-goal." *Anonymous*

Gordon Wilson, father of Marie Wilson, a nurse killed by the IRA's Enniskillen bomb on Remembrance Day, 1987. *Brendan Murphy, Irish News*

Above: Two IRA suspects arrested after discovery of a bomb, Belfast City Center, mid-eighties. *Brendan Murphy, Irish News*
Below: RUC man with a crossbow dart in his neck fired by a hostile nationalist during an Orange march in Portadown, Belfast, late eighties. *Brendan Murphy, Irish News*

Above: Ordnance-disposal officer inspecting wreckage from IRA booby-trap bomb that killed a retired soldier as he got into his car, downtown Belfast, 1987. *Brendan Murphy, Irish News*
Below: UFF show of force, Shankill, 1993. *Brendan Murphy, Irish News*

One of the three Catholics killed by UFF gunman Michael Stone at Milltown Cemetery, 1988, during the funeral of the three IRA volunteers shot dead by the SAS in Gibraltar. *Brendan Murphy, Irish News*

Kevin McQuillan after murder attempt by IPLO during a republican feud, Ballymurphy, 1987. *Brendan Murphy, Irish News*

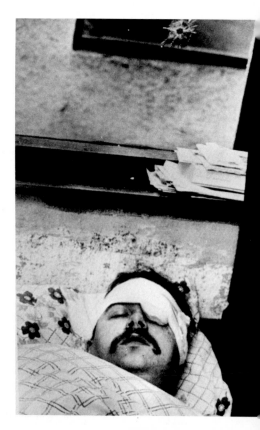

Right: The mother of the victim of a UFF shooting, north Belfast, after hearing from the hospital that her son had died. *Brendan Murphy, Irish News*

Below: Sinn Fein vice-president Martin McGuinness, 1994. *Brendan Murphy, Irish News*

The Most Rev. Patrick Walsh, Bishop of Down and Connor, in County Antrim church after loyalist petrol-bomb attack. *Brendan Murphy, Irish News*

are in English maximum-security prisons like Durham or Whitemoor. Whereas IRA prisoners might still occasionally be singled out for maltreatment in England, in Northern Ireland they are prison royalty. "If you were a terrorist prisoner with a life sentence or a very long fixed sentence in Northern Ireland and you had served eleven years of your sentence," says Duncan McLaughlan, "you would be getting much, much more freedom than a guy in England or anywhere else I know in the world would get." That is not because terrorist prisoners here are considered low-risk. Rather, he explains, "it's because we recognize in Northern Ireland that you can't divorce prisoners totally from the outside world. In Northern Ireland, prisoners are much more a part of the community, and we recognize the value of prisoners in public relations."

Paramilitary prisoners can be difficult to work with, he adds, because of the power their organizations wield in the community, which is dangerously intimate in Northern Ireland. Prisoners still threaten prison officers: "I see your daughter just started a new school. . . ." Because the Maze prisoners are members of outside paramilitary organizations that can gather intelligence and make good on personal threats, they completely skew Northern Ireland's prison budget. To attract people to the Prison Service, the government has to throw money at them. Keeping a person incarcerated in Northern Ireland costs over £70,000 ($110,000) per year, compared to about £20,000 on the mainland. Security against organized escape attempts is also expensive in manpower. For the 700 or so prisoners in the Maze, the Prison Service employs over 1,250 prison staff, 550 of whom might be on duty in a high-security profile. By the same token, says the official of republican prisoners, "you can do business with them."

For posterity, the second strike produced the cathartic blood sacrifice that Patrick Pearse had signaled in 1915 when he raged that "life springs from death." The practical effects, though, were far more important. Inside, the strike established a secure, well-appointed base for the intellectual and political war. Outside, it injected the republican movement with political and economic vitality.

REPUBLICAN TRIUMPHALISM

While the 1977 strike and criminalization had politically enervated the loyalists, the hunger strike and criminalization had politically energized the republicans. Autodidacticism and then sharing the wealth had been part of the republican tradition since internment. The urgent team spirit fostered by the blanket protest and the hunger strikes brought these qualities into full blossom. Tommy Gorman was on the blanket and the dirty protest for almost two years, and released shortly before Bobby Sands began his fast. He speaks of that time nostalgically, reverently. "The whole thing during the blanket—some people talk about it like a religious experience. It's a strange thing—you're in these surroundings and you were completely surrounded by shit, yet your mind was crystal clear. It's this paradox—you're right here now in these clean surroundings, but your mind's full of shit; in there you're surrounded by shit but your mind's crystal clear. You were getting beat maybe three or four times a day, but you were constantly focused on what you were actually at, what you were fighting. And the solidarity and camaraderie between everyone on the blanket was something that's never been recaptured, like, you know?"

Old hands, like Gorman and Sands, learned Irish in the compounds during internment and taught it to newer inmates on the blanket. McIntyre and Roberts left jail fluent, and Roberts is now a teacher in Belfast's only Irish-language primary school. The practical reason IRA leadership encouraged volunteers inside to learn Irish was that screws didn't know the language. Communicating in Irish facilitated jailhouse intelligence. (Speaking Irish was against prison rules, and those who spoke it openly were often singled out for beatings during the blanket protest.) But by illuminating just what the British had supposedly suppressed, learning Irish also clarified many prisoners' perception that British occupiers had stolen their Gaelic culture and deepened their conviction that this culture in its entirety must be wrested back. Irish is the first language for barely over 1 percent of the Republic of Ireland's population. Its revival in Northern Ireland is largely due to ex-prisoners. "I was able to take back what had been taken from my ancestors hundreds of years ago," says Roberts, sonorously. Even when talking with non-Irish speakers, most republican ex-prisoners will end a meeting or a telephone conversation with "Slan"—Irish for goodbye.

The blanket also generated a psychological demand for stamina, which required a deeper appreciation of republicanism. In seminars they arranged themselves—called "rangs," which means "classes" in Irish—republicans honed their understanding of Irish history and other conflicts purportedly akin to Northern Ireland's. The more erudite educated the unschooled with the help of pages of books smuggled in by visitors, lec-

turing "out the door" of their cells in Irish. Again, most republicans before
going to jail had only an impressionistic view that unionism hurt them
where a united Ireland would help them. Jail gave their experiences some
context.

During the troubles, "you seen all what's going on around you, but you
weren't politicized enough to know exactly why you were [fighting]," recalls Donncha O'Hara. "At the same time, you knew that there was something wrong—you weren't just doing it for the fun of it—although you
mightn't have been able to articulate it then. If you grow up in that sort of
environment, then you obviously react to it. And then when you go inside
[prison] and you do set up these structures and you go through an educational process, you can read into things." O'Hara himself is reminded of
his politics twenty-four hours a day. Over twenty years ago, the bomb he
was handling exploded prematurely. He was left paralyzed down his right
side, with only half a right arm, and blind in his right eye. His pain is constant. It is easy for the movement to keep him a true believer: republicanism gives his battered condition a high purpose.

But even for those who weren't maimed, pride was abundant in the H-
blocks. Republican ex-prisoners profess to being much more worldly than
anyone else in the north, particularly their loyalist counterparts. John
Pickering ridicules a loyalist prisoner for not knowing who Che Guevara
was and, upon finding out, ignorantly calling the Cuban revolutionary a
"fucking commie bastard." Tommy Gorman decries the Protestants'
downgrading of the Irish potato famine as "some fucking blip in history."
Gary Roberts imperiously likens the Ulster Prod to "the poor white
cracker in the southern states of America." By contrast, he beams, "republicans in jail started reading about what happened in Cuba, what happened in Nicaragua, what happened in the Second World War, First
World War."

Undertaken in a partisan fever, the process of indoctrination often
yielded exaggerated comparisons which made the plight of northern
Catholics seem far worse than it really was. Tommy Gorman: "These
unionists from up in Ballymena* somewhere—I'm not joking you, they
were just like white South Africans. You mention parity of esteem and
they take apoplexy. You can't mention equality, parity of esteem, recognition of our Irishness—they just go buck-mad. They just can't contemplate

---

*Paisley's home town.

it at all. And this is what we're up against." Even strong nationalists admit that South Africa is "another planet," but however inaccurate the melodrama, it only heightens the republican commitment. Unsurprisingly, Nelson Mandela is now republicans' consensus favorite among contemporary world leaders, having surpassed Yasser Arafat.

Republicans rarely acknowledge that the two egregious wrongs that occurred in Palestine and South Africa—respectively, forcible ouster and coerced segregation—never remotely took place in Northern Ireland. Republicans also gloss over the fact that, unlike the Northern Ireland conflict, the one in South Africa involved rule by a minority that had no appreciable demographic stronghold in any region of the country. Yet republicans do not criticize their supporters, even when such parties commit acts that republicans would stridently condemn had the British committed them. In the early eighties, for example, the Sinn Fein newspaper issued in Belfast condemned the United States' involvement in Nicaragua, but the reference was carefully airbrushed out in the American version. At the same time, Sinn Fein's vilification of Britain over the Falklands war was left undeleted.

As unartful as republican propaganda was, the hunger strike convinced enough sympathetic nationalists to make an electoral difference that republicans could move the British without hurting anyone. In doing so, the strike empowered northern leaders of Sinn Fein—notably, Gerry Adams, who was elected to Parliament in 1983. Thanks to the hunger strike, Sinn Fein director of publicity Danny Morrison, a Belfast man, was able to say at the 1981 party conference: "Who here really believes that we can win the war through the ballot box? But will anyone here object if, with a ballot paper in this hand and an Armalite* in this hand, we take power in Ireland?" Although republican and loyalist violence escalated during the hunger strike and in the two subsequent years, once Sinn Fein had consolidated electoral support, troubles deaths dipped to unprecedentedly low levels in 1984, 1985, and 1986. Thereafter, the annual body count exceeded one hundred only once—in 1988—in the wake of the Enniskillen bombing in 1987.

In 1983, Gerry Adams assumed the presidency of Sinn Fein from southerner Ruairi O Bradaigh. Sinn Fein decided to stand routinely for elections in the north. Since partition, the party had participated in elec-

---

*A powerful, lightweight assault rifle made by Colt in the United States, the Armalite is a version of the M-16. The gun was the IRA's weapon of choice in the seventies.

tions in the Irish Republic but abstained from taking its elected seats in the Dail, as the Republic's parliament is known. In 1986, Sinn Fein ended that policy as well. A few southern traditionalists led by O Bradaigh objected vehemently to the latter move and left to form Republican Sinn Fein, but these defections had a negligible effect on Sinn Fein's overall electoral support in the north, which has hovered around 10 percent since the hunger strike.

Sinn Fein's post-1981 empowerment did not forthwith lead to greater solidarity in the larger nationalist community. Initially, the constitutional nationalists of the SDLP saw the Shinners'* new legitimacy as a threat to its own constituency. Furthermore, the SDLP's support for the hunger strikers had been passive, and in the heat of the moment republicans branded the party "lickspittle" for continuing formal relations with Whitehall.[9] In November 1985, the British and Irish governments signed the Anglo-Irish Agreement, which gave Dublin a consultative role in Northern Ireland governance but also firmly acknowledged the requirement of six-county consent to constitutional change. The SDLP had worked hard for the agreement and applauded it. Sinn Fein condemned it as a "partitionist solution" to the border question. For the next seven years, bullheaded nationalist infighting precluded any rapprochement between the SDLP and Sinn Fein.

Finally, in 1993, SDLP leader John Hume and Gerry Adams began secret talks. Although the substance of their meetings has not been made public, Hume appeared to convince Gerry Adams that the Anglo-Irish Agreement indicated British neutrality—or, at least, fatigue. The Downing Street declaration in December 1993, whereby London as well as Dublin relaxed its sovereign claim on Northern Ireland, seemed to confirm this inference. On August 31, 1994, Adams announced the IRA ceasefire. Post-ceasefire, in both local and international media, Hume has played second fiddle to Adams, who has been portrayed as a spokesman for the entire nationalist community.

Former Northern Ireland Secretary of State Douglas Hurd used to refer derisively to Adams as "Mr. Ten Percent." But it is difficult to avoid the conclusion that the dual "Armalite and ballot box" strategy led to the 1994 IRA ceasefire. Sinn Fein's successful resort to the polls eventually gave the republican movement sufficient political confidence to form a tentative front with the SDLP—in effect, to share Irish nationalism with

---

*Members of Sinn Fein.

those it once deemed too squeamish to carry the fight. Combining the mandates of the SDLP and Sinn Fein, in turn, made the political threat posed by nationalism to unionism sufficiently formidable to sell IRA leadership on a cessation.

THE LEGACY OF THE H-BLOCKS

Republicans' greatest battle against Britain was waged in prison, and the combatants quite rationally regard the outcome as victory. Upon release, they carry the sense of triumph with them—usually through Sinn Fein. Green, McMullan, O'Hara, and Pickering all work for Sinn Fein, and most of Sinn Fein's Belfast city councillors have prison records. The council leader, Alex Maskey, is widely believed to have been recruiting sergeant for the Belfast Brigade of the IRA, although he denies any paramilitary involvement. Another leading councillor, Pat McGeown, participated in the 1981 hunger strike. He was taken off for medical reasons after forty-seven days, and has continued to have health problems sufficiently grave to require a liver transplant. Sinn Fein vice-president Martin McGuinness has done time in the Republic and was chief of staff of the IRA's Northern Command. Jail is a virtual rite of passage for a political career with Sinn Fein. Republican prisoners and city councillors all drink at the Felons' Club on the upper Falls Road. Notwithstanding his hilariously disingenuous claim that he was never a member of the IRA,* Gerry Adams, Sinn Fein party president and messiah, was interned twice, convicted of attempting to escape, and imprisoned on remand in the H-blocks on an IRA membership charge which was ultimately dismissed.

The mass adulation of Adams—"God," as Kevin McQuillan acerbically calls him—hints at the secret of the Provos' success. The IRA is, at bottom, a totalitarian organization which punishes dissent and encourages sycophancy. As an "own-goal," Donncha O'Hara crippled himself. IRA violence in that way insinuated itself inexorably into his life. He says the most difficult thing about leaving prison was finding himself amidst people who didn't agree with him. Gary Roberts, who confessed under

---

*In fairness, his insistence on this point seems to be mainly for overseas consumption. American newspapers have now tacitly acknowledged, however, that there is no material difference between Sinn Fein and the IRA. See, for example, "Dublin Urges IRA Accord on London," *International Herald Tribune*, November 13, 1995, p. 5 (New York Times News Service). For their part, IRA men usually snigger at Adams's disclaimers.

the RUC's rough third degree to a murder to which he was merely an accessory, was a typical joiner and drew inordinate strength from group association. Admitting easily that he was not mentally strong enough to volunteer for the hunger strike, he elevates his brethren by his own self-effacement. "You were asked if you were volunteering for a hunger strike, were you prepared to die on hunger strike. I don't think I could have died on hunger strike. It was open, of course—anybody could have volunteered for it. But you had to be strong enough to go through with it. I didn't have that strength." It is enough for him simply to be connected with them.

John Pickering—"Pickles"—has a distinguished republican pedigree. His grandfather was in the old IRA, and John was interned before he was sentenced to life. With McMullan, Pickering was one of the republicans' leaders in the H-blocks. He was a hunger striker, having pushed to get on the strike even though he was coming off an ear operation. With his prematurely white hair and spare mustache, he fills the role of prison sage perfectly. And he seems to realize that as a republican, his days of personal glory were spent in jail. Pickering speaks of the blanket as "the great leveler" which cleansed the IRA of intramural bullying and elitism. But his analysis proves too much.

"Say there was some guy who was a great sniper, some guy who was a master bomb-maker or something—it might have went to his head a bit," Pickering eagerly explains. "On the blanket that's no good, because on the blanket what makes your reputation is quite simply your capacity to hang in, your mental capacity to resist, your will to resist. It's no use having any past sort of reputation. The blanket killed off a lot of military reputations." Some blanketmen derisively called those who quit the protest "squeaky-booters" on account of the sounds their prison-issued footwear made when they walked down the linoleum floors of the wings, though McMullan and Pickering say they found this hazing practice distasteful. The blanket didn't really eliminate the elite nature of the republican movement; it simply changed the criterion of prestige from military accomplishment to blanket stamina. According to McMullan, the blanket also eradicated any vestiges of authoritarianism in IRA prison culture. McIntyre denies this. Although "it's not the strategy of this leadership to isolate," he says, "arguments are marginalized. My arguments in jail they tried to say were fucking heresy."

Whereas McMullan and Pickering might confess to a certain longing for the heady days of the blanket, McIntyre has no such memories. "I never experienced the camaraderie, I experienced the in-fighting, and I certainly don't miss that. I have never had rose-tinted glasses about camaraderie or comradeship. To me in many ways it was always functional—you're working towards the same agenda with people you'd rather not be there with. It was an environment that was forced upon us. We found ourselves on wings, and it was through proximity rather than choice. And quite often that closed environment, total institution as Erving Goffman wrote about, gives people enormous power over others, and there was a constant struggle to create your own space and resist that power. Out here it's much easier, so I miss it like cancer."

For an active IRA volunteer, of course, life is tougher. Even if there's no arrest warrant out for him, a member of an active service unit must behave as if he is on the run, hopping from one safe house to another and surviving on handouts and a small stipend. If married, he is not permitted a normal conjugal lifestyle. He has to keep his trap carefully shut (hence poet Seamus Heaney's by now trite admonition "whatever you say, say nothing") lest the internal security unit or "nutting squad"* punish the volunteer. Ex-volunteers resist pity, reminding their interlocutors that they were told up front they would end up maimed, dead, or in jail. But the prime source of the group's resilience has always been an ability to romanticize the experience.

Not McIntyre. "Romance?" he chortles. "No. Going to jail—there's no romance in it. The IRA's a slog." Likewise, he mundanely characterizes the experience of the blanket protest as "boring." So it fits that he's an aloof loner, given to quiet study and views that challenge the republican purity of mainstream IRA thinking. In brief, his argument is that Sinn Fein has made a strategic mistake in allowing its goal to revert from forging a united Ireland to merely defending the Catholic community. The novelty of this polemic is his contention that Sinn Fein should have enlisted the *British,* and not the Irish, electorate to persuade Britain to drop Northern Ireland as a colony.

"I think that the problem with the IRA armed struggle is that it has always been linked to a goal which people—particularly in Britain and elsewhere—don't see as being reasonable: a British declaration of intent to withdraw," declares McIntyre. "My argument is that the armed struggle should have been linked to getting rid of the unionist veto, and not by

---

*In argot, "nut" means "head." The "nutting squad" is so called because the most severe punishment it administers is a fatal bullet in the head.

bringing it to Dublin as republicans argue, but by taking it to London. Then the political space would be opened up where Sinn Fein could argue to a largely disinterested British audience who don't want the place anyway."[10] He concludes angrily: "That would act as a powerful spur to unionists to stop their discrimination policies, because they couldn't go over and say, look, we're discriminating against our 'Catholic niggers.'"

The notion of a sovereign nation (especially Britain) simply deciding to eject territory is bizarre and legally dubious. But McIntyre's strategy is clever in that it accounts for both Britain's renunciation of the strategic and economic value of Northern Ireland and the colonial pride that still keeps Westminster from withdrawing its guarantee of majority rule to the unionists in the province. Even if British voters elected to hold onto Northern Ireland, says McIntyre, a frontal embrace forced by Sinn Fein would at least make them dilute unionist bigotry and improve the lot of Catholics. Now, however, Sinn Fein official policy appears to favor an interim devolved government with power sharing and strong executive links to Dublin, leading to John Hume's "agreed Ireland." Such a solution sticks in McIntyre's craw. "I mean, really what's on offer here is Sunningdale [the devolved power-sharing government brought down by the loyalist strike in 1974]. Now, the problem with that would be that I went to jail in 1974 prior to the power-sharing executive of Sunningdale collapsing, and my activity throughout 1974 in the IRA was as a result of the IRA leadership taking a decision to resist Sunningdale." McIntyre was not terribly surprised by Canary Wharf.

When he got out of jail, McIntyre and Jackie McMullan started the Bobby Sands Discussion Group, which met occasionally to discuss the republican strategy. More outspoken ex-prisoners, among them Gorman and Pickering, participated. At these meetings and in print, McIntyre advanced the view that the peace process was a cop-out. A few months after the ceasefire, another ex-prisoner, named Bobby Storey, started visiting members of the discussion group, asking them "offhand" what they were talking about at their meetings. Storey is about six foot three, broad and rangy, with short black hair. He runs well over 220 pounds. But his most fearsome features are his eyes—they are grey-blue, the color of dirty ice, and they dart constantly and balefully over the landscape.

Storey is known as "the brain surgeon" because of his reputedly distinguished performance on the nutting squad, and, less morbidly, because he was one of five IRA prisoners who planned the 1983 escape. There is also a sardonic aspect to the nickname: Storey is not the cerebral type. He simply does what he's told. One of the things he was told to do was police the ceasefire. Now, with his doorstep queries, discussion group members regarded him as the "thought police," using "subtle intimidation." Pickering stopped coming to group meetings. Tommy Gorman, whom Storey had visited at home, noted that "Bobby Storey's been whispering in Pickles's ear." Storey was discouraging open divergence from official Sinn Fein policy. This was part of his brief in policing the ceasefire. Yet the discussion participants were mostly ex-lifers, who have an infinitesimal recidivism rate; they posed no threat to the ceasefire.

In ensuing months, the attendance of the group dwindled. McIntyre, earlier promised membership on the editorial board of the *Starry Plough,* a monthly republican magazine, was now denied it—because of his views, a senior Sinn Feiner official told him. "They give up on me," smiles McIntyre. "Otherwise I wouldn't be talking to you now." Aside from McIntyre, Gorman, and a few others, the devil's advocates had been silenced. McIntyre was more than irritated by this tyranny of middle management. "It's quite often leadership groupies that are hated more than leadership," he comments obliquely, "probably because they feel threatened given that they depend on leadership to keep them in their positions. And as the leadership goes, we go. The leadership themselves might not like the arguments, but at least they understand them. Some of the apparatchiks hate them—oh, God, what's this, what's this, how can anybody think Gerry's wrong?"

Tommy Gorman is a pugnacious ideologue who favors Republican Sinn Fein's "Eire Nua" plan of a federated Ireland with four separate parliaments, one for each of the ancient provinces, institutionally rejected by Sinn Fein in 1986. He feels that Sinn Fein is engaged in a "dodgy strategy" that derogates some of its traditional ideals (like socialism), and that certain members are behaving like "careerist politicians" instead of revolutionary idealists. His reaction to being muzzled was similar to McIntyre's. "Sinn Fein has been hostile to the discussion group. Bobby's one of these fucking right-wing dog soldiers who follows the leader no matter what the leader says. There's no room left for criticism within the movement. That's a big problem."

Gorman's grievances extend beyond strategy all the way to the republican vision. "It's always been the case that we're not out to establish a thirty-two-county nationalist, Catholic-ridden Ireland. We're out to establish a thirty-two-county socialist republic. That's supposed to be in our constitution. The one who cobbled together the thing with Hume and Adams, Al-

bert Reynolds, doesn't even allow trade union representation in his factories. It's things like this here; they're contradictions which can't be hidden
for long. We established a socialist philosophy, but we sort of affect this
schizophrenic image where our people go to America and they're staunch
nationalists and they go to fucking Europe and they're staunch socialists.
You know what I mean? I can't fucking understand this; I mean, it's fucking bad. St. Patrick's Day dinners at the White House—it's a load of crap."

Kevin McQuillan, a pure socialist and emphatically not a Sinn Fein
member, has found the Provisional IRA dishonorably pragmatic all along.
Like Gorman, he finds Adams's courtship of America with $1,000-a-plate
Plaza dinners subversive of republican ideals. "They've never been honest
in their approach, but such is the nature of the beast. Adams is just being
true to the nature of the bourgeois leadership of the republican movement." McQuillan suggests that Adams's conciliatoriness has more to do
with maintaining Sinn Fein's power in the north than winning a united
Ireland. "If I can draw a parallel with the ongoing negotiations between
the Palestinians and the Israelis—the very fact that Yasser Arafat settled
for the pittance that he did settle for, which isn't even autonomy, in effect
puts him in a position to police the peace."

McQuillan is Belfast's leading member of the Irish Republican Socialist
Party (IRSP)—which, unlike Sinn Fein or the IRA, is militantly socialist.
The IRSP's military wing, the INLA, launched some of the republican
movement's most high-impact operations in the late seventies and early
eighties, including the 1979 assassination of MP and Thatcher confidant
Airey Neave in London. Though never convicted, he has been arrested
and detained over fifty times and imprisoned for eighteen months on remand in the Irish Republic for INLA membership and a suspected bombing in Dublin. Nicknamed "Bap" because his crew-cut head resembles a
local sandwich roll of the same name, McQuillan fancies himself a cheerful, work-a-day revolutionary. He lives with his wife and two kids on the
peace line. Despite three paramilitary attacks and several bullet wounds
(his brother was crippled), he remains squat, muscular, undiminished. In
the wake of what he sees as IRA acquiescence to partition, he has tried to
revive the IRSP as "a rallying point" for other disenchanted republicans.
The INLA has never formally declared a ceasefire. Gino Gallagher, the
INLA's chief of staff and a close friend of McQuillan's, was shot dead in
January 1996 as he picked up a welfare check at a Falls Road social security office. McQuillan blamed the Provisionals, and McIntyre agreed he
had "good reasons" to suspect them.

The IRA, like the Mafia and the loyalist paramilitaries, stays on top by eliminating head-to-head competition rather than beating it on the merits. The Provos killed eight members of rival republican guerrilla groups during the early part of the troubles. On February 10, 1994, nearly seven months before the IRA ceasefire, Dominic "Mad Dog" McGlinchey was executed with ten shotgun blasts as he stood in a telephone booth in Dundalk. Nobody claimed responsibility, but McGlinchey, former INLA chief of staff and one of the fabled killers of the troubles, had been tagged the hard man who might rally republicans disenchanted with Sinn Fein's flirtation with peace since his release from Portlaoise prison a year earlier. He had ideological as well as military firepower, as he was engaged in drafting a constitution for a united Ireland with Bernadette Devlin McAliskey, a venerated republican. At McGlinchey's funeral in Derry, McAliskey called him "the finest republican the struggle has ever produced."[11]

Given his formidable bearing and the nature of the McGlinchey hit—shotguns can't be traced ballistically—Gorman and McQuillan, who were both his friends, figure the IRA executed him. "The republican movement under Adams's leadership is very thorough, very organized, and it sets in motion things now that it may want to see realized in a number of years' time. Undoubtedly, in anyone's configuration, Dominic McGlinchey could have been a pole to which a number of disaffected elements could have been attracted," McQuillan comments elliptically.

Sinn Fein suppresses and masks whatever dissent exists within the "republican family," as the faithful like to call it. The dissenters and the mainstream, though, are basically united in their belief that the armed struggle is what has taken Irish nationalism as far as it has come in the north. "Any improvements that have come about under direct rule have come about as a direct result of the IRA," McIntyre declaims. "The Anglo-Irish Agreement, if we're to regard it as a political improvement, came about as a result of the British state's attempts to marginalize, isolate, and ultimately defeat, or render ineffectual the military capacity of the IRA to be reproduced and its political-military capacity to effect political change. The Downing Street declaration is the same thing. All these things, all this stifling of what has been called the nationalist agenda came by tilting the axis towards the nationalist agenda, and has come about as a direct result of the IRA. The catalyst, the dynamic for change in politics, the dynamic for the evolution of economic structures that safeguard Catholic interests and start to recognize Catholic interests have always been located within the IRA. The IRA must take credit."

This is the view almost universally held among republicans, and it explains the IRA's intractability on disarmament. The Provos are not afraid that decommissioning will scotch their military ability to wage war—they could rearm in a matter of months. Rather, they're afraid that even a hint of surrender will give Britain a sovereign victory, negating the political gains nationalism has made over the past twenty-five years and leaving the armed struggle the task of doing it all over again. The republicans' refusal to disarm is certainly reflexive, even visceral, but it is also intelligent.

If the war percolated up from the streets, the IRA ceasefire gestated in the prison. It was in jail that IRA men became collectively politicized and pushed each day for a renewed consensus to fortify them for the blanket protest. In one way, the process was a pernicious form of programming that produced what McIntyre calls "apparatchiks" who didn't really think for themselves. In another way, though, it was a kind of rehabilitation: republicans insisted that they weren't merely murderers, and by rooting their political beliefs made sure that was a sustainable position. Politicization lent credibility to the distinction they urged between criminality and political rebellion.

Although prisoners and ex-prisoners in general do not have any formal input into IRA or Sinn Fein executive decisions, Gary Roberts predicted the ceasefire six months in advance. "It's not because I had inside information. It was because jail is a few years ahead of what's happening outside. And the conclusion that led to the ceasefire in September was the sort of conclusion that we had discussed in jail three or four years previously. You know, one of the things that we always discussed in prison was alternatives." McIntyre, ever the iconoclast, obstinately refused to see anything for republicans in the Downing Street declaration since it preserved the unionist veto, and pointedly predicted that there would be no ceasefire.[12]

Notwithstanding their willingness to fight again, republicans are collectively disinclined to rejuvenate the armed struggle. "There's no way the IRA's going to give up the ceasefire, believe me," said Gorman in early 1995. Even the IRA's Canary Wharf bombing a year later he wrote off as an aberrational "one-off" and "a shot across the bow" of the British government. Gorman's friendship with Adams goes back to internment, when Gorman was OC of Adams's cage. When "streaking" was the rage in the early seventies, Adams and Gorman brought the fad to Long Kesh. Despite his ideological discomfort with some of Adams's tactics, Gorman is resigned to his leadership. "The war's over for this generation," he says conclusively. Even McIntyre, skeptical as he is of the IRA ceasefire's premises, believes that though the rank and file may have the will to return to the armed struggle, they haven't the political way. "A certain logic developed that they cannot go back, and they've crossed the Rubicon on that this year," he mutters. "The political cost of going back would be terrible. But the leadership knew this before they started out, so my argument is it's a case of positioning people. They were trying to position us into saying, we can't get any more through violence, and this [the ceasefire] is what we have to do to get more."

At this early stage, even the unionist chattering class doesn't object strenuously to IRA muscle enforcing the ceasefire. When an active service unit appeared to break the ceasefire in November 1994 in Newry by killing postal worker Frank Kerr in a robbery, Gerry Adams was genuinely shaken. He soon announced that the operation had not been sanctioned by the IRA command and that the IRA would handle the matter internally. The zeitgeist is that the nutting squad did and *should have* killed, banished, or at least kneecapped the Newry culprits. Yet the IRA's violent virtual government extends not only to its own people, but to the entire Catholic working-class community. There, drug dealers and teenage car thieves are frequently beaten with baseball bats, hurley sticks,* or iron bars. Occasionally, they are issued with "exclusion orders" requiring them to leave Northern Ireland on pain of death. In extreme cases, they are killed by the IRA.

Republicans trot out excuses. The police won't come into Catholic areas, so the Provos are the only source of law and order, and common folk beg them to keep a lid on local hoodlums. "If the neighborhoods didn't go out and ask the IRA, it wouldn't happen. It's almost a form of blackmail," says Carol Cullen, who lives with McIntyre and her two children in Ballymurphy, where much of the punishment is meted out. "This happens year in, year out, and we haven't got rid of these hoods; you've got to do something—and they're right. It's painful, but if they didn't ask for it, it wouldn't happen. I don't know what would be the alternative. You go to any public meeting or any community meeting and the main topic is the hoods, and [people] want them pulled limb from limb. The biggest criticism is that the IRA don't do enough to them. You ask them about the peace process and they might give you an answer, but you ask them what they think about the hoods and they will articulate themselves from here down the street, and they will say that the IRA is very weak and

---

*Sticks used in hurling, an Irish game resembling field hockey.

that they are not doing enough about the hoods." At the same time, Tommy Gorman contends, the hoods get what's coming to them. "These are republicans in republican areas. You have these kids who are a product of these areas, whose sort of anarchist fucking feelings bring hate and suffering into these areas. That's when the IRA act."

There are perhaps grains of truth in each statement. The IRA gets some community encouragement, and their victims are often public nuisances. But for every Provo booster there is at least one nationalist (especially outside of Belfast) who considers Provos common thugs, and the "punishments" they administer invariably outweigh the "crimes" committed. In any case, the claim that the Provos impose their virtual government in Catholic areas without enthusiasm strains credibility. In addition to the 167 punishment beatings they issued between the IRA ceasefire and the end of 1995, by mid-January 1996 they had killed eight people (all Catholics) for their alleged involvement in drug dealing or petty crime.*

Cullen, however, has been been programmed into an irrational belief in the Provos' fundamental benevolence that belies her obvious intelligence. She is an attractive woman, sandy-haired with a broad smile and almondine eyes. She is hospitable as well. Yet hard times seem to have resigned her to more of the same. She craves a "normal life" but doubts she'll ever have one. Her day-to-day imperatives are insulation and security. Though comfortable enough in west Belfast, at a lecture McIntyre gave at Queen's University—just a mile across town—she might as well have been in Nairobi. Carol could not stop looking over her shoulder and nestled with other republicans. On account of her frightened insularity, she contributes a ridiculous conspiracy theory to the desk set of justifications for IRA punishment beatings. "I think the RUC encourage joyriding in these communities because they see it as undermining the community and undermining the IRA," she says.

Roberts admits that any such "encouragement" comes from simply "not acting," and that the RUC's failure to act is that "they are a-feared of an IRA ambush." They have good reasons to be—every nationalist neigh-

---

*The group that actually claimed responsibility for these executions was "Direct Action Against Drugs" or DAAD. Under Northern Ireland street rules, no vigilante group could operate in a nationalist area without IRA knowledge, sanction, and cooperation. It is widely believed that DAAD was simply a Provo flag of convenience, created to give the IRA nominal deniability against accusations that it had broken the ceasefire.

borhood in Belfast has signs posted depicting a circled "RUC" with a red slash through it, and republicans proudly killed 298 RUC personnel during the troubles. Punishment beatings could just as well be read as the IRA's baiting the RUC. And Gorman is being disingenuous when he casts IRA punishments as selfless acts against interest. "It's a public-relations disaster for them, so they're hardly going to do something that troubles them willingly," he argues.

Republicans have a juvenile and resentful attitude toward the RUC. The force is 93 percent Protestant, but that is in significant part because not many Catholics applied during the troubles, when any Catholic policeman from republican areas became a high-priority target for execution by the Provos. (Recall Jackie McMullan's policeman neighbor, the late James Heaney.) Catholic RUC men would still be stigmatized in nationalist areas, as the RUC remains irrationally reviled in west Belfast.* One incident illustrates the point. In Northern Ireland, pedestrians must push buttons at crosswalks for a "walk" signal. One day in November 1995, a three-year old, Joseph McGinn, pressed such a button on Grosvenor Road in west Belfast without crossing the street. A passing RUC van broke to a halt, and an officer got out and scolded the boy, who went home terrified. When his mother confronted the officers involved, they said Joseph had "committed an offense" and that she "should have the child under control." Now, maybe upbraiding the tyke was uncalled for. But post-ceasefire and pre–Canary Wharf, policemen had too much time on their hands. They are finding it somewhat trying to make the switch from antiterrorist militia to peacetime police force. They sometimes overreact to minor transgressions, and they do not confine their hypersensitivity to Catholic west Belfast.

Sinn Fein councillor Fra McCann's response, however, was unhelpfully arch. "This incident demonstrates once again that the RUC simply is not suitable to patrol nationalist areas," he said.[13] Two weeks later, Sinn Fein and a republican prisoners' group (an obvious front) pressured a west Belfast soccer club, Donegal Celtic, to withdraw from the Bass Irish Cup tournament. The reason: Celtic was to play the RUC team in the first game. Though reluctant, Celtic felt compelled to withdraw from the

---

*West Belfast natives derisively refer to policemen as "Peelers." The expression dates back to the Peace Preservation Police established in 1814 by Sir Robert Peel, then chief secretary for Ireland and British prime minister at the outbreak of the famine, to quell public disorder emanating from the Catholic emancipation movement. The force developed into an all-Ireland constabulary.

competition. The following January, similar pressure from the Shinners—including home visits to team members—moved the Newington soccer club from nationalist north Belfast to pull out of an Amateur League match with the RUC. One disgusted Newington supporter drolly speculated that Sinn Fein had christened yet another front—"DAFT," for "Direct Action Against Football Teams."*

This mix of paranoia and coercion sets the table for a Sinn Fein political initiative. Since the ceasefire, Sinn Fein has urged the government to disband the RUC and vest day-to-day law enforcement duties in community police forces. Who the Shinners have in mind as the first recruits for the Catholic area groups is transparent.† The larger agenda is to establish subsovereign authority in Catholic areas from which Sinn Fein's power can expand under a devolved government increasingly controlled by nationalists. It's quite understandable—Sinn Fein is the only substantial nationalist party which also has a paramilitary capability, and it is merely playing to its strength.‡ But even law-abiding nationalists, like people elsewhere, revile admitted cop killers and thugs. The politician who has spoken out most vehemently against punishment beatings is not a union-

---

*An elaborate pun: "daft" is U.K. slang for "nuts" or "crazy."

†In November 1995, the *Irish News* reported, with its usual suggestive bias, that a small company in Dorset, England, was producing hand-chiseled figurines of RUC men and selling them for between £36 and £63, and that they were expected to appreciate in value should the RUC be disbanded. One of the sculptors clearly thought Sinn Fein held sway in Ulster: "We don't have time to follow the peace process properly," she said, "but if Sinn Fein are planning some changes we'd like to know in advance. That way we can prepare for any last minute rush." See "Model Police Force Set for Boom if Real-life RUC Men Stand Down," *Irish News* (Belfast), November 3, 1995, p. 1. The story hints at mainland Brits' ignorance and apathy about Northern Ireland.

‡The other part of the explanation is that punishment squads are simply "jobs for the boys." Just as young men join the U.S. Navy to see the world, lads who joined the IRA only shortly before the ceasefire did so to do some damage. Going in, many were no more politicized than the 1969-vintage recruits. They were simply discouraged souls who wanted to belong. Shankill bomber Thomas Begley, for example, was educationally subnormal and played in a republican band. Now that killing people is not as acceptable as it was during the troubles, fledgling Provos need an adventure. IRA leadership doesn't want to lose reserves, so it provides one. The same thing happened after the pre-split IRA border campaign lost steam in 1962 and the leadership switched from physical force to peaceful demonstrations as the preferred form of republican agitation. Desperate to pacify the rank and file, chief of staff Cathal Goulding reluctantly authorized several meaningless and embarrassing military operations between 1965 and 1968—including the fatuous bombing of Nelson's Pillar in downtown Dublin in March 1966. See Patrick Bishop and Eamonn Mallie, *The Provisional IRA* (London: Corgi Books, 1988), pp. 58–60.

ist, but Dr. Joe Hendron, SDLP member of Parliament from west Belfast. He barely wrested the seat from Gerry Adams in 1992 by 589 votes, and seemed likely to face stiff opposition from the living legend again in 1997. "Sinn Fein is a fascist organization," he says. "They say they are on the road to democracy, but they have a long way to go. Breaking young fellows' arms—that's hardly democracy."

Sinn Fein also operates in more insidious ways. For example, concerted Catholic resistance to Orange marches on the lower Ormeau Road was not a product of the "community democracy" that Sinn Fein marketed. It resulted instead from Sinn Fein's manipulation and peer pressure. The Lower Ormeau Concerned Community, another Shinner front, excluded reporters from its July 11 meeting on whether to allow the marches. Two journalists sneaked in anyway. Gerard Rice of Sinn Fein, an IRA ex-prisoner, then took a rough sounding by acclamation. About a third of the crowd were in favor of letting the parade pass through, but Rice decided no vote was needed and told waiting reporters that the group was unanimously against allowing the marchers. "It is cruel," concluded Malachi O'Doherty, one of the enterprising spies, "that the people who do not share the conveniently agreed identity of the imagined community are regarded as nonexistent."[14] Or, worse, they are simply *made* nonexistent, as the supposed drug dealers have been.

Whether in the form of Bobby Storey's "thought police," "Direct Action Against Drugs," or the Lower Ormeau Concerned Community, Sinn Fein is quintessentially McCarthyist. Republicans may talk left-wing, but they act right-wing. Punishment is administered on the basis of word of mouth and attenuated suspicion. Thus, DAAD threatened a nightclub owner with death unless he stopped playing "rave" music, which is associated with the drug Ecstasy. He was later "pardoned." Sinn Fein and the IRA, then, are populist in only the most corrupt and invidious sense. The standard progression in republican politics—IRA volunteer, prison, Sinn Fein worker, elected office—may appear to run from less to more democratic. But Sinn Fein politics remain predominantly revolutionary and ruthlessly centralized. One prominent ex-prisoner admits that she finds Adams's dalliance with the Clinton administration troublesome because it entails an apology. "We're a revolutionary party," she rails. "We'll apologize when they apologize." Whether Sinn Fein can adapt to incremental peacetime politics, in which the Armalite can't be used in aid of the ballot box, is the pivotal question for Northern Ireland's future.

Watching Gerry Adams could not help even the most incisive prognosticator—he is so evasive and dissembling that it's impossible to tell whether he leans toward bullying or democracy as the means to an eventual united Ireland. While the IRA ceasefire itself superficially suggests the latter, Adams's threats, the IRA's censorship of its own, and punishment beatings since the ceasefire would give anyone pause. And he continues to insist coyly that Sinn Fein and the IRA are functionally separate. Nobody believes this—Adams has "spoken for the IRA" with no sign of a challenger for over a decade—but continuing the charade enables him to cast his periodic warnings of the IRA's return to violence as reports from the messenger rather than personal threats. By implication, he wants to keep the military option alive without committing political suicide. Conversely, in 1993 Adams found himself unable to say that it was wrong for the IRA to execute *Catholic* contractor Adrian McGovern in front of his children for supplying the security forces with building materials.[15] At best, he is a go-for-broke statesman. At worst, he is a terrorist playing at politics when it suits him.*

---

*For the record, in Northern Ireland the received facts about Gerry Adams are as follows: He was born in the lower Falls in 1948, and his father—"Old Gerry"—was a well-loved old IRA man jailed in the forties and interned briefly in 1971. In 1964 young Gerry joined Sinn Fein, then the Republican Clubs (the northern political wing of the pre-split IRA and later the Official IRA), and, by 1969, the IRA itself. By the time he was first interned in March 1972, Adams had progressed in rank from officer commanding of the Provisional IRA's Ballymurphy company to OC of the entire Second Battalion and second in command on Belfast Brigade Staff. He was released from Long Kesh on July 7, 1972 to negotiate with the British government the continuation of the IRA ceasefire, which broke down two days later. On July 21—"Bloody Friday"—the IRA set off twenty-six bombs in Belfast, killing eleven and injuring 130. Bishop and Mallie, writing in 1987, reported that the operation was planned by three men, including "a leading Belfast Provisional who is now a senior member of Sinn Fein" (*The Provisional IRA*, p. 232). Between his release on July 7, 1972 and his reinternment on July 19, 1973, Adams held executive rank in the IRA and from March 1973, at the latest, was also OC of the Belfast Brigade. During that one-year span, the IRA killed at least 183 people, fifty-three of them civilians. In March through mid-July 1973 alone—when Adams was in overall charge of Belfast IRA operations, then authorized from the top down—Provo units in the city killed fourteen soldiers, one Catholic civilian, and one Protestant civilian. Adams was released from the compounds in 1976 after serving eighteen months for trying to escape. In 1978, he was charged with IRA membership and spent seven months in the H-blocks on remand before the case was dismissed. Thereupon he became the republican movement's dominant political leader. In 1978, he was elected vice-president of Provisional Sinn Fein. Since 1983, he has been president of the party and, until the Canary Wharf bombing in February 1996, held plenary power in Sinn Fein and the IRA. In the twelve years of Adams's supremacy—which witnessed Enniskillen, the Teebane ambush, and the Shankill bomb, among other republican atrocities against civilians—the IRA killed at least 535 people. For ten of those years, 1983 to 1992, he was member of Parliament for west Belfast. Gerry Adams has never been convicted of committing or abetting a violent crime.

Unionist skepticism about Adams and Sinn Fein is all but indelible. "I don't know how Sinn Fein can take on civil politics," says Chris McGimpsey, the unionist Belfast city councillor from Belfast who represents the Shankill. "I don't see it. They just hate our guts. They just hate Prods. I think that's their motivation. I mean, I'm not going to say that everybody that votes for them—you know, seventy thousand people there—are all the same, but I think the leadership of Sinn Fein are virulently anti-Protestant." The realpolitik is still daunting: before the claim of "undefeated" can really stick, Sinn Fein has a great deal to prove to people it constitutionally abhors—all the more so after Canary Wharf.

CHAPTER 5

"ABJECT AND TRUE REMORSE"

LAUNDERING LOYALIST TERRORISM

The Provos have always had a larger-than-life tradition, they have always had a jaunty buzz about them. The loyalists went straight from sullen to earnest and skipped the swagger. In the ceasefire statement of the Combined Loyalist Military Command, read by Gusty Spence on October 13, 1994, there is watchfulness, defensiveness, and regret.

> The permanence of our ceasefire will be completely dependent upon the continued cessation of all nationalist/republican violence. The sole responsibility for a return to war lies with them. In the genuine hope that peace will be permanent, we take the opportunity to pay homage to all our fighters, commandos and volunteers who have paid the supreme sacrifice. They did not die in vain. The union is safe. . . . In all sincerity, we offer to the loved ones of all innocent victims over the last twenty-five years, abject and true remorse. No words of ours will compensate for the intolerable suffering they have undergone during the conflict.[1]

Unlike Gerry Adams's pride in the IRA's being "undefeated," the notion that the loyalist paramilitaries have been victorious is only faintly suggested, and then in the detached, almost spectatorial observation that "the union is safe." The men who composed this statement, like those who came up with the IRA ceasefire, were mainly ex-prisoners. The UVF group—Spence, Ervine, Hutchinson, Kinner, Mitchell, Smith—all joined the Progressive Unionist Party. The UDA veterans, including John White and Tommy Kirkham, joined the Ulster Democratic Party. Unlike the IRA veterans who staff Sinn Fein, every one of these loyalist stars served the bulk of his time in the compounds rather than the H-blocks. It's a telling difference: while republicans grew from the oppressiveness of the criminalization, loyalists thrived in the freedom of special-category status. Culturally, it scans. The H-block prison regime gave rise to the IRA volunteers' group martyrdom, which fit with the republican tradition of sacrifice. The relative laxity of the cages gave the loyalist paramilitaries room to impose their own military structures, so as to realize the regimented individualism that the Protestant ethic promoted.

Though he puts down much of his legend as "a load of crap," without question the father of loyalist prison culture is Gusty Spence. Sentenced to life in 1966 and released in 1985, he recognizes that loyalists then were, by comparison to republicans, a bit retarded. "There were no intelligentsia, no middle class, within the ranks of the loyalist paramilitaries, so intelligent debate took that little bit longer to manifest itself. Whenever one finds oneself in prison for a length of time, everything is questioned, your cause is tested, you are tested, society is tested. Loyalist violence was looked upon as a necessity. Whereas in the main it has been reactionary, I would say the main aim of loyalist violence was to maintain the union—simple, cut-and-dried. So it's not just a yes-or-no question of renunciation of violence. There was and is a better way."

Spence himself came around to this point of view gradually, but the pace of his transformation was hardly glacial. He began to suggest a non-violent approach for loyalism in 1974, after the first IRA ceasefire broke down. Housed during what he calls "the wilderness years" in Belfast's Crumlin Road Prison,* a labyrinthine Victorian hulk, until sentenced prisoners were moved to Long Kesh at the end of 1974, he had protested in prison along with republicans (whose numbers were far greater in those days) for prisoner-of-war status. Spence, now in his mid-sixties, is a

---

*Located in central Belfast, Crumlin Road Prison is officially designated "Belfast Prison" and popularly known as "the Crum." It has also been called "Ulster's San Quentin." Throughout the troubles, Crumlin Road Prison was used mainly to house unsentenced prisoners awaiting trial. The Crum, unlike the compounds and the H-blocks, was politically integrated. The prison was built in the 1850s along the classical lines of a London "Bridewell" prison, with four wings radiating to form a single X shape. The Crum had an optimal single-cell capacity of only 433, which made complete segregation physically impossible during most of the troubles period, when thousands of arrestees were circulating through the system. Makeshift segregation of republicans and loyalists was accomplished by lock-down and alternating use of facilities rather than permanent physical separation in functionally independent blocks. As a result, riots, brawls, and rooftop protests were frequent occurrences. The last round of disturbances, in 1994, produced extensive damage. After July 1994, the Prison Service sent remand prisoners suspected of paramilitary involvement directly to the Maze and made plans to hold remand prisoners in new units at Maghaberry. Rat-ridden and in irremediable disrepair, Crumlin Road Prison closed, to little regret, on April 1, 1996.

lantern-jawed mesomorph who sports an expansive, grandfatherly smile. The crude, bleeding tattoos that cover his arms are incongruous with the scholarly pipe he smokes. "Crumlin Road Prison was one of the most austere in western Europe," says Spence. "It was certainly worse than the prisons in England. My first seven months spent in prison were in solitary confinement, because I wouldn't work for the prison authorities. They actually—the cheek of the bastards—they wanted me to contribute towards my imprisonment by working for them for a half an ounce of tobacco a week. They wanted me to work for them. It was bad enough being in prison, but that added insult to injury." He also went on several hunger strikes, one lasting thirty-five days, until the paramilitary prisoners got special-category status in 1972—although, he says, "to hear a republican speaking, it was only them who did it."*

The compounds were like military barracks. Though loyalists and republicans were segregated, all of the prisoners were visible to one another through the wire fences that separated them. Each compound contained three Nissen huts (similar to Quonset huts). There were about ninety people housed in a compound, thirty in each hut. Within each compound, the prisoners had completely free association from eight o'clock in the morning until nine at night. After that they were confined to the huts, but there were no cells in them—only separate cubicles. For twenty-four hours a day, then, each prisoner was allowed to circulate among at least twenty-nine others. The prisoners were responsible for maintaining the compounds themselves. For the republicans, these conditions generated a communal, cooperative way of life. They presented the loyalists with an opportunity to legitimize themselves through military discipline.

Breidge Gadd, Chief Probation Officer for Northern Ireland, considers the compounds the ideal milieu for self-rehabilitation. "In terms of how prison should work, Compound Maze was a model prison. An intelligent governor who knows what he's doing and is seriously interested in resettlement of prisoners would have seen Compound Maze as a dream, because it was about prisoners forcing themselves to manage their own lives. It should have been observed, it was not. Because they had to get through all the *Lord of the Flies* stuff, you know, they had to live everything. They had to go through the bit where nobody got up in the morning. They had to

---

*The proximate cause of the introduction of special-category status was the hunger strike of Billy McKee, OC of the Provisional IRA's Belfast Brigade, who was close to death when William Whitelaw, the first Northern Ireland secretary of state under direct rule, gave in on June 19, 1972.

elect their own leader, they had to look at how natural leaders evolved. A fascinating experiment. There's no doubt now that the guys who came out of Compound Maze have this tremendous self-awareness, self-confidence."

Spence established a regime based on the British army—a five-mile run before breakfast, mess, neatly made up bedpacks, washing and shaving, inspection, marching, and drill, every day. "Gusty Spence created the culture within the compounds," says Billy Hutchinson, who succeeded Spence as UVF officer commanding in the compounds. "And the reason was his emphasis was on how you structured your day. Physical fitness and education were the things that he stressed, and things like handicrafts to extricate people's minds from prison doldrums when they were actually laying about and doing nothing. So he had this rule where during certain hours of the day you had to be doing something rather than laying about."[2] Marty Snoddon ran his first marathon in prison.

UVF discipline was also military. Spence held makeshift courts-martial. There was no corporal punishment, however. The worst penalty anyone drew was the equivalent of "KP" duty, which Spence recalls "nine times out of ten was looked upon as a kind of a joke." Eddie Kinner remembers that "if somebody came into your cage during inspection time and there was dust in some places where there shouldn't have been, if a cup hadn't been washed properly, you got a half-hour's fatigues—wee extra jobs like washing out the toilets, or maybe peeling potatoes." Each UVF prisoner was also given regular, nonpunitive chores to do.

The UDA emulated the UVF, though it took longer to establish genuine discipline and never achieved quite the same level of regimentation. "Really, the strongest man in their compounds tended to rule. Around about that period Jimmy Craig would have been in charge, so it was down into the boxing ring and a thumping in the nose as a military code," says Kinner, a bit disdainfully. Tommy Kirkham, an upright sort with an ascetic countenance and a soldierly gameness, recalls stepping in with Craig, who had once boxed for Ireland's national amateur team. "As soon as you put the gloves on you thought you were in the ring with a killer and he started to punch. Effectively, he had to be dragged off me that day. He just got punching as if a bell went in his head." Craig is also reputed to have wielded a hammer with which he threatened to break wayward UDA men's fingers, and to have knifed a man who hit him with a broom.[3]

The republican prisoners got to watch all this. They dismissed UDA prisoners as thugs. UVF prisoners they regarded as comical martinets. "Gusty Spence and these other senior people in jail had these people to brush their cell out, shine their shoes, iron their clothes," Tommy Gorman scoffs. "That would never be tolerated in the IRA. They actually called people 'sir.' There were no 'sirs' in the IRA." He had no time for it, and neither did other IRA men. "It was a wee empire—they had batmen [military valets], they had colonels and captains and majors and regimental sergeant-majors in their compounds, and we all thought they were dickheads," says Anthony McIntyre, who was convicted of a murder that occurred two days before criminalization and did his time in the compounds until he was sent to the H-blocks in 1978 for trying to escape. "Like this was pretty much a joke. The criminals were theirs, in our view. See, the UVF really had no tradition in Belfast, and the UDA had even less of a tradition. The IRA never had the identity problem of having to unite themselves against Britain, and against the prison regime. Instinct told us that we're all on this side and they're all on that side. So there was a common motivation, a common purpose. I think the loyalists had a more difficult time in getting unity. The IRA didn't really need an overarching structure to the extent that the loyalists did."*

Derision aside, McIntyre's inferences are well observed. Unlike Provos, loyalists faced the perversity of being incarcerated by the very authority they wanted to uphold. Recalling his first months in prison, David Ervine says: "I went to Crumlin Road Prison, where I found it a Dickensian hole. I was locked up by people who were defending the status quo—just like me. I think at some point you've got to see the foundation of your justification rocked." Now Ervine walks tall and speaks with the sure, deep voice of

---

*The IRA, of course, is also structured along military lines both in prison and on the outside, but the Provos frown on martial formality. Whereas the UVF and the UDA consciously emulate the British army, the IRA sees itself as fundamentally egalitarian and as establishing differential ranks strictly for operational purposes. As chapter 4 suggests, this self-image is mildly delusional. In any event, military inclinations have produced a degree of practical tolerance among paramilitaries in prison. In the seventies, Spence and the OCs of the other groups established a "Camp Council" which presented grievances to the prison administration on behalf of all paramilitary prisoners. Through this type of setup, prisoners also negotiated "peace treaties" among themselves. In October 1974, for example, joint agitation over conditions in the Long Kesh compounds culminated in republican prisoners' burning down forty huts and fighting en masse with prison officers. Dozens of republicans were injured. The loyalists set up a field hospital to care for them, gave three hundred republican prisoners refuge in loyalist compounds, and negotiated safe passage for them back to their own area. Until recently, loyalist and republican prisoners had agreed not to confront one another during visits at the Maze. The arrangement worked until loyalists beat up Shankill bomber Sean Kelly, whereupon the OCs accepted segregated visiting areas.

a beloved mayor. Then he needed Spence's counsel and his structures. "I had an interesting first meeting with Mr. Spence. We arrived in compound twenty, and Mr. Spence came from the sentence compounds and spoke with us. Where are you from? East Belfast. Oh, he says, that's where they eat the missionaries. Jocular. He says, why are you here? And I says, possession of explosives. And he says, no, no, no, no. Why are you here? I actually thought that he was being extremely arrogant, but then I suppose most commanding officers are. But it caused me a great degree of thought."

Like Socrates with the slave, Spence goaded his charge into self-examination. In pondering his question, Ervine would either recognize his political ignorance or attest to his political sophistication. In any case, Spence calculated, Ervine would see incarceration as an opportunity to educate himself. Spence's question was the standard inauguration for new UVF prisoners. And it worked.

Loyalists, like IRA volunteers, were told to expect prison, maiming, or death upon their induction, yet the prospect of jail did not seem real to them on the outside. "Basically," says Billy Mitchell, "you were caught up in the romance of paramilitarism. You didn't have time to think." What enabled loyalists, as opposed to republicans, to function on autopilot was the odd fact that their brand of terrorism was both reactive and pro-state. Their brief was simply to keep hitting the IRA for as long as they hit the unionist community, and their political objective was already defined as the existing state. It was only once they got in jail that they began to doubt the sanctity of that objective. "In jail you had one enemy and that was the system," Mitchell explains. "The command structure gave you a sense of purpose for being there—a sense that you weren't there to vegetate, that you weren't there to feel the stigma of being a prisoner."

Like the Provos, Spence, Mitchell, and other older inmates held informal seminars on politics and working-class social issues, but these took hold with relatively few of the loyalist prisoners. "Remember, this is the first time loyalists was actually in prison," admonishes Plum Smith. "Republicans had been through this all before in the twenties, you know, and all that there. But loyalists never had to fight before, this was the first time loyalists had to go outside the law, so they found it different and difficult to adapt. They adapted as they went along, whereas republicans could draw on experience from past campaigns." Both loyalists and republicans agitated for formal education. When the Prison Service began to offer courses after internment, the UVF command was given another means of rousing the rank and file.

Spence appointed an education officer, who in turn required each prisoner to enroll in at least one course. (Smith was the first education officer; Billy Mitchell succeeded him; Mitchell's successor later got a Ph.D. and is now a lecturer at the University of Ulster at Jordanstown.) Though some UVF men resented the rule, Hutchinson reckons that 60 to 70 percent of the two hundred men under his command got some kind of educational qualification in the compounds. "You must not get the impression there was anything oppressive about it," says Spence. "It was oppressive when people wanted to lie on their beds all day and feel sorry for themselves and surround themselves with self-pity." UDA performance was not as impressive, but still a respectable 20 percent, according to John White.

Whereas IRA men tended to stay close to their political roots even as they availed themselves of prison-sponsored courses, loyalists were less doctrinaire. "For the republicans, their education, everything was geared to developing republican ideology and strategy," says Mitchell. "I think maybe the difference in the UVF compounds was that it was a broad church, so to speak. You weren't encouraged to become a UVF man in prison. You were just encouraged to develop your mind." Loyalist prisoners often attended to more practical concerns, as well. Eddie Kinner and Marty Snoddon, for example, both earned O-levels and B.A. degrees in computer science from the Open University with an eye toward getting jobs when they got out.

Republicans would claim this difference reflects their greater political sophistication. The attitude is merely knee-jerk snobbery. There is nothing inherently unsophisticated about being practical. Besides, both Kinner and Snoddon decided on computers in part because it cost the Prison Service more money. Like Pickering and McMullan, Kinner and Snoddon are best friends. Kinner stands five foot six, with a bald pate, a broad frame, and an even broader smile that lights up a room with cheerful mischief. He and the tall, Rotarian Snoddon make a Mutt-and-Jeff pair. But the salient differences stop at physical appearances: both men are resolutely honest and self-consciously unpretentious. Unlike most co-accused prisoners, they have maintained their bond, throughout prison and on the outside, for over twenty years. Whatever the contrasts in the intellectual climates of the loyalist compounds and the republican H-blocks, Kinner and Snoddon are living proof that the UVF compounds engendered solidarity to match the bonding in the H-blocks to which Pickering and McMullan's friendship attests.

To whatever extent educational selection reflects intellect, it also reflects simple expectation. Most loyalist paramilitaries, being Protestant and therefore better positioned, had jobs on the outside and had difficulty imagining an existence without a living wage; they were only part-time paramilitaries. Most IRA men couldn't find jobs, didn't really want them, and lived like guerrillas all the time—ideologically as well as logistically. And some loyalists did get college degrees in less vocational subjects—Hutchinson and White in social sciences, McMurray in psychology. Loyalists also had their fair share of honors graduates, including Snoddon, White, McMurray, and Hutchinson.

Regardless of what courses loyalist compound prisoners chose, most did come away with a political education that had been sorely lacking. This, too, was a legacy of Gusty Spence. But it blossomed because of the openness of the compounds. "Gusty Spence probably planted the seeds," says Marty Snoddon. "But at the same time, there was a group of people involved in education within the cages, and we spoke a lot amongst ourselves. I think most of us came to the conclusion that it was a tragedy that we were there, but we'd like to do something to prevent other people having to go through the same thing as we had to go through." Along with this came a modified attitude toward bloodshed. Snoddon continues: "My view on violence didn't change overnight. I suppose it was just a process of being removed from the conflict, sitting back and seeing what was going on, having a look at Irish history. The troubles were just going on year after year and nobody was getting anywhere. Nobody was making any gains in the military sense. So I didn't believe that violence was achieving anything. That's not to say that I didn't feel that I could resort to violence. I didn't become a pacifist. If my family was being attacked again, then certainly I would do what I felt that I had to do—reluctantly."

THE STRUGGLE FOR RESPECTABILITY

Loyalist compound alumni, like republican blanketmen, wax sentimental about their coming of age. "It was a very good culture, and it was a sharing culture, because kind of ironically, it was a very nonviolent culture," says Ron McMurray. "Here were some sixty guys who society said were lunatics and psychopaths, but we could live with each other and talk about our differences. There always were a few fistfights, especially around Christmas, Easter, but it was a far less violent place than it is out in this world. There was a disagreement with the prison staff one day, quite a big one. People weren't letting parcels in, so we couldn't get food in and stuff like that. The first reaction was, we're not going to let these bastards get us down. So the people who were getting parcels in actually shared with everybody else who didn't get them. That was a good experience. Everything was put out together on a table and pooled about. People felt so close to each other. I suppose if you think about it, we had all committed different things in the name of the union, and we all believed in the same thing. We were all there together, and it was a very clean, strong bond."

But loyalists differed from republicans in that political ideology was not always dispositive of social relationships. Marty Snoddon fondly remembers sharing recipes for "poteen"—Irish moonshine—and getting ceremonially drunk with the Official IRA prisoners, who were in the adjacent compound.*

Spence's followers—who comprised most UVF prisoners and a good many UDA men in the compounds—emerged with the view that sectarian violence of the kind the loyalists had admittedly engaged in was pointless. Correspondingly, many of those who had committed sectarian acts came to confront their guilt unprotected by the excuse of war. Billy Mitchell, who helped coin the phrase "abject and true remorse," is particularly frank. "We were counterterrorists. Morally, I was guilty of offenses against humanity. It was no problem going to prison; I don't have a chip on my shoulder about that." For prisoners like him, the contradiction between being locked up in a British jail and being a "loyalist" disappeared. Like Calderwood, Mitchell resigned from the paramilitaries in 1982, and served out his sentence in the H-blocks, and later at H.M.P. Maghaberry with non-paramilitary inmates.

Not all loyalist prisoners went that far, but some still admitted their moral guilt. Concerning the Wilson-Andrews murders, John White whispers, "I held the knife. But in later years after the offense, I come to realize that it didn't further the cause any. It was really a futile act, to a great extent.

---

*Because the Official IRA split with the Provisional IRA in 1970, declared a ceasefire in 1972 that it has never broken, and successfully made the transition to socialist politics through the Workers Party and the Democratic Left, loyalists generally did not regard Official IRA men as military enemies. In fact, UVF men found the Officials' entrenched socialist views edifying. Although once republican purists—they are called "Stickies" because of their practice of fixing gum-backed Easter lilies in their lapels to commemorate the 1916 Easter Rising—the Officials early on disavowed the "physical force" tradition on the ground that it would increase sectarianism and inhibit class politics. Socializing among UVF and Official IRA prisoners, and even some covert cooperation on the outside, were natural extensions of the relationship that began in the compounds as a logistical accident.

That undermined my resilience during police interrogation." A suspected gunrunner and one of very few loyalist internees, White had been taken a hundred times to the RUC's main interrogation center in east Belfast, Castlereagh, where he'd been beaten and humiliated without breaking. He confessed to the Wilson-Andrews murders after sixteen hours of purely psychological questioning. Ron McMurray voluntarily confessed as well.

William Giles is presently in the Maze, serving a life sentence for shooting dead a man, Michael Fay, who he still believes was a "long-time Provo." Nonetheless, he feels intense remorse over the killing. "When you take someone's life," he says, "a piece of you goes with him." Though hackneyed, this sentiment is not mere show. The physically unimposing Giles gives off a nervous, energetic sincerity. He did not participate in the UVF prison flare-up in March 1995, and one prison officer characterizes him as "unusually docile." Giles has thought of approaching Fay's family, and at the time of the murder his parents wanted to meet with the victim's family, but the UVF advised against it. "Of course I'm sorry," Giles acknowledges, as if it should be obvious, "but I wouldn't have anything to say to them."

Not every loyalist personally felt the kind of guilt that Calderwood, Mitchell, and McMurray did. Hutchinson believes the two young men he was convicted of killing were IRA volunteers, whom he considered legitimate targets. Kinner, Snoddon, and Smith say they were behaviorally programmed by their society, and did the inevitable. There is a corresponding moral gap in some of the loyalists' thinking: while they do not believe terrorism is the proper course now, they do not condemn those who perpetrated it because their intentions were defensible and the circumstances compelling. Thus, John White is able to say, without balking, that the troubles were "futile" while the UFF's 1993 Greysteel massacre in retaliation for the IRA's Shankill bombing was "understandable" (though he is quick to say he does not condone it). Plum Smith insists that violence is not the way forward, yet *he* had no choice but to spill blood in 1972 to keep the union safe.

These men are reluctant to say even that, knowing what they know now, they would have opted out then. This dilemma is psychological rather than philosophical. The prisoner cannot bring himself to pronounce killing and jail a waste of time and conscience, yet he also cannot block out the panorama of waste spreading across Northern Ireland that he saw from the prison yard. Loyalists like Mitchell and Hutchinson resolve the problem imperfectly, but workably—by contending that violent conflict can be transformed into nonviolent dialogue. And loyalists exhibit different shades of thinking on violence—Snoddon would take up arms again if he felt the Protestant community truly threatened, Mitchell could not do so. But none of them seems proud of what he did, and every man regrets the loss of life in the troubles generally.

Republicans are never too apologetic about their past, and would never hint that the armed struggle was morally or conceptually misguided. Gary Roberts's position is typical. "I do accept, incidentally, that the IRA did kill innocent civilians, both Catholic and Protestant. I do accept that they did that in the heat of the moment, after something happened—I know people who went in and beat a Protestant to death when they just heard that their friend was shot dead. I don't support that but I understand. But what I don't believe is that the IRA as an organization set down and said, we're going to kill innocent Protestants, we're going to go up the Shankill Road and kill the first Protestant we see. Because if the IRA would have done that, the death toll would have been thirty thousand, not three thousand." He starts with an admission, then excuses it into obscurity, and finally congratulates the IRA for not killing more Prods than they did.

Tommy Gorman was never charged with murder, but he was field operations commander for the IRA's First Battalion (Andersonstown) and admits that bombings and shootings he helped perpetrate may have killed people. If any innocents died on his account, he says, he regrets the loss of life. But on the Wilson-Andrews murder, he gets squeamish and suggests the IRA have a morally higher way of killing. "I could never do it. Stabbing someone like that is very, very personal to me. If I move to hit a Brit or RUC people, it's very impersonal, I'm shooting at a uniform, I'm not saying, 'That's Joe Soap.' Cutting someone up is very, very, very personal."

Loyalists do not play these games. At most, they say that the IRA can be and has been as sectarian as they've been, and that they've actually killed more "legitimate targets"—IRA men—than they've been credited with. Both claims are defensible.* Roberts, though, finesses any challenge

---

*Several times, Sinn Fein has denied that a loyalist murder victim was an IRA member, but later quietly added his name to a memorial scroll of departed volunteers. In the most celebrated case, the IRA claimed that Loughlin Maginn, shot dead by the UFF in 1989, was just an innocent Catholic. The UFF then showed a BBC reporter intelligence files on republican suspects—including Maginn—that the organization had obtained from the security forces. The revelation proved that loyalist paramilitaries' targeting was not exclusively sectarian, but also led to the damaging Stevens Enquiry on security-force collusion with the UFF and the UVF. More recently, in 1991, three Catholics killed by the UVF in Cappagh, County Tyrone, were later revealed to be IRA men.

that the loyalists' "abject and true remorse" poses to the republican con-science. "Gusty Spence says when he declares the loyalist ceasefire that we apologize to all our innocent victims. What does he mean by 'innocent victims'? Was my cousin an innocent victim—thirteen years of age, blew to pieces? The only thing left of him in the coffin was his head; the rest was lead. So, did he mean by 'innocent victims' the Protestants they shot mistaken for Catholics? Was he apologizing for shooting Peter Ward, a barman out for a drink?" Spence believes these people were indeed inno-cent victims, but Roberts's question was rhetorical. No apology from him is forthcoming. And certainly nothing comparable to the remorse ex-pressed by Spence on behalf of all loyalist paramilitaries has emerged from republicans as group.

It may be easier for loyalists to show remorse because they still have the union and the "veto," and can claim some palpable return on their moral investment. Republicans can argue persuasively that they helped em-power nationalists, but they are still a long way from a united Ireland and may not feel that mere "parity of esteem" is enough to merit apologies. They also think because their operations were on balance less obviously sectarian, they have far less to apologize for. Republicans' overriding mes-sage is that they and their people have suffered the most. It's as if the blan-ket protest and hunger strikes, having yielded the blood sacrifice prophe-sied by Pearse, cauterized any moral wound they might have endured. "Fourteen and a half years in jail changed my republicanism. It made it richer, it made it deeper," says Roberts. "When people joined the IRA, and they says, I'm going to go out and shoot the Brits tonight, there was always the chance that the soldiers would shoot back. Everybody runs that risk, but nobody ever thinks it's going to happen to them. Here was Bobby [Sands] who knew that within a short space of time this was going to happen to him, and he stuck with it."

The essential comparison is that while some loyalists are willing to admit that their strategy of violence has been a mistake, there are almost no republicans that would likewise question the efficacy of the armed struggle. Those few that have completely renounced republican methods—like Shane Paul O'Doherty, who served a life sentence for the London letter-bomb campaign that maimed several British civil servants—are excluded from the movement. For a loyalist, the renunciation of violence is often genuine reconsideration; for a republican, it is almost always a tactic.

Ironically, compound-era loyalists give H-block-era republicans a great deal of credit for the hunger strikes, and tacitly concede republicans' greater strength in adversity. "In the compounds there was a sense that, you know, that the whole thing was senseless, and that the government could have given republicans and loyalists in the blocks some concessions which wouldn't really have meant that much," says Billy Hutchinson. "But I think there was a grudging respect for those people who were willing to die to get special-category status. To be perfectly honest, I was in the compounds and I was saying loyalists in the blocks should be doing the same thing to get it as well. It's easy to say, but I thought that the whole special-category thing in the blocks—the blanket, the dirty protest, and the hunger strikes—was something that should have been done by loyalists as well."

Hutchinson adds dutifully that "loyalists didn't do it because those things were seen as republican." John White admits having "some empathy" with the hunger strikers, and appends the same disclaimer. But some first-hand observers doubt that the loyalists as a group could have conjured the collective will needed for a hunger strike even if they wanted to. They had actually begun one during the first republican fast, but ended it after four days. Pickering openly ridicules this sad showing. McIntyre recalls seeing loyalist prisoners betting new sneakers they'd been sent, in a card game; he shudders at such profligacy with practical gifts, and sees it as evidence of frivolity that doesn't lend itself to sustained protest. Sean Lynch, the Provos' present OC in the H-blocks, snarls that the loyalists "sat on their backsides" while republicans were on the blanket, and now enjoy the fruits of the republican protests without having made comparable sacrifices.

Duncan McLaughlan has worked in Northern Ireland's Prison Service since 1971, and was governor of the compounds when they closed in 1988. He is British. Yet he agrees with Lynch. "The republican side has always been much better organized, well-disciplined; it has really thought out what it was about. Republicans generally speaking are working from an ideological base. The loyalists are a reactive group—they have reacted to the actions of the republicans, so they haven't had an ideological base. So they have never been well-organized. Republicans are a hundred percent there as an organization and every guy will subjugate his own personal views to accept the leadership's views and so on; that is not true, that is nowhere near true of the loyalist side in prison. It takes a pretty severe mistake by us, if you like, to get them to work as a group."

Even when loyalists do operate en masse, it's not always by way of calculated disobedience or negotiation. In March 1995, prison officers decided to search the UVF blocks for drugs and cellular telephones they suspected were being smuggled in. One prisoner took exception to a particularly enthusiastic search and hit a screw. An individual confrontation spiraled into a full-blown riot, as over one hundred UVF men closed off the block and collected on the roof, lighting a fire and waving mock rifles. McLaughlan is confident that the situation would never have occurred on republican blocks. "I think it might have happened twenty years ago had circumstances been like that, when there were compounds," he says. "But the republicans have moved on. I hesitate to use the phrase 'they know how to play the game,' but that is what has happened."

In 1992, McLaughlan was governor of the Maze. As he walked the wings, several UVF prisoners attacked him and beat him up badly, nearly managing to pour scalding water on him and breaking another prison officer's nose before they were subdued. The incident demonstrates the demise of the command structure that was so robust in the compounds. "You don't know how many you have to satisfy on the loyalist wings," McIntyre comments. "There's so many commanders, all chiefs and no Indians." Despite the absence of a rigid chain of command, IRA prisoners have learned that they get more accomplished by taking the guidance of consensual leaders and behaving collectively. They all say that screws would much rather walk down a republican wing than a loyalist wing. McLaughlan confirms the point, and he is quick to add that the loyalists are farther down on the learning curve. "The loyalists still have the view that, I want more baked beans now, and in half an hour if you haven't given them to me I'll thump you. They haven't learned that we can be seduced. But I think the loyalist side will arrive at that point."

The fact is, however, that there are substantially more loyalists than republicans that were incarcerated for nonpolitical offenses before going down for paramilitary activities. They have not nurtured their politics as well as republicans have in the H-blocks, and have more of the inclinations and problems associated with regular criminals in American prisons. Whereas more IRA men than loyalist prisoners will choose political documentaries to watch on the VCR, more loyalists than republicans will look at sports or sex movies. A republican will usually prefer a team sport for recreation, while a loyalist might pump iron. "They were more interested in doing their whack and trying to get out of jail," boasts John Pickering. "Our system in there was dynamic. You had to invent ways of keeping people focused. And also you wanted to play an active role in the struggle that was going on outside—you can still do that inside through training people inside and also playing an active part in the campaigns on the outside."

In the loyalist wings there is also a drug problem. "Unfortunately—and it actually embarrasses me to say it—there have been a lot of drugs that has reached the prisons as well as the communities at large on the outside," says Marty Snoddon. "There's a lot of prisoners taking these drugs. There's a whole different attitude to drugs than there would have been in my time in prison. Drugs were frowned upon by I would say a hundred percent of the UVF prisoners in Long Kesh." The UVF riot in March 1995 started over a drug search. On the IRA wings, drugs aren't a problem; according to McLaughlan, they simply wouldn't be permitted. Homosexual rape has not yet afflicted the Maze, and it will probably never happen in the republican wings. One loyalist, however, allegedly threatened to assault a prison officer sexually. Loyalists tend to flaunt the relative freedom paramilitary prisoners have in the Maze. Several have cellular telephones and use them quite openly despite the official prohibition.

Republicans appear to have the superior prison culture, but it is not quite that simple. From one perspective, the loyalist prison tradition has had a generation to ripen and actually prosper in the compounds, and has retrogressed in the H-blocks. Certainly in terms of co-opting the prison authority, republicans have the upper hand. The H-blocks clearly do not match loyalists' collective psyche as well as they do the republicans'. Whereas McMurray cherishes the warmth of sharing food in the UVF compounds, William Giles disdains the IRA's communal system in the H-blocks because it makes sharing mandatory. "For loyalists," he says defensively, "it's matter of individual choice."

So, theoretically, is killing. In 1988, during the funeral at Milltown Cemetery for the three IRA volunteers shot dead by the SAS in Gibraltar, UFF freelancer Michael Stone killed three mourners and wounded sixty-eight in a prolonged grenade and gun attack before he was beaten unconscious by the crowd and arrested. Known as "Rambo," Stone quit school at fifteen without qualifications and went to work as a "hammer boy" at Harland and Wolff, guiding a piston onto a huge anvil and developing seventeen-inch biceps, further sculpted by weight lifting in jail, which he proudly displays. He sports a goatee and thick hair that is close-cropped on the sides but falls in a long, frenetic ponytail in the back. Stone's self-image is clearly that of a warrior. His was a suicide mission, and he became a loyalist hero. Naturally, republicans derogate this brand of individualism. Jackie McMullan merely wonders what narcotics Stone was on. But Stone, now serving a life sentence in the Maze, and OC of UDA from east Belfast, does have remorse for his victims, whereas McMullan will reveal none for casualties of republican violence.*

It is far from baseless for Giles to conclude, as he does, that all IRA men are told they are soldiers fighting a war and cannot feel (or at least express) remorse, while loyalist prisoners deal with guilt individually. Giles considers it psychologically impossible not to feel some remorse after killing people. "When you go to bed at night," he says, "you've only got yourself." Loyalists' greater individuality makes them more regretful than republicans. But republicans' greater unity makes them more civilized than loyalists. From a prison administrator's standpoint—from a social standpoint—republicans aren't better. They are merely more savvy.

In grappling with criminalization, loyalists were politically hobbled by more than just the tactical absurdity of aligning themselves with the republicans. When they had special-category status, their means of safeguarding the union was at least partially legitimized, and it was easier for them to coax a wink and nod from the system that they were nominally fighting. And screws undoubtedly treated loyalists better than republicans during the the days of the compounds. Loyalists had the psychological advantage of being favored. Criminalization, though, took away that advantage by saying to them, you're no better than the Provos. The Provos wholeheartedly invited the disdain of the system they unambiguously despised, but the loyalists needed the anodyne of political status to make imprisonment a bearable cost of loyalty. Where criminalization galvanized republicans, it demoralized loyalists. Again, the reason is politics, not inherent weakness.

The blanket protest spiraled into the hunger strikes. The 1981 hunger strike itself then evolved from pressure tactic, with coercion of the British as the objective, into propaganda tool with death, per se, as its end. The republicans were fanatical, perhaps outright brainwashed. They responded sequentially to stimuli from a hated enemy. The loyalists lacked not the capacity but the reason to generate and harness this type of momentum. They did not hate the British, to whom they were supposedly

---

*The standard republican view is that loyalists' contrition is not genuine, and that they express remorse for purely cynical reasons—either to get an earlier release or for good publicity. For a life-sentence prisoner to be released on license, the Life Sentence Review Board requires him to express remorse.

loyal, and couldn't logically even regard their warders as enemies. Loyalists had an equivalent target of hatred in the Provos, but in prison they had no outlet for fighting them. And emotionally, they had much more in common with other prisoners—including IRA men—than with agents of the state. In the H-blocks, loyalist prisoners have felt paralyzed.

All along, they have searched for reasons to be loyal. It has become difficult in recent years. Peter Brooke, Sir Patrick Mayhew's predecessor as secretary of state for Northern Ireland, in November 1990 announced that Britain no longer had any strategic or economic interest in the province, and repeated the point. Mayhew proffered a tepid commitment to the principle of unionist consent, saying that Westminster would present "no obstacle" to a united Ireland as long as unionists agreed to it. Then came the Downing Street declaration, enshrining British neutrality with respect to a united Ireland. Paisley likened Britain-Ulster relations to those between a husband and an estranged wife whom he hasn't the heart to evict but no longer wants to sleep with. Polls show that a majority of mainland voters would like Northern Ireland to remain administratively—if not constitutionally—separate from Great Britain. At this point, Britain can hardly be called an ally. She is simply a guarantor. Loyalists accordingly have had to shift their allegiance from Britain herself to British institutions—a far shakier foundation for the union.

THE SCOURGE OF HISTORY

When asked why he does not want Ulster to become part of the Republic of Ireland, Billy Hutchinson simply says, "Because I'm British." As he proceeds, his tone takes on the petulance born of uncertainty. "If I can draw an analogy with America and Canada, why is everybody in Canada not American? There's a false border between America and Canada, as if somebody drew a line and said this is the border and these are Americans and you're Canadian. It happens all over the world. And I would argue that what republicans or nationalists have to remember is that the whole of the British Isles was under the rule of Britain at one time, we were all British. The twenty-six counties abdicated, dropped out, and the six counties didn't. The twenty-six counties decided to be no longer British, while the six counties decided that they wanted to be British. But I am British—my allegiance is to the British state, rather than to any monarchy or any government."

Hutchinson is forthrightly pointing out that nationality has an emotive element which, although arbitrary and irrational, is inexorable. It is simply there, like a birthmark, and there's no point in questioning its validity or arguing against it. He is not spurious enough to suggest, as republicans like Pickering would, that nationhood has any inherent moral component. Instead, constitutional preference has to do with habit and indoctrination and, consequently, with comfort. Billy Hutchinson grew up being told that British institutions were superior to Irish ones, that his forebears had died in British wars. He felt secure in the knowledge that Northern Ireland had the might of the United Kingdom behind it, and he felt frightened when the Ulster-British connection was threatened by the IRA. Unfortunately, republicans learned just the opposite: that the Catholic-Gaelic culture and traditions embraced by the Irish Free State belonged naturally to northern Catholics as well, yet had always condemned them to penalty at the hands of the British and the Ascendancy Protestants.

Republicans often contend that Ulster Protestants are looked upon as second-class citizens by mainland Brits. Basically, they're right. But on the constitutional question, it doesn't matter even a little: northern Protestants would rather be British than Irish. Ask a welfare mother from Harlem or a shoeless white cracker from Appalachia whether she would just as soon be Canadian as American. Despite her lot, chances are she will say no. As Hutchinson notes, very few of those who call themselves Americans would submit to being called Canadians, much less to becoming Canadians by consenting to have the border redrawn. That is not because they hate Canada or Canadians. It is because they are, irreducibly and nonnegotiably, Americans. Period.

Thus, say the new loyalists, the Ulster conflict—being about nationality—cannot be eliminated or circumvented. At best, it can be transformed from bloodshed into dialogue. Honest as it is, though, Hutchinson's logic leaves republicans cold: I can't be Irish because I've grown up British. He doesn't quite take on board the outrage nationalists feel over *how* the six counties stayed British. Yet he has a strong argument that such outrage is unjustified.

Republicans tend to have a completely self-serving view of partition. Gary Roberts is roughly representative. "But sure, it's an artificial majority. And what they're saying is that we have no say in this country—they're saying that the rest of this country, the majority of the twenty-six counties, have no say in it. You know the unionist population isn't just northeast Ulster, the unionist population was throughout Ireland. They didn't want to accept partition—they wanted all of Ireland to be ruled by

Britain. But in the aftermath of the First World War, they had made such a contribution to the British government—well, that's the story, anyway—that the Brits weren't going to leave them high and dry. They weren't going to put in the Home Rule Bill, they were going to put in partition. The unionist population in the north turned their backs on the unionists down south and left them 'uns to what they wouldn't accept." John Pickering chimes in that partition is "immoral."

To staunch antipartitionists, the creation of Northern Ireland, though ratified with the rest of the Anglo-Irish treaty in January 1922 by the second Dail, was nonetheless a backroom deal orchestrated by a duplicitous British operator (Lloyd George). For this reason, republicans like Pickering, whose grandfather was an old IRA man in the twenties, consider partition "morally wrong." Why do loyalists express no remorse for *that,* they ask? It may be smug to say "because I'm British," but it's not illogical—the parliamentary way, after all, is the British way. As far as loyalists are concerned, partition was democratically arrived at.* The Government of Ireland Act of 1914, as passed by the House of Commons, allowed individual counties to opt out for six years only; the House of Lords amended it to exclude the nine original counties of Ulster forever. An amending bill permitting temporary six-county exclusion was passed by both houses of Parliament in 1914, but had not been given the royal assent needed to make it law. The guns of August preempted a resolution of the matter, which was taken up again after the war and disposed of in due course, following a year of debate, in 1920.[4] Republicans had a chance to voice their opinion, but on account of the abstention policy did not. Unionists did. According to one historian, in abstaining Sinn Fein was "consumed with its sacred egoism," and effectively "collaborated" with the British in bringing about partition.[5]

Roberts's notion that Ulster unionists in some sharp, literal sense betrayed unionists elsewhere is a disingenuous (or perhaps merely whimsically ignorant) attempt to make partition look roundly dishonorable to unionists as well as nationalists. Factually, the claim is ridiculous. Irish unionists had substantially written off keeping the union of Ireland and Britain intact and accepted home rule in principle before the war had even ended (though rhetorically they regarded the concession as "the

---

*To maintain consistency, loyalists would have to concede that the Anglo-Irish Agreement—which was approved by Parliament—also was a legitimate product of democracy. Many do not make this concession, however.

supreme sacrifice"). The most ardent of southern Irish unionists, Sir Edward Carson, had supported an amendment to the 1912 Home Rule Bill excluding four Ulster counties; threatened London with the forcible installment of a "provisional government" in Ulster and established the UVF in 1912; proposed a nine-county exclusion in 1913; agreed to partition with Lloyd George in 1916; and resigned from Lloyd George's cabinet in 1918 only under the specter (transitory, as it turned out) of thirty-two-county home rule.

Unionists were a firm majority in Ulster, but a hopeless minority in the rest of Ireland. Once the House of Lords' veto was curtailed in 1911, the last constitutional obstacle to home rule had been removed. At this point—long before Sinn Fein supplanted the Irish Parliamentary Party as the voice of Irish nationalism in 1918—most unionists north and south recognized that wholesale unionist resistance to home rule would inevitably collapse under the democratic weight of the nationalist majority. While Carson originally conceived of Ulster resistance in 1912 as a blocking tactic that might cow Parliament into dropping home rule for good, by the end of 1913 even he realized that it lacked the democratic potency and integrity to accomplish any such thing. It is for precisely this reason that statutory partition was mooted so early in the game. In 1920, northern unionists hardly "turned their backs" on anyone. After a protracted fight, they simply took, politically, what they could get with other unionists' wistful blessings.[6]

Northern constitutional nationalists today are in a position broadly analogous to that of the Ulster unionists in 1920: faced with democratic realities, they reluctantly accept the principle of unionist consent, just as the Ulster unionists grudgingly conceded twenty-six-county home rule. In rejecting the consent principle, republicans have refused to embrace the majoritarian considerations that southern unionists accepted when they deferred to their Ulster brethren at partition. It is, therefore, the hypocrisy and intransigence of republicans, not unionists, that are so galling in the fullness of history.

Loyalists can close the historical argument there. Their position still doesn't satisfy republicans. The only tenable historical argument left to republicans is that they didn't have any real political clout until after de facto partition had occurred in 1914. Factually, that is true: Sinn Fein's populist appeal didn't ripen until the Easter Rising in 1916, and the party was not electorally empowered until the elections of 1917 and 1918. It is also irrelevant. Three indisputable facts remain. First, the six-county partition contemplated in the amendment to the Government of Ireland Act of 1914 was the democratic product of parliamentary debate among unionists, mainland parties, and the *nonabstaining* nationalists of the Irish Parliamentary Party; the latter were democratically elected representatives of the Irish people, and their bargaining power was sufficient to win home rule for the southern twenty-six counties. Second, Sinn Fein in 1919 had substantial representation in the British parliament; in abstaining, it forsook the "last clear chance" to maneuver around partition when the new home rule bill was being debated in 1919 and 1920. Third, the Dail approved partition by ratifying the treaty. Twice Sinn Fein and the IRA chose war rather than British *or Irish* parliamentary politics to thwart partition. Twice they failed.

Today's republicans must resort to the fundamentally nonhistorical claim that Northern Ireland embodies a rigged Protestant majority that trumps the will of other Irishmen. Yet the idea that Northern Ireland has an artificial majority is true only in the trivial sense that any polity that decides to bound itself and become a nation has an artificial majority of those who favor nationhood. In that light, the fact that unionists in 1920 decided to drop the three of Ulster's original counties that were most heavily Catholic to maintain Protestant dominance is neither surprising nor especially noteworthy. Republicans, however, contend that partition doomed majoritarian democracy by signaling future generations of Protestants that the perpetuation of their state required unified unionist voting, thereby guaranteeing that the two communities would always vote tribally and making both the Protestant majority and the Catholic minority permanent. This argument assumes its own conclusion by equating constitutional irreconcilability in 1920 with subconstitutional irreconcilability in 1996. That is, those who make the argument are really saying that groups who do not agree about the border cannot agree about anything else that matters politically.

The republican position also ignores the fact that the troubles only drove Catholics and Protestants farther apart by artificially heightening the importance of the border. With guns silent, the two communities will inevitably inch closer together and create more common ground. However just or unjust partition might have been three-quarters of a century ago, since then three generations of Protestants have grown up in Northern Ireland thinking, acting, and feeling British. People alive today are the ones who matter *now*. Republicans cannot sweep them away merely by crying foul play. Partition was political. It was amoral, not immoral.

So: loyalists feel compelled to revere the British system because it got them the statelet that their ancestors insisted on. To avoid the appearance of pure power politics, though, they couch their argument in metaphysical terms. "What I'm saying is, no matter what the Republic of Ireland would do—you know, if they painted the place red, white, and blue, and gave me an extra forty pound a week—I still wouldn't be interested in living in a united Ireland," says Hutchinson. "That's what I'm saying. See, no matter what they do, the Catholic church and the Irish government can't make the Irish Republic any more acceptable. I'm interested in living in the United Kingdom and remaining a part of Britain."

Republicans rightly answer that the argument begs the question of how Stormont and its remnants treated nationalists. To this Hutchinson has a fairly conciliatory response. "My political allegiance is to Britain," he says, "but I was born in the northeastern part of Ireland, which geographically makes me Irish. A Scotsman says he's Scottish, but he's British. If somebody asked me what my nationality was, I would say I was Irish, I would say I was British. You can't say the Giant's Causeway* is British—you know, the Giant's Causeway is part of Irish history and Irish culture and Irish mythology, and I accept that. Yet people feel more British now than they ever did because of the IRA campaign, and a lot of people feel more Irish now because of the loyalist campaign against them. So we actually have overemphasized our Irishness and our Britishness." But he adds a cruel kicker. "We all live in the British Isles; why can't we have friendly relationships?"

Republicans don't want to be part of anything known as the "British Isles." Their distaste for the adjective "British" is as visceral as loyalists' affection for it, and they see loyalism as The Big Lie. Tommy Gorman on loyalist prisoners: "There's all this stuff on the walls—it's a wee dog pissing on a lamppost. Marking out their territory, you know? That strikes me as being very fucking immature. You have these loyalist murals inside prison, and they've got 'Loyalist Prisoners' written all over the place, tattoos. I mean, you've got big fucking tattoos and stuff all over the walls.† I don't know, they seem to have an identity crisis or something like that, where they have to say, I am, I am, I am, I am, you know."

---

*A spectacular natural geologic formation on the north coast of County Antrim.

†Incidentally, Tommy Gorman does have on his arms tattoos of a cross with superimposed anchor and heart (for faith, hope, and charity), an eagle's head, and "Mother." He got them in the merchant navy. They have nothing to do with republicanism.

Most loyalists do have several tattoos of paramilitary insignias or loyalist slogans. IRA men as a rule do not. Gorman is probably correct that loyalists have to remind themselves what their politics are more than republicans do, as they are the less politicized of the two groups. But he also has a problem with the substance of what they claim to be their Protestant identity. "This isn't to downgrade any Protestant or anything, but I have trouble finding out what their culture is. They keep talking about their individual culture—I can't find it, I don't know what it is. What's the difference between their culture and English culture, or their culture and the Scottish culture? I find it strange, because the people who we look back to, sort of the fathers of republicanism, were all Presbyterian. Most of them were ministers who fought against the British in the eighteenth century: 1780, 1798—Wolf Tone, Henry Joy McCracken, all great Presbyterians. They were the people who seen that the only way you were going to get peace and unite Irishmen, Protestant, Catholic, and Dissenter, was to get the Brits out. I just want to know what happened in between times. Presbyterians nowadays would burn fucking Catholics at the stake."

Gorman's rant is somewhat *ad hominem*—he ascribes Paisley's bigotry to all Presbyterians—but he has a small point. Two of Ireland's greatest nationalists—Theobald Wolf Tone and Charles Stewart Parnell, not to mention literary types like William Butler Yeats—were Protestant. The Brits historically abused Presbyterians along with Catholics during penal times (1695–1829) and regard the contemporary Protestant working class (substantially Presbyterian) as second-class citizens. Why, indeed, should non-Ascendancy Prods feel beholden to the British?

If only working-class solidarity between Catholics and Protestants were that simple. Even from a nationalist point of view, Britain and the Protestant Ascendancy co-opted Presbyterians gradually with preferential treatment through the nineteenth century ultimately *on account of* Wolf Tone's 1798 rebellion. Presbyterians won the right to participate in politics some fifty years earlier than Catholics. In the nineteenth century, Ascendancy business owners bought Presbyterian votes with employment. By 1911, Protestants constituted 76 percent of Belfast's population and held 90 percent of the city's industrial jobs.[7] With this, Presbyterians had little more to complain about. Furthermore, Brit-assisted industrialization to a degree insulated Ulster against the famine, and northern Protestants came to attribute their economic good fortunes to Britain. Catholic emancipation and the home-rule movement threatened the union. Trade and war fostered economic and strategic interdependence between Ulster and

Britain. By the time partition came about, there was nothing to recommend nationalism to working-class Protestants. Gorman's little polemic skips these steps, and, in unfortunately typical republican fashion, sanctions an atavistic grudge.

In addition, Ulster Protestants do have a distinct culture, benign and noble as anyone else's. It extends far beyond the jingoism and pomp of the Orange Order, the Ascendancy elitism of Stormont, and the droning "border question" itself. They are ascetic and orderly, and proud of their vaunted work ethic. They value stability as a backdrop for industry. This characteristic translates into a social and political conservatism: Ulster Protestants prefer to keep things the way they have been. They emphasize duty and honor to enduring institutions and pay corresponding attention to tradition and ceremony. Thus, they exalt the British monarchy and, almost to the point of caricature, revere those Ulstermen who died in Her Majesty's service. Historically, they have not shared northern Catholics' defiant sense of being oppressed. The Anglo-Irish Agreement gave them a taste of victimhood by evidencing British abandonment. Nevertheless, due to the more entrenched feelings of loyalty, northern Prods tend to suppress the reality that they are not treated like full partners in the United Kingdom. They choose instead to believe that their fidelity to the Crown will eventually earn them the esteem they deserve.

At the same time, of course, both Protestants and Catholics in Ulster have defined themselves repeatedly and cumulatively in bold, ugly strokes which have often overwhelmed their more respectable features. The sectarian geography of Ulster has changed very little in three hundred years. This stasis is both the cause and the effect of the historical struggle over political power: blood has invested land with a territorial imperative, and vice versa. Young Northern Irish men and women today may recollect of the troubles only the Shankill bomb and the Milltown Cemetery massacre, but the importance of these events to them will be monumental because of the countless incidents of violence that occurred on the Shankill and on the Falls long ago. It's no wonder some of the loyalist prisoners Gorman talks about had a hard time spotting the nuggets of their heritage in this gravel of tribal memory.

Unfortunately, so have some of their "betters." To support Glen Barr's idea of an independent Ulster—which is quite consistent with the Ulster Protestant culture—some unionists have recently trotted out the historical contention that the Gaels were not the first settlers of Ireland, but instead displaced the pictish "Cruthin," who evolved into the Scots and returned during the seventeenth-century plantations to reclaim lands they had occupied first a thousand years earlier.[8] This scenario—which, by the way, appears to be largely true—is designed to take colonialism out of the troubles with the revelation that Ulster Scots got here first after all. In this feature, the loyalist intellectual initiative is sincerely, but indisputably, naive. The structural flaw is that it attempts to impose an ancient historical justification on a modern historical circumstance. Epochal shifts in population are not timeless claims of right; some principle of repose cuts off any such claims. Virtually all history is a chain of domination and submission, and unless there is some temporal limit to the equities of ownership, Scandinavians and Frenchmen as well as Brits and Irishmen will be laying claim to Ulster.

Nationalists carry analogously irrelevant baggage. Some will claim that the Gaels having preceded the Normans in Ireland yields the twenty-six counties a right to Ulster. Patrick Pearse ingenuously dredged up non sequiturs like the Red Branch saga cycle (c. 200 A.D., and myth rather than history, anyway) and the O'Neill rebellions (c. 1600) as counterweights to the reality of Ulster unionism.[9] There is enough mixed ancestry in Northern Ireland to make the notion of "first in time, first in right" hopelessly unworkable. While both the Cruthin and the Gaelic legends may well provide a rich vein to tap for Protestant and Catholic cultural identity in Ulster, they have no promise as political resolutions. Neither does Gorman's point about Presbyterians. When smugly presented to silence the other side, these observations simply demonstrate what Steve Bruce calls "the sad pointlessness of historical nitpicking."[10] They miss the main point: partition happened. Like it or not, it is a colonial problem. Independence, if it worked at all, would work only as a solution to the border issue. But it provides no vindication for a people that has been transformed almost beyond recognition from the plantation days when English and Scottish Protestants ousted Gaelic Catholics.

NEW LEAVES: POST-CEASEFIRE LOYALISM

Loyalists as well as republicans have selected history and used it as a basis for maintaining the opposition between Catholics and Protestants. The difference is in spin. Republicans scroll out a heritage of valiant rebellion that seems to justify the division between Protestants and Catholics. Unionists' vehicle of history has been primarily the Orange Order and like organizations such as the Apprentice Boys of Derry. Although religious and civil liberty is a stated concern of these groups, owing to the political climate of Ulster the organizations have functioned along effectively anti-Catholic lines. Accordingly, "modern unionism" has presented mainly a history of sectarian intolerance itself that makes the division between Catholics and Protestants look like the perpetuation of a tradition that was ignoble to begin with.

Loyalist groups dominate the so-called "marching season," which lasts from April through September. In 1995, republican parades numbered only 285 province-wide, but loyalist institutions* staged 2,508 marches.[11] The ratio—now almost ten to one in favor of the loyalist organizations—used to be even higher. Orangemen like Chris McGimpsey argue that "it's just our community celebrating itself, the other side never come into it." Understandably, it often does not feel that way to Catholics. It does not seem unreasonable for Catholics living on the lower Ormeau Road to ask the Orange Order to reroute their parades away from the scene of a UFF massacre, yet the Order has insensitively refused to do so. (The RUC had to force some of the parades to detour in 1995 and 1996.)

Virtually every loyalist ex-prisoner admits that the three main Protestant organizations are sectarian, exclusionary, and triumphalist. Alex Calderwood, among others, has learned that tribalism has duped Ulster into needless self-destruction. "People believe that the conflict in Northern Ireland is a religious thing, and it's not. Theologies may disagree, but the reality is that a practicing Catholic and a practicing Protestant will not do each other any harm. My views now would be completely different than they were years ago. I know how to define a Protestant now, and on the Shankill Road I can see at least three different types of Protestants, because there's a tribal Protestant, a political Protestant, and a Biblical Protestant. I believe that two of those three are counterfeit—the tribal and the political. Exactly the same goes for Catholics."

Calderwood's point is that in terms of religious doctrine and practice, Catholics and Protestants are not terribly different—certainly not so different as to preclude peaceful coexistence. After all, Catholics and Protestants get along virtually everywhere else in the world. Most Christians are merely "Biblical"; their religion does not strictly govern their politics or social groupings. In Northern Ireland, it does. Thus, Calderwood beholds "political" and "tribal" Protestants and Catholics. The corresponding po-

---

*The Orange Order, the Royal Black Preceptory, and the Apprentice Boys of Derry.

litical and tribal alignments started with disagreements about religious doctrine in the seventeenth century and before. Long ago, however, they turned into conflicts over bad blood itself—fights about earlier fights. Theological differences caused the original bloodbaths, but not the vestigial ones that came later. Yet the religious alignments endured. Thus, Catholics hate Protestants because of Cromwell and Greysteel, and not because Protestants disdain confession. Likewise, Protestants hate Catholics because of the 1641 rebellion and the Shankill bomb, and not because Catholics believe in transsubstantiation. That is Northern Irish tribalism in a nutshell.

Tribal institutions like the Orange Order only perpetuate the problem, and Calderwood and other prison alumni would just as soon do away with them. Owing partly to its close and continuous alignment with the middle-class Ulster Unionist Party, the Orange Order has generally crowded out working-class elements. The organization also expelled anyone arrested for paramilitary involvement, so most loyalist ex-prisoners have little affection for it. Marty Snoddon considers the Orange Order "a spent force" that has "not done anything to benefit the working-class Protestant people." Plum Smith likewise believes it has "outlived its usefulness."

Yet the Protestant mainstream repudiates loyalist violence, and therefore has a distorted assessment of the balance of fault. This mechanism of denial is what enables the Orange Order to protest its innocence in the ongoing controversy over marches through a Catholic stretch of the Ormeau Road. They say "we did nothing," yet blame republican violence on the entire Catholic community and not just the IRA or Sinn Fein. They do not accord the Catholic community the same right to disown its violence that they claim for themselves, even though only about 25 percent of the Catholic population supports Sinn Fein. What has materialized from this gestalt is a sort of Maginot Line of stiffly and unimaginatively defiant Protestantism which, from a public relations standpoint, republicans have successfully perforated.

But now the loyalist ex-prisoners that lead the fringe parties are slowly abandoning reactionary Protestantism and the chauvinistic Protestant traditions. Notwithstanding the military hierarchy in loyalist prison culture, loyalist leadership did not pressure prisoners to think uniformly or take courses in furtherance of unionist doctrine or tradition. Though communal in form and approach, republican leadership aggressively encouraged group-think. Somewhat paradoxically, therefore, loyalist compound culture yielded greater individuality in loyalists than the H-blocks did in republicans. While most republican prisoners took social sciences courses in jail, loyalists chose far more varied curricula. This divergence seems to have yielded in loyalist ex-prisoners a greater degree of open-mindedness than republicans have shown. Gusty Spence on Ian Paisley: "Whenever a person makes a statement at his party conference that Catholic women are incubators for Rome, it's grossly offensive to everyone—a little pup would take offense at it, you know; it's not even human. This is a man who loves his Catholic neighbors?"

Spence and his followers have also grasped an obvious fact which the rest of the Protestant working class is only now beginning to entertain: that Paisley, populist that he may be, did them no great service. "The DUP was shrewd enough to know that if they challenged unionism, they would have to be [constitutionally] more extreme than unionism itself, or they'd have no hope of electoral success," says Spence. "The politics of right, left, and center has never been allowed to develop." Here, for once, there is a constructive dimension in an Ulsterman's historical memory. Whereas Tommy Gorman might urge the predominantly Presbyterian working class to recall how the Ascendancy disenfranchised Dissenters in penal times, Spence suggests instead that they look at how Paisley more recently has left their right to political power effectively unfulfilled. Plum Smith fleshes out Spence's view: "When our politicians went up for office in elections, the issues weren't housing or social issues or welfare issues. The issue was the border. The thing is that ordinary Protestants had no one to speak for them. And when people accuse the Protestant Ascendancy of misrule and all, we feel offended because we didn't rule anything."

Loyalists are also ditching the myth that after partition Protestants in the south were mistreated.* Instead, their argument for a continued

---

*Before partition, Protestants made up 10 percent of the south's population. Open IRA hostility forced a great many Protestants to flee the south after the civil war of 1922–23, but by the mid-twenties the emigration rate of Catholics and Protestants had equaled out. Thereafter, it was primarily the relative youth of the Catholic population and mixed marriages that eroded the Protestant population in the Republic to its current 3 percent. Yet Protestants still own a disproportionate percentage of Ireland's farmland and are overrepresented in professional and managerial occupations. Comments former taoiseach Garret FitzGerald: "The simple fact is that where a well-endowed minority is small enough not to be seen as a threat by the majority, the advantages that for historical reasons it may enjoy are not likely to be contested." See "Statistics Show Protestants Enjoying Privileged Lifestyle in the Republic," *Belfast Telegraph,* December 13, 1995, p. 17. Of course, were the Protestant minority to rise to 25 percent upon reunification, Catholic resentment could set in.

union rests on an incipient blue-collar politics which holds that the whole working class would get a raw deal in a united Ireland. "The south is just a mirror image of the north," says Smith. "One of them's a Protestant polity that's supposed to be for a Protestant people, and one is a Catholic polity for a Catholic people. Middle-class Catholics ruled the south in the same way that the Protestant upper classes ruled the north. And that was to keep the working class down, and you know, let them die whenever there weren't profits to come out of the factories. So there was a class thing, but tribalism was used all the way around. Being part of Ireland does no favors for the working class in both communities, because all you're doing is swapping orange tories for green tories."

The new loyalists exhibit some understanding even towards republicans. "They believe that they're trying to liberate their country," says Billy Mitchell. "I happen to disagree with them, but I mean, if it's okay for me to shoot you for political reasons, then I can't object to you shooting me for political reasons. What I've got to work for today is when neither of the two of us shoot each other. I'm not asking republicans to give up their aspirations. All I'm saying is that we don't believe in conflict resolution. We don't believe you can resolve this polarity of republicanism and unionism, but we do believe you can transform conflict from violence to dialogue."

There remains in loyalism a strong overlay of defensive British nationalism that Hutchinson displays. At the same time, the new loyalists—including Hutchinson himself—are more receptive than they once were to Irish nationalism as a cultural and political force in Ulster. Listen to Mitchell again. "You are what you are," Mitchell reflects. "Just because the unionist Ascendancy was corrupt, that's no reason to give up your nationality. As we progressed into modern socialism, then we were able to identify with the working-class people of England and the Scots. Also, historically, the cream of our forefathers gave their lives on two battlefields, two European theaters of war, for the British Crown. So it's hard for a man to say, I want to disengage from everything that my forefathers lived or died for. The Protestant working class today aren't simply who we are now. In Ulster here we've been molded by Calvinism in the religious sense, we've been molded by unionism, we've been molded by all the ties of Ulster Scots heritage and culture. We've been molded by English influences. And we've been molded by Gaelic and Irish influences, you know; we can't deny that. What we're really doing at the moment, we're sitting down and analyzing our past and our present, and getting rid of the bad baggage and keeping the good baggage."

Neither Hutchinson nor Mitchell would go quietly to a united Ireland. But both claim, on the record, to respect nationalist aspirations sufficiently to accede to the will of a nationalist majority in Northern Ireland—should one ever materialize. The shelving of Orangeism and a more sympathetic view of the south and of republicanism on the part of these new loyalists should enable them to present their case for the union less encumbered by sectarian anachronisms, and less vulnerable to republican bombast. On these merits, the Protestant community could have mounted a far better defense to the republicans than they did during the troubles. In their "abject and true remorse," perhaps the loyalists are apologizing not only for the over nine hundred deaths they've caused, but also for taking so long to realize how strong their political position really is.

Partition wasn't just a gift, it was as hard-earned as the Free State. The notion first caught light in the wake of the Wolf Tone rebellion, and after the first home rule bill was introduced in 1886 it continued unabated until it was a reality.[12] Similarly, loyalism has always been premised on the distinct culture that Ulster Scots have had throughout modern Irish history, and therefore conditioned on Britain's recognition of the same. Loyalists now apprehend a cultural heritage that extends far deeper than the pageantry of the Orange Order, and feel justified in insisting that dismissive republicans like Tommy Gorman take that on board. If the hunger strikes of 1980–81 recalled the blood sacrifice of the Easter Rising of 1916, then the muscular 1974 Ulster Workers Council strike equally harked back to the UVF's massive mobilization against home rule in 1914. In terms of *relevant* pre-partition history, call the contest between nationalists and unionists a standoff.

After partition, the unionists blew it with Stormont, and the new loyalists admit it. A lazy, unchallenged government looked the other way when Orangemen taunted Catholics on the 12th of July, gangs beat up kids who couldn't sing *God Save the Queen,* and employers kept "Taigs" off the payroll. Now the new loyalists are testifying that this would not happen again. They are asking the nationalist community to give unionism a chance to make amends.

CHAPTER 6

FOLK HEROES

A CREDIT TO THE REBEL COMMUNITY

Both republican and loyalist ex-prisoners consistently attest that prison gave them an ideal political vantage point as well as educational opportunities they would not have exploited on the outside. On the one hand, prisoners had been deeply involved in carrying the fight; on the other, they had been sidelined and forced to make constructive use of their time in jail. Their room and board were taken care of by Her Majesty. Prisoners were able, therefore, to see the troubles unfold with literal detachment, but without distraction and without losing their interest. The result was a far more mature view of the nationalist-unionist debate than the paramilitaries had going in. IRA men came to see their fight as primarily (though excessively) against the British rather than against Ulster's Protestant majority, while loyalists realized that they had grievances against the Protestant Ascendancy as well as the IRA. It is no accident that the IRA's ceasefire came only after its older prisoners had debated and tested the direction of republicanism for years, or that since the loyalist ceasefire Protestant ex-prisoners rather than middle-class unionist politicians have voiced the most conciliatory attitude toward nationalists.

There are, of course, some differences. Whereas the Protestant community generally eschews the loyalist paramilitaries, the nationalist community tends to regard members of the IRA as folk heroes. Recidivism among fixed-sentence republican prisoners, like Tommy Gorman, who went to jail four separate times, was rather high. Joe Clarke was on active service for over twenty years after being interned. Before they were sentenced to life, McIntyre and Pickering were repeat offenders. Yet they were never ostracized.

"'Recidivism,'" snickers McMullan—"There seems to be some sort of criminal undertone to that term. The community here, they wouldn't see it like that. And if you can get past that and understand that, well then you'd be better able to comprehend the differences between here and America. You know, in America I imagine that people who have been in prison and ex-prisoners would be sort of social outcasts and would be treated with mistrust. That isn't the case here amongst our own communities, and there has never been any break in the bond between ourselves and the communities in which we live."

The difference between republicans and nonpolitical offenders does lie in political motivation. Indeed, after the intense politicization of the H-block protest and the hunger strikes, ex-prisoners' reinvolvement in illegal paramilitary activity increased in spite of the stiffer penalties that had come with criminalization.

Recidivism among paroled life-sentence prisoners, on the other hand, is virtually nil. This is partly because their "license" makes them subject to reincarceration without trial and therefore more susceptible to breaking under interrogation, partly because the paramilitary organizations consider them too conspicuous to be useful, and because released lifers don't want to jeopardize the chances of release for those still inside. But ex-lifers' capacity to stay clean is perhaps just as substantially due to their inclination to wind up in school, politics, or community work, which Sinn Fein encourages.

Leo Green, Jackie McMullan, Donncha O'Hara, and John Pickering all work for Sinn Fein. Green and McMullan head the POW department, and participate regularly in public debates and seminars. O'Hara is a press officer. Pickering was sent to San Francisco to testify on behalf of four republican prisoners, now facing extradition back to Northern Ireland, who escaped from the Maze in 1983. Anthony McIntyre, though a dissenting voice, has lent Sinn Fein his brain upon occasion, and is writing his doctoral dissertation on Irish republicanism since 1969. His cellmate and one of his closest friends from jail, Laurence McKeown, a hunger striker who lasted seventy-one days without food, is writing his Ph.D. thesis on republican education in prison—also at Queen's University of Belfast, in the sociology department. Carol Cullen has two children to care for—like many women in the Catholic working class, she was a single parent before she reached twenty—but has opened up a community advice center for republican ex-prisoners on the Falls Road. Again, Tommy Gorman—probably the most energetic of the bunch—runs the Springfield Inter-community Development Project with Billy Hutchinson. Kevin McQuillan is a paramedic, and chairman of the Springfield Park Residents

Association, which is active in cross-community reconciliation on the peace line.

Much of this activity is voluntary (Sinn Fein, for example, doesn't pay ex-prisoners a wage), and many former prisoners draw public aid. But they do not fit the Andy Capp stereotype of the working-class bloke on the dole—they would be unlikely to drink all day, gamble away their money, or sit idly while their wives and mothers work. The anti-establishment twist to their activities is often snide. Gerry Adams outraged unionists in 1994 when he applied for public legal aid to fight a denial of unemployment benefits, claiming he was just an unemployed barman. Republicans remain political animals, accepted in their communities.

Even before the ceasefires, the republican tradition was to serve one's time in an IRA active service unit, do a stretch in Long Kesh, and then go legitimate in Sinn Fein. Gerry Adams and Martin McGuinness are typical examples. Thus, loyalists concede that the nationalist community is better able to certify its ex-paramilitaries as political leaders because that community subsumes a "prison culture" that the unionist community has never had. In the Protestant community, ex-prisoners are commonly ostracized. The working-class Catholic community has been more widely traumatized by the troubles—in particular, by the aggressive methods used by the army and the police, like internment and an unacknowledged but sporadically evident shoot-to-kill policy. The security forces have killed some 167 Catholic civilians, versus only twenty-three Protestants, over the past twenty-five years.

Nationalists also have a long history of revolt, whereas loyalists do not. Republican ex-prisoners, then, take their acceptance back into their communities to be an affirmation of their cause. "Our communities are constructed of people who are ex-prisoners, who are family members of ex-prisoners," says Carol Cullen. "It's no different, it's no big deal. The IRA could not have kept up the campaign without the cooperation and indeed the support from these communities, but they need to move on now."

Ex-prisoners have not always been so well integrated. The split between the Provisional IRA and the Official IRA occurred partly as a result of community disgust with the pre-split IRA's unimpressive performance as neighborhood guardians during the disturbances on the lower Falls in August 1969. Only during the hunger strikes, in strongly republican areas like north and west Belfast, did the IRA replace the church in popular perception as the preferred source of protection for Catholics.

"I think the hunger strikes destroyed any sort of aspirations I had towards the Catholic church," says Carol Cullen. "The hunger strikes literally changed all people's lives.* I resented the Catholic church for letting the men and women in jail rot. I actually resented [then Archbishop, later Cardinal] Cahal Daly and his cohorts telling hunger strikers, there are other hunger strikers dying. The whole republican movement was trying to change the conditions inside jails through hunger strikes, and a massive amount of people supported their demands. But the Catholic church, along with the British government, kept calling them criminals. The Catholic church collaborated with the British government, and that was really low. I can remember standing on the Antrim Road at a Youths Against H-blocks protest and the RUC beating fifteen-, sixteen-year-olds and the priests literally walking past them and doing nothing to help them. I became totally disillusioned with them. It was a myth that they were the people who had the standing and the power in the community, and that's why I was so disappointed—I thought they could do something, and their attitude was just, be a Catholic. They had power because we had given them special status and a special place, but as an organization they didn't get anything done. I just lost the whole urge to go to Mass."

The IRA's present role as enforcer of community mores is strong evidence that it has displaced most other mechanisms of social control in Catholic working-class areas. Brendan Hughes, like Cullen, McIntyre, McMullan, and Pickering, is "a lapsed Catholic. I'm totally antagonistic towards the Catholic hierarchy. I am very, very suspicious of Catholic priests. I respect people who are genuinely religious. I reject people who call themselves religious and stand and watch injustice. They can be pious and religious and preach all the charity to the world, and stand and watch another man being oppressed, another woman being oppressed." The IRA and Sinn Fein, of course, did nothing of the sort. While Gerry Adams is outwardly a devout Catholic—apparently he attends Mass regularly—he opposes Church orthodoxy insofar as it will not qualify the republican armed struggle as a "just war."

Hughes is forty-eight, Cullen thirty-two. The 1981 hunger strike produced a radical, multigenerational shift towards a secular brand of republicanism in the entire Catholic community. The republican movement acquired a moral dimension and force of conscience that it had not previously had. As Fionnuala O'Connor puts it, "the upheaval of the

---

*A telling manifestation of Cullen's insularity. To her, "all people" means Belfast Catholics.

hunger strike renewed the IRA's roots in the Northern Catholic soul with fresh grievance and sense of isolation."[1] Cullen was barely seventeen years old when Bobby Sands began his fast. Her parents were passive nationalists. Although they were rarely employed, she was earning excellent grades in secondary school, passed six O-levels and two A-levels, was admitted to art school, and seemed to have a realistic chance of bettering her station. On account of the H-block protests, though, she completely lost interest in traditional advancement. She joined the IRA in 1982 and stayed on "active service" until she was arrested in January 1989, caught red-handed trying to blow up an RUC station in the town of Crumlin, County Antrim.

The hunger strikes not only increased the IRA's recruiting strength in Northern Ireland, they also broadened it geographically. In March 1981, Ella O'Dwyer was twenty-two and an English literature student at University College, Dublin. She had come from a rural village in County Tipperary, some two hundred miles from Belfast, which she has never visited. Her father worked in a meat-packing plant, and struggled to make ends meet for his family of nine. Despite her working-class roots,[2] she remained essentially apolitical like the rest of her family, and knew little about the troubles or the constitutional question when growing up. Her aim was to extend her horizons beyond her trappings, and she went to Denmark and Germany to earn money to pay for college. As a student, she developed sympathy with republicans by way of the H-block marches and demonstrations in Dublin during the second hunger strike. Thereafter, her interest in republicanism as a political movement piqued, O'Dwyer traced Ireland's poverty to British colonialism.

In 1982, like Cullen, O'Dwyer joined the Provisional IRA. She was arrested in Glasgow in 1985 and fingered as a member of the active service unit that tried to kill Margaret Thatcher, and did kill five others, in Brighton. Though the Crown prosecution couldn't connect her to that operation, she was convicted of conspiracy to cause explosions and sentenced to life imprisonment. She spent ten years in British jails, and was transferred to H.M.P. Maghaberry in Northern Ireland in 1994. O'Dwyer is a strikingly pretty woman—her lush red hair, a sprinkling of freckles, and delicate features conjure cinematic images of milkmaid "colleens." She will spend the prime of her life and more in prison. Four years ago, while he was still inside, she married Jackie McMullan by special arrangement. They never spent a night together. Yet Ella O'Dwyer claims she does not regret her choice and is not angry over her circumstances. "There are some things I can't do, but they can wait," she says, blushing. "I'm happy with my choice, and happy I can contribute to the struggle." Such is the renewed strength of the republican tradition of sacrifice.

That tradition is continually reinforced, regardless of the ceasefires. During 1995, the three biggest legal news stories in Northern Ireland were Private Lee Clegg's appeal and release; the European Court of Human Rights' 10-to-9 decision that SAS commandos illegally used excessive force in 1988 when they gunned down three unarmed IRA volunteers in Gibraltar on a bombing reconnaissance operation, violating their "right to life"; and the inquest into the 1987 incident in Loughgall, where the SAS ambushed eight Provos who were trying to blow up an RUC station and shot all of them (plus one innocent passerby) dead. Each story involved republican martyrdom in one form or another.

Clegg was a life sentence prisoner out in four years, while IRA lifers generally serve at least fourteen years. The three dead Provos in Gibraltar included Daniel McCann, a former blanketman, and Mairead Farrell, one of three Armagh jail hunger strikers who joined the men's fast in 1981; the third, Sean Savage, was shot repeatedly after he was down, taking sixteen of the twenty-seven bullets fired. The eight IRA men who died in Loughgall were some of the organization's most experienced guerrillas; the fact that the security forces had been tipped off and laid in wait made the Provos seem more like victims than terrorists caught, as they were, *in flagrante delicto.* Both the Gibraltar and the Loughgall proceedings revived nationalist outrage over the security forces' apparent "shoot-to-kill" policy.

While the republicans' propaganda sense is very sharp indeed, the principal reasons behind their folk-hero status are structural. First, the IRA was fighting a far stronger foe with a palpable tradition of bullying and severity towards its many colonies which it tended not to acknowledge. "The security forces were a bunch of sneaks," says Andy Tyrie. "When they were doing the shoot-to-kill policy, they should have said, from Monday morning, if you want to be a paramilitary and you turn up with a gun somewhere, we'll shoot you. They didn't do that, and they tried to deny there was a shoot-to-kill policy when there had to be a shoot-to-kill policy. You know, they said there is no shoot-to-kill policy but they were not such big sneaks that anybody believed them."

Second, the loyalist paramilitaries rarely came up against the security forces head-to-head, having lost only thirteen members to the police and army during the troubles, versus the republicans' 141. Because they are not loyalist targets, the police and army do not have as great an operational incentive to seek out loyalist terrorists as republican ones. The security forces also pay less attention to loyalists because they do not pose a direct threat to the state. But nationalists tally it all up to collusion. They have some reason to do so. In 1989 the UFF revealed that it possessed official files on suspected IRA men, and the ensuing Stevens Enquiry traced leaks to several UDR members. Such revelations *ex proprio vigore* preserve the IRA's status as defenders of their community. And they are fine grist for Sinn Fein's public relations mill.*

SINN FEIN: IMAGE VERSUS REALITY

After the ceasefires, IRA misdeeds faded into the background, while perceived transgressions of the security forces against the IRA did not—much to the benefit of the republican image. Loyalists can't compete because they cannot credibly claim persecution. Moreover, the Protestant community looks upon the loyalist paramilitaries as a sort of "Dad's army" run amok, and concedes the Provos' professional and ideological superiority. "I used to say to them, you know, give me any Protestant paramilitary who's prepared to get out and lie in a ditch for two weeks living on tins," says Glen Barr. "The Provos can do that, you know. Youse boys have had it far too easy. Unless you have that sort of commitment to your cause, then, you know, it's just a pastime for you. The Provos are totally committed and dedicated. You know, you take the Provos, you take them into jail—the political education those guys get! How many times do they pull these guys out of a hat and all of a sudden stick them in front of a television, and these guys can quite eloquently put forward the Provo case?"

---

*Nevertheless, security force collusion with loyalist paramilitaries appears to have been aberrational rather than institutional, and has usually been perpetrated by low-level misfits or renegades. (See Steve Bruce, *The Red Hand* [Oxford: Oxford University Press, 1992], pp. 199–225.) RUC officers generally will not look the other way when they find out about a past or planned loyalist hit. It is rumored that when the father of a UVF suspect boasted to RUC officers he presumed to be sympathetic that he had blown up McGurk's Bar in 1971—"the big one," he called it—they arrested him and put him away. Just before the loyalist ceasefire, RUC men roused Gary Roberts and his family at five in the morning and moved him to a safe house, on the basis of intelligence that the UFF was planning to execute him. In 1994, the RUC staged an elaborate operation to gather evidence against the elusive Johnny "Mad Dog" Adair, UFF commander and allegedly the Shankill bomb's specific target. Thinking RUC officers were at heart comrades-in-arms, Adair jocularly told covertly wired uniformed policemen to "shove your dove." They put him away for sixteen years for directing terrorism.

Barr recalls that in the late seventies the UDA tried to politicize the rank and file by appointing political education officers. "It was quite a revolution," he cracks sarcastically. UDA prisoners attempting to match the IRA inmates' first hunger strike in 1980 lasted five days. As Robert Cooper and Ron McMurray suggest, law-abiding unionists will not openly support the UVF and the UFF, but some privately cringe at their failures. One Protestant from Suffolk remembers his mother's classically ambivalent reaction to the UFF's botched attempt to kill Gerry Adams in 1984, during which the would-be assassin literally shot himself in the foot. Of the loyalist paramilitaries she said: "I hate them, son, but sure they let you down." Where Brendan Hughes makes a dramatic and successful escape from Long Kesh in a garbage truck, the UDA's unfortunate Benjamin Redfern gets crushed to death when he tries it.

As Barr suggests, the other feature of republicanism that invites admiration for ex-prisoners is their political uniformity. When they emerge from jail as they do, spouting the same ideas, it is difficult to regard them as mere criminals. At the very least, they get plaudits for becoming politicized *and politically fungible* in jail from the likes of Glen Barr—a hardened loyalist.

John Pickering, describing the educational process in jail, strongly implies that the objective was to install pat answers in future Shinners. "When your opponent is trying to nail you in a corner, if you have combined the knowledge with your experience and your intelligence, you're able to reply to them. You know, like if somebody asks us about this decommissioning of arms at the minute—if you're following this here, if you're enthusiastic about the struggle, you can nail that argument to the floor in two seconds flat." He also illuminates the pressure to conform. "Some republican who just thinks it's good enough to go out and booze all the time and fart about all the time but not educate himself—it suddenly hits him: isn't it logical for the British to say to the IRA, hand down your guns and we'll talk to you, nobody's going to let you go to a table with a gun. Then he'll get stuck for an answer simply because he's not educating himself about how it's ridiculous to ask the IRA to hand in their guns prior to the negotiations."

To anyone who has observed Gerry Adams, it should come as no surprise that republicans are programmed. His manner is robotic, his voice a sonorous monotone, his verbiage standardized. Carriage, delivery, and rhetoric hardly vary from one public appearance to another. Adams has no demonstrated capacity for ad-libbing or thinking on his feet, since the media have customarily lobbed him generic questions designed to pick up tried-and-true lines like "unionist intransigence" and "the British government is jeopardizing the peace process." On the odd occasion when an enterprising journalist does ask him a question to which Adams has no set-piece response, he simply feeds the reporter a prepared answer to a different question. For months, the press asked Adams whether the IRA ceasefire was "permanent." For months, the Sinn Fein president responded blankly that it was the party's objective "to remove the gun from Irish politics once and for all." In the wake of Canary Wharf, he was still mouthing the same incantation.

Gerry Adams is a sly and effective politician. His principal weapon is unblinking repetition. Adams knows that if even a dubious point is reiterated long and ingenuously enough, it becomes plausible to onlookers. Sinn Fein, for example, has insisted that British army and RUC weapons be put on a par with paramilitary armaments for decommissioning purposes. This position is logically unsound. While Sinn Fein can defensibly push for greater restraint and evenhandedness in the use of state force, for the party to decree state emasculation redefines modern civil government altogether. Yet security force disarmament became one of the views entertained by the international advisory commission chaired by George Mitchell. In advancing the position, Adams never betrayed so much as a wink. Neither did any other Sinn Fein spokesman. Republican unanimity, contrived though it was, helped Sinn Fein.

Sinn Fein encourages team play at least as forcefully as IRA OCs do in jail. Bobby Storey became a chastising omnipresence over the Bobby Sands Discussion Group. For the May 1995 Northern Ireland investment conference in Washington, the Sinn Fein delegation had to swear off drink. Even in their private affairs, republicans toe the line. Gary Roberts, as stalwart a republican as there is, concedes that he will have to take care not to "brainwash" his children in telling them about his past, though he will present them with "no apologies" and characterize the beginning of the troubles as "merely defensive." Yet it is clear that the Provisional IRA's inaugural campaign was no more "merely defensive" than the loyalist campaign of counterterrorism was "merely reactive." Republican propaganda has dyed the wool of most IRA volunteers.

The few independent thinkers among republican ex-prisoners see the conformity that jailhouse and outside leaders enforce as potentially stagnating for the republican movement. "Prisoners will come out by-and-large slotted into what's going on," says McIntyre. "They will make no transformative impact. Because I tend to think, since Adam's day, there's no sort of organized caucus that has identified itself as being opposed to any leadership. The jails have always been conditioned by the [IRA] staffs to articulate republican arguments, as opposed to articulating arguments that might run counter to those held by the leadership." Carol Cullen states openly that the IRA has been an "undemocratic" and "sexist" organization, and that despite some advances it still waffles unsatisfactorily on women's issues like abortion. But there's no denying the value of a united front to the republican argument. When loyalists might appear to be wrestling with their own unformed views, republicans will speak in polished paragraphs. "In many ways you find that the majority come out able to argue the given line much better than their own line," offers McIntyre.

Whereas the nationalist community views all Provos as dedicated (if misguided) republicans, the unionist community regards the leading lights among loyalist ex-paramilitaries (like Hutchinson, Ervine, and Kinner) as exceptions. The fact that virtually all of them served their time in the compounds supports the public perception that there won't be many more where they came from. That may well be accurate. But more importantly, owing to Irish history, nationalists can readily accept rebels as heroes. Unionists cannot. Since they began to court partition in earnest, they have had official might in one form or another—from the 1912 UVF (effectively sanctioned by the British government) all the way up to the Royal Irish Regiment in 1992—behind them. This has engendered a law-abiding mentality. Unionists prefer to hear an admission of *reform* before granting loyalist ex-prisoners a legitimate voice. Because reform implies criminality before it, loyalists are willing to admit only to "transformation" and not "reform" as such. The nationalist community, though, doesn't require such humility of republican ex-prisoners. Sinn Fein built up its electoral strength without an IRA ceasefire. All that was required to bring them inside the larger nationalist political fold was the ceasefire itself.

Corresponding ideological adjustments have, of course, eased the republican shift from Armalite to ballot-box. Ella O'Dwyer believes that the entire island of Eire needs to be rid of Britain's colonial shackles, which means ending partition and forming a true thirty-two-county republic. This is republican fundamentalism, and at some point every republican has embraced it. Plainly not every republican holds fast to such an absolutist ideology now, however. The ceasefire suggested that the Provos might settle for being sentries for the Catholic community—the role they claimed at the start of the troubles in 1969—and no longer consider a united Ireland the sine qua non of Catholic empowerment in Northern Ireland. Again, the rhetoric of republicanism has not changed—Adams still champions the goal of a united Ireland. But the realpolitik of republicanism, as embodied in the IRA's unilateral cessation of the military campaign, has outgrown the old verbiage. The more modest vision emerged from a long evolution, which Canary Wharf does not necessarily negate. Now, as in 1969, the consensus republican imperative is protecting the nationalist community rather than marching to Dublin.

The lowered trajectory of the struggle distresses a few, like McIntyre, but most ex-prisoners support Sinn Fein's dialing back the objective to a level that does not require a military campaign. And the republican rank and file has not, of course, dropped a united Ireland as an aspiration. "I'm not saying that I want to see a devolved government," clarifies McMullan. "I do think a united Ireland is inevitable. It might take twenty, twenty-five years to come about, but I think it's happening. There's obviously going to be some interim setup. There isn't going to be a united Ireland tomorrow morning, I don't believe. Of most immediate importance to me would be things like equality, an end to religious discrimination—just generally equality for everyone in the six counties. A united Ireland's going to come anyway, you know. It just isn't going to happen, and the republican movement has stated that it isn't going to happen, by forcing the British army out of Ireland, pushing them into the sea or something—it's not going to come about like that. But a united Ireland by itself isn't the answer, you know. You fly the green flag over Dublin Castle, you fly it over Stormont Castle."

McMullan reflects some understanding that nationalists' chief gripe is nothing as merely symbolic as a flag. Their real concerns now, as they were in 1969, are civil rights and equality of treatment. In a sense, the Provisional IRA leadership used reunification to bootstrap community protection into a grand issue of sovereignty, worthy of international attention, from the essentially humdrum domestic problem that it really is. Republicans' willingness to relax their insistence on a united Ireland is conditioned in part by the Irish Republic's passivity on the matter. But the more affirmative influence is the credit accorded republicans by the larger nationalist community for winning the advances in Catholic welfare that have come under direct rule. What many outsiders don't realize is that to secure respect from that community as well as the unionist side, they must lay down their arms. The romantic resonance of the hunger strikes was far less durable for the Catholic middle class than it was for the working class and for republican ideologues.

A middle-class Catholic woman from Derry blames primarily the British for the troubles, and remembers, like most Derry people, Bloody Sunday as the epitome of British excess. She also has a deep-seated distrust of unionists, and believes they will continue to try to hold on to any remnant of the power they enjoyed in Stormont. But she came to detest the IRA as well—because, she says, "they became just as fascist as the unionists were." On a more practical level, they ruined their own people's lives, Catholic as well as Protestant, in Derry in the seventies. The Derry woman resented being stopped by "hoods" in IRA "no-go areas" who asked her who she was and where she lived, demanding identification. About fourteen years ago, her house was taken over by the Provos in classic fashion. They broke in with weapons and held the woman, her husband, and her children prisoner. They took the family car and used it in an operation in which an RUC man was murdered. Witnesses identified the car, and the police arrested the woman and her husband and held them under the Prevention of Terrorism Act—in equally classic style— putting guns to their heads during aggressive questioning. They were cleared and released, resenting the IRA as well as the police.*

She considers Gerry Adams "crafty but not smart" and remembers Martin McGuinness from school days as a "bully." But she admires John Hume more than any other politician in Northern Ireland. She also thinks Shane Paul O'Doherty is "lovely," and it was his renunciation of violence that won her over. Understand, there has always been a remote place for the Provos in the heart of the nonviolent northern Catholic on account of Stormont's outrages. "I think the Catholic population—whilst I'm not saying they endorsed the activities of the IRA—I think there was

---

*On the other hand, the IRA has sometimes been favored by what passes for "radical chic" in Belfast. For example, actor Stephen Rea, of *The Crying Game* fame, is a Belfast Protestant married to Dolours Price. They live in west Belfast. Dolours and her sister Marion served long prison sentences for IRA car bombings in London that occurred in 1973. Protesting against incarceration in Britain, the two sisters went on hunger strike for two hundred days, during which they were force-fed. Finally, they were transferred to Armagh Prison in Northern Ireland. Far from hobbling him, Rea's marriage to a republican ex-prisoner enhances his image by giving him street credibility. In Hollywood, the IRA generally connotes glamour rather than evil. To film an especially terrible "troubles movie," *A Prayer for the Dying*, Mickey Rourke showed up in Belfast with "Tiocfaidh Ar La"—the IRA motto meaning "our day will come" in Irish—tattooed on his forearm. An unabashed contributor to Noraid, Rourke was surprised when local journalists warned him to roll down his sleeves when buying cigarettes in ultra-loyalist Sandy Row. Among the "beautiful people" who have glommed onto Gerry Adams and the republican cause is Bianca Jagger.

a communal sense that there were injustices that needed addressing," observes Marty Rafferty. "They may not have liked that way of doing it, but I think there was more of a latent understanding of what might have motivated somebody to do that." When Sinn Fein moved in Hume's direction, the IRA rejuvenated a public reputation that was flagging with the Catholic middle class.

The republicans also started to realize, as some loyalists did, that they were being used by the unionists to delay indefinitely the resolution of the constitutional issue. "The national question has been put back on the agenda, whereas they were using the armed struggle to fog the issue," says McMullan. "The issue then became the armed struggle itself." For mainstream unionists—who, again, were not materially much affected by the troubles—IRA and loyalist violence became the mechanism for maintaining partition without the risk of serious political dialogue. This, McMullan suggests, was the real stuff of unionist intransigence. Now that former combatants (loyalists included) are themselves insisting on such dialogue, they believe mainstream unionists have been outflanked.

There is a post-Clausewitzean dimension to Sinn Fein's conversion. War was an extension of politics by other means; now politics is an extension of war by other means. To this extent, Sinn Fein is asking everyone in Northern Ireland to concede that terrorism has enfranchised the insurgents. But some prominent nationalists don't buy this line. One of the skeptics is Monsignor Faul. He sardonically contends that the Provos actually want to bypass politics, at which they are neither competent nor comfortable, and go directly into the civil service—namely, by using their muscle to police Catholic areas legally as they have illegally.[3]

"Poor John Hume is a very decent man, an honorable man, but he was so anxious for peace that he built up an immense political profile for them which they were totally unworthy of," says the impish, peremptory Dungannon priest. "They are not public representatives. If I wanted my sewer fixed or I wanted my door fixed and I went to them, well, they might do it. But basically, they love this thing about we are going to replace the police. In some villages in County Armagh they are wearing good suits. They get out of the old jeans and get into the good suits, and the people know that they're now the police because they put on good suits and go up and down the street giving dirty looks at everybody. They're prepared to see themselves in that kind of a role, but I don't think they're people who would talk to you and tolerate your disagreement. A public representative generally will work for his people, he will also tolerate their disagreement and he'll also accept their opinion and try to implement it for them. But a Provo political agitator won't have that flexibility; he'll compel you to follow his opinion because he's essentially fascist."

Monsignor Faul does not believe that the ceasefire was the Provos' attempt to parlay their folk-hero status into political capital. Instead, he thinks it was a desperate lunge at political survival. "The IRA were nearly finished. The people were fed up with them. I always said the IRA would stop when the people said we're getting nowhere with this," he says, drolly assuming a priestly omniscience. "They had enough guns to carry on. Enniskillen did them serious harm. They had no recruits. Derry was getting a lot of prosperity; John Hume brought a lot of money into Derry. They were getting no recruits from Derry. They could keep it going in Belfast because in any big city you'll get an element that will fight; there's always gang warfare in any city. The country people were getting fed up with it, too. And I say that because in the last two or three years the British Army and the police stopped a lot of the harassment on the roads, and the economic border disappeared. They did one disaster, Warrington;* all these things made them dreadfully unpopular. So they were finished, anyway. Another thing, the loyalist campaign had a bad effect on them. The young Turks who go with the loyalists went out and killed men, women, and children; went into these pubs and raked them. The Provos couldn't stand up to that without doing the same thing themselves. I think they weren't prepared to do that. They did it in the seventies. They weren't prepared to do it now. They were lucky enough to get John Hume and Albert Reynolds to get them out on a high political note."

It's all opinionated speculation, of course—Faul was not privy to discussions held by the IRA Army Council or Sinn Fein's inner circle. But his view is as plausible as any other theory about the IRA ceasefire—and more so than the one advanced by republican apologists: that Gerry Adams had it all mapped out in 1986.

Although Faul concedes a higher moral tone to the IRA than to the loyalists, he has little more faith in the republicans as a legitimate political force. Neither do mainstream unionist and nationalist politicians like Chris McGimpsey and Joe Hendron. For McGimpsey, the Provos are just too old for new tricks. "These guys have had twenty-five years of violence,

---

*March 20, 1993. Two boys, ages three and twelve, were killed in Warrington, England, when two IRA bombs placed in trash cans exploded without warning.

so I'm not sure that they can go the way the Workers' Party went after only three years of violence," says McGimpsey, comparing Sinn Fein to the Official IRA's political wing. "I have a lot of friends in the Workers' Party who would in their youth have been members of the Official IRA, but their backs are totally turned on all that stuff and they make a positive contribution. I don't know how Sinn Fein can do that. I don't see it."

Hendron is more measured in his skepticism, but even for him the jury is still a long way from a verdict on the transformation of the republican movement. "It's an important fact that the IRA wanted to stop, but I still see them as a fascist organization. That's how it is today, that's the main difference between them and the SDLP, though we're not talking about five years from now. They still break people's arms and legs and banish them from the country. It's still the jungle law with them. They tend to rule by fear and by indoctrinating young people. It's almost like a sect—'we are the chosen people.' Every social issue extends from that. They don't really care about the old lady who's got problems."

Republicans expect flak from the "troubles establishment," and remain largely undaunted by it. Monsignor Faul talks about harnessing the Provos' dedication for a greater good. "As a Catholic priest, I'm looking for a lever to switch all that allegiance and fidelity into religion. There's a switch somewhere. If I could just pull that lever, and switch it on to the evangelical role of the Church, wonderful things could be done." The armed struggle, he says, is extraneous to Catholic empowerment: "We have the schools, education is our liberator." Resentful over the IRA's banishing him from their wings at Long Kesh, he casts prison leaders like Pickering as incendiary. Pickering was the penultimate hunger striker. Although he was just two months out of the hospital after a major ear operation, Pickering fought to go on the strike, moving Faul to comment that the Provos had "scraped the bottom of the barrel." Pickering sees Catholic chauvinism lurking in Faul's rhetoric and calls him a "Catholic bigot." McMullan labels him "a mirror image of Ian Paisley." Where Monsignor Faul envisions a separate-but-better existence for Catholics in Northern Ireland, republican rhetoric—"parity of esteem"—in theory angles more for mixed-and-equal.

PEACETIME STATIC

The republican position is the politically correct one. Even locally, Monsignor Faul—an Irish priest from central casting, complete with silver hair, rosy cheeks, generous belly, and lilting mutter—seems an obsolescent crank. On the ground, Protestant sectarianism emerges clearly from loyalist paramilitary violence. Catholic sectarianism is not so evident from republican violence, but instead is threaded through Monsignor Faul's more subtle species of rhetoric. For example: "The poor old loyalists know in their heart of hearts that the British despise them. They have no identity. They're not Irish, English, Scottish, or Welsh. They're the people who won the Battle of the Boyne and the siege of Derry. Now, they go berserk when they hear that's a poor identity. I think that's the biggest thing we've got going for us, is an identity. How can you fight over the siege of Derry? How can you fight over the Battle of the Boyne? It's not much of an objective. The Provos had the objective of lifting their people up, of justice—what they call equality of treatment, parity of esteem, and eventually a united Ireland."

The troubles, he says, have diverted Protestants from self-improvement. "The Catholics have the schools. They have done very well in construction, manufacturing, industry, and all that. The Protestants jumped into the UDR and the police and the civil service and all the logistics of the thirty or forty thousand jobs, paid by the Brits, the silly old Brits, the stupid old Brits. But the Brits are beginning to catch on. The Brits are fed up with it—they're sending their soldiers over here to get killed, sending six billion [pounds annually] over; Major gets abused, Thatcher gets bombed, Taylor goes over and insults them. The Brits have had enough of it. The Brits like the Catholics, the Catholics are more their idea of Irish—humorous and jolly and sing-a-song and enjoy themselves and good family people."

As far as Monsignor Faul is concerned, Catholics are more principled, more intelligent, more industrious. In short, they are culturally superior. Come what may, they can't lose. Unionists already sense besiegement by the Irish Republic, which they infer from its theocratic constitution wants to Catholicize Ireland, and by the IRA, which they know from the "Brits Out" strategy wants to de-Anglicize Ulster. Add to these assaults Monsignor Faul's smug determinism, and the threat unionists perceive from the Catholic Church is as potent as the one nationalists see in Paisley. Both clerics resolutely oppose integrated education.

But Faul's condemnation of republican violence has been admirably consistent, and serves the nationalist community as an in-house reminder to be on guard. Any confidence republicans may have in the peace process is due in part to the threat of violence they keep in their pocket and will keep there regardless of how decommissioning or constitutional issues shake out. Canary Wharf was a cynical reminder that republican hard men regard that threat as a permanent feature of Irish politics. Sir Hugh Annesley, RUC Chief Constable, has publicly acknowledged that even if they were to hand in weapons, the Provos are sufficiently driven, inventive, and well-connected* to rearm quickly and wreak havoc with home-made munitions in the meantime.[4]

But Sinn Fein also sees the mainstream parties' dismissiveness as veiled fear of what they actually regard as a formidable threat to their political hegemony. "You can see with the Hume-Adams talks—it's the first time the SDLP recognized Sinn Fein's mandate," says Tony McCabe, a Sinn Fein member and community worker in Ballymurphy. "The SDLP had always determined that they would be the only voice of nationalism, and they tried to strangle Sinn Fein, and they worked with the enemies of the Catholic people in order to strangle that voice. And I think that backfired on them when Sinn Fein's voice didn't go away. I think that was one of the factors in pushing them, because they've suddenly discovered that Sinn Fein had a bloc vote and that it wasn't going to go."

During the troubles, the SDLP used the live threat of physical-force republicanism to heighten their own influence with unionists: give us what we want or the Provos will go buck-mad. After the ceasefires, Sinn Fein can appropriate for itself the threat of violence to increase its own political power without being tainted as the perpetrator. Even so, republicans mindful of the movement's original purpose are afraid that Sinn Fein itself could become co-opted by mainstream elements. "The only problem I have with the ceasefire is that we have aligned ourselves with the SDLP and the Irish government," Tommy Gorman worries. "We're a very minor partner in a tripartite sort of alliance. We could be put out of touch very,

---

*In addition to rackets in Northern Ireland and the Republic, Noraid was a source of substantial funds for the IRA's arsenal, having contributed as much as $10 million over the course of the troubles. The IRA also procured weapons through various illegal U.S. and European arms dealers, and a few through the Palestinian Liberation Organization. The Gaddafi government donated large stocks of weapons in the seventies and, more significantly, after the British-assisted U.S. airstrikes on Libya in 1986, as well as money. See Patrick Bishop and Eamonn Mallie, *The Provisional IRA* (London: Corgi Books, 1988), pp. 246, 293–309. In May 1996, the Russian government announced that Estonia, independent since 1991, had smuggled arms to the IRA. The Estonian government denied the claim. See "Estonia Falls Foul of Moscow Machinations," *Independent* (London), May 14, 1996, p. 8.

very quickly." No doubt this is the kind of thinking that led to Canary Wharf.

Uneasiness about the establishment is one reason old Provos like Gorman place such a high value on street-level communication between the two working-class communities. He sees it as an alternative vector for political empowerment, and one which is more likely to preserve Sinn Fein's prestige as a working-class party. "The old, failed unionists are still there, but maybe these new unionists might come up with some sort of better package—more working-class, more amenable to change. They need to change the situation, whereas Molyneaux and Taylor* don't need to change. They have their wee patch. The loyalists here might break the mold of this Protestant psyche of voting for middle-class people, that working-class heroes don't exist in the Protestant community."

At the same time, most republicans carry at least latent disdain for loyalist ex-prisoners, even though several have become political leaders of the Protestant working class. Leo Green, having watched loyalists in prison, is suspicious of what has motivated them to become overtly political. "Some of them—lifers, in particular—maybe thought that the jail might take a sympathetic view when it come to reviewing their cases. You know, here are people who've turned away from violence and now they want to better themselves. I think that's very much the norm within the loyalist wings today. Despite what some of them might suggest, you'll not find any great education within the loyalist wings. I daresay over the past six months it has heightened somewhat—only simply in the context of, does this mean we're all getting out?" Green is also unconvinced of loyalists' ability to suppress their selfishness enough to cohere as a unit. "Apart from anything else, the loyalists have never demonstrated any great commitment to, if you like, self-sacrifice in jail and achieving something for a collective."

McIntyre presents a more studied—and a deeper—skepticism about working-class loyalists. To him, they dangle socialism as a carrot in front of Sinn Feiners while behind them loyalists brandish the stick of a perpetual union. "I think that Billy Hutchinson and probably Ervine are genuine as working-class people who want to see working-class solutions within the constitutional setup, and if that constitutional setup is changed, they are quite prepared to return to their sectarian activity, which is murdering innocent Catholics," he says. "Because they see that as

---

*Ulster Unionist Party MPs.

a bona fide way of keeping the IRA in line, of forcing the IRA into a position of weakness, of saying to the IRA there's consequences to whatever you do. I think that's basically how they see it. Having said that, I quite like Billy Hutchinson, but the fact is that the vast political gulf between us is made no more bridgeable by the fact that he might make a few solutions.* You know, you have this nonsense in 1974 when the IRA were calling the UVF socialists and welcoming coming developments, talking about UVF/IRA alliances. All nonsense. Never happen. If it does, it'll happen on the UVF's terms, not the IRA's."

Gorman, McCabe, Green, and Roberts all share these fears in varying degrees. But invariably, they juxtapose their disrespect for the loyalist paramilitaries with a grudging appreciation of their ability to keep a cruel eye on the politico-military ball throughout the troubles, as McIntyre does. Beyond the military context, in the post-ceasefire world, republicans may become open to the possibility that loyalists can broaden their vigilantism into political clout. Some republicans foresee selective political links with the new loyalists—albeit links which assiduously avoid the border issue. "The British don't want to stay here, and as soon as they can get out they'll get out. That's my belief, anyway," says Joe Clarke. "And I think people like David Ervine are shrewd enough to realize this. Gusty Spence said a couple of years back that he could see a united Ireland coming, you know. I could see David Ervine trying to push socialist development in his community. At a later date whether he would want to come across and have joint ventures with Sinn Fein, I just don't know. It would be nice at the end of the day if this was to happen. The main thing is that republicans still have the thirty-two-county socialist republic as their ultimate goal. If taking these people on board and working with them brings it that much closer, fair enough."

Each side tends to regard the other's apparent commitment to socialism as window dressing for the border issue, or at least as subservient to it. Why this mutual suspicion should exist is no mystery. It is an article of faith that all political issues in Northern Ireland pale next to that of the border. "There cannot be such a thing as a unionist socialist," rails Kevin McQuillan. "The politics that people such as the PUP are espousing are confused Strasserite, pre-Hitler politics—basically, they're national social-

---

*Some republicans also believe that Hutchinson is in fact too reasonable to weather a crisis in loyalist leadership. "If things go wrong," says Kevin McQuillan, "Hutchinson will get it in the ear. There's no doubt about it, and it will not be from republicans."

ists who don't want to use that term. The PUP and parties like them are neofascists. No matter what anyone says about putting class and the interests of socialism above the tribal sort of unionism and nationalism, until such time as the divisions in this country on the issue of partition is resolved, they will never be able to make any attempt at resolving and putting into practice here true class politics." Yet McQuillan calls himself a revolutionary socialist who is aiming for a united Ireland. For all his talk about the loyalists' limitations, he can't divorce his economics from his nationalism, either. Neither could James Connolly at the inception of modern Irish republicanism.

Tommy Gorman hawks much the same line as McQuillan when he talks about the cross-community project he runs with Billy Hutchinson. "I have invested a lot in the struggle, so I'm not just going to throw it away for a mere job. Billy and I have built up a good rapport. He's a sound man. It's just that—and maybe I'm being ethnocentric—he's still got a way to go yet. Billy would claim to be a socialist. To me, you can't be a socialist in an imperial context, you can't be a socialist and a colonialist. And I find it hard to equate the two sort of things." As is the Provos' wont, Gorman is personally warm but doctrinally obdurate, having seemingly overlooked completely the British Labour Party that has held power for much of the post-partition era.

Gary Roberts doesn't even bother with warmth. He is simply convinced that no unionist could possibly have good intentions toward nationalists, no matter what material benefits he contemplates for the working class. "I don't think there's politics there. I think what we have is people coming forward, masquerading as a political group. I don't think David Ervine, Gary McMichael, people like that, I don't think there's a political theory in their heads. I think it's just loyalist thuggery trying to be diplomatic. I'm totally skeptical. We heard in the past that Protestants—loyalists, sorry—or unionists tried to reach out at socialism. Okay, they're saying that we're prepared to talk about this, that, and the other thing, but again their defined limits haven't changed." In other words, they still want the union, so they must only mean harm to nationalists.

Passionate Northern Irish socialists will sometimes claim that the troubles were a middle-class ploy to keep the working class from uniting in the pursuit of their common interests. That takes matters to a conspiratorial extreme, but undoubtedly the constitutional question has been employed to keep the lower classes on board in regard to economic and social issues that have nothing to do with the border. Unionists and nationalists have basically created one-issue blocs, like the pro-life voters in the United States: party leaders could throw anything else they wanted onto the platform, and their constituencies would swallow the whole package. Single-issue politics created a false cohesion. McQuillan and Gorman know this, yet they are painfully myopic in their explication of the republican dilemma. They can't see the hypocrisy of taking unionists to task for their inability to set aside an issue—the border—which republicans have made paramount. While some, like McMullan, pay lip service to the Republic's "vibrant economy," their argument for reunification is at bottom based on an impressionistic notion of natural law—on the moral and cultural rightness of a united Ireland.

Loyalists, at least rhetorically, do not commit the equal and opposite mistake. Their economic argument for the union is in essence empirical rather than ideological. But Monsignor Faul, for all his derision of the Provos, swears their hearts are in the right place. "Bobby Sands said, 'Greater love hath no man than this—that a man lay down his life for his friends.'* That sums up an awful lot of Provo philosophy. While their methods are fascist, basically they do it for the poor." Taken literally, this view is somewhat naive. Republicans have not shown much concern for impoverished Protestants, and have done no more for destitute Catholics than the SDLP. Although the Provisional IRA began in 1970 with the limited objective of defending the poor Catholic community, republicans lost their focus on that goal after they and the Brits turned up the military heat in 1971. During the remainder of the troubles, republicans simply presumed that the well-being of the Catholic working class was an incident of a united Ireland. Now, however, Shinners like McMullan realize that reunification will be a long time in coming. Accordingly, republican community workers, Gorman among them, are now inclined to concentrate their efforts more on ground-level conditions in nationalist areas than on agitation over the border question. It was Gorman who insisted most vehemently and hopefully that the IRA's breach of the ceasefire with Canary Wharf was an isolated event, intended merely to focus minds.

Perhaps, therefore, Sinn Fein is prepared to work within civil strictures to develop a working-class politics. Breidge Gadd, chief probation officer in Northern Ireland, tells an amusing story that suggests as much. Fed up

---

*The same quote, verbatim, is embossed on a bronze memorial plaque for British soldiers who served and died in the two World Wars. It was recently emplaced in a small park on the corner of the Shankill Road and Wilton Street.

with the Provos kneecapping hoods, she and her deputy went to Gerry Adams and suggested that instead of taking a baseball bat or a lead pipe to local delinquents, the IRA send them to the Probation Board to get help. Shortly after this visit, Gadd learned that orders had been issued stating that anyone buttonholed by the IRA must seek the services of the Probation Board—or be kneecapped.

There is certainly enough common subconstitutional ground between republicans and loyalists to yield qualified optimism for a rapprochement. For example, both republicans and loyalists distinctly lack the mentality of the upwardly mobile: neither would want ever to be considered middle-class. They tend to stay in their old neighborhoods and live humbly. This is true even of those who have probably profited from paramilitary involvement. This phenomenon reflects pride in and identity with a working-class heritage on the loyalist side, and in a revolutionary (i.e., persecuted) background on the republican side—a sort of pride that is not nearly so sticky in the United States or other places which offer more realistic opportunities to become "nouveau riche." With ceasefires in place, there would be an incentive for loyalists and republicans to get together on economic issues.

But the border looms uniquely large in Northern Ireland. Minority communities in the United States do not take up arms against each other. Upward mobility seems possible to them, and they do not want to soil what they perceive as their eventual bed. There is no sovereignty question for American minorities, only an equality issue. Right-wing militiamen may vow, "I love my country, I fear my government," but they have no serious dispute about where that country's boundaries lie. Many American blacks are as patriotic as rednecks, and the Black Panthers never turned into anything equivalent to the IRA. Neither will the Michigan Militia. Yet the Catholic civil rights movement that spawned the Provisional IRA derived its principal inspiration from the American black movement, which then appeared on the verge of armed revolution.

The difference in Northern Ireland is that the two working-class communities there did not really consider the possibility of a better economic lot for both of them under a single flag. Working-class loyalism embraces British Labour Party socialism to benefit blue-collar Protestants, crowding out the Protestant middle class. Likewise, republicanism aspires to a socialist state, excluding the Catholic middle class. The two sides share a proletarian reverse snobbery. But neither republicans nor loyalists have been willing to lower the border's profile sufficiently to bring the working classes together. First republicans would have to admit that social justice, not ideology, drives the nationalist side of the border issue. Loyalists, to justify their defense of the six-county state, would have to show that the state has a capacity for thoroughgoing impartiality that it did not have under Stormont. These developments would deflate the significance of the border in both communities. They are, therefore, the keys to turning the idiom of this conflict decisively from coercion to negotiation.

That agenda may not sit well with ex-prisoners. Their pedigrees give them a loud voice, but also prima facie limit their capacity and their range as politicians. They are revolutionaries and counterrevolutionaries by mind-set, and therefore by nature less interested in conventional politics. Their violent pasts also make their communities' acceptance of them as leaders more tenuous and perishable than it would be with ordinary politicians (though this tentativeness applies less to republicans than to loyalists). Ex-prisoners have been inspirational and influential in the early stages of post-ceasefire Northern Ireland, but they fear that as time goes on they may recede into the supporting role of retired folk heroes. As such, they would still occupy a far more honored place than ex-convicts in almost any other society.

The very feature that makes terrorism take hold as a cultural force—namely, revolution—makes political success for a terrorist group almost impossible. Terrorists, as opposed to ordinary criminals and ordinary politicians, like "special category status." Thus, Sinn Fein boycotted the May 1995 economic conference in Belfast, and old republicans lament any attempt by Sinn Fein to build bridges with the SDLP. Just as soldiers don't like peacetime, guerrillas don't like reconciliation. Omar Bradley said it was just as well Patton died at the end of World War II. If a political settlement is achieved, mightn't some nationalists likewise say that Gerry Adams and company have reached the end of their useful lives?

Adams would hope to convince them otherwise. From a republican point of view, standing down as politicians would mean either giving up the goal of a united Ireland or going back to the armed struggle. Neither alternative is palatable to Sinn Fein. Unless republicans are somehow allowed to remain a political force over the long term, Northern Ireland as a whole will be more vulnerable to the *military* reassertion of that objective, and a commensurate loyalist "reaction." This dynamic has been reiterated in Ulster throughout recent history. One of the key reasons was always the political relegation of the combatants after the smoke cleared. During sustained rioting in Northern Ireland on account of partition in 1920–22, over five hundred people were killed. Most were Catholics, but two of the new parliament's unionist MPs also were murdered. The government interned four hundred people, mainly suspected IRA men. Stormont commissioned the brutal and all-Protestant "B-Specials" to fight the IRA and entrenched itself against nationalism.[5] Constitutional nationalists never really participated fully in the assembly, and the IRA rose in each subsequent decade until it brought Stormont down in 1972.[6]

Against the unforgiving polarity between the aims of unionism and nationalism during the partition era—nationalists were convinced until the Free State became a republic in 1949 that reunification was an impending inevitability—the political inertia of Stormont was virtually unavoidable. Now that even republicans' insistence on a united Ireland has relaxed, there is some political room for enterprising people from both sides to maneuver.

Brendan Hughes, who at the start of the IRA ceasefire smelled a sellout, has changed his mind. "When I first got involved in the republican movement I wouldn't accept anything from the British establishment because it was British. But I came to accept that the whole structure of Britain is built upon the blood, sweat, and tears of my father, my mother, all the rest of my family, and all the rest of the people. So that whole outlook has changed. Look at City Hall, which we've never seen as ours. But it's just as much ours. Just because there's a Union Jack flying over it doesn't mean it isn't ours, and we've started to express and deal with what is ours, where before we were totally distanced from it. We had the idea that it doesn't belong to us—sort of a foggy notion that when this new Ireland comes about, right, you sink the one we have here and create this new one."

For a republican of Hughes's vintage and distinction even *provisionally* to recognize British institutions is no small thing. In Crown prosecutions, republican defendants—including Hughes in 1974—for years refused to recognize the jurisdiction of the court and stood mute, as a matter of course. But on November 8, 1995, to the chagrin of some unionists, Sinn Fein held a rally in downtown Belfast at the Ulster Hall, the public auditorium where the first meeting of the Ulster Unionist Party was held ninety years earlier. Gerry Adams and Martin McGuinness emerged from black-taxis to rousing applause. Against a ceiling-high tapestry of Bobby Sands, the Lagan Valley Martyrs Flute Band played the Irish national anthem, and closed the evening with a ballad for the ten dead hunger strikers of 1981. Pre-ceasefire, the Belfast City Council would have found a way to cancel the Sinn Fein booking. This time, unionist councillors thought about it but dropped the idea. The RUC established check-points, but stayed a healthy block away on all sides, leaving building security to republican muscle.

Everyone was learning. But unless nationalists and unionists can put aside triumphalism and countertriumphalism, and get down to the humble politics of no-smoking-on-buses, the perils of fluoridated water, and "mad cow disease," events like Sinn Fein's rally at Ulster Hall will amount to nothing more than fleeting photo opportunities for Sinn Fein. What is remarkable is not that the Shinners invaded a unionist institution, but that the City Council didn't stop them. The Shinners' having a rally at the Ulster Hall is not republican progress; it is unionist progress.

THE REPUBLICAN DILEMMA

Sinn Fein claims that its gains in political confidence, and not loyalist violence or republican fatigue, produced the ceasefire. The proof would be for republicans to unite with loyalists on working-class issues. In the bargain, such a move would also act as a hedge against marginalization by the mainstream nationalists. Sinn Fein in politics, though, is a stubborn novice. Even in peace, it will not stop demonizing the British. This penchant will, of course, safeguard the Brits' excessively exalted place in nationalist heritage. Many republicans find the obsession with the Crown shortsighted. "At the end of the day, getting the Brits out of the country is wee buns," says Tommy Gorman. "But it's hard to convince nine hundred thousand loyalists* that their destiny lies in a united socialist republic. It's okay getting Brits out, but at the same time you have to start convincing these people that their destiny, where their true destiny lies. I mean, they don't trust the Brits, they don't trust anyone, you know."

Gorman is a bit wishful here. Sinn Fein doesn't trust anyone, either. Although Sinn Fein and the new loyalists are trying to learn "the language of trust," as David Ervine calls it, it's a hard sell. To the extent "trust" means faith in promises as yet unfulfilled, it is a chimera in Northern Ireland, where talk is cheap and history is loaded. Again, Canary Wharf proved delusional any notion that seventeen months of peace had generated genuine trust between republicans and unionists.

---

*Gorman misspeaks. Like most republicans, he ascribes to all unionists the more militant mindset of the "loyalist." The *New York Times* makes the same error, but Gorman knows better.

Trust requires common ground, and most republicans still think that is extremely narrow. "The problem in all our communities is poverty," says Carol Cullen. "We all demand the redistribution of wealth, we've all got the same sort of economic demands as that. But that's where the commonality ends. The loyalists are just demanding that the people who are living in poverty in their own areas have a better standard of life, a better quality of life. And that's our demand also. Some sort of strategy for an economic development will certainly compliment both communities, but it will not be done in tandem. You know, it's not like there's going to be cooperation. I can't imagine it. There are cross-community groups, but I think at this stage we're all still skeptical, we're still paranoid, cynical—we just don't trust each other." In this atmosphere, the most either side can hope to get from the other is forbearance for as long as the realization of a mutual goal—like, say, forming a devolved government—remains possible. Indeed, this is why Britain's requirement of decommissioning was so singularly unrealistic.

The irony here is that republicans, hitherto unbendable, have been the ones to give a little on their constitutional aspiration. Peace can't proceed without their compromise. To an extent, again, flexibility is simply an imperative of the modern-day Republic of Ireland's zeitgeist—the citizenry of the south is in no great hurry to absorb a 35 percent increase in population, two-thirds of it angry and fearful Prods. But flexibility is a luxury Sinn Fein does have. Even in a devolved government under British dominion, Sinn Fein could maintain that improved conditions for and official attitudes towards northern Catholics during direct rule came mainly because of the armed struggle, and *a fortiori* take credit for subsequent improvements as well. In a united Ireland, on the other hand, unionists would unequivocally be the vanquished. Sinn Fein can always insist that any devolved government is "interim" or "transitional," while unionists could scarcely make the same claim of a unitary Irish state. If, then, an empowered nationalist community lets a devolved government have another chance, both sides win—at least temporarily. If it demands a united Ireland, the province is stuck in a zero-sum game once again.

So far, however, Sinn Fein has rested on the laurels of its superior propaganda. Republicans keep their political edge over the new loyalists only because they're better at revolutionary politics. Unless Sinn Fein gets smarter, though, that advantage will only last for as long as politics in Northern Ireland pivot on the threat of terrorism. Even now, their edge is based on military issues of temporary importance. Sinn Fein can insist on amnesty for republican prisoners on the ground that British soldiers and RUC men didn't have to serve time for murdering Catholic civilians. Loyalists can't credibly assert the same claim, so they ask merely for phased early release of politically motivated prisoners. Similarly, Sinn Fein can refuse to decommission on the ground that northern Catholics have no other defenders—a claim the loyalists can't make about Protestants.

Partial victories for Sinn Fein on either issue will give republicans bragging rights—any British compromise can be packaged as an admission that the IRA was justified in waging the armed struggle. But such symbolic intangibles are merely decorative and will fade quickly. In December 1995, a survey in Dublin's *Sunday Tribune* found that 76 percent of Irish citizens sided with the Brits' requirement of some disarmament before talks. Given that attitude, the people of the Republic—Sinn Fein's supposed larger constituency—are unlikely to be impressed by republican rigidity for very long. In any event, once the prisoner and weapons issues are resolved, the easy propaganda victories for Sinn Fein will be exhausted. The party will either have to get down to real politics or become an unsightly relic of a futile war.

Sinn Fein's long-term strategy meandered after the IRA ceasefire. Since Canary Wharf, even its short-term strategy has been in disarray. To rescue the past, the republican movement has become myopically obsessed with winning the disarmament and prisoner debates, and has lost sight of the political future. Despite declaring the ceasefire, Sinn Fein and the IRA have not been satisfied to take credit for progress in civil rights. Instead, republicans have continued to insist that whatever progress has been made hasn't been enough. This tack undermines the only sensible rationale for the ceasefire—namely, that republicans have won something worth keeping. If they continue along the same path—and Canary Wharf suggests some still lean that way—republicans will not develop the ability to participate constructively in unarmed politics under a devolved government. Within the nationalist community, their obdurately "revolutionary" approach will appear anachronistic, and likewise their prestige will derive only from the past. Progress in Irish politics has usually occurred when stubborn old men have finally let go of impractical ideals—as when de Valera gave up on reunification as a consuming aim and got on with the business of nourishing a twenty-six-county republic. Insofar as Adams's propaganda coup in the United States is based on a sanitized presentation of the Provisional IRA's eventful history, it will lose momentum fairly rapidly. Without violence, Gerry Adams is just another monotonic politician with a shady past. Yet with the IRA's regression to violence, he became a pariah to all but the hard-core faithful.

In devolution, McIntyre will say all that's on offer is Sunningdale, and therefore that there has been no progress in twenty-five years. He might say that *all* republicans have won is a beguiling mystique. Yet power sharing means more to nationalists than it did in 1974. Sinn Fein then had no mandate in the north; now it has a solid 10 percent. The SDLP's present support, at almost 25 percent, is slightly higher than it was twenty years ago. Thus, nationalists now have a much bigger piece of the power-sharing pie. One key reason for this, in addition to Sinn Fein's post-1981 empowerment, is that the proportion of Catholics to Protestants in Northern Ireland has gone up. This trend is predicted to continue. Consequently, nationalist constituencies may become even larger in the future.*

Beyond relative strengths on the constitutional question, each side has faced the harsh reality that its putative sovereign is not its salvation. Northern Ireland is not "as British as Finchley," as Eddie Kinner learned when he was labeled a "Paddy" on a trip to England. Neither is Catholic west Belfast just like the Irish Republic; a Sinn Fein councillor reportedly told a visiting southern nationalist politician to "fuck away off to the Free State where you belong." What marks these understandings now is that they are equable and mature rather than sullen and resentful. "I realize that it's a very, very difficult decision for the United Kingdom to rule a divided society, and that to a certain degree they have to placate the nationalists," says John White. Tommy Gorman, for his part, is uncomfortable with the powers that be in the Republic, and considers southern capitalist politicians like Albert Reynolds† incompatible with true Irish republicanism. "We would question whether their priorities would be for working-

---

*There are three main reasons for the demographic shift: (1) a slightly higher birth rate among Catholics; (2) a higher emigration rate among Protestants; and (3) a higher median age for Protestants. Many unionists dispute projections of a secular increase in the Catholics' share of Ulster's population.

†Albert Reynolds, Irish taoiseach and leader of Fianna Fail from February 1992 to November 1994, owns nonunion bacon-processing plants. He is widely credited with brokering the rapprochement between John Hume and Gerry Adams, producing the joint Downing Street declaration, and facilitating the IRA ceasefire. After Reynolds's government toppled, from the sidelines he officiously warned Major that his failure to budge on decommissioning was jeopardizing the peace process. When Major did budge and the IRA staged Canary Wharf anyway, Reynolds blamed the prime minister's election proposal.

class Catholics or working-class anyone. Allying ourselves with people like this is dangerous in the extreme, people whose main priority is their own political dynasty."

Sinn Fein is not without competent peacetime politicians. Mitchel McLaughlin, the party's northern chairman and a Derry councillor, has shown some taste for the give and take of ordinary politics. On television in October 1995, he said the fringe loyalist parties have shown that "unionism is not a monolith," and were "a breath of fresh air" whom republicans "could do business with in the future."[7] Neither Adams nor McGuinness would have ventured that far. But McLaughlin has never been to jail. His earnest intensity contrasts uneasily with the flashy, seditious preening of, say, an Alex Maskey or a Martin McGuinness. Their shtick represents the Sinn Fein status quo. Maskey's bearded smirk and McGuinness's carrot-topped gaze of righteousness fit the romantic image of republicanism. Whether Sinn Fein can make the drastic shift toward the style of a Mitchel McLaughlin remains in doubt. McGuinness, not McLaughlin, is Adams's heir apparent. In any case, Adams seems to have no plans to step down, and dissidents within the republican movement are neither numerous nor vehement enough to summon the will to take him out permanently.

With its 10 percent, Sinn Fein has a far firmer electoral base than the new loyalists. Neither the PUP nor the UDP has any electoral mandate at all, much less support to match Sinn Fein's. Tommy Kirkham finished a disappointing fourth in the February 1995 Newtownabbey council election in Rathcoole—a Protestant estate and UDA stronghold just north of Belfast. Chris McGimpsey, a liberal member of the Ulster Unionist Party, won over Glencairn's voters in the 1993 election for the Belfast city council. Historically, working-class Protestants have voted for the professional politicians who operate from the comfort of their endowed churches, small businesses, or law practices. So far, these voters have shown little inclination to change their ways, in spite of the exhortations of the new loyalists. It would hardly be an unprecedented event in republican history for Sinn Fein to send out political feelers to the loyalists—the Official IRA, through the Workers' Party, has done it with the UVF. On the other hand, due to their political weakness, the new loyalists are disinclined to risk support by approaching Sinn Fein.

Unionists in general, of course, hold a comfortable majority in Northern Ireland. They do not need to convert Sinn Fein to unionism. It is Sinn Fein that needs to convert unionists to nationalism. Both the Anglo-Irish

Agreement in 1985 and the Downing Street declaration in 1993 reinforced the requirement that Northern Ireland's majority consent to the reunification of Ireland. In speeches, republicans derisively call this condition the "unionist veto," and condemn any framework embracing it as quisling "partitionist nationalism." But the reality is that the unionist consent requirement, in one form or another, is here to stay. Although Sinn Fein has repeatedly rejected it since the IRA ceasefire and still employs the threat of violence, the ceasefire itself was tacit acknowledgment that unionists cannot be coerced into a united Ireland and a clear demonstration that the party now prefers a constitutional solution. Canary Wharf was at bottom a frustrated act of near political nihilism, not a calculated step toward a united Ireland. Even Adams and McGuinness concede that unionists must be "persuaded."

The British government in 1990 renounced its economic and strategic interest in Northern Ireland. Sinn Fein has thus implored the Brits to "join the ranks of the persuaders" in selling unionists on a united Ireland. In the best of all possible republican worlds, British apathy—or antipathy— would convince unionists that Ireland was their only feasible sovereign and present them with a Hobson's choice. But Sinn Fein has discovered that unionists are too stubborn to let Britain off the hook, and Britain is too proud to abandon unionists altogether. Republicans cannot count on unionists to take the path of least resistance. Nor can Sinn Fein rely on the British government to do its bidding. When republicans believed they could shoot and bomb their way to reunification, they didn't need to placate unionists or the British. Now, whether they like it or not, they have to be charming to prevail.

CHAPTER 7

SHAKY PILLARS

THE PALL OF UNIONISM

Ulster Protestant culture is at bottom too prudish to assign loyalist para-militaries the status of heroes. "That's all to do with the Protestant psy-che," says Marty Snoddon. "The Protestant people are by and large law-abiding people. The majority of them would say that those Protestant prisoners, for whatever reason, broke the law." Protestants generally be-lieve that killing is bad. Nationalists are less likely to think that way, tend-ing instead to see the republican cause as understandable in the cold light of history.*

The fact that loyalists' faith in violence is more easily shaken than re-publicans' has not, so far, translated into political success. Tommy Kirkham was elected to the Newtownabbey district council as a member of Paisley's DUP in 1990, but when he jumped ship in 1995 to the UDP (accepted to be the UDA's political arm), he was beaten badly. Chris McGimpsey thinks Kirkham committed political suicide in making the switch. "With that type of candidate, fighting a vigorous campaign, who had a track record and was a nice guy, the best he could manage was 18 percent of the vote. That's as good a candidate as they could have got in a sympathetic area—it's traditionally a strong UDA area. So if Tommy couldn't win a seat there, I don't think the UDP will win a seat anywhere," McGimpsey remarks. Kirkham disagrees. "It was by no means courageous,"

---

*The loyalist paramilitaries, however, probably have not been any more crippled than the IRA by informers precisely because law-abiding Protestants maintain more distance than uninvolved Catholics from "men of violence." Informers on both sides have tended to be active paramilitaries squeezed or bribed by the security forces. The IRA has caught more "touts" due to better internal security. Through 1993, the Provos had killed fifty-nine al-leged informers, compared to the loyalist groups' combined total of sixteen.

he says. "It was a move that we wanted to make because the DUP was getting absolutely nowhere, and we believe the DUP are going down the tubes. They're the people who continue to say no, they're the people who continue to criticize everything and everyone else." The jury's out on who is right. However unionist politics shake out, the new loyalists have an uphill climb in front of them.

The republican version of the troubles euphemizes the IRA and demonizes the loyalist paramilitaries. If an IRA man gets caught with his mates trying to blow up a van full of construction workers on their way home from their army base work site, according to Sinn Fein he is a "volunteer" in an "active service unit" engaged in the "armed struggle." If a loyalist is apprehended strafing Sinn Fein's Falls Road offices, he is a "gunman" in a "death squad" committing an act of "terrorism." The republicans have far more stroke with the international media than the loyalists—particularly in the United States, where Sinn Fein's weekly newspaper *An Phoblacht/Republican News,* bowdlerized of any socialist messages or anti-American allusions, is imported, and Noraid publishes the *Irish People* for the Irish-American faithful. These are available at any good newsstand in New York, Chicago, or Boston. The UDA's *New Ulster Defender* and the UVF's *Combat* aren't distributed beyond Lisburn.

The republican account gets global exposure, which then boomerangs back to the province. The hunger strikes did not change the fact that the Provos murdered hundreds of innocent civilians. But nonviolent prison protests obscured these realities to a distant audience, and locally at least made republicans look dashing next to the pouting, withdrawn loyalists. The best recent example of this dynamic is Gerry Adams's pre–Canary Wharf series of pilgrimages to the United States. He secures visas over John Major's objections, meets with the National Security Advisor, spends St. Patrick's Day at the White House, and hosts $1,000-a-plate fundraisers at the Plaza Hotel (he raised $600,000 in total).* Reports come back that Adams is acting like a statesman and being treated like one. *Quod erat demonstrandum,* say the Provos, and the nationalist community hails Adams as their Mandela, ignoring the fact that his new status was achieved with American smoke and transatlantic mirrors. Republicans collectively bask in Adams's prestige, and the whole movement looks good.

---

*From February through October 1995, Sinn Fein raised $1,117,081.12, according to a filing submitted to the U.S. Department of Justice by Friends of Sinn Fein, the party's U.S. lobby, under the U.S. Foreign Agents Registration Act.

Unionists, mainstream or otherwise, cannot hope to counter Sinn Fein's appeal in the United States, and they know it. The visions of unionism are a terrific turnoff. Image-wise, the trim, handsome Gerry Adams—with his neat beard, natty tweeds, and studious pipe—beats colorless, fat, stodgy unionists like John Taylor hands-down in the beauty contest. As a result, local wit favors republicans. David Ervine's loud sweater is labeled crass by the *Irish News*. But Sinn Fein's emerging sartorial splendor moves BBC producer Francis Gorman to convert the Irish republican slogan "tiocfaidh ar la"—pronounced "chucky ar la" and meaning "our day will come"—into "Chucky Armani." On the substantive side, Adams enjoys the inherent advantage of opposition: Sinn Fein has no record of serious governance, and its terrorist record is peddled as romantic rebellion. Unionists, on the other hand, are burdened with their once unyielding and still reticent incumbency. Adams can hurl thunderbolts of a "new Ireland" which glisten with bold promise, while unionists squat inside the drab, familiar garrison of the unionist majority.

Any nationalist politician would welcome American political meddling in Northern Ireland, knowing that it will have a "green"* tint. To get help in Congress, a U.S. president often must curry favor with Washington's "Irish mafia"—the Kennedys, Senators Moynihan and D'Amato, Representative Peter King, ex-Representative Bruce Morrison. They are all Catholic and all nationalist. Some, like D'Amato and King, seem to bask in veiled associations with the IRA. As a tactical matter, any unionist politician *must* discourage close U.S. involvement. When President Clinton prefaced his back-to-my-roots sojourn to County Fermanagh in December 1995 with the hope that all-party talks would have been scheduled by the time he arrived, UUP deputy leader John Taylor shot back a particularly sour rebuke. "No party should allow itself to be rushed into talks merely to suit the ambitions of candidates in next year's U.S.A. presidential election," he said. "President Clinton has found a cottage in County Fermanagh; that should be sufficient."[1] As it happened, Clinton never even made it to Fermanagh, casting a wee bit of doubt on the genuineness of his intentions. The Protestant people correctly consider their politicians' trips to the United States nothing more than damage control. By default, they fall back on the same turgid images of the same staid politicians they've seen for years.

---

*In Northern Ireland, the adjective "green" connotes nationalist bias, "orange" unionist bias.

Mainstream unionists initially responded to the prospect of long-term peace unimaginatively, remaining immobile and banking on the Brits' refusal to enter all-party talks until the IRA showed its bona fides by handing in some weapons. In typical fashion, they almost snatched defeat from the jaws of victory, and failed to comprehend the dynamic at work. The British government felt bad about alienating the unionists when, in February 1995, it promulgated a distinctly green template for a political settlement. Known as the "framework document," it recommends, in addition to devolution, the symbolically evil "cross-border institutions with executive powers." Unionists fear that such bodies will lead to "a united Ireland through the back door," or to joint authority, which would be almost as opprobrious. The Brits' subsequent insistence on decommissioning was an olive branch to the unionists. Accordingly, if the unionists would drop the disarmament condition, so would the Brits. All-party talks could then begin, and unionists would be free to attack unacceptable aspects of the framework document.

But no. Emotionally, the unionists cannot see the ceasefires as anything but a victory for the IRA. This sort of shortsightedness plainly impedes the peace process without materially helping the unionists' bargaining position. The new loyalists grasped this fact and soft-pedaled the decommissioning condition. The larger unionist community, however, still maintained that not requiring the Provos to forfeit some weapons could only lead to more concessions. Unionists ascribed the PUP and UDP's softer position solely to their interest in safeguarding the UVF and UDA's arsenals, which also would have to be depleted to match IRA disarmament. Be that as it may, the new loyalists have shown more perspicacity than mainstream unionists in distinguishing victory from defeat. On the wall of brick estate housing on the Shankill Road, graffiti two storeys high reads: "I.R.A.—I Ran Away—1969, 1994." In February 1996, UDP leader Gary McMichael participated in a televised debate with Sinn Fein's Pat McGeown. A couple of days later, the IRA bombed Canary Wharf, ending the ceasefire. Nevertheless, both McMichael and David Ervine successfully counseled restraint provided the Provos did not resume violence in Northern Ireland itself.

Some new loyalists may admit they are resigned to an eventual united Ireland, but only in the context of ensuring protection for Ulster Protestants when reunification comes. Marty Snoddon, who is not active in politics and speaks only for himself, offers a particularly brave and measured view. "I'm reasonably hopeful about the peace process, but I'm not reasonably hopeful about the framework document. The British government, and certainly the American government too, know very little about the Protestant people, and are just throwing them crumbs on the table. I hope it doesn't transpire, as it appears to be to some degree, that the Protestant people become the oppressed people of Ireland. I know there's a lot of people starting to feel that way, I know there's a danger of that happening, and certainly a big danger of a backlash as a result. That worries me. I think there has to be a form of power sharing within the six counties. It's going to be a long, slow, painful process. People have to be educated, people have to overcome the fears of the other side. I have no doubt that some day there will be a united Ireland, and I think the Protestant people, if they're smart enough, can make that united Ireland, by using the strength that they would have today, some form of an acceptable united Ireland within an acceptable Europe."

Snoddon confronts the possibility that the voters of Ulster may someday agree to a united Ireland, and sees that the best way to guarantee proper treatment for Protestants is for them to use their present majority anticipatorily so as to make sure they're well treated in *any* constitutional setup. Mainstream unionists will not entertain the same vision because it frightens their constituents. If they are to invigorate unionist politics, then, the new loyalists must carefully straddle the line between reconciliation and abdication. They must build their constituency from the ground up, without the aid of a far-reaching public relations capacity or the swashbuckling aura that paramilitarism carries for nationalists.

These limitations vis-à-vis Sinn Fein have always been the bane of the loyalist paramilitaries, and spelled their failure to develop a political base during the troubles. In matters of form, the new loyalist parties must adhere to local custom. Unlike Sinn Fein, they cannot behave like revolutionary parties. They must undertake reassimilation deliberately and cautiously. Those who are successful must settle for being shaky pillars of the community.

NASTY PIECES OF WORK

When a loyalist gets out of jail, everybody in the neighborhood will want to slap him on the back and buy him a drink. Younger men will mind their tongues when an ex-lifer is within earshot, knowing he has killed and conceding him street seniority. But the deference probably comes more from fear than respect. In any case, admiration is confined mainly to other paramilitaries and their families. Certainly it stops far short of the workplace, the Orange lodge, or the ballot box. Whereas dedicated IRA volunteers or ex-prisoners in the republican community are known affectionately as "the lads," their UVF and UDA counterparts will more likely be indexed in the loyalist community as "nasty pieces of work." The label is often unfair.

Upon his release from prison in 1988, Eddie Kinner went to work as a computer programmer at an engineering firm called F. G. Wilson (Engineering) Limited. There he flourished, writing office management software in-house that would have cost the company £6,000 from an outside source. Fearful that divulging his past to workmates might put his job at risk, Kinner had his "UVF L.P.O.W." tattoo and tattooed UVF insignia covered up with a red, forearm-sized Grim Reaper, but one manager from a "respectable unionist background" found out who he was from a television program. His comment to Kinner: "At least you've learned your lesson." Kinner doesn't see it that way. He believes he was a prisoner of war, and certainly does not think prison taught him anything. Rather, he learned a few things while in prison. He could have explained this nicety to the manager, but held his tongue because he needed the work.

Kinner now runs the Computer Training Center on the Shankill Road for the Northern Ireland Association for the Care and Resettlement of Offenders (NIACRO), which is funded mainly by the Probation Board. Ron McMurray also works for NIACRO, but as a counselor for young offenders convicted of nonpolitical crimes. He fully embraces his employment by a "statutory body" as a means of atoning for terrorist sins. Part of his job is keeping kids from joining paramilitary groups, and it presents no conflict for him. Kinner, though, has problems with working for NIACRO. Although most loyalists and republicans decline help from NIACRO or the Probation Board to preserve the stance that they were strictly political prisoners and not criminals, the odd loyalist will sign on. Jim "Tonto" Watt—the UVF's chief bomber in the seventies and now, after eighteen years in jail, a devout Christian who long ago resigned from the UVF—was one of Kinner's trainees during the working-out phase of his imprisonment. Kinner finds his own participation in the PUP, which is the political wing of the UVF, at cross-purposes with the purported rehabilitation of political prisoners. "I've certainly felt at times that I was doing stuff that I didn't feel that I had NIACRO's approval to do, and therefore felt that I was jeopardizing my job by doing it," he says.

Through a cross-community charity, Bryson House, Marty Snoddon provides computer training and services gratis to anyone who needs them but can't afford to pay for them. Snoddon, Kinner, and Tony Catney, a cousin of Kevin McQuillan and ex-IRA lifer who took charge of Sinn Fein's Brussels office in May 1995, started a prisoner self-help project called PROPP, which stands for Progressive Release of Political Prisoners, at the encouragement of Marty Rafferty. The project aims to ease prisoners' readjustment to the outside world. Politically motivated prisoners seldom use state organs like the Probation Board and NIACRO because they imply rehabilitation. The welfare arms of the paramilitary groups, which by law are denied state funds, can't draw money from customary private sources and simply aren't up to the job. PROPP aims to fill the gap between the two. Under PROPP, the republicans have already opened a center on the Falls Road, which provides reference services, counseling, training, family support, and day care.

A planned twin on the Shankill Road has taken longer to get up and running, but Marty Rafferty is at pains to explain that this is not because of any shiftlessness on the part of the loyalists. "A lot of the republicans are unemployed, so they are free to go and do their counseling courses and volunteer their services and form their network—they have nothing else to spend their day on. Whereas the loyalists—I mean, Eddie has a job, Marty has a job, Billy has a job." Granted, loyalists do look to conventional avenues of self-fulfillment to a far greater extent than republicans do. As a result, the loyalists are spread thinner. But it is unfair for republicans to denigrate the loyalists' conventionality by characterizing it as selfishness. In fact, loyalists get more flak from the Protestant community when they try to reassimilate than republicans get from the Catholic community. Again, republicans are generally seen as heroes, loyalists as wayward lads who didn't know what to do with their anger.

Despite his wispy frame and thick glasses, Jimmy Creighton was for six years Andy Tyrie's "minder," or bodyguard. His legendary moment came when he barred a tardy Ian Paisley from entering the meeting of the coordinating committee during the 1974 strike. He left the UDA in 1980, and is now community development officer for the Glencairn Community Redevelopment Association. His brief is to improve housing and economic conditions in Belfast's most depressed Protestant area, where unemployment runs about 60 percent. A chain-smoker with a voice like a chain saw, he has maintained a no-bullshit reputation with plain, crude talk about the plight of working-class Prods. Creighton is hopeful that the new loyalists will gain support, but knows that neighborhood service is a hard way to generate it. "Community work you don't get medals for. You get a big slap on the back of the neck," he says. "You can do people ninety-nine good turns, and the hundredth time they come and ask you to do something and you can't do it, then you become the biggest bastard that ever walked. And maybe that's when they turn around and say, well, sure he was a UDA cunt."

Under the "Hurd statement," issued in 1985 by Douglas Hurd when he was Northern Ireland secretary of state, community projects are denied funding if shown to have paramilitary links—a factor which discourages them from employing ex-paramilitaries. In 1989 Creighton's project, along with a couple on the Falls Road, had its funding yanked on account of perceived paramilitary connections. The government restored the money only in 1993. Loyalist ex-prisoners get little if any more rhythm from the state than republicans do. When Tommy Kirkham was chairman of the Whitewell Community Center through 1988, the RUC interrogated him for three days at Castlereagh, convinced that the Center was a UDA front. Finally, he resigned for the good of the project.

A republican's hope for a better material life putatively lies in revolution itself—a wholesale rejection of Northern Ireland as it is presently constituted. Thus, he was probably a full-time guerrilla, and is more likely now to be a full-time political activist. But a loyalist's great expectations flow from keeping society closer to what it has been. His active service as a paramilitary was likely part-time, and odds are that cause will still compete with career for his time. Occasionally, the two are neatly wedded. With substantial church funding, Billy Mitchell has started a project in north Belfast, the LINC Resource Center, which arranges training employment for ex-prisoners and people from economically stigmatized areas. Whether new loyalists like Mitchell become a major force in community politics depends on whether working-class loyalism can offer a vision of self-help more attractive than the paternalism of middle-class unionists.

THE UNSHACKLING OF LOYALISM

New loyalism began in the 1970s, with Gusty Spence in the Long Kesh compounds. Now, it stands not only for the union, but for the end of Protestant sectarianism and the political rebirth of the Protestant working class. But as with any faction in Northern Ireland, how the new loyalists got where they are is as important as what they represent.

The new loyalists disavow Stormont and claim that the unionist establishment has treated them like second-class citizens. Mainstream unionists regard this polemic as simplistic and somewhat craven. Chris McGimpsey holds a B.A. from Syracuse University, which makes him twice an Orangeman. He also has a doctorate in Irish history from the University of Edinburgh, but his mother is from a Shankill Road family. McGimpsey has more sympathy with the working class than most members of the predominantly middle-class UUP. As a Belfast city councilman, he represents the depressed Glencairn area. But McGimpsey still says the new loyalists' analysis "over-eggs the cake" by failing to acknowledge the complicity of the Protestant working class in its own fate.

"Stormont did not work as effectively and as efficiently as it should have because there was a permanent government with a permanent opposition," he admits. "People got lazy, and there was no imaginative thinking. Stormont was not responsive to social and economic issues. It was not a socialist government; it was not a government that expressed enough concern, I would say, for working-class people. But it's too easy to simply blame the unionists. There is an undercurrent in Protestant working-class thinking that you always blame somebody else. It's the Catholics, the Brits, it's the unionist government in Stormont, it's the Protestant middle classes. And I always say, well, fair enough, you're right in all your criticisms, but it's about time we start blaming ourselves as well. If we didn't want to vote for a unionist who lived in a big house and had no empathy with people who lived in mill houses, why did we? Oh, well, they come down and waved the flag at us. You know, that's not a rational argument. I've had this discussion with Eddie Kinner and Billy Hutchinson, David Ervine."

These new loyalists forget, says McGimpsey, that before the troubles there were alternatives to the mainstream unionists for the working class—including the expressly socialist option of trade unionism through the Northern Ireland Labour Party. They also discount the political influence during the Stormont period of middle-income farmers, who were economically more important then than they are now. "Even people who were unemployed got the sort of representatives they wanted. Now, it's easy now for their sons or grandsons to say, oh, my grandda was misled and betrayed by unionism, you know. Nobody's going to believe their own grandda was nuts and he voted for the wrong type of unionist. It's easier to say, my grandda had the wool pulled over his eyes."

Bob Cooper, now the chairman of the Fair Employment Commission and a long-time Alliance Party member, goes farther than McGimpsey in contending that the working class actually intimidated middle-class unionists and, to an extent, dictated their political agenda. "They are almost going along with the republican myth that we were conned. What they don't recognize is that the [Ulster] Unionist Party was scared of them, scared of loyalist working-class people. The Unionist Party, far from attempting to con them, didn't allow itself to make progress in certain areas because they believed that they couldn't carry the loyalist working-class people with them. And one of the things which people forget is that the first Official Unionist politician to win a majority of votes in the Shankill district was John McQuade in 1965. Up until then, it would have been represented by labour politicians or by Independent Unionists, and the Independent Unionist who represented it was a real hard-line former policeman who'd been expelled from the police because of his bigotry. So they were not conned. They shaped their destiny to a greater extent than they would now attempt to argue."

The truth probably lies in the middle ground: during Stormont, the Protestant working class accepted the primacy of the border in exchange for economic security; during the troubles, thanks to Paisley and the right-hand side of the Ulster Unionist Party, the Protestant working class accepted the primacy of the border as the price of mere economic hope. Quid pro quo was transformed into coerced loyalty. Unionists promised to save loyalists from Irish unification provided the loyalists vote as if they were economic conservatives even though, being generally poor and unlanded, they were at heart socialists. This arrangement made them not only genuinely incompatible with nationalists on the constitutional question, but artificially incompatible on social policy as well.

Consequently, one factor that tipped the balance in favor of violence was that the troubles ensured political participation for everyone without cost to the mainstream parties. Consigning armed conflict to the working classes enabled the mainstream nationalist and unionist groups to carry on their own battle for hegemony without worrying about more mundane blue-collar problems. As long as the main concerns of republicanism and loyalism remained military, their socialist embellishments posed no threat to the SDLP, the UUP, and the DUP. The fact that loyalists and unionists, and nationalists and republicans, agreed on the border issue did not create interclass solidarity. Instead, because the border was really the only issue, agreement tended to cancel out the political voice of the working classes.

The new loyalists are left with the not insubstantial argument that at least since direct rule began, the constitutional issue was forced down their throats and kept them from developing the working-class politics that had been suppressed, if democratically, all along.[2] And indeed, their principal complaint is that it was Paisleyism, not so much Stormont, that sucked them in. From the new loyalists' perspective, the received view of the troubles as a fight between two minorities is too simplistic; working-class Protestants carved out a third one. Imagine the "poor white trash" of the United States fighting a reactionary war against economically competitive blacks with the tacit encouragement of "the power elite," realizing they were duped, then registering their displeasure in the form of a nascent working-class politics that embraces those competitors and ignores the "betters" who used them. This notional course is roughly analogous to the new loyalists' actual one.

But loyalism's inherent conservatism on the border has made it difficult for loyalists to embrace socialism openly. During the troubles, Northern Ireland's economy grew inordinately dependent on Britain's subsidy in general, the security budget in particular. In 1994, 40 percent of the province's jobs were government-related. The troubles depressed overseas investment, the only noteworthy flash being maverick entrepreneur John DeLorean's short-lived automobile plant south of Belfast. Wanted by the police, he fled the province in 1982 leaving massive debts which he still has not repaid. Northern Ireland was neither socialist nor capitalist; it was freakishly pragmatic.

Insofar as the Ulster Unionist Party is at core middle-class, its natural alliance is with the British Conservative Party. Before 1969, the two parties had been solidly aligned ever since the Conservatives had supported Ulster MPs against home rule in the late eighteenth century. But after the troubles started and direct rule was imposed, unionist MPs used their bargaining power as swing voters to gain support for the union—in particular, the reinstitution of a devolved government—from whichever party held power. The UUP executive voted narrowly to restore its special relationship with the Conservative Party in 1983, but recanted in 1985 when Thatcher signed the Anglo-Irish Agreement. In February 1995, unionist MPs threatened to withdraw support for John Major in his fight against party Euro-skeptics and switch unionist allegiance to Labour on account of the nationalist slant of the framework document. Once again, economic ideology was strictly subordinate to the border.

Unionists were especially cool toward the British Labour Party in the eighties and early nineties, when the party, in opposition, promoted a united Ireland by Northern Irish consent.* Conservatives have always supported unionism. Accordingly, to the extent that unionism embraced any salient economic philosophy during the troubles, it was Thatcherite capitalism, which overwhelmed British Labour Party socialism throughout the United Kingdom. Although republicans were largely to blame for Northern Ireland's particular distortions, as revolutionaries they could comfortably flog left-wing politics as the antidote for the statelet's economic woes and impugn Margaret Thatcher to boot. Loyalists could not. As pro-state terrorists, they were stuck with the economic agenda of the British government. Thus, in Thatcher's era and after, they muted their socialism.

The UVF grew its socialist roots in the compounds—Billy Hutchinson's favorite book remains Robert Trestle's *The Raggedy-Trousered Philanthropist*, a socialist polemic which he read in prison. David Ervine quotes George Bernard Shaw. But loyalist socialism lay dormant for twenty years, until the new loyalists came of political age. The UDA, being larger than the UVF, has always been more diffuse and pragmatic in its politics, but Glen Barr started out as president of a trade union in Derry and continues to advocate a mixed economy. The new loyalists have some faith in British socialism, despite its recent difficulties. Republicans cannot afford to have the same view, since it would not support their argument for dropping the union with Britain. Consequently, their public assessment of Britain's economy is that it is conceptually unsound—that true socialism is impossible in a unionist context. The new loyalists take the inverse position. They argue that the majority of people in Northern Ireland should *and will* vote to maintain the union because it is economically the best option. This position is straightforward, but shrewd. The argument turns on everyone's welfare. It has no sectarian undertone, and is not vulnerable to demographic projections of a Catholic voting majority in the next generation.

"People have stated that scientifically they can prove that by the year 2025 there's going to be a nationalist majority," reasons Billy Hutchinson. "I don't believe that there will be a nationalist majority. I believe that there

---

*Since Tony Blair took over as Labour Party leader in 1994, and especially since the cease-fires, Labour has taken a more neutral line on reunification. See Ivan Gibbons, "Realism Essential," *Fortnight* 336 (February 1995), p. 14. Conservatives now generally favor devolution. Post-ceasefire, then, British policy on Northern Ireland has been effectively bipartisan. On Northern Ireland matters, Blair supported John Major unreservedly both before and after Canary Wharf.

will be a majority of people who describe themselves as Catholics. I don't think the majority of people in Northern Ireland, irrespective of whether they're Catholic or Protestant, will ever vote for a united Ireland. When it comes to a crunch, a lot of Catholics know when they're well off. They don't want to go into the Republic of Ireland and start paying 46p on the pound tax, when they only pay 25p on the pound up here. The biggest growth sector in Northern Ireland since direct rule is the Catholic middle class. There will never be a nationalist majority saying they want to go into a united Ireland. They'll stay where they are. Sure, it'd be ludicrous to move. The key is how Catholics fare over the next twenty-five to thirty years. If they fare even better than what's happening now, there's no way— the whole thing about a united Ireland will actually be forgot about."

Ideologically, loyalist socialism easily stands up to the republican charge that it can't coexist with unionism. Billy Mitchell eruditely explains his beliefs: "I would call myself a Christian socialist. The British labor movement owes more to Methodism than it does to Marx. In the early British labor leaders—the like of Keir Hardie and George Lansbury—I would identify my socialism. I wouldn't be too far removed from the British Labour Party, on the side of Tony Blair, Shirley Williams, people like that. As we progressed into modern socialism, then we were able to identify with the working-class people of England and the Scots."

The republican attack on loyalist socialism tends to collapse working-class loyalists into the unionist Ascendancy class. Beyond the inaccuracy of this stance, Mitchell regards it as the pot calling the kettle black. "There's no difference between the green tories of Fianna Fail and the blue tories of the Conservative Party, or the orange tories of the unionist Ascendancy. This is where I can't understand the logic of the republicans. I mean, they claim to be working-class, they claim to be some sort of socialists, yet they'd be prepared to sacrifice their socialism for a state controlled by green capitalism." Again, there is some weight behind this salvo, as the PUP has actually courted the pure socialists among republicans—namely, the Official IRA.

Whereas Hutchinson makes his socialism merely compatible with a continued union, Mitchell does him one better by arguing that a continued union jibes with global economic reality. "I believe that a united Ireland or an independent Ulster is meaningless. No country is independent economically, so what does a united Ireland mean? We paint our postboxes green instead of red?" he laughs. "It's just about symbols, because economically we're dependent on Britain. Ireland is dependent on the whole European economy, and Europe is dependent on the world economy, so the Group of Seven really rule the world. So to me it's not worth fighting and dying for symbols. That's really all the IRA are fighting for." Here again is a loyalist using the economic status quo—in particular, Britain's £5-billion annual subsidy to Northern Ireland and the Republic's heavy economic dependence on the European Union—to full forensic advantage.

Certainly republicans are being disingenuous when they say that socialism is inconsistent with unionism. The British Labour Party, even with recent dilutions on matters such as privatization, is undeniably socialist. In fact, the welfare state the party instituted fifty years ago so compromised British capitalism that eighteen years of aggressive Conservative rule has not succeeded in completely resurrecting the free market. Labour may well regain power in Westminster in 1997. Republican economic arguments will be correspondingly weaker. On the other hand, loyalists are also playing cute when they deny that their socialism is merely incidental to their unionism. If, as Mitchell says, the border is "just about symbols" and global economics is what really matters, would he forsake the union if the Irish Republic could offer Ulster Protestants a better welfare state? Plainly not. Loyalism means loyalty to the Crown. It is semantically about being British. Republicanism, likewise, means a thirty-two-county Irish republic. It is semantically about being Irish.

For loyalists as well as Sinn Fein, socialism is a tactic of persuasion, not an immutable principle. And if republicans still see loyalists as deluded stooges of the Protestant Ascendancy, then loyalists see republicans as Machiavellian demagogues who merely feign populism. Ideologically, it's a standoff.

THE NEW LOYALIST ALTERNATIVE

The new loyalists' preferred argument for the vitality of loyalism itself pivots on the practical advantages of British institutions rather than on any romantic attachment to Great Britain. It also draws strength from the present numerical majority unionists enjoy in Northern Ireland. Obviously, republicans are deprived of this advantage. Indeed, they cannot even be sure that voters in the Republic, faced with a referendum, would endorse a unitary Irish state outright. A pre-ceasefire poll in the *Irish Times* showed that those voters overwhelmingly preferred an internal solution prior to reunification. This result strongly suggests that the southern electorate sides with *unionists* rather than republicans on the issue of consent.

Yet the voters who shy away from immediate reunification will not give up the *aspiration* of a united Ireland. According to the same poll, 58 percent opposed any repeal of article 2 of the Irish Constitution, which claims all thirty-two counties as the national territory, or article 3, which obligates Dublin to effect reunification.[3] To southerners, a united Ireland is theoretically attractive because it is resonant of the ideal that inspired independence. But reunification is practically daunting. The Republic is struggling economically and wants no part of the sectarian ugliness that has plagued Northern Ireland. It follows that Sinn Fein's support in the south is a minuscule 2 percent.

By the same token, as Anthony McIntyre suspects, loyalists cannot be sure of Britain's unalloyed support. Ever since Prime Minister Harold Wilson referred to striking loyalists in 1974 as people "purporting to act as though they were an elected government, spending their lives sponging on Westminster,"[4] the handwriting has been on the wall. The fact remains that while unionists can be reasonably sure of Britain's guarantee that a united Ireland must have unionist consent, that is all they can be sure of. In Britain, they behold a flagging international power whose fatigue stops short of exhaustion only on account of national self-regard and the weight of history. London's resolve is simply too brittle to bear the weight of Paisley's heavy-handed guilt trips. His day has come and gone. New loyalists like Kirkham recognize that much. But are they dextrous enough to massage the Brits in the right places?

At first blush, it appears so. The political imperative is for the new loyalists to make their case within the system. This need has moved them to sanitize their pedigrees—Spence by a public conversion to nonviolence long before the ceasefires, Ervine and White by earnest political leadership, Hutchinson by getting a college degree in jail and taking up community service outside. Whereas republicans thrive on reminding people of what they have done, loyalists must strive to make them forget it. Anthony McIntyre loses nothing for the movement in characterizing peace as merely "a cold war," while Hutchinson feels compelled to say resolutely that "the war is over." Troubles-era politics reflected the difference: neither the Ulster Unionist Party nor Paisley's DUP felt it could get close to the paramilitaries without losing support, whereas the SDLP did not consider a rapprochement with Sinn Fein impermissibly risky.

Even now the new loyalists remain without any firm electoral base, while Sinn Fein's has been secure, though limited, since the hunger strikes. At a conference sponsored by the Peace People in late 1994, David

Trimble, an MP and now UUP party leader, condescendingly told Billy Hutchinson that working-class people should "leave politics to the people who know what they're doing."

Loyalists have more to lose by reaching out to republicans than republicans chance by reaching out to loyalists. The nationalist community acknowledges that IRA men had their reasons for killing, and grudgingly concedes political motivation to loyalists as well. Thus, a detente between ex-prisoners from each community seems more or less natural to nationalists. But the unionist community generally regards loyalist paramilitaries as murdererous criminals, and holds republican ex-prisoners in even lower esteem. Unionists are reluctant enough to embrace loyalist ex-prisoners as politicians. When they seek accommodation with their republican counterparts, they court political doom.

Thus, Falls Road Catholics trust Tommy Gorman while Shankill Road Protestants do not trust Billy Hutchinson. Gorman can guarantee Hutchinson's safety in Catholic west Belfast, but Hutchinson does not feel he can protect Gorman on the Shankill. Some working-class Prods have taken to calling Hutchinson "the Protestant Provo" on account of his involvement (indeed, his friendship) with Gorman and his innocuous admission that the Giant's Causeway is part of Ireland. Protestant church leaders had been meeting with Sinn Fein about cross-community issues monthly for three years between 1992 and 1995, yet the new loyalists, though invited, had to decline participation for fear of politically self-aborting. "There's a healing process, and it's too soon to forgive and forget," says John White. "We're certainly open to it, but there's a lot of people still grieving in our communities, and we wouldn't gain widespread support at all for talking to Sinn Fein."

Despite these inherent constraints on new loyalist initiative, David Ervine and Billy Hutchinson say that the loyalists' open-ended ceasefire might have come before the IRA's, but for the Provos' desire to steal the loyalists' thunder and provoke them into an upsurge of violence instead. There is some circumstantial evidence to support this theory. In summer 1994, republicans assassinated two high-ranking loyalists—Trevor King of the UVF and Ray Smallwoods of the UDP. On July 15, the day after they were buried, the Combined Loyalist Military Command issued a statement saying it would declare a ceasefire if the IRA would reciprocate. The IRA rejected the offer. In the ensuing six weeks, the IRA killed two leading UDA men, launched ten attacks on security force installations, and bombed two pubs in Protestant areas. During that period, the Provos

Gerry Adams announcing IRA ceasefire in west Belfast, August 31, 1994. *Brendan Murphy, Irish News*

Celebratory Falls Road menu. *Brendan Murphy, Irish News*

Top: Schoolchildren on the "peace line," ten days before the loyalist ceasefire. *Brendan Murphy, Irish News*

Middle: Schoolchildren on the Falls Road, the first day of the IRA ceasefire. *Brendan Murphy, Irish News*

Bottom: "Edited" post-ceasefire road sign near the border. *Brendan Murphy, Irish News*

Three cops and a Sinn Fein protester, north Belfast, 1995. *Hugh Russell, Irish News*

An Orangeman scolding the RUC for blocking the Orange parade from proceeding down the Ormeau Road, June 1995. *Hugh Russell, Irish News*

Monsignor Denis Faul. *Ann McManus, Irish News*

Martin McGuinness speaking at a Sinn Fein rally, in front of a poster of Bobby Sands, Ulster Hall, November 1995. *Hugh Russell, Irish News*

Above: Kevin McQuillan and Gino Gallagher, chief of staff of the hardline INLA, at a press conference held by the IRSP, 1996. Weeks later, on January 30, Gallagher was shot dead at a Falls Road welfare office. *Brendan Murphy, Irish News*
Left: John White in front of a loyalist mural, Shankill Road, 1995. *Brendan Murphy, Irish News*

Augustus "Gusty" Spence before reading the loyalist ceasefire announcement. *Brendan Murphy, Irish News*

Spokesmen for the Combined Loyalist Military Command announcing the loyalist ceasefire, October 13, 1994, Glencairn, Belfast. Left to right: David Adams, David Ervine, Gary McMichael, William "Plum" Smith, Gusty Spence, John White, Jim McDonald. *Brendan Murphy, Irish News*

Tommy Gorman, 1996. *Brendan Murphy, Irish News*

Ward, October 1994, holding picture of son Peter
, sometimes called the first victim of the troubles,
m Gusty Spence was convicted of murdering in
. *Brendan Murphy, Irish News*

Billy Hutchinson addressing a conference in republican west Belfast, 1995. *Hugh Russell, Irish News*

Carol Cullen at her drop-in center for republican ex-prisoners, 1996. *Ann McManus, Irish News*

Loyalist mural, Shore Road, north Belfast. *Brendan Murphy, Irish News*

Provisional IRA mural, lower Falls. *Brendan Murphy, Irish News*

A milk truck on fire during Clegg disturbances, lower Falls, July 1995. Unrest in the summer of 1996 was far worse. *Brendan Murphy, Irish News*

killed five people versus the loyalists' seven victims, and injured dozens. Then they stole the limelight of peace by declaring their own ceasefire.

The slow pace of the new loyalists' empowerment, of course, is not entirely due to Sinn Fein's nimble manipulations and other political externalities. Working-class Protestants, ex-prisoners in particular, are conditioned to be less expansive and more cautious in expressing themselves than working-class Catholics. Long-term imprisonment makes anyone withdrawn and in need of shepherding on the outside at first, and the network of social support for released loyalist prisoners doesn't compare to the open arms that republicans find waiting for them. It follows that they are also far less cocky about testing their new intellectual and political wings, with good reason. "In the Protestant community, there was always some sort of belief that there was a class that was born to rule, and if you came from a working-class background you weren't born to rule," says Hutchinson. "People say, you really need educated people in your party— I mean, I have a degree in social science, but because I got my education in prison, it's knocked down a notch or two. That has been the problem within the Protestant community—that people do feel that there was a class that was born to rule and that class should be there. It's the David Trimbles of this world."

Yet not all of the negative energy towards the new loyalists emanates from Ascendancy Prods like Trimble or Shankill escapees like McGimpsey. Some of it comes from working-class folks themselves, who—perhaps in deference to their "granddas"—can't rally themselves to any calling higher than soldier. "I'd warned Tommy [Kirkham] to be ready for a big disappointment, you know, there in the heartland of Rathcoole, the UDA's own area," says Glen Barr, a working-class Derry Prod and scarred veteran of the UDA's attempts to go political. "You know, the UDA's grand when the guys are drinking in pubs and all, but when they get to the ballot-box there's no guarantee how they're going to vote. And there's a lot of jealousy you see, as well; rivalry within them. Tommy Kirkham's a nice guy, a very nice fellow, but I'm sure there's some UDA guys who'll say, I'm not voting for him, he's getting too big for his boots."

As Barr suggests, there is a truculent anti-cosmopolitan backlash from blue-collar Protestants against the new loyalists' calls to political engagement. UVF man William Giles, still serving a life sentence in the Maze, estimates that of ninety people in his block, sixty have earned some form of educational qualification in prison. This is new loyalism at work. By contrast, most teenagers on the Shankill Road leave school with *no* qualifications. Giles himself has a B.A. in psychology, with second-class honors,* from the Open University. He sees the main problem in the Protestant working-class community as low expectations for children, and he would like to help change that when he gets out. Although he attributes his anti-academic, politically ignorant, work-driven upbringing—old loyalism—to "the Protestant ethic," he is extremely reluctant to blame anyone. On the Shankill Road itself, this refusal to denigrate one's heritage, however debased, is writ large. With it often comes a persistent wish to replicate the past and nothing more—to get blue-collar jobs in whatever replaces the shipyard and the linen mills, but with no advancement to management or government.

Eddie Kinner himself shows traces of this stultifyingly provincial mentality. Even as he became educated, he says, "I always attempted to maintain me own accent. I didn't want to lose the Shankill Road accent or anything like that. When you're learning all of those kind of words, even in mathematics and computing, you learn how to pronounce them from the tutors or from television programs from the tapes, so actually there's a certain amount of politeness that starts to creep in if you're not aware. For some reason I just didn't want to be superior. I didn't want to move away from my roots in that way. I just didn't feel it was anything I was quite capable of doing."

Kinner skipped school about a third of the time during the height of the troubles in the early seventies, often because it was unsafe to go out. Although a good chess player with obvious aptitude for abstract thinking (he was in the chess club), in secondary school he was never encouraged even to think about college. His sole outside inspiration came on the last day of school, when a teacher told him offhand that he could have taken O-levels. With so little urging in school, working-class Protestants came to regard intellectual endeavors with the hostility that comes with lack of confidence. As Breidge Gadd, chief probation officer, puts it: "They weren't given any choice—you don't do education if you're a real man."

Perhaps because the Catholic community hasn't known even the humble security of reliable menial work, it doesn't suffer the same neurosis. "On the Shankill Road, if anyone makes it either educationally or employment-wise, they pretty much get out if they can," notes Marty Rafferty. "Those who become qualified teachers move off the Shankill Road.

---

*Equivalent to *magna cum laude*.

Those who become social workers move off the Shankill Road. On the Falls Road, you have your social worker living around the corner from your client. You have your doctor still living in the road, you have your teacher still living on the road. So there's much more of a cross-section of abilities, of educational development, of occupations, of leadership. On the Shankill, on the whole, people are likely to be unemployed and less educated because once people do succeed they move out. The Catholic community can embrace its whole community a bit more than the Protestant community seems to be able to."

Appreciably more working-class Catholics than Protestants emerge from school with some qualifications. At university level, the Protestant rather than the Catholic community is experiencing a "brain drain." The enrollment of Queen's University of Belfast, once a Protestant stronghold, is now over 50 percent Catholic. Those Protestants who qualify for university tend to flee to England or Scotland and stay there. Catholics who make good—like Joe Hendron, a practicing medical doctor as well as a politician—are more likely to stay local.

To counter the Protestant working class's timidity, Hutchinson offers an important, if setpiece, declaration: "I think politics is too important to be left to the politicians." Of all the new loyalists, Hutchinson is the one who has searched his soul the hardest and put it smack dab on the line for his community. Even the most skeptical republicans—Kevin McQuillan, for instance—single out Hutchinson for his courage and enterprise. Yet he does not himself believe that the new loyalists will ever develop a mainstream following. "I don't think we'll ever get the mandate that Sinn Fein has. I don't think we'll ever reach those dizzy heights."

Notwithstanding their mandate, Shinners are hardly true democrats. Sinn Fein will not, for example, concede that republicans would docilely abide by a Northern Ireland referendum on the reunification. Why? Because the party maintains that the only proper democratic majority is island-wide. Yet Sinn Fein's claim to political weight is premised on its 10-percent support in a state it considers illegal. With a 2-percent mandate in the Republic, the party's all-Ireland support would come to less than 5 percent. The new loyalists, on the other hand, do not have the luxury of switching from one political context to another when it suits them. They are compelled to admit that they would shuffle to Dublin if perchance an Ulster majority were to approve reunification.

Although the same constraint nominally applies to mainstream unionists, they are more practiced at using sidelong arguments to put the possibility of a united Ireland out of sight and out of mind. Hutchinson handles the prospect of a Catholic majority by arguing that the union with Britain would be economically attractive even to Catholics. In contrast, unionist MP John Taylor murmurs that Catholic emigration will drive out any Catholics who might otherwise vote for a united Ireland. From Taylor, republicans draw the inference that unionists will make staying unpalatable to Catholic nationalists. "I mean, he can state this here; had he said it somewhere else he'd have been down for being a racist,"* fumes Tommy Gorman. "They get away with murder, some of them politicians." Were Hutchinson to support Taylor's argument, he would alienate Gorman and sacrifice cross-community reconciliation—potentially a big part of the new loyalist agenda. At the same time, Hutchinson's guileless argument is less reassuring to many unionist voters than Taylor's dismissive one.

NEW LOYALIST PROSPECTS

The new loyalists are not naive about their intramural disadvantages, and there are even some indications of a compensating political astuteness. For a parade and rally on October 13, 1995, celebrating the first anniversary of the loyalist ceasefire, UDP and PUP organizers instructed marchers to avoid nationalist areas, particularly the Ormeau Road, and placed a strict prohibition on alcohol. Thousands congregated on cordoned-off Royal Avenue in downtown Belfast, and the event proceeded without incident. David Ervine has been consciously groomed as the PUP's favorite son.[5] He was never convicted of killing or maiming anyone, just possession of explosives. He almost always wears a coat and tie, sports a dark mustache, and smokes a pipe. He has a ready smile and a polished accent, and seems older than his forty-two years. Beneath a respectably receding hairline, he looks the part of a unionist politician rather than a loyalist paramilitary. He is bright and articulate.

UDP leader Gary McMichael has never spent a minute in jail. His father, John, was vice-chairman of the UDA, but the IRA made him a troubles martyr in 1987, wiring a bomb to the ignition of his car outside his home in Lisburn. Gary, then eighteen, was at a rock concert in Belfast and

---

*Republicans sometimes say "racist" when they mean "sectarian" or "bigoted." Cross-community bias in Northern Ireland, of course, has nothing to do with race. The term "racist," though, carries a greater stigma than the other two.

was summoned over the public-address system to hear the bad news. He is heavyset, somewhat boyish, and projects hard-earned sincerity, if not great intellect. The new loyalists are fully aware that they have no real mandate as yet, and have remained modest. They do not beg for credit for statesmanship that has not yet been certified at the ballot box.

On the other hand, John White on the face of things would have to be considered a net liability for the UDP. He went to jail for two very ugly murders. Despite his seemingly genuine contrition and studious countenance—he is quite bald, wears round rimless glasses, and appears rather shy—many Protestants cannot accept him as a politician. Andy Tyrie, a friend of White's and generally a very savvy character, seems to have more faith than he should in the forgiveness of the loyalist working class for what many perceive as the paramilitaries' besmirching of the Protestant people. "I told him when he decided to take an interest in politics, I said, John, you'd be good for politics because you live in the area, you have a good brain on you, you know how to treat people and work with them. I says, first of all, you have to accept the fact that you spent time for murder. I says, don't deny it, I says, and then nobody will have anything against you."

White himself is too optimistic in his belief that "prisoners certainly are viewed as folk heroes, and they will be viewed as veterans," and David Ervine suggests it's more prudent to regard them as "bad messengers with a good message." But the fact that the new loyalists have not visibly discouraged White's participation suggests a certain stubbornness about the validity of their original quarrel, which may prove counterproductive. In stark contrast, the IRA wisely prohibited prisoners convicted of putatively sectarian murders—including Bik McFarlane and Anthony McIntyre—from participating in the 1981 hunger strike on the theory that they'd make unconvincing martyrs.

While IRA prisoners or ex-prisoners take great pains to conceal any sectarian influences and invariably cite political or quality-of-life factors as their inspiration, loyalist prisoners are almost perversely frank. IRA prisoner OC Sean Lynch says he joined the struggle on account of unequal job opportrites in his rural home town. But Michael Stone, OC of UDA prisoners from East Belfast and UDA prison spokesman, for example, openly admits that in his youth he was a member of one of the "Tartan gangs"—UDA forerunners that would force Catholic families out of the neighborhood first by throwing bricks through their windows; then, if they didn't leave, by waiting until they went to Mass and petrol-bombing the houses, which would sometimes be burned to the ground. In the next breath, he calls the Ulster Protestant heritage that sustained his paramilitary motivation "the wealth of history."

A similar hunkered-down quality emerges in the extreme tentativeness (with the notable exception of Hutchinson) of the new loyalists in what personal contacts they have had with republicans. Post–Canary Wharf, it is hard to blame loyalists for their standoffishness. But Eddie Kinner and Anthony McIntyre met at a seminar on education in early 1995, when the IRA ceasefire was intact. While McIntyre came away from the meeting liking Kinner, Kinner felt upstaged and put off on account of what he took to be McIntyre's high tone. "He talked way above everybody's head," says Kinner. "He's not practical, he's not real." There is a haughty naiveté operating here. While he would like the PUP to become the source of plain loyalist truth, Kinner finds the political machinations required to reach that end distasteful. "I think it's dangerous to get involved in chasing support," he says, "because your motivations are wrong then. You start to look for what's going to be popular, and doing what's popular. For me, getting involved in political imagery implies some kind of falsehood. We have not engaged in presenting issues different from what we're actually about. If you start to get involved in con games, you'll get caught out or you'll start to believe them yourselves."

Kinner's pre-political innocence is admirable, but unhelpful when it comes to competing with mainstream unionists or countering Sinn Fein. Kinner took offense when, on a radio program, David Trimble interpreted a question Kinner didn't understand for Kinner's benefit. Gary McMichael was the only unionist to attend the St. Patrick's Day celebration at the White House in 1995, Paisley and James Molyneaux (then UUP party leader) having declined on account of Gerry Adams's and Northern Ireland Secretary of State Sir Patrick Mayhew's simultaneous presence. The best assessment Chris McGimpsey could muster was that McMichael had "put country before party" in trying to draw a human face on unionism. "Unfortunately," he added, "in Northern Ireland there's too many politicians prepared to put personal position before party, and party before country." By implication, they're all mainstream unionists, with whom new loyalists are the underdog competitors.

While McMichael took the kind of forward-looking risk that underdogs need to take, parochialism puts an offsetting retrograde twist on new loyalism. Tommy Kirkham, also a UDP man, talks nice about reconciling the two communities, but part of him remains insular and petulant. He tells a story about a Catholic civil rights worker whose house in north Belfast was burned down by loyalist paramilitaries in the late sixties, when Kirkham was in his early teens. "I remember the house of a guy called Grogary who was a dentist in the Duncairn Gardens. He was involved in the civil rights campaign and he lived in a large house in Fortwilliam, and the Rooftop Youth Club that I attended was on Fortwilliam. I remember leaving the club on a Friday night, walking down past the house. There was a group of us, and all of a sudden this guy threw a couple of bottles out the window of the house. You know—he was a civil-righter living in a Protestant area. What did he expect? Of course we got involved. Later on that night the house was being attacked by people in combat gear. The house was burnt to the ground. But he caused that incident that night. I watched it, and I took some glory in the fact that his house was burnt to the ground, because it was him that started it as far as I was concerned."

Republicans have the extraordinary ability to remember back to medieval times, but forget, say, the 1975 "ceasefire." Loyalists, on the other hand, tend to have acute and candid memories of recent troubles history. In the post-ceasefire atmosphere, frank talk like Kirkham's may amount to an admission against interest. Undeniably, there is still an abundance of sectarianism permeating both communities. The richest mixture by far is produced in Belfast, where loyalist paramilitaries were very intensely concentrated. Belfast is the most heavily segregated area in Northern Ireland, and in Northern Ireland segregation breeds bigotry, just as it does in the United States. A Protestant teenager growing up in north Belfast, as Tommy Kirkham did, might not meet a Catholic until he starts working at age seventeen. Similarly, a Catholic kid from Andersonstown might not encounter a Protestant until he leaves school. In the meantime, they've been imbued with prejudices telescoped for generations and nurtured by the troubles, and aired them with free rein, unchecked by counterexamples or counterarguments.

The growing Prod finds out that Catholics are drunken libertines who will steal a Protestant's wallet, salve their guilt with a trip to the confessional, then go do it again. As the Catholic comes of age, he learns that Protestants are uptight puritans who will begrudge a man a drink on Sundays, and damn the man who takes one anyway. These stereotypes lie a fair distance from the whole truth, but once exposed the preconditioned will selectively incorporate those experiences that substantiate and perpetuate their biases rather than those that disprove them. It takes a serendipitous turn of fate—like Alex Calderwood's meeting a singularly genial

Catholic in the young-offenders center and running a protection racket with him—to turn a young sectarian bigot around.

The same points apply to bigoted groups in the United States. The big difference is that they have physical space in which they can throw round-house punches and still miss everyone they hate, where Catholics and Protestants in Belfast do not. Michigan Militia types can always find their kind of town if they want to—95 percent white, no immigrants, far away from New York and the pernicious United Nations, with big forest preserves for barbecues and target practice. They have *Lebensraum.* But in Northern Ireland, people had nowhere else to go. One atrocity begat others, then others.

Because the loyalist paramilitaries launched a more overtly sectarian armed campaign than the IRA, the entire loyalist community gets tagged with the label "sectarian" while the Catholic community often escapes that stigma. "It's worse than patronizing," says Jackie Redpath, for over twenty years a community development worker on the Shankill Road. "I don't think that republicanism has ever faced up to the sectarianism that exists within it. They'd be afraid to face up to it. But if you're a wee lad from the Shankill going down to the city center and getting the shit kicked out of you at Millfield [Technical College] by Catholic kids because you happen to have the wrong football shirt on, that's sectarian. And I don't think that's ever been faced up to, and therefore it's a total put-down. I mean, Martin McGuinness always talks about the loyalist 'death squads,' and the IRA death squads are exactly the same. It's a put-down, and it's not useful." In Redpath's view, mutual presumptions of sectarianism present the biggest barrier to peace in Northern Ireland. If the new loyalists have a major shortcoming, it would be their failure to stay focused on this sort of cross-community problem, and their tendency instead to become preoccupied with defining themselves as the untapped working-class voice of unionism.

As iconoclasts, of course, the new loyalists are not even on the same planet as Sinn Fein. Constitutionally, they are satisfied with the status quo; economically, they are pragmatic and urge no wholesale changes. Moreover, they are inhibited by the political cautiousness of the Protestant community, and some of the bridge building has to be done indirectly. David Ervine, for example, is fond of observing that the Catholic was abused for his disloyalty, while the Protestant was used for his loyalty. This is a favorite theme of loyalist ex-prisoners, and republicans grudgingly take their point: under Stormont working-class Protestants as well as

Catholics were partially disenfranchised and severely underprivileged, though unlike Catholics they were conditioned to accept their position at the risk of losing even more. They did benefit from industry in their neighborhoods and jobs inherited through nepotism, so at the polls they chose the devil they knew and kept quiet. As Billy Mitchell says, if the Catholics hadn't turned the civil rights protests into a sectarian crusade, the Prods probably would have joined them. The idea now is to supplant illusory sectarian differences with solid common ground.

Obviously, this is a far more constructive approach than loyalists had before the ceasefires, and it has made republicans somewhat more receptive to them. Hutchinson and Gorman's project, for instance, is not a hands-on social welfare organization, but instead exchanges information between the Catholic and Protestant working-class communities with an eye toward better understanding and coordination. Both ex-prisoners freely acknowledge that their political objectives—to remain British and to unite with the Republic—are as diametrically opposed as ever. Yet their shared prison experience has forged a bond, albeit a tense one. Gorman sees Hutchinson as a fellow political casualty. Recall that Hutchinson goes so far as to admit that loyalists should have supported republicans in the H-block protests for special-category status after it was withdrawn in 1976. While neither styles himself a pacifist, the project is a ground-level reflection of their agreed view that the conflict must be transformed from violence to negotiation to be resolved.

Underpinning Hutchinson and Gorman's work is the recognition that the two groups at the sharp ends of the conflict—the Catholic and Protestant working classes—have common social problems that have long been neglected by the mainstream parties and can at least develop a harmonious economic outlook. More ambitiously, Hutchinson is hopeful that "parallel social, economic, and cultural economic development" can make the two communities disinclined to poison their own waters with bloodshed, and confine the constitutional debate to politics. In this attitude, Hutchinson shows a positive residue of loyalist paramilitary thinking: it is the nationalist community that needs to be convinced of the peaceful way, and not just the hard men of the IRA.

The project, in sum, is a community enterprise which aims to fulfill a ground-level political role. Both ex-prisoners understand that the less advantaged people of the north are tired of having their welfare subordinated to the constitutional issue. The enterprise also reveals the deeper truth about paramilitaries: that they were and are driven by a reverential sense of community. At the most malignant extreme, these strong ties to the neighborhood spelled institutionalized sectarian murder. Now the perpetrators are marshaling the same communitarian motivation and energy by more benevolent means. Hutchinson and his wife live near the "peace line" where Catholic and Protestant west Belfast meet, and recently chose to send their twelve-year-old son to one of the few "integrated" Northern Irish schools with both Catholic and Protestant students. An Orangeman or a Paisleyite would be unlikely to follow the Hutchinsons' lead.

At the same time, progressive elements among the mainstream unionists are beginning to awaken to the reality that the new loyalists have already grasped—that while unionism is eminently defensible, its trappings are objectionable enough to put off potential Catholic converts. In October 1995, David McDowell, secretary of the Unionist Graduates Association, told the Ulster Young Unionist Council that the UUP had to divorce itself from the Orange Order and get wise to the exigencies of public relations: "I would, I must confess, question the sanity and moral integrity of any Roman Catholic who joined our party at present," he said. "How could he honestly live with himself knowing that a seventh of the people at this conference represent a folk tradition that defines itself by opposition to his religion? How many times have you been ashamed to be in this party when some councillor gets up on his hind legs and, in barely comprehensible tones of Biblical wrath, denounces President Robinson* as a witch or claims that extending pub opening hours will sap the Protestant will to fight popery? We must have an efficient selection system which weeds out the inarticulate, the embarrassing, and the downright barking [loony], while simultaneously promoting the intelligent, the rational, and the media aware."[6]

David Trimble himself is trying gently to distance the Ulster Unionist Party from the Orange Order. At this point, the Order's image may be irretrievably tarnished. On October 30, 1995, the Irish-American Unity Conference ran a $20,000 quarter-page advertisement in the *New York Times* likening Orange marches to Ku Klux Klan rallies and calling David Trimble, who is an Orangeman, "the David Duke of Ireland." Trimble resented the comparison, but so did celebrated ex-Klan member and Louisiana politician David Duke. He pointed out that the Klan has not institutionally hated Catholics for years, and said the implied connection between him and the Orange Order had "blackened" his name. "There's

---

*Mary Robinson, president of the Republic of Ireland.

been too much fratricidal conflict in Northern Ireland," said Duke. "There is no reason for white Christians to kill each other."[7] On that, he was embarrassingly right. But during the troubles nobody was ever killed in the name of the Orange Order, which in fact expelled convicted loyalist paramilitaries.

The Unity Conference's hate-mongering was reprehensible and the *Times*'s complicity equally galling, but, as McDowell points out, the Orange Order itself has done precious little to counter the nationalist-marketed view that it is a front for bigots. The "Two Davids" saga was either a wake-up call or a death knell.* McDowell's rhetoric embodies the guts, panache, and inventiveness that unionism has lacked, but it merely encapsulates what the new loyalists had been saying for months earlier. If his views carry the day, the PUP and the UDP may well "meld into" the larger unionist parties, as McGimpsey believes they will. Some members of the DUP are even beginning to soften, and mainstream unionists are finally starting to acknowledge that Orange Order grandstanding is unhelpfully triumphalist.[8]

Regardless of whether the fringe parties stay intact, the new loyalists will be able to take some credit for resuscitating unionism by keeping the old pols on their toes. The evaporation of the fringe loyalist parties, if it happens, would not mean the disappearance of new loyalism as a political force, any more than the nonexistence of a "Neocon Party" in the United States renders neoconservatives voiceless. Whatever party David Ervine is in, he'll probably win a council seat in the next few years. Gary McMichael has already taken a seat on the Lisburn district council. Possibly, Tommy Kirkham will get elected as well. Hutchinson, Kinner, and Mitchell will bring new loyalist viewpoints to the community—buffeted

---

*Don't bet on unionists' acquiring cachet terribly soon. As of November 1995, they were still far behind Sinn Fein in the area of political finesse. Sinn Fein's new Washington lobby group, Friends of Sinn Fein, had an office in Dupont Circle and a budget of $200,000 (thanks to Gerry Adams's fundraiser at the Plaza) and was run by Mairead Keane, a true believer with Irish citizenship but long a resident in the United States. Meanwhile, the Ulster Unionist Party's stateside outfit was ensconced at Dulles Airport outside Washington, D.C., under the stewardship of a Scottish expatriate who has spent only a few days in Nothern Ireland and came to the United States recently by way of her husband, an American pilot. The poor woman drew a blank when a caller asked about ex-Congressman Bruce Morrison—Sinn Fein's most vigorous and conspicuous American supporter. See "In Black and White," *Irish News* (Belfast), November 2, 1995, p. 8. On the other hand, the UUP may just be following the law of diminishing returns, realizing that they are rowing upstream against the green tide in the United States.

though they are by the consternation of law-abiding Protestants, the sanctimony of the mainstream unionists, and the reticence of the republicans, and hindered though they are by their own callowness, obdurateness, and history. New loyalism is not an irresistible force. But it is proof that the former loyalist paramilitaries are at least as capable as the Shinners of civilized unarmed politics.

CHAPTER 8

AT THE END OF THE DAY

Republican violence and the loyalist violence it provoked alienated both Great Britain and the Republic of Ireland from Northern Ireland. It was the bankruptcy of republican terrorism, not some newfound beneficence on the part of the IRA, that forced the Provos into a tactical shift. Catholics had tasted a socially more benevolent government and over twenty years had acquired some of the political power that Stormont denied them. (For example, Derry is no longer gerrymandered, is run by a Catholic-dominated city council, and is known by official road signs as "Free Derry.") Catholics didn't need the Provos to pursue their civil rights. By 1993, Gerry Adams had apparently absorbed these realities. Rather than stepping up the armed campaign, he started talking with John Hume, Northern Ireland's ranking nonviolent nationalist.

The result of these talks was the Downing Street declaration in December 1993, issued jointly by the British and Irish governments, which officially established their neutrality on the reunification of the island. In particular, the declaration reiterated that Britain had "no selfish strategic or economic interest in Northern Ireland," and stated that the right of self-determination was "for the people of the island of Ireland alone, by agreement between the two parts respectively . . . on the basis of consent, freely and concurrently given, North and South." Mainstream unionists were unsupportive, but muted. Nationalists became more hopeful.

On the strength of the Downing Street declaration, the IRA declared a ceasefire on August 31, 1994. This ceasefire was unilateral: it was not conditional on any reciprocal military restraint on the part of the security forces. The IRA's two earlier ceasefires in 1972 and 1975 were both bilateral in that they were premised on the security forces' agreed relaxation of anti-terrorist measures. Both of the earlier ceasefires were designed merely to test the political waters, and contemplated a relatively quick military solution—namely, a declaration of intent to withdraw by the British. When this was not forthcoming, the IRA went back to violence with an emphatic vengeance. The 1994 cessation, by contrast, simply invited responses from both the British and the loyalists. On account of these unprecedented aspects, the IRA ceasefire was an act of diplomacy which in both moment and vision exceeded anything the constitutional nationalists had done.*

Protestants, though sentimentally disheartened by a cooler Britain, took comfort in the sanctity of Ulster majority rule reaffirmed by the Downing Street declaration. By the end of 1993, loyalists had out-killed republicans, forty-eight to thirty-eight, for the first time since 1976. The loyalist paramilitaries figured they could go out winners. Moreover, loyalists had always maintained that their campaign was strictly reactive. Thus, IRA leadership was reasonably confident that loyalists would have to respond with their own ceasefire simply as a matter of credibility. The day after the IRA's declaration, loyalist paramilitaries killed one person, John O'Hanlon, a Catholic carpenter. He was the last official victim of the troubles. For the next six weeks, nobody died at loyalist hands. Then, on October 13, 1994, Gusty Spence announced the Combined Loyalist Military Command's cessation of all military operations for as long as the IRA ceasefire was in effect.

Surprisingly, the loyalists maintained better discipline than the IRA. During the first year of peace, maverick IRA volunteers took the only major step out of bounds. In November 1994, they robbed a post office of about £150,000 and murdered the employee who tried to stop them.

Passions remained, but were contained. The Falls Road Easter Parade and Sinn Fein vice-president Martin McGuinness's accompanying speech at Milltown Cemetery, traditionally a soaring tribute to the old IRA's siege of downtown Dublin in the 1916 Easter Rising, seemed "flat" to Anthony McIntyre. Brendan Hughes, the Belfast IRA's inspirational leader during the peak of the troubles, confirmed that "not many people were listening. They read about it the next morning in the paper. It was so low-key compared to all the other years that we were there." Joe Clarke didn't even bother to attend. "Dinner was ready," he said.

---

*In fact, the Anglo-Irish Agreement had transmogrified the SDLP. The party became triumphalist, with the result that whenever unionists would make a conciliatory move, Hume would hold out for more. Thus, the Brooke talks on an internal political settlement in 1991 and 1992 collapsed because Hume turned down a devolved government with power sharing—two-thirds of Sunningdale—cold. Ironically, history some day may credit Adams with breaking an impasse that Hume helped cause.

British officials held preliminary talks with Sinn Fein negotiators at Stormont in December 1994, less than four months after the IRA ceasefire. Similar meetings with the loyalist fringe parties followed soon after. Periodic bilateral conferences occurred throughout 1995. Daytime army foot patrols in republican west Belfast ended in March 1995. RUC officers took off their flak jackets and stowed their machine guns. For the first time, the RUC stopped the marches by loyalist "Orange" institutions on the lower Ormeau Road—McIntyre's and McMurray's old neighborhood—at the behest of nationalist residents traumatized by the UFF's execution of five Catholics at a betting shop there three years earlier. Some Protestants objected, but only perfunctorily. During the 1995 marching season, there were 3,057 parades, over 80 percent of them Protestant; eighteen were rerouted, and only twelve resulted in disorder.[1]

In the first year of peace, the entire gestalt of the Northern Irish people changed from reckoning to transformation. When Shankill bomber Sean Kelly refused to recognize the jurisdiction of the Crown Court and proclaimed his eagerness to serve time with his comrades in "Long Kesh," even nationalists saw him as passé. Before the ceasefires, Torrens Knight, who was ultimately given consecutive life sentences for the Greysteel massacre, had struck many loyalists as an embarrassing throwback when after being charged with the killings, he clenched his fist on the steps of the courthouse and bellowed, "No surrender!" Once in the Maze, Knight objected to murals signifying peace that his fellow prisoners had composed; they muscled him off the wing, and he was transferred to H.M.P. Maghaberry to serve his time ignominiously with non-paramilitary prisoners.[2] Now he has found religion. In June 1995, the Belfast City Council, one of the most persistently sectarian institutions in the province, elected a Catholic nationalist deputy lord mayor for the first time. The Union Jack still flies high at Belfast City Hall, but after the IRA ceasefire the "Ulster Says No" banner rejecting the Anglo-Irish Agreement was quietly removed from the cupola.

In February 1995, the British and Irish governments published the long-awaited "framework document," which contained their recommendations for a political settlement in Northern Ireland. Conceptually, it dated back to the Brooke talks of 1991 and 1992, in which the British and Irish governments met with all "constitutional" (i.e., nonviolent) political parties to fashion an internal settlement. The talks collapsed because the unionists and the Brits would not agree to a devolved government with a sufficiently substantial "Irish dimension" to satisfy the SDLP.

In early 1995, however, the British were acutely afraid that the IRA would resume terrorism—in particular, its London bombing campaign. Westminster did not consult the unionists or any of the other political groups in Northern Ireland. Consequently, the framework document catered to the nationalist agenda. In fact, it expressly stated that "the Anglo-Irish Agreement would be replaced by a new *and more broadly based agreement.*" [Emphasis mine] Although the document was not binding, it was detailed enough—twenty-four pages long—to indicate that London and Dublin intended to present a working draft rather than one proposal among several possible ones.

In particular, the framework document prescribed an Irish dimension in the form of cross-border institutions with executive powers (for which Conor Cruise O'Brien has coined the useful abbreviation "CROBIEPs"[3]). CROBIEPs would cover the environment, tourism, and economic and cultural development. Most discomfitingly, they would also have a supervisory role in health matters (e.g., birth control and abortion) and education. Moreover, the executive powers would be expandable by agreement between the Dail and a new Northern Ireland parliament, which to unionists looks more like rolling joint authority than mere devolution.

The SDLP's response to the framework document was, predictably, the contented silence of the cat that ate the canary. Although republicans posture publicly that the document is far too orange in that it makes the "veto" permanent, Sinn Fein was uncharacteristically quiescent when the proposal was floated in February 1995 and did not reject it out of hand. Tommy Gorman had a visceral reaction to the document because it tenders the repeal of articles 2 and 3 of the Irish Constitution, which make the six counties of Northern Ireland the Republic's legal territory, as a quid pro quo for the CROBIEPs. Anthony McIntyre sees the document as Sunningdale in drag. But Brendan Hughes's perspective is roughly representative: "The framework document was the white tape to start the Grand National. That's all it was." In other words, to republicans it's unsatisfactory but negotiable. Unsurprisingly, mainstream unionists rejected the document as "an eviction notice" from Britain, Paisley going his usual extra mile and labeling it a "declaration of war" on unionists.[4]

To the new loyalists the framework document was disappointingly green. Yet their overall response was hopeful and statesmanlike. Rather than dwelling on CROBIEPS, they reiterated confidence that the consent principle kept the union safe, and focused on bipartisan problems with the document.

In particular, the framework document posits a panel of three representatives elected from a single Northern Ireland constituency who would have veto power over important decisions of the new devolved assembly. Undoubtedly, the three people so elected would be a UUP leader (probably David Trimble), DUP leader Ian Paisley, and SDLP leader John Hume. The two unionists would inevitably vote down the one nationalist, and power sharing in the assembly would be neutered. That is the principal conceptual flaw.

Structurally, the framework document is byzantine enough to make an American founding father blush. The devolved assembly would consist of about ninety members, elected according to proportional representation for terms of four or five years. It would function like a British-model parliament, combining legislative and executive functions. To fashion a functioning executive department, multipartisan committees would be formed in the assembly, and their chairmen would act as department heads in a new Northern Ireland Office, roughly equivalent to the Cabinet in the United States. But candidates for each chair would have to be nominated unanimously by the panel and voted on by the assembly.

Most legislation pertaining to Northern Ireland's internal affairs, including enabling legislation for a CROBIEP and legislation delegating executive functions to the CROBIEP, would originate in the assembly. To become law, a bill would have to be passed by majorities of both the relevant committees and the full assembly, but "contentious legislation" with major constitutional, community, or financial implications would require 65 or 75 percent super-majorities *plus* the unanimous approval of the panel. Presumably CROBIEP legislation would qualify as contentious. The panel would also have the power to demand judicial review of any proposed legislation—in effect, that is, to seek advisory opinions.

Although executive power would derive ultimately from the assembly, that power on anything more than a quotidian scale could only be put into effect through the panel. The panel would function like a tripartite presidency. Because decisions are euphemistically supposed to be "by consensus," each of the three members carries an effective veto. In its basic contours, the panel would not be unlike the United Nations Security Council, which has always been subject to paralysis at the whim of a single permanent member. By the terms of the framework document, the panel's powers of nomination, judicial referral, and direct legislative review would likely handcuff the government of Northern Ireland.

The drafters of the framework document apparently mistook Ulster for Belgium. In fact, the factions in Northern Ireland are not the great compromisers that the contemplated government would need to operate, and never will be. While participation in CROBIEPs by department heads from both Northern Ireland and the Republic would be "a duty of service" under the framework document, the substantive content and extent of its duties could only be determined by enabling and delegating legislation passed by *each* assembly but agreed on by *both*. Given the barriers to passing anything on the Northern Irish side, much less agreeing with the south on it, this is hardly a prescription for joint authority, much less a united Ireland through the back door. The fundamental problem with the framework document is not that it tilts Northern Ireland on a slippery slope to Dublin, but that it holds the province in suspended animation. On the strength of Whitehall's published version of the document—the 11,000-word "Frameworks for the Future"—John Major was awarded the Golden Rhubarb Trophy for the most baffling document of 1995 by the Plain Language Commission, an anti-gobbledygook watchdog lobby.

By summer 1995 the framework document had been stuffed into a closet. But the accepted inference from the document, impracticable though it is, was that the Brits in theory would dilute their position as sovereign power through joint structures, as Sinn Fein had urged. Even Thatcher with the Anglo-Irish Agreement had never gone that far. On the other hand, with the constitutional requirement of unionist consent still intact, neither Sinn Fein nor the SDLP were sanguine. Both were anxious for the British government to convene all-party talks to see how much of the framework document they could salvage for the nationalist minority. Consequently, mainstream unionists refused to engage in such talks unless the IRA handed over some of its weapons. The issue of the day became "decommissioning."

Having angered unionists with the green tint of the framework document, the Brits sought to appease those same unionists by supporting their insistence on IRA disarmament before all-party talks began, though they whittled down the requirement from a substantial handover to a token one. David Trimble argued, logically, that since Sinn Fein itself had put forward the "Armalite and ballot-box" strategy, the IRA should relinquish a few guns to certify their alleged dedication to the democratic process.[5] But since only the threat of IRA arms gave Sinn Fein its bargaining power and folk appeal, the requirement was unrealistic. Moreover, the Brits and unionists, per custom, had unwittingly put Sinn Fein in the driver's seat. Adams reiterated his standard retort: he couldn't deliver the IRA.[6]* In an effort to outflank the nationalists, Trimble proposed an alternative to their Holy Grail of all-party talks. Backed by some of the new loyalists, he suggested a Northern Ireland assembly elected according to proportional representation—as a basis not for a devolved government per se but rather for a constitutional convention to determine what form such a government might take and how it might be democratically generated. Still slavering for the framework document and its CROBIEPs, the SDLP and Sinn Fein flatly refused to consider the idea. Now they were the obstructionists. By hooking nationalists, the framework document had hindered the peace process.

Throughout this first round of bickering, mainstream unionists pointed out that no party to talks will say anything that the others haven't heard before. They also noted that talks are premised on the possibility of consensus, which among current political leaders remains dim in Northern Ireland. More selfishly, but understandably, unionists wanted to ensure that going into talks on Northern Ireland's constitutional future, they had something concrete to show for their six-county numerical superiority. Though a constitutional convention proved fruitless once before,† the device is theoretically less vulnerable to failure than all-party talks in that it would produce a palpable majority (or super-majority) position. But Sinn Fein and the SDLP knew that they would lose out in any cut-and-

---

*This posture serves two purposes. First, rhetorically it marshals republican history—no incarnation of the IRA has ever voluntarily disarmed. Second, the claim upholds the legal distinction between Sinn Fein and the IRA. Until the Canary Wharf bombing, the distinction seemed a benign fiction. It gave the IRA a facilitating link with nonviolent politics, eased Sinn Fein's slink towards the SDLP, and rewarded Adams for producing the IRA ceasefire. The deception also enabled Adams himself to appear to the world "romantically ambiguous," in Conor Cruise O'Brien's apt phrase. See "A Fox Loose in the Henhouse," *The Independent* (London), February 3, 1994, p. 21. Canary Wharf, however, showed that since the IRA ceasefire a gap had indeed arisen between Sinn Fein and the IRA.

†In 1975, after the loyalist strike brought down the power-sharing executive, the British authorized the election of convention delegates to devise a form of devolved government which, in the words of the Government White Paper, "is likely to command the most widespread acceptance throughout the community." This chastising circumscription and unionist hypersensitivity to power sharing doomed the project. Westminster rejected the majority report of the convention, which recommended a restoration of Stormont powers with power sharing only at committee level and not Cabinet level. Now that most unionists are resigned to more equitable power sharing, a convention presumably would not face such high hurdles.

dried voting procedure. Their determination to avoid an assembly was re-inforced by the fact that President Clinton had put talks on his pre-visit wish list. Conferences between the NIO and Sinn Fein failed to break the stalemate.

In November 1995, Irish police near the border arrested two men in a van carrying 1,300 pounds of homemade explosives. The men were members of a new military faction called the "Irish National Republican Army," which was connected to "Republican Sinn Fein," a dissident offshoot of Gerry Adams's mainstream Provisionals. Republican Sinn Fein president Ruairi O Bradaigh confirmed the possibility of renewed republican vio-lence, and backhandedly certified the IRA's commitment to peace. "The present leadership of Provisional Sinn Fein and the IRA has been constitu-tionalized, and once the constitutional bug bites there is no escape," he said. "It is an incurable disease."[7] Still, rumblings of an IRA resumption got louder. Wary constitutional nationalists welcomed the feel-good hoopla bracketing President Clinton's visit as a safe interval in which to dissuade the Brits from supporting elections, and thus pacify the IRA.

On November 30, Clinton arrived in Northern Ireland to genuine (if sycophantic) euphoria but no scheduled talks. In the eleventh hour, the Irish and British governments managed to squeeze out a palliative "peace deal." In their joint communiqué, Major and Irish taoiseach John Bruton formally inaugurated the "twin-track" approach to the peace process, whereby disarmament and political settlement would be handled in paral-lel rather than in series. In substance, the two leaders merely certified an international advisory commission on disarmament that unionists and nationalists had agreed on in principle months earlier, and took aim at all-party talks by late February 1996.

Former U.S. senator George Mitchell was appointed chairman of the three-member commission. But despite this bow to President Clinton and, by implication, to nationalists, the Brits were becoming less afraid of an IRA backslide by the day. John Major still refused to lift the precondition of some IRA disarmament, which had been the only real impediment to peace negotiations since the IRA and loyalist ceasefires were declared in fall 1994. Yet during his visit, Clinton repeatedly characterized the agreement as "a risk for peace," and demurely accepted a measure of credit for it. Two weeks after the presidential visit, Mitchell came to Belfast to convene the commission for the first time. Adams promptly revoked his approval of the twin-track approach, branding it "a formula for disaster."[8] Bill Clinton's catalytic power in Northern Ireland had been grossly exaggerated.

Senator Mitchell's report was released on January 22, 1996. In pertinent part, the report recommended that the decommissioning precondition be dropped, but added that Sinn Fein should be required to declare the IRA ceasefire permanent, to submit in advance to the outcome of all-party talks before entering them, and to agree to IRA disarmament simultaneously with talks. The loyalist paramilitaries would be held to the same requirements. The British government accepted the recommendations of the report. In particular, John Major agreed that all-party talks could proceed in tandem with paramilitary disarmament. He further proposed that negotiators first be determined by province-wide elections, provided such elections were, per Mitchell, "broadly acceptable" to both communities. Both the SDLP and Sinn Fein considered this a new precondition to replace decommissioning, and a sop to unionists. The two nationalist parties rejected the suggestion out of hand, despite a *Belfast Telegraph* poll indicating that 68 percent of SDLP voters and 50 percent of Sinn Fein supporters favored elections.[9]

On February 3, the Forum for Peace and Reconciliation, convened in Dublin after the ceasefires, issued its own recommendations for a political settlement on the border issue. Twelve political parties from Northern Ireland and the Republic participated in the forum. Sinn Fein was the only party that would not endorse the requirement of six-county consent to reunification. Yet since partition, that requirement has been incorporated in every important document relating to reunification—the Government of Ireland Act of 1920, the Treaty of 1921, the Northern Ireland (Temporary Provisions) Act of 1974, the Sunningdale agreement, the Anglo-Irish Agreement, the Downing Street declaration, and the framework document. Meantime, President Clinton encouraged nationalists to agree to the elections Whitehall was urging.

With these last two developments, republicans found themselves more fettered than ever by the consent requirement. Seventeen months had passed since the IRA ceasefire, and no permanent military or political solution was remotely in evidence. Frustrated IRA hard-liners lost patience and ended the ceasefire. On Friday, February 9, 1996, at 5:35 P.M. Greenwich Mean Time, the IRA called the Irish Republic's state television station and said that the ceasefire was over. At 5:40 P.M., the Metropolitan Police received warnings from Irish sources that a bomb had been placed in the South Quay area of east London, and began to evacuate the area. At 7:00 P.M., a one-thousand-pound homemade fertilizer bomb went off under the Docklands Light Railway Station, next to the Canary Wharf office buildings. Two people were killed, and over one hundred were injured, six seriously. Property damage came to about $140 million. This was the notorious "Canary Wharf" bombing.

The response, especially in Northern Ireland, was remarkably measured. Although many unionists had predicted an IRA relapse, they left the door of peace open to the IRA and Sinn Fein, insisting only on a reinstatement of the ceasefire to get the process back on track. Within hours of the bombing, the RUC put their flak jackets back on and broke out their assault rifles. British troops began cruising the streets again in armored vans. The British government sent five hundred Royal Irish Regiment soldiers back to Northern Ireland. These were natural enough security precautions, and in context rather modest. Brendan Hughes, however, found them "most insensitive"—indicating that even dovish republicans would stick by the more bellicose members of the movement, at least publicly. Gerry Adams denied prior knowledge of the attack but refused to condemn it, blaming the British and unionist dilatoriness. Dublin felt betrayed and, like London, refused to talk to Sinn Fein at ministerial level until the IRA announced another ceasefire and vowed its permanence. After seventeen months of broad acceptance, Sinn Fein appeared isolated from all sides—mistrusted by republican hard men, unionists, and the two sovereign governments. SDLP nationalists were also shattered, as they seemed to have lost a constitutional partner.

On the other hand, a year and a half without terrorism was unprecedented in post-1969 Northern Ireland. For the first time in twenty-five years, Northern Irish civilians sensed a way out. Although they had faced earlier breakdowns with morbid resignation, now they did not easily let go of the prospect of peace. "No Going Back" demonstrations congested Belfast and other towns. Belfast's three dailies established a peace hotline, which at one point was drawing seven thousand callers per hour. Yet despite overwhelming popular opposition to the IRA's return to violence—north and south, east and west—Gerry Adams continued to characterize the resumption as an assertion of the Irish people's national right to self-determination.

Before Canary Wharf, Adams had claimed a division between Sinn Fein and the IRA to maintain the threat of violence and increase Sinn Fein's bargaining power. Now he used the apparent rift to exculpate himself for the bombing. At the same time, both Adams and the IRA indicated a preference for negotiation. Nobody in the republican movement would admit to a "split" as such; maintaining the appearance of unity remains a key lesson of republican prison indoctrination. Yet four months passed between Canary Wharf and the next significant IRA operation—the June 15 bombing of a Manchester shopping center, leaving over 200 people injured and property damage exceeding $300 million. This long gap suggested that support for the resumption of the armed struggle was far from unanimous. Ervine, Hutchinson, and McMichael urged the loyalist paramilitaries to refrain from retaliatory violence.

Many loyalists had feared that once the rest of the world no longer listened to Gerry Adams, he would try to resume the armed struggle if dissatisfied with the portents of the peace process. "I would worry about when people get bored with Gerry Adams's rants and raves, and it comes to the point where we're all equal and the same opportunities are there," said Andy Tyrie in June 1995. "And maybe there's an assembly elected here. If he's unhappy about it, what is he going to do? When he arrives at the stage when he's faced with democracy, and he's being blocked all the time through democracy, what's going to happen?" Canary Wharf vindicated such fears. Republicans are angry. But the grating aspect of the breakdown is that Catholics and nationalists in general are not comparably aggrieved. So why did the republicans call off the ceasefire?

Because for all republicans, doves as well as hawks, nonviolence was a tactic, not a principle. Adams could not have changed that even if he had wanted to.

Adams had every reason to keep the IRA from committing the Canary Wharf bombing. The deed contradicted the raison d'être of the 1994 IRA ceasefire that he brought about—namely, that the British government and Ulster unionists can't be terrorized into a united Ireland. Canary Wharf also undermines the "international dimension" of Adams's strategy—President Clinton must have felt as though he'd been hornswoggled. The IRA's peaceful options were far from exhausted. The bombing occurred long before the late-February talks deadline established by London and Dublin's joint communiqué last November. Canary Wharf made the abandoned disarmament requirement look sensible.

The only logical inference was that, contrary to received wisdom before Canary Wharf, Adams did not have complete control of the republican movement. The movement appeared to have fragmented. This revelation has devalued Adams diplomatically. His persuasive power with both the Brits and the unionists rests on his capacity ultimately to deliver the IRA and in the meantime to keep it at bay, which the bombing negated. But those who called for Adams to condemn the atrocity and prove his ignorance of plans for the bombing were missing the point. It is his shameless hypocrisy that in and of itself carries his appeal within the republican movement. Republicans and their sympathizers know that the image—the pipe, the beard, the tweed—gives brutality a suave face. They find it gratifying that Adams literally got away with murder. When his followers see Adams palm himself off as a statesman, they feel a warm, smug complicity.

As distasteful as this phenomenon is, without it Adams could not have conjured the IRA ceasefire and goaded the IRA onto the political path. Only he had the pedigree within the movement to do that. As both a high-ranking IRA man during the peak of the troubles and the architect of Sinn Fein's political strategy, Adams is unique in recent republican history. If the unionists, London, and Dublin are to keep the IRA on board, it has to be through Adams. He has no heir apparent. They have to let him have his hypocrisy. In granting Adams a visa after Canary Wharf, President Clinton recognized this unpleasant reality. Without Adams's duplicity, Britain's long-term goal of drawing the IRA away from the armed campaign and into nonviolent politics has no prayer of being fulfilled. Indeed, the most disturbing aspect of the London bombing was not that the friendly side of Adams's Janus face was looking dubious to his political opponents. That will always be the case. It was more troubling that the nasty side was losing currency among republicans.

According to Anthony McIntyre, Adams's "high-wire act" eventually alienated the republican rank and file. Adams, he says, did not explain to the little people in the movement how the incremental political approach he had sold to IRA leadership would produce a united Ireland. Instead of paying attention to the folks on the ground, Adams flew off to America for meetings with Anthony Lake and $1,000-a-plate fundraisers at the Plaza. When the peace process dragged on for seventeen months without tangible political progress, popular frustration trickled up to the "hard men" of the IRA. Thus, McIntyre maintains that republicans fatalistically anticipated the London bombing. "It was like waiting for somebody to die of cancer. You know it's going to happen, but it's a shock when it does."

McIntyre thinks Adams allowed Britain and the unionists to delay all-party talks long enough to turn the peace process into "a republican retreat disguised as a strategic initiative" that has "hammered away at the morale of republicans." Kevin McQuillan is even more critical. "Adams is crassly stupid or he's deviously cynical, and he's walked us into this knowing full well where it's going to get us," says McQuillan. "At the end of the day, what's it going to get us, after twenty-five years of horrendous sacrifice, struggle, and suffering we have had to endure, as well as the suffering we have made other people endure? It's going to end up with the republican family becoming partitionist republicans. We've de facto recognized something that we say is an illegal statelet that we were working to undermine to the point where we will accept the mere right to *argue* our case for an eventual thirty-two-county republic."

While Adams outwardly paints John Major as a clumsy miscalculator of IRA will, McIntyre sees the prime minister as a sophisticated tactician. The Brits, says McIntyre, knew that all-party negotiations a month after the IRA ceasefire would inevitably have failed, and that a resumption after such a short period would not have rained much political fallout on Sinn Fein. Thus, London protracted the peace process to allow Clinton and local optimism to co-opt Sinn Fein and the IRA's military capability to rust, upping the political ante for an IRA resumption. This analysis appears largely correct. If so, Major's was an entirely sensible strategy from any standpoint except a republican's. Along with almost everyone else, the prime minister simply believed that Adams's influence within the republican movement was stronger than it now appears to be.

Consensus and common sense favor exonerating Adams as a partial dupe of his own people, rather than indicting him as an unreconstructed Machiavellian. Given the debilitating blow Canary Wharf dealt to Sinn Fein's credibility, the terrorists responsible could not have been particularly interested in a united Ireland. Their devotion was merely to the IRA itself, and to the posterity of rebellion for its own sake. There will likely always be a few of these types on both sides, and they will irrationally step out of line every so often. Thus, Canary Wharf may have been surprising, but it was not shocking. Indeed, many unionists had been predicting it for eight months. While the IRA ceasefire was in place, Adams showed them that, for all his faults, killing Brits and Protestants is unfulfilling to him and his followers. He really does want a united Ireland. That is a defensible political aspiration.

Even in the worst case, the disrupted peace process has likely tempered the military inclinations of the republican movement. Sinn Fein members, led by Adams, are still apt to favor a political solution to the border question. Adams may sometimes talk a hard, pessimistic line to woo militant republicans back to his fold, but his threatening rhetoric may belie more peaceful intentions. It is doubtful that the nihilism of Canary Wharf convinced him that a purely military approach works better than politics. He simply needs his hypocrisy to survive as a political force both within republican circles and outside them. If a few recalcitrant hard men continue terrorist operations, the two governments and the unionists are likely to treat them as a separate, strictly military problem. But all three will still deal with Adams. They need him as much as he needs them.

In both communities, of course, there was lamebrained tribal support for a reprise of the troubles. A sullen gentleman in Andersonstown proclaimed the London bombing "brilliant. We got frig-all from the Brits." On the Shankill Road, as David Ervine urged restraint, new graffiti petulantly asked, "Who gave Ervine permission to speak for the men on the ground?" But the seventeen months of peace in 1994, 1995, and 1996 were more than just a cruel tease to the people of Northern Ireland. That span produced a collective resolve to salvage a solution and overwhelm periodic (and perhaps inevitable) seizures of violence.

Although the IRA ceasefire did break down, all politicians were less alarmist than they had been after past disappointments and showed substantial capacities for damage control. This is evidence of a new robustness and rationality in Northern Irish politics. As Canary Wharf and Manchester demonstrate, nobody has foresworn terrorism for good. But thanks to the ceasefires, and seventeen months of authentic peace, there is, at least, political daylight. Consequently, there remains a far stronger incentive than there was before the IRA ceasefire for the paramilitaries to avoid violence.

The summer of 1996 began fitfully, but not without hope. The British government followed through on its pre–Canary Wharf plan in an effort to resurrect the crippled peace process. On May 30, Northern Ireland's voters elected 110 representatives from more than twenty political parties to a consultative "peace forum." Whitehall required the parties to select from the forum delegates to multiparty political negotiations that began on June 10.

Sinn Fein emerged from the elections with an unprecedentedly high 15.5 percent mandate, but was not permitted to participate in the talks unless the IRA reinstated its ceasefire. Although Gerry Adams protested that Sinn Fein's exclusion was undemocratic, *vox populi* indicated that nationalists had given Sinn Fein that extra quantum of support not to embolden the IRA but rather to produce another ceasefire.[10]

Nevertheless, five days after the talks began, the IRA bombed Manchester. Yet the loyalist paramilitary groups refrained from striking back at the nationalist community in Northern Ireland, and the talks proceeded without Sinn Fein. Neither loyalist patience nor popular determination is infinite. (Paisley was the other big winner in the May 30 election, showing that the province was as divided as ever on the constitutional question.) Still, the immediate aftermath of the Manchester bombing confirmed the desire of everyone but IRA militants to break the spiral of retaliation and boycott that sustained the troubles.

POST-CEASEFIRE REALITIES

Despite Ulster's sharp divisions, the rhetoric of politics is finally evolving from the recriminative into the substantive. Some of the verbiage remains coy and precious. These symptoms are growing pains and should be expected. Each side, for instance, uses Europe to minimize the other's claim to national identity, and to deride the notion of independence. Sinn Fein argues that since the European Union and the Maastricht Treaty* are weakening sovereignty throughout Europe, erasing the border should logically become less objectionable to unionists. Jackie McMullan talks about a united Ireland "through Europeanization." The new loyalists run the argument the other way, saying that the dilution of nationhood via east-west links ought to make reunification a dead letter. "No country is independent economically, so what does a united Ireland mean?" asks Billy Mitchell. Tactically, the ploy is more effective for nationalists than for unionists, as nationalists tend to want any sort of movement away from the status quo other than full integration with Great Britain—a Progressive Unionist Party fantasy that will never happen. But both arguments gloss over the terminally emotive character of the Northern Ireland problem.

The economics of European unity alone won't change anybody's mind about the border. Neither will the subsumed economic debate over a continued union versus a united Ireland. Unionists argue that the Republic, with less than 5 percent of the United Kingdom's national budget and a higher rate of taxation,[11] could not afford the £5-billion annual subsidy that Britain provides. Nationalists counter that the need for subvention will soon diminish because almost half of that amount goes for security,[12] and that in any event the financial requirement is partially offset by the huge European Union subsidy (£7.2 billion in structural funds for 1994–99, plus eight- to nine-figure levels annually from Common Agricultural Policy price supports[13]) that Ireland enjoys. In 1995 alone, the EU subsidy came to nearly £2 billion, and helped produce a 7 percent growth rate in the Republic.

---

*The Maastricht Treaty went into effect on November 1, 1993, and now applies to the fifteen full member states of the European Union. The treaty calls for common citizenship, coordinated foreign and defense policies, and harmonized social policies, as well as a single currency and European central bank by 1999. In a referendum, the Republic of Ireland comfortably ratified the treaty by a 2:1 margin. Great Britain also adopted the treaty, but with far greater ambivalence, having negotiated some dilution of the treaty's original concept of federalization and an opt-out clause regarding the single currency. In Northern Ireland, nationalist MPs strongly supported the treaty, while most unionist MPs opposed it on the ground that it eroded national sovereignty.

This is only half a case. Losses in security jobs will mean greater pressure on an already-struggling private sector in Northern Ireland. Unlike the British subvention, which includes matching grants for new industrial ventures, Ireland's European Union subsidy is skewed heavily towards agriculture, which absorbs a far lower percentage of Northern Ireland's labor force than the Republic's (8 percent versus 14 percent).[14] Moreover, agriculture in the Republic and Northern Ireland already has been substantially integrated through the European Union and existing cross-border arrangements, which would make the positive economic impact of reunification smaller still. Finally, the EU subsidy will inevitably shrink precisely because the robustness the money brings to the Republic will diminish its future need.

Nationalists deride unionists' heavy reliance on the subvention as static, while unionists put down dynamic nationalist speculation as pie-in-the-sky.[15] Given the fact that without the subvention, Northern Ireland would be worse off than, say, Liverpool, unionists do come out decisively on top. Although the historical industrialization gap between north and south is closing, Northern Ireland's economy remains structurally so different from the Republic's—65 percent versus 49 percent employed in services as of 1986[16]—that economically viable reunification seems more wishful than realistic on the face of it. As for the nationalists' other pet argument—the vaunted "peace dividend" of heightened international (read: American) industrial investment—despite the fireworks and afterglow over the May 1995 Washington investment conference, the ultimate level of investment cannot yet be estimated, and may well be negligibly small given the number of foreign firms that already have branches in Northern Ireland.[17]* Foreign

---

*The MacBride Principles, which effectively require affirmative action in favor of Catholics, constitute another potential hindrance to foreign investment. These guidelines derive from the Sullivan Principles, which the U.S. anti-apartheid lobby in 1977 campaigned to have applied to American firms doing business in South Africa. They were adopted by the Irish-American lobby in 1984, and renamed after Sean MacBride, chief of staff of the old IRA in the thirties, later Irish foreign minister, a barrister, founder of Amnesty International, and Nobel Peace laureate in 1974. The U.S. Congress and at least sixteen states have enacted legislation imposing the MacBride Principles on firms employing persons in Northern Ireland. Northern Ireland's fair employment laws require equal opportunity only, and the Fair Employment Commission opposes affirmative action (i.e., fixed goals or quotas) on account of what Northern Irish perceive as a societal disaster in the United States. More modest FEC reforms have already produced a backlash in the Protestant working class. Standing on a street corner in east Belfast before the ceasefires, one UDA man pointed to the UDA's former headquarters and cracked, "We'd rather get [FEC chairman] Bob Cooper in there than Gerry Adams." John Hume has campaigned against the MacBride Principles precisely because he fears they will discourage overseas investment in Northern Ireland.

lenders would not be much more enthusiastic about bridging a nascent unified economy to viability.[18]

Economically, fast reunification ends up infeasible for roughly the same reasons independence does. When they're being candid, even nationalist economists realize that the north, facing the double whammy of diminishing private-sector and soon public-sector employment, will need a decent interval of continued British support.[19] The IRA ceasefire suggests that even republicans agree. In parallel with the devolution issue itself, the economic debate will come down to whether this interval is indefinite or not. Unionists will say yes, nationalists no. As the new loyalists seem to realize, only time—and secular economic trends in Britain, Ireland, and Northern Ireland—will tell.

Economics, in any case, is tangential in Northern Ireland. The reality is that with the consent principle now all but irrevocable, Protestants in Ulster will stay British de jure for as long as they are a majority.

Both republicans and loyalists know implicitly that the Republic and Britain will no longer be proactive players in forging a political solution. In the short term, as the two sides negotiate, the two sovereigns are little more than persuaders. In the long term, after the two sides have found a constitutional parking space (i.e., a devolved government), the two sovereigns will act as alternate guarantors: London will back up a unionist majority in Northern Ireland by maintaining the union, while Dublin will probably support a nationalist majority by accepting reunification. Implicit in a successful settlement are an admission by unionists that the continuation of the union is merely one of several possibilities, and an admission by nationalists that reunification is not a territorial inevitability.

Serendipitously, this situation would honor history. Protestants' loyalism always has been conditioned on the benefits Britain could bring them, and the Crown's maintenance of the union has depended on unionist consent ever since partition; only Paisley turned the relationship on its head by conjuring an obligation (mainly on account of the military and industrial dividends Ulster has paid to Britain since partition) that ran from Britain to Ulster, and now the new loyalists regard him as a real-life Elmer Gantry. Likewise, Catholic claims to reunification as a right have always pivoted on deeply woven injustices to Catholics in a "gerrymandered" statelet; as direct rule has progressively unraveled those injustices, logic has weakened the republican position from equitable claim to cultural preference.

The principal tic that members of each group still have to shake off is the painfully circular notion that because they suffered during the troubles, they deserve special consideration. Loyalists have started to admit their own complicity and to profess remorse. Republicans are unlikely to reciprocate publicly—their subculture of the "undefeated" permits neither shame nor regret—yet their insistence that they were soldiers allows many, like Leo Green and Tommy Gorman, to let their foes off the hook now that the guns are silent. These overt shifts in attitude have helped render moot the debate over fault and moral desert. Thus, the IRA's Canary Wharf bombing was labeled "atavistic" by MP Seamus Mallon of the SDLP. Despite British and unionist foot dragging and republican testiness, the idiom of Northern Irish politics has turned mainly political. If Protestant loyalty is really only to Ulster, and Catholic nationalism is at bottom merely self-protective, devolution will afford both sides plenty of room to coexist.

Although the Provisional IRA is a fundamentally coercive organization, they have practiced their coercion with passive Catholic support; they got the support not because northern Catholics insisted on a united Ireland, but because they had been socially marginalized by Stormont. Take away the social inequities, you take away the Provisional IRA's very purpose. And if direct rule is any indication, institutionalized discrimination will continue to evaporate.

But Sinn Fein's and the IRA's standing problem is innate rather than environmental. Republicans are uncomfortable with incremental, nonrevolutionary politics. Yet their near-evangelical confidence that republicanism will win out remains unabated. "People are going to discover that [the republican movement] is not a big, fantastic, mysterious, hidden bank with all these geniuses in it thinking up all these ideas about how to publicize itself," says John Pickering. "We are right. We're morally right, we're politically right. We're not coming from any bullshit background. We're just ordinary people who are committed to a just cause. Once all the disinformation is cut out of the road and people can just see what we're about, after a while they're going to realize that we're just ordinary guys who have the right argument. It's really very simple." The republican mantra of "ordinary people in extraordinary circumstances" at best explains the troubles; it does not excuse them. But despite the waning of their support, republicans cling to their status as folk heroes. That drains their ability to participate in a nonrevolutionary arena. As Canary Wharf demonstrated, even post-ceasefire too many are prone to resort to bloodshed when they don't get their way fast enough.

Gusty Spence conveys the appropriate spirit of compromise: "My aspiration is to be integrated into the United Kingdom. I know that that's not on, because if that aspiration is fulfilled it nullifies the other person's aspiration, and he rightly will be up in arms. Maybe with understanding that they can't have what they want, and we can't have what we want, we'll settle for somewhere in between." The Irish would be lost without someone to be Irish at. Confrontation in Ireland is a matter not merely of politics but of habit. What's needed, of course, is for the two sides not to be too Irish at each other. Unionists and nationalists could always put up with a little spirited backsliding because the center always held in Northern Ireland: they had a functioning civil society in spite of the troubles. This foundation enabled the peace process, though diminished, to survive the Canary Wharf bombing.

In fact, the most conspicuous peculiarity of the troubles was the easy fusion of terrorists with burghers. Gusty Spence's favorite joke: Before the troubles if a man applied for a job and said he had a prison record, he was told he had no chance; now if the same man says he has no record, he's asked why not. "It looked at one time in Northern Ireland," he says, "like one half of the population was going to be in prison and the other half was going to keep them there." The problem in Northern Ireland is not that Catholics and Protestants can't live together. They do and have for centuries—but, in Sir Walter Scott's evocative phrase, "like people fighting with daggers in a hogshead." The problem is that they have been content to live together *and* remain willfully ignorant about each other—in particular, about how similar they are.

Ulster Protestants and northern Catholics are both Christian, both white European. Both groups believe in hard work and leftish social policies, and (save for a few Paisleyite teetotalers) like their drink and "the crack"* after hours. Both groups are strong on "family values." Neither really favors abortion or divorce,† though Protestants have exaggerated the

---

*An Irish expression encompassing jocular banter, jaunty give-and-take, and frivolity for the sake of mere fun.

†Abortion is legal in mainland Great Britain, illegal in the Republic. In Northern Ireland, the law is so vague that it is interpreted by a conservative—and largely Protestant—judiciary as a prohibition. Virtually no doctor in the north is willing to perform the procedure without official sanction. Recently, the legal guardian of a seventeen-year-old retarded girl was compelled to go to court to determine whether she should get an abortion, after all doctors consulted had refused to perform one. When the judge permitted it, both communities were outraged. See "Storm Over Abortion on a Mentally Handicapped Girl," *Irish News* (Belfast), October 5, 1995, p. 1. Divorce is now legal in Ireland as well as Great Britain and Northern Ireland.

precious difference between mere disapproval and outright prohibition for political reasons. In an international context, Catholics and Protestants are cut from very similar cloth. The border issue has kept them culturally, and to an extent physically, segregated. Indeed, the central absurdity of the troubles is that they started as a fight against sectarianism and ended up embedding it even more deeply.

Nobel Peace laureate Mairead Corrigan-Maguire suggests that the key to fixing Northern Ireland is not so much to forget history and both sides' morbid collusion, but instead to accept the blood on their hands as something they have in common. The ceasefires make it possible for the people of Northern Ireland to lighten up. With no guns blazing or bombs exploding, even the Northern Irish can be more exacting about what segments of history are most relevant to political remedies, and relegate the rest to the local conceits of parades and murals. That is where the "reconciliation industry" can actually be useful. In December 1995, the Church of Ireland's Belvoir Parish Church Hall—rebuilt after the IRA blew it up in 1992—held a day-long Irish dance festival involving hundreds of Catholic and Protestant children. Corny and obvious? Perhaps. But the event neatly reflected which parts of the past should be celebrated and which should be interred. It is the intercommunity dance festivals that will enable the Northern Irish to be Irish at the rest of the world without blowing it up.

Even in peace, Northern Ireland needs to see itself as a tangibly divided society. Neither Protestants nor Catholics want reconciliation to be seamless. There are two reasons for this. First, under devolution, there will be no united Ireland; neither will there be any closer link with Britain. There will be instead a government functionally separate from both London and Dublin in which nationalists and unionists share power. In this grey limbo, each side needs some permanent symbols that it has won something to justify twenty-five years of violence. Thus, the Belfast city council is paying for public signs on the Falls Road to be in Gaelic as well as English, and the Crown is funding Irish language schools. In the Protestant estate of Glencairn, the International Fund for Ireland is financing a million-dollar museum for the Battle of the Somme. Irish tricolors and murals of Bobby Sands and the Easter Rising will grace the Falls Road for years to come. Union Jacks, King Billy paintings, and Red Hand stencils will adorn the Shankill Road for just as long.

Second, the Northern Irish derive distinctions both honorable and notorious from the troubles. They want to keep their prestige. So during "the marching season" (April through September), Catholic communities will continue to stop Orange processions from passing through Catholic areas, while Protestant groups will still block the few republican parades. The two communities in Northern Ireland will not completely meld. What they probably will do is turn the memory of the troubles into a brooding omnipresence that acts as a self-deterrent—somewhat like a nuclear arsenal. Various devices are already taking shape: dance festivals founded on irony, the morbidly nostalgic warp of the arts and letters, academic dispute-resolution centers. In sum, the post-ceasefire "reconciliation industry" is cheerfully resigned to something far short of complete success.

At the same time, Belfast's own "Generation X" does not find paramilitarism sexy anymore. The troubles have forced the youth of Northern Ireland to lag behind all the other kids in the area of popular culture, and the Thatcherite promotion of healthy self-interest seems to have brought their resentment to a head. Disaffected teenagers in west Belfast are more interested in stealing cars than in joining the IRA. "In them days, my generation joined the IRA and got involved politically, whereas this generation now is getting involved in drugs and joyriding," says Umberto Scappaticci. "We were young and we had to show our frustrations somehow."

An ex-IRA lifer convicted of killing a UDR man, Scappaticci now runs an independent community project in Twinbrook, The Lynx Project, which through constructive activities helps young people inclined to steal cars or use drugs resist the temptation. In the true spirit of reconciliation, the Probation Board of Northern Ireland funds the project—by way of the "Duke of Edinburgh Award," no less. Yet Twinbrook is the home of Bobby Sands and perhaps the most saturatedly republican area in Northern Ireland; dogs bark rabidly when the rare RUC man shows his face on the street there. Scappaticci takes referrals from the local IRA, who often condition a car thief's health on his subsequent participation in The Lynx Project. Despite his bodybuilder's physique and a cleft of fortitude in his chin, he wears the harried look of a scoutmaster.

Former IRA volunteers will never be accepted by the state as official lawmen, but the RUC has reached an uneasy truce with the Provos in places like Twinbrook. This will likely be the *modus vivendi* for a number of years, until the RUC is accepted in Catholic estates. But the situation does have a positive, if attenuated, influence on policy. David Cook, then chairman of the Police Authority of Northern Ireland, announced firmly in late 1995 that the post-ceasefire RUC must be tightly insulated against political—which, in historical context, means *unionist*—control. Ingrained prejudice will take time to gouge out. Though Catholics made up 21.5 percent of the RUC's new applicants during the year following the ceasefires, they made up only 16.5 percent of those accepted. The force is about 8 percent Catholic overall, and has encouraged more Catholics to join.[20] The Northern Irish establishment, of course, is by nature conservative, and not exclusively along sectarian lines. Female RUC officers have been allowed to carry weapons only since April Fool's Day, 1995.

The people of Northern Ireland are tired of death, but they still need its legacy. Life in post-troubles Northern Ireland will be more tolerant of coexistence than harmonious interaction. Both Catholics and Protestants are committed to the artificial perpetuation of the community divide rather than its dissolution, but this objective can be served without spilling over into violence. Various community leaders on both sides wax eloquent about cross-community cooperation, but in fact it is severely limited. The one state-funded welfare and counseling organization that assists both republican and loyalist prisoners is Quaker Service, and that is an accident of history. "I know this sounds crazy, but this is Northern Ireland—historically the republicans accept us because the Quakers helped Catholics out during the famine. All we have to do is not blow the image," says Marty Rafferty, laughing. "And on the loyalist side—well, we're not Catholic. I mean, we came from a reforming tradition, so there was something there, and also we'd done some work during the war years and stuff in Protestant areas." Usually, history works against sharing.

Republicans have a ready constituency, but they are dispositionally unsuited to statesmanship without bombs. The Canary Wharf job proved it, perhaps conclusively. Either Sinn Fein will become functionally indistinguishable from the SDLP and hang on to history as a reason to stay separate, or it will disappear as a political force on account of IRA obstinacy. Conversely, the new loyalists have the right attitude for normal politics, but they lack the constituency. They will either blend osmotically into the left-hand side of the Ulster Unionist Party, or remain small and decoratively separate.

Yet the ceasefires were no small dispensation. As the guns were distanced from Northern Ireland politics, so was the canker of self-importance that allowed pointless bloodshed to proceed for a quarter-century. For as long as totemistic murder persisted, the people of Northern Ireland felt exempt from the moral compulsion of free will and effectively convinced themselves that sectarian conflict was an immutable law of their unique nature. "The integrity of their quarrel," in Winston Churchill's

unfortunate phrase of ennoblement, permitted the population to celebrate their stoicism and their strife and to solicit pity from the rest of the
world. They became spoiled, and expected special treatment. When the
killing stopped, the bubble burst. The Northern Irish had to awake to
their own foolishness. Now many understand that the "war" achieved literally nothing—that the border hasn't changed, that cultural chauvinisms
remain intact, that Catholic civil rights could have been won by peaceful
means. Of course, it was the paramilitaries who started the troubles and
kept them going. Any thanks they get is, and should be, backhanded.
After all, it is humiliating to have to thank someone for not shooting you.

The conflict gave an otherwise obscure people their day in the sun and
refined their taste for morbid nostalgia. What other place would have celebrated Harland and Wolff's building of the *Titanic*—the biggest prod-
uct-liability tort of the twentieth century—with a plaque at Belfast City
Hall, on the logo of Belfast Gin, and now in a proposed *Titanic* cultural
center? With the sharpening stone of international attention, each community honed its tribal identity to its finest and most poignant edge: the
nationalists were oppressed, the unionists besieged. It has been correspondingly hard for both paramilitaries and noncombatants to give up
the troubles.

When the contrapuntal political killings stopped after the ceasefires,
newspapers had to resort to parochialism of the local-man-killed-in-
Hiroshima-explosion variety. Five traffic deaths amount to "a weekend of
carnage."[21] The day after Israeli Prime Minister Yitzhak Rabin was assassinated, as circumstances brought Clinton, Major, and Bruton together in
Tel Aviv for his funeral, one *Irish News* headline read: "Israel Summit May
Promote Peace in North."[22] There was no meeting formally scheduled, and
the entire article was written in the subjunctive. Seriously. Post-ceasefire,
there was a slight aura of mourning over the fact that the Northern Ireland
problem was no longer so weighty or so worthy of attention. When the
IRA bombed Canary Wharf, some journalists betrayed a retrograde thirst
for blood. Within ten days, the IRA had planted one more bomb (successfully disarmed) in London and exploded another. Although the loyalist
paramilitaries had refrained from retaliating, London's *Independent* effectively threw down the gauntlet to them with the headline, "The Nightmare Slide to War."[23] If post-ceasefire news coverage had been wishfully
desperate, post-resumption coverage was recklessly sensationalist.

Yet Ulster's rank and file are finally demonstrating a mutual willingness
to compromise, and a genuine desire for peace. An October 1995 editor-

ial in the staunchly republican *Andersonstown News* recommended that Catholic west Belfast not hold out unrealistic hope for all-party talks and a ready constitutional solution, and instead concentrate on firming up equal rights.[24] At the same time, almost half of Shankill residents surveyed said they believed unionists should participate in all-party talks even if the IRA did not decommission.[25] Even prison officers are resigned to shortened careers. "The Prison Service is like the French Foreign Legion," says one official wistfully. "We have a glorious past, but our future is fuck-all."

When the IRA ceasefire was declared, republicans leaders probably considered it a way of replenishing political capital they were fast depleting. They did not bargain for a population uncharacteristically enthusiastic for peace, loyalist discipline, and the high political cost that American sponsorship has imposed on an IRA return to violence. Due to these three factors, Sinn Fein, mainstream unionists, and the British government have been denied any defensible pretext for abandoning the goal of a permanent settlement.

While the Northern Irish are singular in their fondness for "the crack" they are equally proud of their capacity to recognize their own folly and "catch themselves on." Between the lines of the ex-paramilitaries' rhetoric, there is some recognition that for twenty-five years they choreographed intercommunal murder with enough cynical precision and restraint to turn what began as civil strife into a purposeless, self-renewing banality. Now loyalists and republicans would like to see themselves as something better than working-class corner-boys moved to terrorism. Some loyalist ex-paramilitaries acknowledge their unsavory history, and want to be part of a purged future. Some former IRA volunteers aim to carry the glory of their violent past into the political forefront of a pacified Ireland. In different ways, their respective rap sheets limit their capacities to achieve these ends. But on account of the ceasefires alone, ex-paramilitaries have already bartered infamy for a small measure of dignity.

CHAPTER 9

THE WEAK SMILE AND THE
HARD SWALLOW

For both sides, notwithstanding Canary Wharf, the current peace process is the most earnest effort at peaceful persuasion to date. But as forces in civil politics, the two groups are equally limited from different directions. Republican ex-prisoners are more accepted by their community, but temperamentally less comfortable as ordinary politicians. Loyalist ex-convicts are less accepted by their community, but more at ease with conventional politics.

In 1969, the most respectable calling available to a young northern Catholic was to become a rebel. Loyalists, by contrast, had jobs. Now, republicans still extract most of their self-respect from "the armed struggle," while new loyalists have the nonviolent culture of the Protestant ethic to nestle back into. Loyalists can tolerate the unavoidable humbling of paramilitaries in post-ceasefire Northern Ireland. Sinn Fein has a harder time. Thus, while republicans exasperated by the slow pace of constitutional politics blow up Canary Wharf in frustration, the new loyalists ask Protestant paramilitaries to resist the temptation to retaliate lest the gains of peace be squandered. Yet nationalists give Sinn Fein 25 percent of their votes, while the unionist electorate throws its support to mainstream politicians.

The political handicaps republicans and loyalists suffer are profound. But the greatest political benefits ever bestowed on the people of Northern Ireland were the ceasefires, and the paramilitaries delivered them. Like it or not, the men who did the dirty work during the troubles are now essential for keeping the peace.

Gerry Fitt founded the SDLP and now sits in the House of Lords. One of the victims of the troubles, Paddy Wilson, was his best friend. Fitt had to identify Wilson's body. His views on the participation of ex-prisoners in the governance of a peacetime Northern Ireland are sweeping. When he saw ex-terrorist John White in the loyalist delegation announcing the

241

ceasefire, he was disgusted. "It made my blood run cold to see him there," said Lord Fitt. "Under no circumstances should he be involved in talks because he brutally and savagely murdered Paddy Wilson and Irene Andrews. Paddy Wilson was almost decapitated, he was stabbed so many times. Are those the credentials you need to be involved in talks?" Fitt represented Catholic west Belfast in Parliament for seventeen years, yet IRA supporters, displeased with his gentle approach to Irish nationalism, attacked his house in August 1976. He fended them off with a gun for twenty-five minutes. He believes ex-prisoners made a choice—violence— which should disqualify them from politics. "There are still deep, gaping wounds on the body politic of Northern Ireland among Protestants and Catholics. To ask them to forget these murders is in defiance of human nature."[1]

Robert Cooper was also a close friend of Wilson's. Yet his most interesting conviction is that he must find it in his heart to take people like White on board if peace is to stick in Northern Ireland. "If we don't accept that people who've done terrible things have to be treated as ordinary decent members of society who have to be listened to, then there's not much hope for the peace process. I have to accept that someone like him may have a role to play just as other people of the unionist community have to accept that some of the major figures in Sinn Fein who may have had IRA connections in the past may have a role to play as well." Cooper, now chairman of the Fair Employment Commission, is an Ascendancy Protestant who *a priori* would be unlikely to accord political legitimacy to ex-paramilitaries.

Even some direct victims are ready to include the former terrorists in a political solution. Thomas Clarke, whose son Malachy hanged himself after an IRA punishment beating, says: "I just want to see the silent majority of Northern Ireland speaking out. I don't give a damn who they support. Until they do, the proper political influences won't be set into motion. We can't just leave it to the UVF or the IRA. By my speaking out, I'm trying to encourage other people to speak out. Don't let the beatings hold you back. I'm a long way from forgiving them. Before you can forgive somebody you've got to vent your anger, and you've also got to be given some modicum of justice as well."

The ceasefires have liberated a great deal of latent grief. One cross-community bereavement counseling group reported that since the ceasefires, calls from victims have increased 80 percent, some of them from people whose loved ones were killed as long as twenty years earlier.[2] The current exchange is far less inflamed, and favors a more thoughtful brand of human interest than the bathos hurled back and forth during the troubles.

The loyalists have stated publicly their "abject and true remorse" for ritual murder. Unlike republicans, loyalists will use the words "murder" and "terrorism" in referring to their past. The preponderance of people in Northern Ireland see their contrition as genuine. And it has the weight of symbol—the same people regard the gesture as a bellwether of peace. But even though the statement is an admission coming from hitherto unrepentant hard men, it threatens to ring hollow to those who lost people close to them. Most loyalist prisoners and ex-prisoners recognize this fact. Several have considered approaching the survivors of their victims in person.

"The reason [I don't] is that I don't want to open a can of worms," says Alex Calderwood, now a dedicated Christian. "I would have no problem meeting them if they wanted to meet me. But I didn't want to probe into somebody else's life. There've been people who've had the same experience as me—about going to the media and going to the press and doing different things, and saying they're sorry and things like that. But people have wrote in: 'Okay, you're sorry; let us get on with our life. You're out of prison, you're living your life; I don't have my husband, or I don't have my son.' That's why I didn't do it." Ron McMurray feels the same way. "There was one stage I thought, should I actually write to these people expressing my sorrow, but it does seem a bit shallow, so I never did contact them. If some of the survivors said, look, I really want to talk to him, I want to get it off my chest and see who done this, I would consider meeting them." John White also considered contacting the families of his victims, but decided against it. "I don't think it would achieve anything in the way of alleviating their suffering," he says.

Sinn Fein and the fringe loyalist parties will continue to stress their prisoner-of-war status, and argue that their special category warrants special treatment. The government will retort that they are felons. Since the criminalization policy began in 1976, paramilitaries in Northern Ireland have officially been common criminals. Yet virtually every aspect of the law enforcement regime mocks that designation.

The Emergency Provisions Act, which applies solely to Northern Ireland, distinguishes "scheduled terrorist offenses" from other crimes, and subjects them exclusively to nonjury trials before a one-judge "Diplock court" (named for Lord Diplock, who conceived of it) designed to circumvent juror intimidation by paramilitary groups. The act raises a presumption of intent to use explosives found in a suspect's possession, authorizes warrantless arrests of terrorist suspects, and allows the security forces to hold them without charge for three days. And the act makes it a crime to collect information useful to terrorists, to provide unauthorized weapons training, or to wear paramilitary garb (including hoods or masks) in public.[3] Sentenced prisoners in Northern Ireland jails in 1972 totaled 745; in 1979 the number had reached 2,300; the inmate population at the time of the IRA ceasefire stood at 1,941.[4] The Maze is a purpose-built prison, specifically intended to replace Long Kesh after internment. It houses only republican and loyalist paramilitary prisoners. By a factor of two, the Maze is the largest of Northern Ireland's three prisons for sentenced prisoners.[5] The prison regime there is more liberal than it is elsewhere. The Prison Service spends over $100,000 on each prisoner per year; by contrast, the U.S. government spends about $21,000 per year per inmate in federal prisons, which include accommodating "Club Fed" pens.[6] In short, paramilitaries have tyrannized the administration of justice in Northern Ireland. In fact if not in name, they do occupy a special category.

The law-abiding society responds to this reality in different ways. Like Green, most ex-prisoners are philosophical. They regard lost comrades as casualties of war, and decline to exact blame. Dan McCann, one of the three IRA volunteers killed by the SAS in Gibraltar, was Tommy Gorman's best friend. They were on the blanket together in prison. "The old thing about nature's gentlemen is true about a lot of people, but Big Dan really was a gentle man," Gorman reminisces, his voice cracking. "He was religious in his own way, and very, very funny. Oh, I was shattered by the three deaths, especially Dan's. I knew Dan extraordinarily well. But I mean, people are on about their relatives and sons being murdered and stuff like that. IRA people never say that*—they were just taken, caught, and executed. If we got them 'uns we would murder them 'uns. It's as simple as that. It's just that they caught us on the hop. And that was it." They ask no forgiveness, and extend none.

At the same time, former paramilitaries tend not to believe in a statute of limitations for culprits in what they regard as senseless sectarian hits. In 1992, the UFF gunned down Joe Clarke's brother, Padraic O Cleirigh, in

---

*This, of course, is a convenient fiction of Gorman's. In the matter of taking life, republicans frequently impose on their foes a stricter moral standard than they apply to the IRA. Both Sinn Fein officially and IRA prisoners individually have bitterly condemned the Gibraltar shootings as an instance of the security forces' "shoot-to-kill" policy, even though the IRA has manifestly carried out a "shoot-to-kill" policy of its own.

his living room as his wife and son stood by. The man was a Falls Road black-taxi driver and a promoter of the Irish language, but he was not an IRA volunteer. Although Joe Clarke himself has not been on active service for the IRA for several years, he would avenge his brother whenever the opportunity arose. "He wasn't an active republican at all. He just lived in a bad area in north Belfast. If I had the people who done it, I would do the same to them with no qualms about it at all," he says matter-of-factly. "That's the way things are in Northern Ireland, you know."

Ron McMurray understands that revenge, as a dish savored cold, likely will not be taken off Ulster's menu. "If tomorrow the majority of the people in this country voted to have a united Ireland, I would abide by that. I'd accept it. But I'll be on the first boat out. I would fear for my safety, I would fear for my family. I would be living in a society which would know that I'm a convicted loyalist killer. Life could be made tough. It's not so much about me. It would be about my family. My family never committed any atrocity."

Most noncombatant survivors want nothing to do with the people who killed their loved ones. Yet most cannot truly forgive the culprits. With respect to these people, Sinn Fein's disinterested stance seems unobjectionable, as does the loyalists' view that survivors should be left alone. The rub is that survivors whose losses are fresh generally want to see the state punish paramilitary killers, unimpeded by the euphoria of peace. At a conference held by a reconciliation group called Protestant and Catholic Encounter (PACE) in May 1995, Alan McBride professed his inability to forgive the IRA for the Shankill bomb, which killed his twenty-nine-year-old wife, Sharon. "I hope I can arrive at forgiveness sometime," he said, trembling. "When I arrive there, I'll make a public statement and I'll say I can forgive. But while these people remain unrepentant, I find it very difficult, even though the terrorists have swapped a balaclava for a shirt and tie."

Gary McMichael (for the UDP), Jackie McMullan (for Sinn Fein), and Ron McMurray were at the PACE conference as well. So was Leo Green, and he offered a response to McBride. Green pointed out that his brother, an IRA man, had been killed by loyalists in 1975, yet he had "no wish to see them in jail." Later, in private, he explained his position. "I have no concern about punishing the people who killed my brother. I mean, I'm not happy with the fact that he's dead, but I agree that there's some sort of political rationale behind what they did. Certainly at this point in time, it would serve absolutely no purpose in anyone being put in jail for it. And if there was someone in jail for it, I would be arguing just as strongly that they should be released. I wouldn't state it simply in terms of forgiveness. The notion of forgiveness implies like, here I am offering my own forgiveness and we all feel better about it. They're obviously not interested in my forgiveness, but equally I'm not particularly interested in theirs. All I'm simply saying is that several thousand people have died, and if you start to get into this notion of him, her, him, who, this, that, and the other, it doesn't serve any purpose at all."

McMichael, whose father was killed by the IRA in 1987, basically agrees. "I'm bitter towards the people who killed my father," he says. "I wouldn't be human if I wasn't. One alternative was to do nothing, to just go on with life as normal, which I couldn't do. Another alternative that was probably the easiest choice would have been to become involved in the UDA myself perhaps to try and take physical retribution. But I didn't do that. And the last alternative was to become involved in politics." Sure enough, McMichael sounds like a politician, but a sensible one. "It's a matter of trying to rise above things and doing what's right. I'll give you a very stark example. I was in the White House on St. Patrick's Day. Gerry Adams was in the room. There were 350 other people, right, but I felt extremely uncomfortable because he was there. It was very emotive for me. But I was there to do a job, and we've got to understand that everybody suffered. Everybody has suffered in this conflict. Absolutely everybody— perhaps not directly by losing people in their families, but they've all suffered the consequences of violence, socially if not physically. At the end of the day, it's not really about me, and it's not about Gerry Adams, and it's not about the guy who lives down the street—it's about everybody."

Thus Sinn Fein argues for a complete amnesty for all paramilitary prisoners, and the new loyalists ask for early release at minimum. Green's and McMichael's arguments sound eminently sensible. Yet amnesty would leave innocent victims—that is, those whose dead were uninvolved in any paramilitary or security activity—with no retribution, and without a sense of social control. As Oliver Wilkinson, chief executive of Victims Support Northern Ireland, put it at the conference, they would be forced to take peace with only "a weak smile and a hard swallow."

Emotionally, amnesty would be too much for the province to bear. As a compromise, prisoners will be let out sooner than they would have in the absence of peace. Parliament, at Mayhew's request, has increased remission from one-third to one-half for determinate sentence prisoners, and will probably accelerate review for lifers.

For most, this moderate mode of dispensation is acceptable. Noncombatants whose losses occurred long ago seem to have reached a point of repose. What they tender is something short of forgiveness—perhaps a kind of moral amnesty. Ann McCann, a Catholic but no relation to Dan, lost her brother Gerard Duddy, twenty, in 1972. He was killed on a Saturday night in Andersonstown by a crew of loyalists in a drive-by shooting as he walked home from a discotheque. Nobody has ever been charged with his murder. "My Christian belief tells me I should be forgiving, but my human nature tells me that I don't really forgive the person that killed Gerard. I don't, at this moment in my life, want him to be up in court and put behind bars, and know that he's there for fifteen years or whatever. I don't have a wish for that anymore—I never did have it. But forgiving is a very difficult thing to do. They've never got anybody for Gerard's death, and I find it difficult to know how I would feel. I don't want to be given that opportunity." Similarly, after the loyalist ceasefire, Mary Ward, a seventy-four-year-old Catholic widow whose son, Peter, Gusty Spence was convicted of killing as he walked out of a Shankill Road bar over thirty years ago, took his statement of "abject and true remorse" at face value. "I said I wouldn't forgive him but as the days have gone by I've been thinking, what's the point in keeping the whole thing going? It's peace we all want."[7] McCann and Ward's message is that they can't forget, but it's time to move on.

The Protestant community has also come to handle republican atrocities philosophically, with gallows humor. One joke circulated shortly after the Shankill bomb. Begley's mother is escorted by the RUC into the morgue to identify his body, which is arrayed in pieces on a metal slab. The cop picks up his head and says, "Is that your son?" "No," she responds, "he was taller than that." Loyalists also have the capacity to make macabre fun of themselves. One UVF man was sent to jail when he botched a hit and shot himself. "What'd you get done for," his mates inside asked him, "attempted suicide?" Plum Smith put fourteen bullets into his victim without killing him; friends ask Smith whether his *modus operandi* was lead poisoning.

THE END OF INDIGNATION

Recent survivors like McBride are the most easily seduced by institutionalized finger-pointing. The most visible abettor is an organization known as FAIT, for Families Against Intimidation and Terror. It does quite a bit of good—in particular, by dogging Sinn Fein and the fringe loyalist parties about the persistent punishment beatings that their paramilitary counterparts have carried out since the ceasefires,* chronicling these rough tactics, and keeping international human rights outfits abreast of the situation. But FAIT also indulges in a degree of reconciliation hucksterism. During the seventeen months before Canary Wharf, the director of the organization was Henry Robinson, a former member of the Official IRA who shot a Provisional three times in the legs in 1982, then served two and a half years in the Maze, where he became a vegetarian and a pacifist. The bespectacled Robinson looks like a sedate schoolteacher, but the technique he favors to make his point is histrionically confrontational. He thrusts people who have just lost their loved ones up in the faces of ex-paramilitaries in public, and has the victims yell abuse at them. He employed this device with both Gerry Adams and the new loyalists at Dublin Airport as they returned from trips to the United States in late 1994.

Such aggressive shaming only makes the targets turn their backs, and keeps the victims themselves wallowing in their misfortune. Robinson's less-than-pristine resume also gets on the nerves of ex-prisoners. "He talks about punishment shootings when he went and shot someone ten years after his own organization called a ceasefire," snorts Jackie McMullan. Echoes Billy Hutchinson: "I'd put my record in community affairs up against his any day." Nevertheless, Robinson wants the paramilitary groups to quit violence cold turkey. "There's evidence that both sets of terrorists have converted to democracy," he says. "We're calling for them to stop these violations of human rights. We are not fully convinced that they've converted to democracy. We don't believe that they can convert to democracy until these beatings stop."

Analytically, that's true: punishment beatings are fascistic and undemocratic. But it makes little sense to link the political acceptance of Sinn Fein and the loyalist fringe parties unconditionally to a cessation of the paramilitaries' enforcement activities, as Robinson wants to do. Like all addicts, they will wean themselves off violence only gradually. The best medicine is a healthy, fluent political process. Robinson's methods interpose victims between the people of Northern Ireland and general peace, which neither the victims nor their countrymen want.

One of Robinson's recruits is Sandra Peacock. On September 1, 1993, three UVF gunmen took a sledgehammer to the door of her house in north

---

*Between the IRA ceasefire and the end of 1995, republicans committed 167 punishment beatings, loyalists 92. (Royal Ulster Constabulary Press Office, January 5, 1996.)

Belfast and shot her husband dead in front of her and her daughter. Jim Peacock was a prison officer—the last one killed in Northern Ireland—and by all accounts a particularly professional and civilized one. John White remembers him as "a really decent bloke." Even John Pickering, who took digs from as many screws as any republican prisoner did, says Peacock gave him "no hassle whatsoever." Most likely, the UVF just considered him a soft target and took him out to get the prison administration to relax disciplinary or security measures in the jail. The irony is that Sandra Peacock is exactly the sort of *non*-Ascendancy Protestant the new loyalists would want to win over. She was born in 1946 in Ballymoney, a Protestant town, to an unwed mother. The proper folk considered her an embarrassment, and she was not allowed to take the "eleven-plus" examination to qualify for college preparatory education on account of her wayward birth. According to Peacock, her eventual stepfather sexually abused her and her first husband was "a nasty piece of work" who battered her, and left her and their three children for another woman in 1972. Sandra Peacock knew Billy Hutchinson before he went to prison, and liked him.

In 1974, this tough, resilient woman married Jim Peacock—a "lovely big man" from Liverpool—and had another child by him. He joined the Prison Service in 1977, and found the work worthy and agreeable. After the hunger strikes, the Provos targeted him and they had to move. A local UVF man, now dead, assured them they'd be protected in their new neighborhood. The Peacocks' politics were solidly unionist. But now Sandra Peacock is convinced that the new loyalists are all still actively involved in the organization that killed her husband, though Gusty Spence has claimed the hit was unsanctioned. "I have done everything I can since Jim died to agitate them and aggravate them," she says matter-of-factly. "Did you see the way Hutchy looked at me in Dublin? He looked at me with pure hatred, because he knows that I am the weak spot." Barely five feet tall and a gaunt hundred pounds, the plainly heartsick Sandra Peacock made them all look presumptively big and bad.

The UVF has made her not only bitter, but politically dissonant. "Gerry Adams is the smartest, the most charismatic, the best politician in Ireland," she declares. "There's times when Gerry Adams has me nearly convinced. If ever a day comes when I'm in the same room as Sinn Fein and the loyalists, I'll shake Sinn Fein's hand." On the peace process: "I laugh my head off, because I'm so vindictive and so nasty and so different from the woman that I once was. I don't give a damn. I hate them all." By her own admission, after FAIT tires her out Sandra Peacock will simply isolate herself and sneer bitterly at the paramilitary front parties she says are conning the public. But she will die in Northern Ireland. "I've got six foot two* coming to me out of this country," she says, "and the bastards'll not do me out of it."

Thomas Clarke, another member of Robinson's army, is a fifty-one-year-old Catholic artist who paints cityscapes of Belfast. Tall, dark, and earringed, he admits to once having "republican sympathies," though he has never approved of their methods. He lives in the middle Falls, near Tommy Gorman's boyhood home, with his twenty-two-year-old girlfriend, Lisa O'Hagan. Her brother Dee was beaten by the IRA several times for joyriding in Twinbrook, which she left after the IRA occupied her mother's house. Clarke's sixteen-year-old son Malachy had problems with drinking and glue sniffing, though he did not sell drugs. On October 24, 1994—almost two months after the IRA ceasefire—several Provos saw him standing on a street corner with a glue bag, jumped out of a car, chased him into an alley, and beat him up. They broke his nose, ruptured his eardrum, and scarred his face. The Clarkes pressed charges. Although word on the street was that the beating was unsanctioned, and despite six witnesses, nobody fingered Malachy's assailants. Six weeks later, after periodic intimidation from "a handful of chuckies,"† Malachy Clarke hanged himself.

Some republicans conceded that his beating was regrettable, but attributed his suicide to his father's lifestyle and his mother's purported drinking. A few months later, graffiti on a lower Falls brick wall read: "Tom Clarke Drove His Son To Suicide." For his part, Thomas Clarke has adopted proactive realism rather than Sandra Peacock's abject cynicism to face the future. Convinced that once paramilitaries have materialized in a society they cannot be eradicated, he believes that they need to be co-opted by partial empowerment. "As long as other people with different affiliations are allowed to function with them and keep an eye on them and create a sense of balance, that's all right. It's only whenever they're going to be put en bloc into a police administration that you're running a real big risk." The problem with paramilitary organizations, says Clarke, is that sometimes it's the scum rather than the cream that rises to the top. One of the men who beat Malachy is "an emaciated wee toe-rag who if it wasn't

---

*The United Kingdom's statutory gravesite allotment.

†"Chucky" or "chuck" is nationalist slang for Provisional IRA members; the term is a corruption of the first word of the Irish phrase "tiocfaidh ar la," the republican motto meaning "our day will come."

for the political situation here he'd be nothing but a turd under your foot." Clarke, for good reasons, does not believe that Sinn Fein and the new loyalists are the true voices of the working class, or the best sources of hope for Northern Ireland.

Focusing excessively on direct victims in an effort to cement peace runs the risk of alienating ex-prisoners. Robinson dismisses out of hand all former prisoners who haven't utterly renounced violence, and some that have. "There are three categories of former paramilitaries," he says. "One is the born-again Christian type, who are absolutely fucking useless—no good to anybody because everything's redemption, everything's God, and you can't get any sense out of them in practical terms. Another type is the likes of republican and loyalist former prisoners who still maintain links with those organizations and say, well, we don't agree with violence but we understand why it happens, and they're not proactively against the human rights violations which these groups continue to carry out. Then there's other people like myself who have rejected violence, and who say that it was never right and say that in order to move forward what we've got to do is campaign against these guys."

Given that ex-prisoners also have generally been more conciliatory than the mainstream politicians (particularly on the unionist side) since the ceasefires were declared, ostracizing ex-prisoners makes no sense. Doing so reintroduces the kind of negative spiral that perpetuated the troubles: people like Alan McBride are trotted out to show up the Provos, then reshelved to leave unbloodied politicians at Northern Ireland's helm. The ex-prisoners are wise to this device. "One of the obstacles that people use to the release of prisoners is the victims," Eddie Kinner told a fringe meeting at the annual British Labour Party Conference in October 1995. "This is something I find very distasteful when I look around at the victims in my own community that have never received any assistance or attention from the people who have decided to use them as political footballs. If they were genuinely concerned about the victims and their families, they would be examining their hardships and needs and trying to address them instead of just using them when it is politically expedient."

Most paramilitaries would agree with Kinner when he says that the paramilitaries were not the sole cause of the troubles, and consequently should not be demonized. Most would also agree intuitively, however, that there are "victims" and there are *victims*. "If the people who are doing the most complaining are the type of upper-middle-class unionists who haven't been affected by it, then I'm simply not interested in what their arguments are," says Anthony McIntyre. "But as regards people who have had relatives killed, who genuinely have a perspective on the victims, I think that their considerations have to be taken on board." Unfortunately, McIntyre's voice is a lonely one among republicans.

GETTING BEYOND RECRIMINATIONS

Now that violence has largely ended, name calling and hyperbole are slowly becoming unnecessary. But that is not the whole battle. Although the troubles' three thousand-plus body count is low by absolute standards, as a percentage of Ulster's population of 1.6 million it is substantial. A relatively large portion of the population has been touched intimately and painfully by the conflict. Was the sacrifice worth the likely result, particularly given that it nearly materialized in 1974? Can these victims live with former terrorists in high places, or is the itch for retribution too acute? On these questions, nationalists are readier to forgive loyalists than vice versa. There is a variety of reasons—an ostensibly greater sectarian element in loyalist violence, the acceptance among nationalists that comes with the "prison culture," nationalists' view that sacrifice is the inevitable cost of change. But both communities are weary of violence and loss. People like Bob Cooper have reached closure on the matter of whether history goes away: it doesn't, especially not in Northern Ireland.

The IRA and the loyalist paramilitaries are part of history, and if political empowerment aids their positive transformation, it can't be dismissed. By the same token, Northern Ireland needs to make room for the inevitable unforgiving. Samuel Malcolmson was until 1995 the chairman of the Disabled Police Officers' Association. On September 22, 1972, en route to the site of the shooting death of a British soldier, he was ambushed by an IRA volunteer, who shot Malcolmson in the back. He was hospitalized for some months, usually unconscious, and emerged paralyzed down his left side and in constant pain. His mother had a heart attack and died when she saw him in the hospital bed. "Those guys who have come out and have committed murder and are now trying to show a face of respectability—I wouldn't vote for them," he says. "In my world, if I had my way and capital punishment was the norm, those people would be dead."*

---

*Britain officially abolished the death penalty in 1965, and the last person actually executed was hanged in 1955. In 1983, conservative MPs spearheaded by unionists attempted to have the death penalty (particularly for terrorists) reinstated, but they were badly, and probably conclusively, defeated in the House of Commons. ("Death Knell For the Gallows," *Belfast Telegraph,* July 14, 1983, p. 5.)

"Obviously, we've got to be sensitive," says Billy Mitchell. "I don't expect people who have been hurt through bereavements, you know, atrocities, to forgive me, or to accept us. Obviously a lot do. Initially people will start off saying, I don't want to know, then I don't mind knowing, then they do want to know, then they get concerned. But I don't expect that to happen right across the board. I don't think it's even right of society to ask them to forgive and to forget. They've got to be allowed to grieve and heal in their own time. And therefore I don't expect them to support the PUP or Sinn Fein." Mitchell has a loyalist working-class perspective. In seeking amnesty, Sinn Fein may be wrongly imputing the greater stoicism of the republican community to the loyalist community as well.

The new loyalists and republicans would like to fashion an intercommunity mandate against violence. Their strongest logical allies would be the living casualties of the troubles: if they can forgo vengeance, and then condemn it, the mandate for peace will be most secure. There are plenty of clichés about how to do that—"building bridges," "breaking down barriers," and "crossing the great divide" are a few—but they merely restate the imperative. The Northern Irish, of all people, should know how precious little diagnostic or prescriptive power slogans carry.

One personality who puts some meat on the brittle bones of truism is Mairead Corrigan-Maguire—a tiny woman with potent, surprisingly hard-nosed opinions. With Betty Williams, she co-founded the Peace People reconciliation group in 1976, after her sister's three children were killed when a car driven by an IRA volunteer, shot dead after trying to ambush an army foot-patrol, careened out of control and hit them as they walked in Andersonstown with their mother, who later killed herself. Maguire and Williams won the Nobel Peace Prize in 1976. Maguire links shared victimhood with the political solution in Northern Ireland. What everyone has in common here, she argues, is partition and the strife that came with it—most recently, the troubles. Therefore, people in Northern Ireland are *all* fundamentally different from people in the Republic of Ireland. It follows that a unitary state will not work. Permanent devolution is the answer. "Irish unity is not on," she says resolutely. "We're seventy years into partition, we are different."

Maguire suggests that both Northern Ireland and the Republic tone down their tempestuous relationship with Irish history and look mainly at the last twenty-five years. Northern Ireland is not the south's business; the divorce referendum of November 1995, which finally made it legal, is. "I think that it's important too that people in the south of Ireland look at their own identity instead of just kind of living with this idea of, oh, Irish unity would be very nice, and be very, very honest and say, well, look, what does this really mean to us in the south? Do we really want to take on Northern Ireland? I think they've got to look at the fact too that seventy years into partition, they have changed as well. You see, I don't find an awful lot of real, in-depth thinking in the south as to what has been happening in Northern Ireland, because they rightly are more interested in their own economy and their own problems and their own society. It's a young society and they've got many problems to deal with. But I think we all now need to be honest and reflect on what has gone on, and have a sense of our own identity and what we would like to see happening in the future, and not just take on board a whole lot of mythology and ideals that other people have had in the past. Narrow nationalism has been very, very destructive." Two weeks before the IRA ceasefire, she aired this view at the Felons' Club, the drinking establishment on the Falls Road run by and for republican ex-prisoners. The applause was polite but pointedly sparse.

Maguire's view also hinges on the notion that everyone in Northern Ireland—middle classes as well as working classes, churches as well as government—has been complicitous in perpetuating the troubles. "It was almost like a tale of two cities in that people in working-class areas carried the brunt of the troubles. They were in the areas where the IRA were operating, or the UVF or the UDA. Those were the areas where the soldiers were brought in in great numbers, and whole areas were cordoned off. Homes were searched by soldiers, brothers were lifted into local camps for two and three days and were never told where they were, who had to suffer really tremendously during the troubles. The middle class just turned a blind eye to them. It didn't cost them much, and there was almost a sense of, keep it there, as long as we're not being affected by it."

Equally, all have been victims because the society that the troubles have created is warped in every quadrant. On this point, Mairead Corrigan-Maguire sounds a bit sentimental. "I think in a sense we are all part of the suffering in Northern Ireland in one way or another. I don't like to think of a small group of people who are somehow *the* victims. I think from the fact that we live in Northern Ireland, twenty-five years of the troubles have in some way touched most all of us and changed us. So we're therefore all part of the problem and therefore all part of the solution. I never think of a small group of people as *the* victims."

Everybody in Northern Ireland, if not a victim in fact, has a victim's mentality. Republicans frame in ornate scrolls the 270-odd volunteers killed in action and the ten dead hunger strikers. They portray British countermeasures in 1969 as a continuation of eight hundred years of colonial subjugation rather than an emergent response to civil unrest. Nationalists protest that all they ever wanted was to liberate oppressed Catholics with the civil rights movement, and that the IRA tainted the effort terminally. Unionists claim Catholics never took Ulster seriously enough to accept the political participation that was offered them, and responded inappropriately with violence. Unionists also feel that the British have spiritually abandoned them by signing the Anglo-Irish Agreement, and that nationalists have unfairly diluted Ulster's unionist majority by manipulating American policy and opinion. Loyalists say they were set up by unionists as the fall guys for Stormont before the war, then allowed to take many of the casualties once it started.

Apportioning blame in this hash of accusations, Corrigan-Maguire says, is pointless. The idea instead is for all Northern Irish people to embrace the troubles as their common bane, however different the effect of the conflict on each group. There is a risk in this strategy, which could merely reinforce the suffering and forestall catharsis. Ex-prisoners can help minimize that risk, and they are doing so. They have both directly inflicted pain and directly endured it. Because of this, they vivify the notion that a person can be both victim and oppressor. As symbols of that duality, they knit together the past, present, and future of Northern Ireland. Compare the reflections of Brendan Hughes and Marty Snoddon—two prisoners, one a republican and the other a loyalist, who served long periods of imprisonment and do not presently speak for any political organization. "Breaking down the tribal traditions is going to take time, just like it's taken us time to come to this position, where I can sit here and say, I don't want a thirty-two-county democratic socialist republic in the morning—because that's the reason I went to jail, fighting for that," says Hughes. "But I mean, we're not going to wake up in the morning and have an all-Ireland. It's just not on the cards. So we have to find another way to do it."

Marty Snoddon has no fear of a united Ireland "as long as it's a united Ireland where people's beliefs and attitudes are protected. There's got to be a bill of rights to protect the individual. If you protect the individual, then people don't need to form into groups. I have a British way of life, just as a Scotsman has a British way of life. I feel as if the British government has betrayed the Protestant people of Northern Ireland, just as they've probably betrayed everyone that they've ever governed. So I don't feel any loyalty to the British crown. I hold loyalty to my British way of life here. I am, after all, an Ulster Protestant. I would like to be able to remain an Ulster Protestant within a European Community. I don't want to be going around and shaking hands with every Catholic I meet just because they're a Catholic. I would like to be going out in the street and saying, well, that guy's okay—it doesn't matter what he is." Hughes rejoins, "Well, okay, he can retain [his British identity]. And we have to retain our identity. But I mean, twenty years down the line, we can have the same combined identity with an objective to move on."

Beyond the shared working-class interests, between Hughes and Snoddon there is room for pragmatic, political convergence. As far as recriminations for past misdeeds are concerned, it's a wash between the two. Their attitudes are both exemplary and realistic. In the past, what has passed for noble rhetoric—republican stridency and sanctimony, loyalist in-the-bunker defiance—has been purely decorative, without any serious political subtext. Unfortunately, some of the hypocrisy still escapes every now and again. When John Hume failed to win the Nobel Peace Prize in 1995, DUP spokesman Ian Paisley, Jr., a chip off the old block, couldn't just say dispassionately that the prize would have been premature. Instead, he had these choice words: "The search for self-glory by Irish nationalists has ended in ignominy. The Academy have had their fingers burnt once in Northern Ireland in 1976 when they handed out the award to the Peace People, who could not deliver. They are obviously not going to get their fingers burnt twice when they know the IRA are involved in a tactical peace process, not in a real peace."[8]

When Canary Wharf appeared to vindicate this view, Billy Hutchinson scolded unionist politicians for "gloating at the killing of British citizens because it meant the end of the IRA ceasefire."[9] To virtually all those who have lost loved ones to the troubles or spent time in prison, Paisley Junior's heaving out a chance for peace that was backed by over a year of quiet from the IRA was not only imperious but grossly offensive. Victims are dismayed enough that the ceasefires didn't come sooner. After feeling the initial wave of euphoria when Adams announced the IRA ceasefire, Ann McCann was hit with disgust over the other message of peace: that terrorist killing over twenty-five years had all been for nought. "The peace, the ceasefires, actually brought an anger out in me that wasn't there. I think when the troubles were continuing, and you switched on your television every night and there was one atrocity after another—listening to things like kids being abducted and maybe tortured for days maybe before their bodies were found and informers being lifted and tortured—we often said, well, thank God Gerard died instantly. It almost made our situation not so bad. There was great joy about the ceasefire, but the sense of anger followed quite quickly—like, what the hell was it for? Now, if I'm thinking that as a victim twenty-two years down the road, what must victims whose sons or husbands died earlier this year or last year be thinking?"

Peace makes the Alan McBrides of Northern Ireland feel like afterthoughts. To give some of them justice, Anthony McIntyre suggests a war crimes tribunal. Such an institution would assume the conclusion that republicans and loyalists were in fact engaged in war rather than terrorism. Under that assumption, it would also rate the morality of the different paramilitary groups. *Ex hypothesi,* the Provos would come out way on top because they hit more military targets—a divisive result rather than a conciliatory one. As Mairead Corrigan-Maguire would say, it's not on. The politics of the open wound was practiced quite enough during the troubles.

McCann's testimony suggests the best course: admit that the troubles do not deserve the label "war," that they rose out of a sectarian miasma, and that anyone lost was not martyred but wasted. After twenty-five years, Northern Ireland has not constitutionally changed. With no gunsmoke to cloud the issue for seventeen months, it became clear that republican and loyalist terrorists killed nearly three thousand people merely to certify sovereign aspirations—in effect, just to make their feelings emphatically known. Neither side has gained a single inch of territory. Neither side has redefined the relevant electorate for Northern Ireland. Republicans have not improved the material lot of the working-class Catholics who make up their constituency; they are still widely unemployed. Loyalists have not made Protestants more secure; most of their traditional industrial strongholds have become moribund over the past twenty-five years. Indeed, the troubles have economically blacklisted Northern Ireland. The civil rights reforms enacted by Britain have brightened Catholics' prospects since the suspension of Stormont, but this legislation merely tracks the trend of reform in the West that began before the troubles.

Like Vietnam for Americans, the fruitlessness of the conflict is hard truth for the Northern Irish. But unlike the mythologies of the past, the revelation might offer some lessons about the futility of runaway righteousness and hypersensitivity to history.

Both sides take secret pride in a conflict of which they should be openly ashamed. The Provos, in their refusal to apologize, are the worst offenders. Gordon Wilson, perhaps the troubles' most famous victim, offered the IRA forgiveness when they asked for none. Wilson, a craggy drapery maker, had a twenty-year-old daughter, Marie, who worked as a nurse in Belfast. On Remembrance Day, 1987, home in Enniskillen to visit her family, she was crushed to death by exploding rock from the bomb that the IRA had planted near a war memorial. Ten other Protestants died as well. In their sublime blend of confusion and stoicism, the words Wilson uttered hours later, after he'd held her hand as she lay buried in rubble and breathed her last conscious breaths, are as throat-catching now as they were then: "I bear no ill will. That sort of talk is not going to bring her back to life. She was a great wee lassie. She loved her profession. She was a pet and she's dead. She's in heaven and we'll meet again. Don't ask me please for a purpose. I don't have a purpose. I don't have an answer but I know there has to be a plan. If I did not think that, I would commit suicide. It is part of a greater plan and God is good and we shall meet again."[10]

Hoping his victim's pedigree and his appointment to the Senate of the Republic could soften the IRA, in 1993 Wilson met with two Provo spokespersons. They handed him a typewritten apology for the death of his daughter, reiterated the IRA's claim that the Enniskillen bombing was a mistake,* but were otherwise unrepentant, blaming the troubles wholly on the British presence in Northern Ireland. He came away from the meeting with no illusions. "I said, I am tired of hearing the IRA talking about their mistakes. And really, it was then we agreed that we weren't getting anywhere," he recounted. "Some called me naive, and said I was made a fool of, and maybe they were right. God knows. But I had hopes. People had told me they couldn't think of anybody more likely to get something from the IRA in the way of a little peace. I thought I might, if only a change of emphasis. I was wrong."[11]

Wilson died in June 1995. Marie's message, and his, is simply that the troubles were pointless heartbreak unrepaid. This is a dignified and conclusive rebuke to the perpetrators. Even without contrition, ceasefires are welcome. Repentance is a bonus. Leave it at that.

---

*In the span of a year beginning with the Enniskillen bombing, the IRA said that twenty of its victims had been "mistakes." Wilson was prompted to seek the meeting by the deaths of the boys in Warrington—two more "mistakes." He also met with loyalist paramilitaries after the UFF had unmistakenly gunned down seven civilians at Greysteel in retaliation for the IRA's nine mistakes in the Shankill bombing.

INTERVIEWEES

Unless otherwise noted, all quoted remarks were made in interviews conducted by the author on the dates specified below. A few quotations in the text are unattributed, and several interviewees unlisted here, at the request of the source or at the author's discretion, to ensure the safety of the source from reprisals.

DAVID ADAMS. Press officer, Ulster Democratic Party (UDP). Former officer, Ulster Defense Association (UDA). February 8, 1995; February 22, 1996.

ANNIE ARMSTRONG. Lisburn district councillor, Twinbrook, Sinn Fein. June 9, 1995.

GLEN BARR. Chief executive officer, Ebrington Business Centre, Waterside, Derry. Political adviser, UDA, 1972–76, 1978–81. Chairman, Coordinating Committee, 1974 Ulster Workers Council strike. February 15, 1995.

ALEX CALDERWOOD. Community worker, The Centre, Shankill Road, Belfast. Former life-sentence prisoner, Ulster Defense Association/Ulster Freedom Fighters (UDA/UFF). February 9, 1995; February 27, 1995.

JOSEPH CLARKE. Resident of west Belfast. Member, Sinn Fein. Former internee, Provisional Irish Republican Army (IRA). April 27, 1995.

JOY CLARKE. Chief education and training officer, Northern Ireland Prison Service. May 9, 1995.

THOMAS CLARKE. Artist, Belfast. Father of Malachy Clarke, IRA punishment-beating victim and a suicide. February 20, 1995.

FERGUS COOPER. Promotions officer, Northern Ireland Association for the Care and Resettlement of Offenders (NIACRO). January 25, 1995.

ROBERT COOPER. Chairman, Fair Employment Commission for Northern Ireland. Head of Department of Manpower Services, Northern Ireland Executive, 1974. Founding member, Alliance Party. Friend of Paddy Wilson, UDA/UFF murder victim, 1973.

MAIREAD CORRIGAN-MAGUIRE. Co-founder, Community of the Peace People. Co-winner, Nobel Peace Prize, 1976. March 27, 1995.

JIMMY CREIGHTON. Community development officer, Glencairn Community Development Association, Belfast. Member, UDA, 1971–83. February 28, 1995.

CAROL CULLEN. Resident of west Belfast. Member, Sinn Fein. Former fixed-sentence prisoner, IRA. March 16, 1995.

DAVID ERVINE. Political spokesman, executive member, Progressive Unionist Party (PUP). Former fixed-sentence prisoner, Ulster Volunteer Force (UVF). February 9, 1995; March 6, 1995; June 12, 1995.

MONSIGNOR DENIS FAUL. Priest and school principal, Dungannon. Human rights activist. May 4, 1995.

BREIDGE GADD. Chief probation officer, Probation Board for Northern Ireland. Former member, Life Sentence Review Board. May 10, 1995.

WILLIAM GILES. Life-sentence prisoner, UVF, Her Majesty's Prison Maze. May 17, 1995.

TOMMY GORMAN. Community worker, Springfield Intercommunity Development Project, Upper Springfield Resource Center. Member, Sinn Fein. Former internee and fixed-sentence prisoner, IRA. February 24, 1995; March 24, 1995; May 5, 1995; December 22, 1995; February 13, 1996.

LEO GREEN. Officer, Sinn Fein P.O.W. Department. Former life-sentence prisoner, IRA. May 15, 1995; February 14, 1996.

DR. JOSEPH HENDRON. Member of Parliament, Social Democratic and Labour Party, west Belfast. Medical doctor. June 6, 1995; June 8, 1995.

BRENDAN HUGHES. Resident of west Belfast. Member, Sinn Fein. Former internee and fixed-sentence prisoner, IRA. April 21, 1995; February 15, 1996.

BILLY HUTCHINSON. Project director, Springfield Intercommunity Development Project, Belfast. Press officer, executive member, PUP. Former life-sentence prisoner, UVF. February 14, 1995; March 1, 1995; May 15, 1995; February 22, 1996.

EDDIE KINNER. Coordinator, Shankill Computer Training Centre, NI-ACRO, Belfast. Executive member, PUP. Former life-sentence prisoner, UVF. February 14, 1995; March 8, 1995; October 12, 1995; February 22, 1996.

TOMMY KIRKHAM. Community worker, Glencairn, Belfast. Member, UDP. Former fixed-sentence prisoner, UDA/UFF. March 16, 1995.

SEAN LYNCH. Officer commanding, IRA prisoners, H.M.P. Maze. June 7, 1995.

TONY MCCABE. Community worker, Ballymurphy, Belfast. Member, Sinn Fein. February 24, 1995.

ANN MCCANN. Administrator, Community of the Peace People. Sister of Gerard Duddy, loyalist murder victim, 1972. February 7, 1995.

HAZEL MCCREADY. Former reserve officer, Royal Ulster Constabulary (RUC). Secretary, Disabled Police Officers' Association. May 25, 1995.

JIM MCDONALD. Director, Loyalist Prisoners' Welfare Association (UVF). February 21, 1995.

CHRISTOPHER MCGIMPSEY. Belfast city councillor, Court, Ulster Unionist Party. June 1, 1995.

ANTHONY MCINTYRE. Doctoral candidate, Politics Department, Queen's University of Belfast. Former life-sentence prisoner, IRA. February 16, 1995; March 9, 1995; April 26, 1995; February 7, 1996; February 13, 1996.

DUNCAN MCLAUGHLAN. Deputy director of operations, Northern Ireland Prison Service. June 16, 1995.

GARY MCMICHAEL. Party leader, UDP. Son of John McMichael, IRA murder victim, 1987. March 30, 1995.

JACKIE MCMULLAN. Officer, Sinn Fein P.O.W. Department. Former life-sentence prisoner, IRA. March 13, 1995; September 19, 1995.

RONALD MCMURRAY. Counselor, NIACRO. Former life-sentence prisoner, UVF. May 2, 1995.

KEVIN MCQUILLAN. Community worker, Ballymurphy, Belfast. Former spokesman, Irish Republican Socialist Party. Former remand prisoner, Irish National Liberation Army. May 10, 1995.

SAMUEL MALCOLMSON. Former officer, RUC. Former chairman, Disabled Police Officers' Association. May 25, 1995.

BILLY MITCHELL. Project coordinator, LINC Resource Centre, Belfast. Executive member, PUP. Former life-sentence prisoner, UVF. February 22, 1995; March 23, 1995.

MALACHI O'DOHERTY. Freelance journalist, Belfast. Various.

ELLA O'DWYER. Life-sentence prisoner, IRA, H.M.P. Maghaberry. September 29, 1995.

PAUL O'DWYER. Irish-American civil rights lawyer and political activist. August 2, 1995.

LISA O'HAGAN. Resident of west Belfast. Victim of IRA strongarm tactics. February 20, 1995.

DONNCHA O'HARA. Press officer, Sinn Fein. Former life-sentence prisoner, IRA. January 30, 1995; February 6, 1995.

SANDRA PEACOCK. Resident of north Belfast. Widow of James Peacock, Northern Ireland Prison Service, UVF murder victim, 1993. February 23, 1995.

JOHN PICKERING. Member, Sinn Fein. Former internee and life-sentence prisoner, IRA. March 13, 1995; September 19, 1995.

DIANA PURCELL. Senior counsellor, The Open University, Belfast. March 15, 1995.

MARTHA "MARTY" RAFFERTY. Social worker, Quaker Service, H.M.P. Maghaberry and H.M.P. Maze. June 19, 1995.

JACKIE REDPATH. Community worker, Greater Shankill Partnership, Belfast. April 5, 1995.

GARY ROBERTS. Instructor, Meanscoil Feirste, Irish Language Centre, Falls Road, Belfast. Former life-sentence prisoner, IRA. February 21, 1995; March 2, 1995.

HENRY ROBINSON. Community worker, Families Against Intimidation and Terror (FAIT). Former fixed-sentence prisoner, Official Irish Republican Army. February 10, 1995.

UMBERTO SCAPPATICCI. Director, The Lynx Project, Twinbrook, Belfast. Former life-sentence prisoner, IRA. June 9, 1995.

WILLIAM "PLUM" SMITH. Coordinator, Woodvale Resource Centre. Chairman, executive member, PUP. Former fixed-sentence prisoner, Red Hand Commando/UVF. March 15, 1995; March 21, 1995.

MARTIN SNODDON. Computer training supervisor, Bryson House, Belfast. Member, PUP. Former life-sentence prisoner, UVF. April 11, 1995.

GUSTY SPENCE. Executive member, PUP; former life-sentence prisoner, UVF. February 3, 1995; February 17, 1995.

MICHAEL STONE. Life-sentence prisoner, UDA/UFF, H.M.P. Maze. Officer commanding, UDA/UFF prisoners, east Belfast. Prison spokesman, UDA/UFF. June 20, 1995.

ANDY TYRIE. Resident of east Belfast. Businessman. Chairman, UDA, 1973–88. Former remand prisoner, UDA/UFF. June 17, 1995.

JOHN WHITE. Spokesman on prisons and for north and west Belfast, UDP. Former internee and life-sentence prisoner, UDA/UFF. January 28, 1995; February 4, 1995; February 25, 1995; June 3, 1995.

NOTES

Prologue

1. The book McIntyre refers to is Malcolm Sutton, *An Index of Deaths from the Conflict in Ireland, 1969–1993* (Belfast: Beyond the Pale Publications, 1994), now the authoritative source on troubles dead. For this book, all pre-1994 figures on deaths resulting from paramilitary attacks, victims' names, and victims' ages were obtained from or verified by Sutton's compilation. Corresponding information for 1994, 1995, and 1996 was gathered by the author through local media reports and inquiries to official sources in Northern Ireland.

Chapter 1

1. A. T. Q. Stewart, *The Narrow Ground* (Belfast: Pretani Press, 1986), 101–10, 128–37.
2. W. D. Flackes and Sydney Elliott, *Northern Ireland: A Political Directory, 1968–1993* (Belfast: Blackstaff Press, 1994), 256–58.
3. John O'Beirne Ranelagh, *A Short History of Ireland,* 2nd ed. (Cambridge, England: Cambridge University Press, 1994), pp. 131–32.
4. R. F. Foster, *Modern Ireland* (New York: Penguin Books, 1989), p. 558.
5. *Ibid.,* pp. 318–44.
6. Christine Kinealy, *This Great Calamity* (Dublin: Gill and Macmillan, 1994). See also Neal Ascherson, "The Lesson from Ireland's Famine Was Clear: The Unfettered Market Kills," *Independent on Sunday,* May 21, 1995, sec. I, p. 26.
7. The irony was publicly noted beyond Northern Ireland. See Cal McCrystal, "Buried by Time," *Independent on Sunday Magazine,* May 14, 1995, pp. 5–6.
8. Foster, *Modern Ireland,* p. 491.
9. See Michael Laffan, *The Partition of Ireland, 1911–1925* (Dundalk, Ireland: Dundalgen Press, 1987), pp. 61–67.
10. Foster, *Modern Ireland,* pp. 505–11.
11. *Ibid.,* pp. 469–71, 502–4; Ranelagh, *A Short History of Ireland,* pp. 198, 255–56.
12. Ranelagh, *A Short History of Ireland,* pp. 163–66, 255.
13. John Lyttle, "In the Name of My Father," *The Independent Magazine,* March

30, 1996, p. 28. Devoid of either sanctimony or apology, Lyttle's brief account of his growing up gay among paramilitary "hard men" during the troubles is perhaps the most vivid, hard-nosed, and frank reminiscence by a first-hand observer that I have read.

14. "Children of North Confound Experts," *Irish News* (Belfast), November 11, 1995, p. 3.

15. Fair Employment Commission for Northern Ireland, *A Profile of the Northern Ireland Workforce,* Monitoring Report No. 6, March 1996, p. 169.

16. "Stop Campaign Against Whiskey Firm Says Hume," *Irish News* (Belfast), February 8, 1996, p. 1.

17. Letter to the author from the Superintendent, Royal Ulster Constabulary, February 2, 1996.

18. P. J. O'Rourke, *Holidays in Hell* (London: Picador, 1989), p. 278.

19. Letter to the author from the Superintendent, Royal Ulster Constabulary, February 2, 1996.

20. Flackes and Elliott, *Northern Ireland: A Political Directory, 1968–93,* p. 458.

21. Foster, *Modern Ireland,* p. 591; Flackes and Elliott, *Northern Ireland: A Political Directory, 1968–93,* pp. 8, 231. Maudling's actual statement was as follows: "You may not totally eliminate the IRA, but the army has the power and certainly the intention of reducing the level of violence to something which is acceptable." "Ulster's Rage Is Justified: Maudling," *Belfast Telegraph,* December 15, 1971, pp. 1, 4. A day later, he tried to clarify his point, saying in substance that he had intended only to point out that the IRA had not been eradicated in the past, and that any military effort needed a political complement. "Maudling Clarifies His IRA Remark," *Belfast Telegraph,* December 16, 1971, p. 1. The damage to posterity, however, was already done.

Chapter 2

1. Ranelagh, *A Short History of Ireland,* p. 262.

2. *Ibid.,* p. 260.

3. *Ibid.* See also Paul Arthur and Keith Jeffery, *Northern Ireland Since 1968* (London: Basil Blackwell, 1988), p. 5.

4. Quoted in Ranelagh, *A Short History of Ireland,* p. 168.

5. Quoted in Patrick Bishop and Eamonn Mallie, *The Provisional IRA* (London: Corgi Books, 1988), p. 137.

6. Quoted in, for example, Ruth Dudley Edwards, *Patrick Pearse: The Triumph of Failure* (Dublin: Poolbeg Press, 1990), pp. 236–37.

7. Lionel Shriver, *Ordinary Decent Criminals* (HarperCollins, Flamingo, 1993), p. 39.

8. "Provos Issue Fresh Threat to Civilians on 'Aiding Military'," *Irish News* (Belfast), January 20, 1992, p. 1.

9. "Adams Blames British Policy," *Sunday Life* (Belfast), January 19, 1992, p. 4.

10. Steve Bruce, *The Edge of the Union* (Oxford: Oxford University Press, 1994), p. 124.

11. Bishop and Mallie, *The Provisional IRA*, p. 313.

12. *Ibid.*, pp. 132–35.

13. Sean O'Callaghan, "Don't Swallow the Provos' Line." *The Independent* (London), May 30, 1996, p. 19.

14. "5 Die and 40 Hurt in Attack on Bar," *Irish News* (Belfast), August 14, 1975, p. 1; "Four Die in Bar Bomb Horror," *Belfast Telegraph*, August 14, 1975, p. 5.

Chapter 3

1. "Victims Stabbed 50 Times," *Irish News* (Belfast), June 27, 1973, p. 1.

2. *Ibid.*

3. Among academics, the "double-minority" view is probably the preferred framework for analyzing the troubles, and certainly the most fruitful one. See Padraig O'Malley, *The Uncivil Wars* (Boston: Houghton Mifflin, 1983), p. 7; Stewart, *The Narrow Ground*, p. 162; John Whyte, *Interpreting Northern Ireland* (Oxford: Oxford University Press, Clarendon Paperbacks, 1991), pp. 100–101.

4. Steve Bruce, *God Save Ulster!* (Oxford: Oxford University Press, 1989), pp. 168–69.

5. Quoted in *ibid.*, p. 67.

6. Quoted in Dervla Murphy, *A Place Apart* (Old Greenwich, Conn.: Devin-Adair, 1978), p. 144.

7. Bruce, *God Save Ulster!*, p. 64.

8. Arthur and Jeffery, *Northern Ireland Since 1968*, p. 27; Bob Rowthorn and Naomi Wayne, *Northern Ireland: The Political Economy of Conflict* (Cambridge, England: Polity Press, 1988), p. 79.

9. See "Drugs Scourge 'Climbing,'" *Belfast Telegraph*, May 2, 1996, p. 6; "UVF Carves Up Drugs Peddling with IPLO," *Irish News* (Belfast), May 10, 1996, p. 7.

10. Flackes and Elliott, *Northern Ireland: A Political Directory, 1968–1993*, p. 329. See also Bishop and Mallie, *The Provisional IRA*, pp. 391–93; Steve Bruce, *The Red Hand* (Oxford University Press, 1992), pp. 189–98.

11. Flackes and Elliott, *Northern Ireland: A Political Directory, 1968–1993*, p. 327.

12. Quoted in O'Malley, *The Uncivil Wars*, p. 373.

Chapter 4

1. "Troubles Chronology," *Fortnight* 332 (October 1994), p. 36–37.

2. "Adams Paints Black Picture of Future of Peace Process," *Irish News* (Belfast), November 25, 1995, p. 1.

3. "Life Sentence on Youth (20) for Police Murder Bid," *Irish News* (Belfast), December 7, 1976, p. 5.

4. David Beresford, *Ten Men Dead* (London: Grafton Books, 1987), pp. 373–76.

5. The earthily innovative methods by which IRA prisoners and outside commanders exchanged directives during the hunger strike are detailed in Beresford, *Ten Men Dead*, p. 30.

6. *Ibid.,* p. 216.
7. Brian Campbell, Laurence McKeown, and Felim O'Hagan, *Nor Meekly Serve My Time* (Belfast: Beyond the Pale Publications, 1994), pp. 260–63.
8. Beresford, *Ten Men Dead,* p. 216.
9. Campbell, McKeown, and O'Hagan, *Nor Meekly Serve My Time,* p. 259.
10. McIntyre also put his argument on the record. See Anthony McIntyre, "Waking Up to Reality," *Fortnight* 332 (October 1994), p. 17.
11. Flackes and Elliott, *Northern Ireland: A Political Directory, 1968–1993,* p. 216.
12. Anthony McIntyre, "Not Worth the Paper," *Fortnight* 325 (February 1994), p. 17.
13. "Mother's Fury As Police Warn Son, 3, Over Prank," *Irish News* (Belfast), November 22, 1995, p. 7.
14. Malachi O'Doherty, "Community Charged," *Fortnight* 342 (September 1995), p. 21.
15. Emily O'Reilly, "Local Hero," *Esquire* (G.B. edition), December 1993/January 1994, p. 122.

Chapter 5

1. Reprinted in, for example, "Militant Protestants in Truce, Lifting Peace Hopes in Ulster," *New York Times,* October 14, 1995, pp. A1, A12.
2. Marty Snoddon recounted the UVF compound culture in a pamphlet published by the Probation Board for Northern Ireland. See Martin Snoddon, "Culture Behind the Wire," *Freedom* (Probation Board for Northern Ireland, 1990), p. 63.
3. Steve Bruce, *The Red Hand,* p. 245.
4. Foster, *Modern Ireland,* pp. 470–71, 503.
5. J. J. Lee, *Ireland, 1912–1985: Politics and Society* (Cambridge, England: Cambridge University Press, 1989), p. 44.
6. Foster, *Modern Ireland,* p. 465; Ranelagh, *A Short History of Ireland,* pp. 187–88.
7. Ranelagh, *A Short History of Ireland,* p. 146.
8. See Ian Adamson, *The Identity of Ulster* (Belfast: Pretani Press, 1987).
9. See Foster, *Modern Ireland,* p. 492.
10. Bruce, *The Edge of the Union,* p. 143.
11. Royal Ulster Constabulary Press Office, November 22, 1995.
12. Stewart, *The Narrow Ground,* pp. 163–67.

Chapter 6

1. Fionnuala O'Connor, *In Search of a State* (Belfast: Blackstaff Press, 1993), p. 101.
2. Bishop and Mallie incorrectly characterize O'Dwyer as "middle-class." Bishop and Mallie, *The Provisional IRA,* p. 428.

3. Some academic commentators have countenanced a two-tier police setup, giving the RUC supervisory province-wide control but vesting ground-level enforcement authority in separate community police forces. See Mike Brogden, "Rank Disagreement," *Fortnight* 334 (December 1994), p. 18.
4. "IRA Has Not Wavered from Peace Path Says Annesley," *Irish News* (Belfast), January 26, 1995, p. 4.
5. Ranelagh, *A Short History of Ireland,* pp. 256–60.
6. Stewart, *The Narrow Ground,* pp. 175–76.
7. *Counterpoint,* Ulster TV, October 12, 1995.

Chapter 7

1. "Taylor Sends a 'Hands Off' Warning to U.S.," *Belfast Telegraph,* October 7, 1995, p. 1; "Taylor Warns Against U.S. Dictating Talks Agenda," *Irish News* (Belfast), October 9, 1995, p. 3.
2. See Paddy Devlin, "Labour's Faltered March," *Fortnight* 337 (March 1995), p. 16.
3. John Ardagh, *Ireland and the Irish* (London: Hamish Hamilton, 1994), pp. 442–43.
4. Flackes and Elliott, *Northern Ireland: A Political Directory, 1968–1993,* p. 354.
5. See, for example, "The Protestant Pretenders," *The Independent* (London), March 6, 1995, p. 21; "RTE to Show Ervine Tribute," *Irish News* (Belfast), May 10, 1995, p. 7; "David Ervine: Doors Opened in Long Kesh," *Faces* (October 1995), p. 16.
6. "Get With It, Young Tell Unionists," *Irish News* (Belfast), October 9, 1995, p. 3.
7. "Comparison with Trimble Upset Former KKK Head," *Irish News* (Belfast), November 1, 1995, p. 1.
8. See "Ulstermen March to a New Drum," *The Independent* (London), October 14, 1994, p. 21; "Loyalists Cross the Line," *Irish News* (Belfast), January 19, 1995, p. 4.

Chapter 8

1. Royal Ulster Constabulary Press Office, November 22, 1995.
2. "Greysteel Killers Are Moved Out of the Maze," *Irish News* (Belfast), June 5, 1995, p. 5. In an interview with the author on June 20, 1995, UDA/UFF prison spokesman Michael Stone corrected certain inaccuracies in the newspaper report.
3. Conor Cruise O'Brien, "Why Unionists Pose No Threat," *The Independent* (London), January 20, 1995, p. 18.
4. "British, Irish Set Peace Plan for Northern Ireland," *Washington Post,* February 23, 1995, pp. A1, A24; "Cabinets Approve Anglo-Irish Plan on Ulster Talks,"

New York Times, February 23, 1995, pp. A1, A9. See also "Unionists 'Sick,'" *Belfast Telegraph,* February 22, 1995, p. 1; "War on the Union, Says DUP Leader," *Belfast Telegraph,* February 22, 1995, p. 7; "Adams and Paisley Poles Apart on Political Fallout," *Irish News* (Belfast), February 23, 1995, p. 4.

5. David Trimble, "The Trap in Sir Patrick's Path," *The Independent* (London), October 19, 1995, p. 20.

6. For one of many examples of Adams's deployment of the IRA's hard line to make Sinn Fein look helpless, see Gerry Adams, "Why the IRA Won't Hand Over Their Weapons," *Belfast Telegraph,* June 14, 1995, p. 10. The republican prisoners' view on decommissioning was equally negative. See the letter to the editor from "Republican Prisoner, H-Block 8" in "British Demands on IRA 'Absurd'," *Irish News* (Belfast), March 28, 1995, p. 8.

7. "Prophet of Death and Destruction," *Belfast Telegraph,* November 10, 1995, p. 3.

8. "Mitchell Team Starts Historic Path to Peace," *Irish News* (Belfast), December 15, 1995, p. 1.

9. *Belfast Telegraph,* January 16, 1996, pp. 1, 8–9; January 17, 1996, pp. 1, 6–7; January 18, 1996, pp. 1, 8–9.

10. See, for example, "A Message from the IRA," *The Economist* (London), June 22–28, 1996, p. 53; "Troops Patrol Belfast Again, Raising the Tension," *New York Times,* June 22, 1996, p. 4.

11. *The World Almanac and Book of Facts, 1996* (Mahwah, N.J.: Funk & Wagnalls, 1995), 775, 828.

12. Ronnie Munck and Douglas Hamilton, "A Disintegrated Economy," *Fortnight* 324 (January 1994), p. 26.

13. Ardagh, *Ireland and the Irish,* pp. 89, 101–102.

14. Kieran A. Kennedy, Thomas Giblin, and Dierdre McHugh, *The Economic Development of Ireland in the Twentieth Century* (London: Routledge, 1988), p. 99; *The World Almanac and Book of Facts, 1996,* p. 775.

15. Compare Ronnie Munck, *The Irish Economy: Results and Prospects* (London: Pluto Press, 1993) with Paddy Roche and Esmond Birnie, *An Economic Lesson for Irish Nationalists and Republicans* (Belfast: Ulster Unionist Information Institute, 1995).

16. Kennedy, Giblin, and McHugh, *The Economic Development of Ireland in the Twentieth Century,* p. 99.

17. Frank Gaffikin and Michael Morrissey, "The Regeneration Game," *Fortnight* 334 (December 1994), p. 27.

18. New Ireland Forum, *The Macroeconomic Consequences of Integrated Economic Policy, Planning and Coordination of Ireland* (Dublin: Stationery Office, 1984), pp. 12–13.

19. See, for example, Rowthorn and Wayne, *Northern Ireland: The Political Economy of Conflict,* pp. 156–57.

20. "RUC 'Less Likely to Accept Catholics'," *Irish News* (Belfast), October 20, 1995, p. 1.

21. "Five Die on Roads in Weekend of Carnage," *Irish News* (Belfast), November 13, 1995, p. 1.

22. "Israel Summit May Promote Peace in North," *Irish News* (Belfast), November 6, 1995, p. 1.
23. "The Nightmare Slide to War," *The Independent* (London), February 20, 1996, p. 1.
24. "Is It Time for the Politics of the Possible?" *Andersonstown News* (Belfast), October 28, 1995, p. 6.
25. "Shankill Ceasefires Poll," *Shankill People* (Belfast), October 1995, p. 3.

Chapter 9

1. "Keep Killers Out of Talks Says Fitt," *Irish News* (Belfast), October 19, 1994, p. 3.
2. "Counterpoint," Ulster TV, October 12, 1995.
3. W. D. Flackes, *Northern Ireland—A Political Directory, 1968–1983* (London: British Broadcasting Corporation, 1983), pp. 316–17.
4. Beresford, *Ten Men Dead,* p. 31; Northern Ireland Prison Service, *Monthly Prison Report,* September 1994, p. 1.
5. Northern Ireland Prison Service, *Annual Report, 1994–1995,* p. 23.
6. See Northern Ireland Prison Service, *Annual Report, 1994–1995,* p. 22; Robert Worth, "A Model Prison," *The Atlantic Monthly,* November 1995, p. 40.
7. "I'll Forgive Spence for Killing My Son," *Irish News* (Belfast), October 18, 1994, p. 1.
8. "Conspiracy Theory Haunts Awards Miss," *Irish News* (Belfast), October 15, 1995, p. 4.
9. "Don't Support 'Gloaters' Says UVF," *Irish News* (Belfast), February 13, 1996, p. 1.
10. Bishop and Mallie, *The Provisional IRA,* pp. 459–60.
11. "'I Asked the IRA If They Were Prepared for 3,000 More Dead. They Said Yes,'" *The Times* (London), November 5, 1993, p. 17.

GLOSSARY

Paramilitary and Political Organizations
and Northern Irish Terms

Alliance Party. Mixed, emphatically nonsectarian, middle-class unionist party. Draws between 8 and 10 percent of the vote in Northern Ireland.* Dr. John Alderdice has been party leader since 1987.

Anglo-Irish Agreement. Agreement between the British and Irish governments signed in 1985, re-establishing six-county majority consent as a prerequisite to reunification and instituting a consultative "Irish dimension" in the form of an Intergovernmental Conference composed of civil servants from both Northern Ireland and the Republic. Regarded as an act of British betrayal by unionists and loyalists, a promising development by constitutional nationalists, and an unwelcome entrenchment of partition by republicans.

The blanket. The mass protest by republican prisoners in the Maze between 1976 and 1981, in which they defied criminal status by refusing to wear prison clothing and instead draping themselves only in blankets. The blanket protest culminated in the hunger strike of 1981, in which ten republican prisoners died.

Canary Wharf bombing. The IRA attack expressly ending the IRA's seventeen-month ceasefire; a 1,000-pound homemade fertilizer bomb exploded underneath the Docklands Light Railway Station near the Canary Wharf office buildings in east London, killing two civilians, injuring more than one hundred, and damaging property estimated at $140 million.

Combined Loyalist Military Command (CLMC). Shadowy umbrella organization for principal loyalist paramilitary groups, including the UDA/UFF, UVF, and Red Hand Commando. Emerged in 1991. Through PUP and UDP representatives, announced the 1994 loyalist ceasefire.

---

*Voting strengths are based on 1992 parliamentary election figures and 1993 district council election figures.

Consent principle. The principle that Ireland cannot be reunited as a thirty-two-county state unless the majority of voters in the six counties of Northern Ireland agree. This requirement was incorporated into the Government of Ireland Act of 1920, the Treaty of 1921, the Northern Ireland (Temporary Provisions) Act of 1974 establishing British direct rule, the Anglo-Irish Agreement of 1985, the Downing Street declaration of 1993, and the framework document of 1995. Republicans refer to the consent principle as the "unionist veto." See *Unionist veto.*

Constitutional nationalist. A nationalist who specifically excludes physical force as a legitimate means of reuniting Ireland, instead espousing nonviolent methods.

Constitutional question. The overriding constant in Northern Irish politics: whether the union between Britain and Northern Ireland should be maintained, or the thirty-two counties of Ireland should be united. Also called "the border question."

Dail Eireann. The parliament of the Republic of Ireland. Usually called simply "the Dail."

Democratic Unionist Party (DUP). The most militantly Protestant of the two mainstream unionist parties. Commands between 13 and 18 percent of the vote in Northern Ireland. The Rev. Ian Paisley has been party leader since the DUP was founded in 1971.

Devolved government. any governing administration in Northern Ireland with substantive legislative and executive authority delegated by Westminster—e.g., the Stormont assembly (1921–72) and Sunningdale (1974). Devolved government is distinguished from direct rule by Westminster, which was instituted in 1972, suspended briefly in favor of Sunningdale in 1973, and then reimposed in 1974. Northern Ireland remains governed, at present, by direct rule.

Downing Street declaration. Statement issued jointly by the British and Irish governments on December 15, 1993, broadly establishing the neutrality of the two sovereign governments on the constitutional question, proclaiming the right of self-determination as belonging to "the people of the island of Ireland alone," conditioning the reunification of Ireland on the "freely given consent of a majority of the people of Northern Ireland," and endorsing "exclusively . . . peaceful political means" for resolving the constitutional question.

Falls Road. Principal thoroughfare of Catholic west Belfast and the vein of the strongest republican support in Belfast. "The Falls" is the ranking geographic metaphor for militant republicanism.

Green. Adjective indicating nationalist bias.

Internal settlement. See *Irish dimension.*

Irish dimension. Shorthand for any role, consultative or executive, for the government of the Republic of Ireland in Northern Irish affairs. Generally spurned by unionists, welcomed by nationalists. The term is used in contradistinction to *internal settlement,* which denotes any political solution by which Northern Ireland would remain constitutionally under exclusive British authority and subject to no Irish authority.

Irish Free State. The formal name for the twenty-six-county independent state created by the Government of Ireland Act of 1920 and the Anglo-Irish Treaty of 1921. The Irish Free State was accorded dominion status within the British commonwealth. Though under the treaty the Free State owed allegiance to the monarchy, it enjoyed total independence in domestic affairs, full fiscal autonomy, and wide latitude in foreign relations—in a word, virtual nationhood. The 1937 constitution did away with the oath of allegiance to the Crown. In 1949, the Dail declared the twenty-six counties the Republic of Ireland—a completely independent nation, outside the British commonwealth, owing no allegiance to the monarchy. The Republic of Ireland is variously called the "Irish Republic," "southern Ireland," "the south." More problematically, the Republic is referred to as "Eire," which the Irish Free State was officially re-named in the 1937 constitution. The word is Irish for "Ireland," and under articles 2 and 3 of the constitution aspirationally embraces the entire island but legally includes only the twenty-six counties. Irish republicans still refer to the twenty-six counties as "the Free State" or "the twenty-six counties" because to them any Irish republic worthy of the label must comprise all thirty-two counties of the island.

Irish National Liberation Army (INLA). Republican paramilitary group active mainly in the late seventies and early eighties, particularly in border areas and Belfast's lower Falls, and the only important group not to declare a ceasefire in 1994. The INLA consisted mostly of ex-Provisionals dissatisfied with the Provisional IRA's authoritarianism, and ex-Officials unhappy with the Official IRA's 1972 ceasefire. Latterly plagued by internal feuds, mainly with the breakaway "Irish People's Liberation Organization."

Irish Republican Socialist Party (IRSP). The (legal) political wing of the INLA. Working-class, rigidly socialist. Negligible electoral support. Critical of IRA ceasefire.

Loyalist. Any unionist who believes that the union between Northern Ireland and Great Britain should be defended by extralegal physical force. Loyalists are generally working-class.

The Maze. Common expression for the penitentiary officially called "Her Majesty's Prison the Maze." South of Belfast, the Maze is the main prison in Northern Ireland for paramilitary convicts. It consists of eight "H-blocks." The Maze was opened in 1976. Before that, paramilitary prisoners were housed in the wire-fenced compounds of an old military camp called "Long Kesh," adjacent to the Maze. Republicans still refer to the Maze as "Long Kesh," "the Kesh," or "the H-blocks," refusing to acknowledge the official name, with its royal trappings and implication of criminality. Loyalists tend to call the Maze, simply, "the jail."

Nationalist. Anyone who believes the island of Ireland should be reunited to form a single thirty-two-county state. Nationalists are overwhelmingly, though not exclusively, Catholic.

Northern Ireland. The six-county state in the northeast of Ireland created by the Government of Ireland Act of 1920 and the Anglo-Irish Treaty of 1921. Northern Ireland is part of the United Kingdom. To unionists, it is "Ulster" or "the province," to constitutional nationalists "the north of Ireland" or "the north," to republicans "the six counties."

Official Irish Republican Army. Republican paramilitary group originating from those who declined to join the militant Provisional IRA in 1970. The Official IRA declared a ceasefire in 1972 and was largely dormant during the remainder of the troubles, its activities limited to local rackets and community defense (sometimes against the Provisional IRA).

Orange. Adjective indicating unionist bias.

Orange Order. The largest of three Protestant fraternal organizations, the other two being the Apprentice Boys of Derry and the Royal Black Preceptory. The Orange Order was founded in 1795 and now has about 100,000 members— roughly one in three Protestant adults. Doctrinally, the Orange Order is anti-Catholic and vehemently unionist, having maintained close institutional links with the Ulster Unionist Party.

Orangeism. The strident and exclusively Protestant brand of unionism espoused by the Orange Order, the Royal Black Preceptory, and the Apprentice Boys of Derry, and (to nationalists) epitomized by the parades these fraternal organizations hold.

Partition. The separation of the island of Ireland, effected by the Government of Ireland Act of 1920 and the Anglo-Irish Treaty of 1921, into the twenty-six-county Irish Free State and six-county Northern Ireland, the latter of which remained part of the United Kingdom. See *Irish Free State* and *Northern Ireland.*

Power sharing. The institutionalized allocation of power between unionists and nationalists in the governance of Northern Ireland. Although some degree of power sharing has been effected through election by proportional representation since 1973, nationalists have pressed for more substantial guarantees of executive control (as in Sunningdale) along with an Irish dimension. Unionists initially resisted such guarantees, but now generally accept them in some degree and focus their defiance on the Irish dimension.

Progressive Unionist Party (PUP). One of the two "loyalist fringe parties," considered to represent the UVF. Working-class, pragmatically socialist. Negligible overall electoral support, but influential on account of high-profile constituency. Although former Belfast Lord Mayor Hugh Smyth founded the party in 1978 and nominally remains party leader, David Ervine is in practice its leader. William "Plum" Smith is the chairman of the party.

Provisional Irish Republican Army (IRA). The principal republican paramilitary group during the troubles, and by far the most destructive, republican or loyalist. Alternatively known as "the Provos," "the Provies," or simply "the IRA." Advocates the creation, by force if deemed necessary, of a thirty-two-county socialist state. The Provisional IRA started in 1970, when militant members of the extant IRA centered in Belfast split to form their own group. Those left over became known as the "Official IRA." See *Official Irish Republican Army.*

Red Hand Commando. Small, ruthless loyalist paramilitary group with close ties to the UVF.

Republic of Ireland. See *Irish Free State.*

Republican. Any nationalist who advocates physical force as a legitimate means of reuniting Ireland.

Republican Sinn Fein. Radical Sinn Fein splinter group based in the Republic of Ireland, founded in 1986 in opposition to Sinn Fein's new policy ending abstention from the Dail. Negligible electoral support. Opposed IRA ceasefire. Believed to be connected with "Irish National Republican Army," an obscure republican paramilitary group that arose briefly and uneventfully in November 1995.

Royal Ulster Constabulary (RUC). Northern Ireland's official police force. Over 90 percent Protestant, the RUC has primary responsibility in the province for antiterrorist measures as well as ordinary law enforcement.

Shankill Road. Main thoroughfare of Protestant west Belfast, and the heart of resolute loyalist support in Belfast. "The Shankill" is the ranking geographic metaphor for militant loyalism.

Sinn Fein. The Provisional IRA's (legal) political wing. Commands between 10 and 12 percent of the vote in Northern Ireland; less than 2 percent in the Republic of Ireland. Working-class, pragmatically socialist. Formal name: Provisional Sinn Fein. Gerry Adams has been party president since 1983.

Social Democratic and Labour Party (SDLP). The largest nationalist party in Northern Ireland, drawing about 22 percent of the vote. Preponderantly middle-class. The SDLP embraces "constitutional nationalism"—that is, the reunification of Ireland by nonviolent political means. John Hume has been party leader since 1979.

Stormont. The term has two meanings. First, it refers to Stormont Castle, the grand building in east Belfast from which, since it opened in 1932, the state has been administered. Second, and metaphorically, "Stormont" refers to the Protestant- and unionist-dominated devolved assembly that ruled Northern Ireland from partition in 1921 until direct rule was imposed in 1972.

Sunningdale. Shorthand for Northern Ireland's devolved power-sharing government, according a consultative role to the Irish government, that controlled Northern Ireland for five months in 1974, until the loyalist strike forced Britain to resume direct rule. The name comes from the Sunningdale (Berkshire) Civil Service College in England, where the British and Irish governments and participating Northern Irish parties hammered out the principles under which the government was to operate.

The troubles. In this book, the approximate quarter-century between the Catholic civil rights protests in 1968 and the loyalist ceasefire on October 13, 1994, during which Catholic and Protestant paramilitary groups engaged in guerrilla conflict in Northern Ireland over the constitutional question.

Ulster Defense Association (UDA). The largest loyalist group, formed from local vigilante organizations in 1970. Outlawed in 1992. The UDA's paramilitary wing, known as the Ulster Freedom Fighters (UFF), arose in 1973 and was immediately declared illegal. In the paramilitary context, the UDA is often referred to as the "UDA/UFF."

Ulster Democratic Party (UDP). One of the two "loyalist fringe parties," considered to represent the UDA/UFF. Working-class. Negligible overall electoral support, but influential on account of high-profile constituency. Gary McMichael has been party leader since 1994.

Ulster Freedom Fighters (UFF). The paramilitary wing of the UDA. See *Ulster Defense Association.*

Ulster Unionist Party (UUP). The largest political party in Northern Ireland. Largely middle-class. Commands between 30 and 34 percent of the vote in Northern Ireland. David Trimble was named party leader in 1995, after Sir James Molyneaux's sixteen-year tenure.

Ulster Volunteer Force (UVF). After the UDA/UFF, the largest loyalist paramilitary group. Founded in 1965, the UVF took the name of the illegal army raised in 1912 to fight Irish home rule. Except for one year in 1974 and 1975, the UVF was illegal throughout the troubles. Unlike the UDA, the UVF has always been entirely clandestine.

Unionist. Anyone who believes that the six counties of Northern Ireland should remain part of the United Kingdom—or, put another way, that the "union" between Northern Ireland and Great Britain should be maintained. Unionists are overwhelmingly, though not exclusively, Protestant.

Unionist veto. Republican term for the consent principle, reflecting the notion that the requirement of six-county majority consent to the reunification of Ireland gives a permanent unionist majority in Northern Ireland an effective "veto" over popular sentiment island-wide.

Workers' Party. The (legal) political counterpart of the Official IRA. Strongly socialist and against violence. Negligible electoral support in Northern Ireland. An offshoot, the Democratic Left, was formed in 1992 by Workers' Party members seeking to sever all links with the Official IRA.

SELECTED BIBLIOGRAPHY

Adams, Gerry. *Cage 11.* Dingle, Ireland: Brandon, 1990.

———. *Falls Memories.* Dingle, Ireland: Brandon, 1983.

———. *Free Ireland: Towards a Lasting Peace.* Dingle, Ireland: Brandon, 1995.

Adamson, Ian. *The Identity of Ulster,* 2nd ed. Belfast: Pretani Press, 1987.

Ardagh, John. *Ireland and the Irish.* London: Hamish Hamilton, 1994.

Arthur, Paul, and Keith Jeffery. *Northern Ireland Since 1968.* London: Basil Blackwell, 1988.

Bardon, Jonathan. *A History of Ulster.* Belfast: Blackstaff Press, 1993.

Beattie, Geoffrey. *We Are the People: Journeys Through the Heart of Protestant Ulster.* London: Mandarin, 1993.

Bell, Desmond. *Acts of Union: Youth Culture and Sectarianism in Northern Ireland.* London: Macmillan, 1990.

Bell, J. Bowyer. *The Irish Troubles: A Generation of Violence, 1967–1992.* Dublin: Gill & Macmillan, 1992.

Bell, Robert, Robert Johnstone, and Robin Wilson, eds. *Troubled Times: Fortnight Magazine and the Troubles in Northern Ireland.* Belfast: Blackstaff Press, 1991.

Beresford, David. *Ten Men Dead.* London: Grafton, 1987.

Bew, Paul, and Henry Patterson. *The British State and the Ulster Crisis: From Wilson to Thatcher.* London: Verso, 1985.

Bishop, Patrick, and Eamonn Mallie. *The Provisional IRA.* London: Corgi Books, 1988.

Brown, Terence. *Ireland: A Social and Cultural History.* London: Fontana Press, 1985.

Bruce, Steve. *The Edge of the Union.* Oxford: Oxford University Press, 1994.

———. *God Save Ulster! The Religion and Politics of Paisleyism.* Oxford: Oxford University Press, 1989.

———. *The Red Hand: Protestant Paramilitaries in Northern Ireland.* Oxford: Oxford University Press, 1992.

Campbell, Brian, Laurence McKeown, and Felim O'Hagan, eds. *Nor Meekly Serve My Time.* Belfast: Beyond the Pale Publications, 1994.

Connolly, Sean. *Religion and Society in Nineteenth-Century Ireland.* Dundalk, Ireland: Dundalgen Press, 1987.

Conroy, John. *Belfast Diary: War as a Way of Life*. Boston: Beacon Press, 1987.

Coogan, Tim Fat. *The IRA*. London: HarperCollins, 1993.

————. *The Troubles: Ireland's Ordeal 1966–1995 and the Search for Peace*. London: Hutchinson, 1995.

Dillon, Martin. *The Dirty War*. London: Hutchinson, 1990.

————. *The Shankill Butchers*. London: Hutchinson, 1989.

Edwards, Ruth Dudley. *Patrick Pearse: The Triumph of Failure*. Dublin: Poolbeg Press, 1990.

Fitzpatrick, Brendan. *Seventeenth-Century Ireland: The War of Religions*. Dublin: Gill and Macmillan, 1988.

Flackes, W. D., and Sydney Elliott. *Northern Ireland: A Political Directory, 1968–1993*. Belfast: Blackstaff Press, 1994.

Foster, R. F. *Modern Ireland, 1600–1972*. New York: Penguin, 1988.

Gormally, Brian, and Kieran McEvoy. *Release and Reintegration of Politically Motivated Prisoners in Northern Ireland*. Belfast: Northern Ireland Association for the Care and Settlement of Offenders, 1995.

Harkness, David. *Northern Ireland Since 1920*. Dublin: Helicon Books, 1983.

Kennedy, Kieran, Thomas Giblin, and Deirdre McHugh. *The Economic Development of Ireland in the Twentieth Century*. London: Routledge, 1988.

Kinealy, Christine. *This Great Calamity*. Dublin: Gill and Macmillan, 1994.

Laffan, Michael. *The Partition of Ireland, 1911–1925*. Dundalk, Ireland: Dundalgen Press, 1987.

Lee, J. J. *Ireland, 1912–1985: Politics and Society*. Cambridge, England: Cambridge University Press, 1989.

Lyons, F. S. L. *Ireland Since the Famine*. London: HarperCollins, Fontana, 1985.

Mallie, Eamonn, and David McKittrick. *The Fight for Peace: The Secret Story Behind the Irish Peace Process*. London: Heinemann, 1996.

McKittrick, David. *Endgame—The Search for Peace in Northern Ireland*. Belfast: Blackstaff Press, 1994.

————. *The Nervous Peace*. Belfast: Blackstaff Press, 1996.

Munck, Ronnie. *The Irish Economy: Results and Prospects*. London: Pluto Press, 1993.

Murphy, Dervla. *A Place Apart*. Old Greenwich, Conn.: Devon-Adair, 1978.

Murray, Dominic. *Worlds Apart: Segregated Schools in Northern Ireland*. Belfast: Appletree Press, 1985.

New Ireland Forum. *The Macroeconomic Consequences of Integrated Economic Policy, Planning and Coordination of Ireland*. Dublin: Stationery Office, 1984.

O'Brien, Conor Cruise. *Ancestral Voices: Religion and Nationalism in Ireland*. Dublin: Poolbeg Press, 1994.

————. *States of Ireland*. London: Hutchinson, 1972.

O'Cleary, Cornelius, Sydney Elliott, and R. A. Wilford. *The Northern Ireland Assembly, 1982–1986: A Constitutional Experiment*. London: C. Hurst & Co., 1988.

O'Connor, Fionnuala. *In Search of a State: Catholics in Northern Ireland*. Belfast: Blackstaff Press, 1993.

O'Doherty, Shane Paul. *The Volunteer*. London: HarperCollins, 1993.

O'Malley, Padraig. *Biting at the Grave.* Boston: Beacon Press, 1990.

————. *Northern Ireland: Questions of Nuance.* Belfast: Blackstaff Press, 1990.

————. *The Uncivil Wars: Ireland Today.* Boston: Houghton Mifflin, 1983.

Parker, Tony. *May the Lord in His Mercy Be Kind to Belfast.* London: Jonathan Cape, 1993.

Ranelagh, John O'Beirne. *A Short History of Ireland,* 2nd ed. Cambridge, England: Cambridge University Press, 1994.

Roche, Paddy, and Esmond Birnie. *An Economic Lesson for Irish Nationalists and Republicans.* Belfast: Ulster Unionist Information Institute, 1995.

Rolston, Bill, and Mike Tomlinson, *Unemployment in West Belfast: The Obair Report.* Belfast: Beyond the Pale Publications, 1988.

Rowan, Brian. *Behind the Lines: The Story of the IRA and Loyalist Ceasefires.* Belfast: Blackstaff Press, 1995.

Rowthorn, Bob, and Naomi Wayne. *Northern Ireland: The Political Economy of Conflict.* Cambridge, England: Polity Press, 1988.

Shriver, Lionel. *Ordinary Decent Criminals.* London: HarperCollins, 1992. (Published in the U.S. as: *The Bleeding Heart.* New York: Farrar Straus Giroux, 1990.)

Stewart, A. T. Q. *The Narrow Ground: Patterns of Ulster History.* Belfast: Pretani Press, 1986.

Sutton, Malcolm. *An Index of Deaths from the Conflict in Ireland, 1969–1993.* Belfast: Beyond the Pale Publications, 1994.

Toolis, Kevin. *Rebel Hearts: Journeys Within the IRA's Soul.* London: Picador, 1995.

Whyte, John. *Interpreting Northern Ireland.* Oxford: Oxford University Press, 1990.

Wilson, Andrew J. *Irish America and the Ulster Conflict, 1968–1995.* Belfast: Blackstaff Press, 1995.

INDEX